The Catholic Tradition

REV. CHARLES J. DOLLEN
DR. JAMES K. McGOWAN
DR. JAMES J. MEGIVERN
EDITORS

The Catholic Tradition

Personal Ethics
Volume 1

A Consortium Book

Library of Congress Card Catalog Number: 79-1977
ISBN: 0-8434-0728-X
ISBN: 0-8434-0725-5 series

The publisher gratefully acknowledges permission to quote from the
following copyrighted sources. In cases where those properties contain
scholarly apparatus such as footnotes, such footnotes have been omitted
in the interest of the general reader.

GEORGES BORCHARDT INC.
Chapters 3 and 5 from *Love and the Person* by Maurice Nédoncelle,
translated by Sr. Ruth Adelaide, S.C., © 1966 Sheed and Ward, Inc.
Reprinted by permission granted on behalf of Desclée de Brouwer by
Georges Borchardt Inc.

BURNS OATES & WASHBOURNE, LTD.
"Of the Order of Charity" from the *Summa Theologica* of St. Thomas
Aquinas translated by Fathers of the English Dominican Province, 1916.

THE CATHOLIC UNIVERSITY OF AMERICA PRESS, INC.
Selections from *The Fathers of the Church*, Volume 23, *Clement of
Alexandria: Christ the Educator*, translated by Simon P. Wood, copy-
right 1954; Selection from *The Fathers of the Church*, Volume 49,
Lactantius: The Divine Institutes, translated by Sister Mary Francis
McDonald, O.P., copyright © 1964; "Confessions: Book Eight" from
The Fathers of the Church, Volume 21, *St. Augustine: Confessions*
translated by Vernon J. Bourke, Ph.D., copyright 1953.

COLUMBIA UNIVERSITY PRESS
Selections from *Medieval Handbooks of Penance* translated by John T.
McNeill and Helena M. Gamer, copyright 1938.

Table of Contents

THE CATHOLIC TRADITION: Personal Ethics

Introduction

The Catholic Tradition is a 14 volume anthology of excerpts from the great Catholic writers from antiquity to the present day. *The Catholic Tradition* is intended for the armchair reader who has not studied theology or church history and has not time to struggle unassisted through 198 books. The publisher's intention is to provide such a reader with a compact home library that will permit him to familiarize himself with the great Catholic writers and their works. The works included in *The Catholic Tradition* are all religious in subject. The publisher did not include fiction or nonfiction books on secular subjects written by Catholic authors.

The Catholic Tradition arranges the writings according to religious subjects. There are seven religious subjects, each of which is covered in two volumes: The Church; Mass and the Sacraments; Sacred Scripture; The Saviour; Personal Ethics; Social Thought; and Spirituality. Within each subject, the writings are arranged in chronological order, which permits the reader to follow the development of Catholic thought across 2000 years.

Each excerpt in *The Catholic Tradition* is preceded by a brief biographical and explanatory introduction to help the reader understand the world in which the writer lived and wrote, and the problems with which he was dealing.

The selection of the excerpts and the writing of the introductions has been a long and difficult process. The task of making the final selections was particularly arduous (as such choices always are); the most modern authors, about whose writing there is yet no final judgment provoking the most debate. The selection of authors was made originally in the publisher's offices and then submitted to the three editors of the series who refined the selection. The editors submitted their selection to an unofficial board of scholars who very kindly made constructive comments.

The process of assembling the many hundreds of books from which to make the final selection was in itself a vast task. Many of the books under consideration were very scarce and not available in bookstores or libraries. The work of collecting the books and then making selections among them stretched over a three year period, and many books were selected for inclusion and later rejected after careful scrutiny and reflection.

The editing of *The Catholic Tradition* was a long and difficult job because the literature of Roman Catholicism is a vast and complex body. Of all the Christian denominations, the Roman Catholic Church is by far the oldest and largest. Its ranks include a tremendous number of saints and scholars, writers and thinkers, mystics and preachers: many of whom felt so strongly about their faith that they were willing to die for it. They have left an incomparably rich legacy of art and writing. Selecting from it is not simple.

The selections that we made are representative of the best of mainstream Catholic writing. Generally, they should be intelligible to a thoughtful layman. Some however, may prove more technical than others, and some of the very recent writers may seem controversial. The reader should bear in mind that some theological questions simply do not admit of facile answers, and that some of the earlier writers were considered controversial in their own days. It is also well to remember that the writings gathered here, brilliant and revered as their authors may be, are not necessarily official statements of Church policy. But they are, all of them, solidly part of the Catholic tradition.

The writers are all Catholics, many of them clergymen, some of them converts to Catholicism. They all wrote as loyal

Introduction

servants of the Church and from a Catholic point of view. When they wrote on personal ethics they proceeded from the assumption that man's goal was to imitate Christ, not simply to follow a secular set of ethical rules. When they wrote on social problems they expressed the need to solve social problems because they loved their neighbors, not for the material enrichment of society. Their writings on Christ reflect an intense struggle to bend human language to divine definition. Taken together, their writings form a literary tradition that is Roman Catholic at heart. That tradition has certain ingredients that are not present in the literary traditions of the other Christian denominations. Particularly, the heritage of liturgical ceremony and mystical contemplation have left an incomparable treasure of literature that is here presented in the volumes entitled *Mass and the Sacraments,* and *Spirituality.*

The whole corpus of Catholic thinking and writing, distilled here in *The Catholic Tradition,* is generally considered by scholars to have three important periods: the ancient, or patristic, period; the high middle-ages, which is the era of St. Thomas Aquinas and sometimes called the scholastic period; finally the time in which we live today, the last 100 years. These three epochs are golden ages of Catholic writing. They are separated from each other by the generally unproductive eras of the dark ages and the Reformation.

Through all these epochs the great Catholic writers have preserved and developed the Christian message: love God; love your fellow man. Each writer wrote conscious of the tradition behind him, conscious that he was building on the work of men before him, adapting their work to changed conditions or continuing their work on the outer edges of human speculation.

The present day writers, those of the third great era of Catholic writing, are the most important part of *The Catholic Tradition.* Here for the first time their thinking is presented along with the work of their predecessors; here can be seen the stunning achievement of today's Catholic writing, and how it follows logically from the writing of the patristic and scholastic thinkers.

The present day writers presented in *The Catholic Tradition* number 114, over half of the total number of writers chosen.

Their writing will probably prove more intelligible to the average reader because they write in today's idiom and they address contemporary problems.

Oddly enough, many if not most of the modern writers are not familiar to the average Catholic. St. Augustine, and St. Thomas Aquinas are household names, but only serious Catholic readers today are familiar with the masterful writings of Karl Rahner, Edward Schillebeeckx, Raymond Brown, and Gustavo Gutiérrez. None the less, these men are representative of a great historical flowering of Catholic writing today and their names may well echo down the ages.

THE PUBLISHER

Clement of Alexandria
150-215

Very little information is available on this Father of the Church who is second only to Origen as a representative of the early development of theology in Alexandria. Clement was well instructed in Greek philosophy, which he used generously in his theological writings. A convert to Christianity, he conducted a school of Christian instruction in Alexandria. He left that city around 202, during a persecution of the Christians. He seems to have spent time in Antioch and Cappadocia before his death.

Clement was highly respected in Christian antiquity for his holiness and learning. He is one of the major contributors to early Christian literature. Perhaps one of Clement's greatest achievements is the ease with which he blended Greek philosophical thought and Christian biblical faith into a complementary whole.

His three most important works are The Exhortation to the Heathen, Christ The Educator and The Stromata. The Exhortation, designed to lead pagans to Christian faith, is an excellent example of how the spirit of philosophy and of the gospel can be brought together. Christ The Educator is a guide to Christian life. The aim of The Stromata (tapestries, miscellanies) is to supply the Christian community with ample material to construct a rich Christian philosophy.

As the Christian communities of the early church developed, it was normal that questions concerning daily conduct should arise. *Dwelling within a predominantly pagan society, Christians wanted to have some guidelines as to how they should act in public. With whom should they associate? How should they dress? To what degree could they participate in the life style of a wealthy city like Alexandria?*

Clement's contribution to the community in relation to questions such as these is his Christ The Educator. *It is a treatise on moral training which presents Christ as the teacher of character. In Book I, Clement sets down his general thesis: Christ is the Educator, the Christians are the children. Guided by a paternal love for all mankind, Christ teaches with a mixture of severity and kindness. As Educator, Christ is most practical. By persuasion and example, He leads the Christian to choose the good and avoid evil.*

Books II and III are full of details on how a Christian should eat and drink, on laughter and conversation, on dress and sleep, on companions, and similar topics. Much of this might appear dull and insignificant to the contemporary reader. However, it is important to realize that norms such as those developed in Christ The Educator *have had a lasting impact on the Christian world's handling of everyday activities.*

The influence of the Greek Stoic philosophy on this moral treatise is obvious. Clement's attention to details and emphasis on the practical reveal his contact with this philosophy. Specifically Stoic virtues such as self-sufficiency, apathy and frugality are presented to the Christian for imitation. Apathy, as a virtue, is clearly Stoic and appears foreign to the Christian concepts of involvement and sensitivity. Yet, Christ is presented as entirely free from passion.

The difficulty of establishing a mature model for Christian conduct is being experienced again today. The practical questions of what to do, what is right or wrong, are still alive. Though knowledge of how earlier generations responded cannot give contemporary Christians a set of answers, it certainly can serve to initiate serious reflection and discussion.

CHRIST THE EDUCATOR

BOOK ONE

CHAPTER 1

O you who are children! An indestructible corner stone of knowledge, holy temple of the great God, has been hewn out especially for us as a foundation for the truth. This corner stone is noble persuasion, or the desire for eternal life aroused by an intelligent response to it, laid in the ground of our minds.

For, be it noted, there are these three things in man: habits, deeds, and passions. Of these, habits come under the influence of the word of persuasion, the guide to godliness. This is the world that underlies and supports, like the keel of a ship, the whole structure of the faith. Under its spell, we surrender, even cheerfully, our old ideas, become young again to gain salvation, and sing in the inspired words of the psalm: 'How good is God to Israel, to those who are upright of heart.' As for deeds, they are affected by the word of counsel, and passions are healed by that of consolation.

These three words, however, are but one: the self-same Word who forcibly draws men from their natural, worldly way of life and educates them to the only true salvation: faith in God. That is to say, the heavenly Guide, the Word, once He begins to call men to salvation, takes to Himself the name of persuasion (this sort of appeal, although only one type, is properly given the name of the whole, that is, word, since the whole service of God has a persuasive appeal, instilling in a receptive mind the desire for life now and for the life to come); but the Word also heals and counsels, all at the same time. In fact, He follows up His own activity by encouraging the one He has already persuaded, and particularly by offering a cure for his passions.

Let us call Him, then, by the one title: Educator of little ones, an Educator who does not simply follow behind, but who leads the way, for His aim is to improve the soul, not just to instruct it; to guide to a life of virtue, not merely to one of knowledge. Yet, that same Word does teach. It is simply that in this work we are not considering Him in that light. As Teacher, He explains and reveals through instruction, but as Educator He is practical. First He persuades men to form habits of life, then He encourages them to fulfill their duties by laying down clear-cut counsels and by holding up, for us who follow, examples of those who have erred in the past. Both are most useful: the advice, that it may be obeyed; the other, given in the form of example, has a twofold object—either that we may choose the good and imitate it or condemn and avoid the bad.

Healing of the passions follows as a consequence. The Educator strengthens souls with the persuasion implied in these examples, and then He gives the nourishing, mild medicine, so to speak, of His loving counsels to the sick man that he may come to a full knowledge of the truth. Health and knowledge are not the same; one is a result of study, the other of healing. In fact, if a person is sick, he cannot master any of the things taught him until he is first completely cured. We give instructions to someone who is sick for an entirely different reason than we do to someone who is learning; the latter, we instruct that he may acquire knowledge, the first, that he may regain health. Just as our body needs a physician when it is sick, so, too, when we are weak, our soul needs the Educator to cure its ills. Only then does it need the Teacher to guide it and develop its capacity to know, once it is made pure and capable of retaining the revelation of the Word.

Therefore, the all-loving Word, anxious to perfect us in a way that leads progressively to salvation, makes effective use of an order well adapted to our development; at first, He persuades, then He educates, and after all this He teaches.

CHAPTER 2

Our Educator, O children, resembles His Father, God, whose Son He is. He is without sin, without blame, without passion of soul, God immaculate in form of man, accomplishing

4

His Father's will. He is God the Word, who is in the bosom of the Father, and also at the right hand of the Father, with even the nature of God.

He it is who is the spotless image. We must try, then, to resemble Him in spirit as far as we are able. It is true that He Himself is entirely free from human passion; that is why He alone is sinless. Yet we must strive, to the best of our ability, to be as sinless as we can. There is nothing more important for us than first to be rid of sin and weakness, and then to uproot any habitual sinful inclination. The highest perfection, of course, is never to sin in any least way; but this can be said of God alone. The next highest is never deliberately to commit wrong; this is the state proper to the man who possesses wisdom. In the third place comes not sinning except on rare occasions; this marks a man who is well educated. Finally, in the lowest degree, we must place delaying in sin for a brief moment; but even this, for those who are called to recover their loss and repent, is a step on the path to salvation.

It seems to me that the Educator expresses it aptly through Moses when He says: 'If anyone die suddenly before him [the priest], the head of his consecration shall be defiled; and he shall immediately shave it.' By 'sudden death' He means an indeliberate sin, and says that it 'defiles' because it pollutes the soul. For the cure He prescribes that the head be shaved on the spot as soon as possible, meaning that the locks of ignorance that darken the reason should be shorn so that the reason (which has its seat in the head), stripped of hair, that is, wickedness, may the better retrace its course to repentance.

A few words afterwards He adds: 'The former days were without reason,' by which He surely means that deliberate sin is an act done contrary to reason. Involuntary sin He calls 'sudden,' but deliberate sin 'without reason.' It is precisely for this purpose that the Word, Reason Itself, has taken upon Himself, as the Educator of little ones, the task of preventing sins against reason. Understand in this light that expression in the Scriptures: 'For this reason, thus speaks the Lord . . . .' The words that follow describe and condemn some sin that has been committed. The judgment contained in these words is just, for it is as if He were giving notice in the words of the Prophet that, if you had not sinned, He would not have made these threats. The same is true of those other words: 'For this reason, the Lord says these things . . . ,' and 'Because you have not heard these words, the Lord says these things . . . ,' and 'Behold, for this reason, the Lord says . . . ' In fact, the inspired Word exists because of both obedience and disobedience: that we may be saved by obeying it, and educated because we have disobeyed.

Therefore, the Word is our Educator who heals the unnatural passions of our soul with His counsel. The art of healing, strictly speaking, is the relief of the ills of the body, an art learned by man's wisdom. Yet, the only true divine Healer of human sickness, the holy Comforter of the soul when it is ill, is the Word of the Father. Scripture says: 'Save Thy servant, O my God, who puts his trust in Thee. Have mercy on me, O Lord, because I have cried to Thee the whole day through.' In the words of Democritus, 'The healer, by his art, cures the body of its diseases, but it is wisdom that rids the spirit of its ills.' The good Educator of little ones, however, Wisdom Himself, the Word of the Father, who created man, concerns Himself with the whole creature, and as the Physician of the whole man heals both body and soul.

'Arise,' the Saviour said to the paralytic, 'take up the bed on which you are lying and go home.' And immediately the sick man regained his health. To the man who was dead He said: 'Lazarus, come forth.' And the dead man came forth from his tomb, the same as he had been before the underwent [death], except for having tasted resurrection.

But the soul He heals in a way suitable to the nature of the soul: by His commandments and by His gifts. We would perhaps expect Him to heal with His counsels, but, generous with His gifts, He also says to us sinners: 'Thy sins are forgiven thee.' With these words we have become little ones in spirit, for by them we share in the magnificent and unvarying order established by His providence. That providence begins by ordering the world and the heavens, the course of the sun's orbit and the movements of the other heavenly bodies, all for the sake of man. Then, it concerns itself with man himself, for whom it had undertaken all these other labors. And because it considers this as its most important work, it guides man's soul on the right path by the virtues of prudence and temperance, and equips his body with beauty and harmony. Finally, into the actions of mankind it infuses uprightness and some of its own good order.

CHAPTER 3

Both as God and as man, the Lord renders us every kind of service and assistance. As God, He forgives sin; as man, He educates us to avoid sin completely.

But, since man is the creation of God, he is naturally dear to Him. Other things God made by a simple word of command, but man He fashioned by His own direct action and breathed into him something proper to Himself. Now, a being which God Himself has fashioned, and in such a way that it resembles Himself closely, must have been created either because it is desirable to God in itself, or because it is useful for some other creature. If man has been created as desirable in himself, then God loves him as good, since He Himself is good, and there is a certain loveableness in man, which is the very quality breathed into him by God.

But, if God made man only because He considered him useful for some other creature, even then He had no other reason for actually creating him than that with him He could become a good Creator, and man could come to a knowledge of God (remember, in this case, unless man has been created, God would not have made the other creature for whose sake man was being created). So, the power which God already possessed, hidden deep within Himself, the power of willing, He was actualizing by this display of the external power of creating, drawing from man a motive for creating him. Thus, He saw what He possessed all along, and the creature whom God had willed to be, actually came into existence. For there is nothing that God cannot do.

Therefore, man, the creation of God, is desirable in himself. But being desirable in oneself means being connatural to the person to whom one is desirable, and being acceptable and pleasing. But what does being pleasing to someone mean, if not being loved by him? Man is, then, an object of love; yes, man is loved by God.

7

It must be so, for it was on man's account that the Only-begotten was sent from the bosom of the Father, as the Word evoking trust. Evoking trust, indeed, trust in abundance, the Lord clearly professes to do when He says: 'The Father Himself loves you, because you have loved Me.' And again: 'And thou hast loved them, just as thou hast loved Me.'

I believe it is already evident what the Educator desires and what He professes to accomplish, what He has in mind in His words and in His deeds when He commands what we are to do and what we are to avoid. It is clear, too, that the other kind of discourse, that of the Teacher, is at once direct and spiritual, in unmistakable language, but meant only for those initiated into the mysteries. But, for the present, let that be.

As for Him who lovingly guides us along the way to the better life, we ought to return Him love and live according to the dictate of His principles. This we should do not only by fulfilling His commandments and obeying His prohibitions, but also by turning away from the evil examples we just mentioned and imitating the good. In this way, we shall make our own actions, as far as we are able, like those of our Educator, that the ancient saying, 'according to His own image and likeness,' may be accomplished.

But we wander in thick darkness; we need an unerring guide in life who will keep us from stumbling. The best guide is not that blind one who, in the words of Scripture, 'leads the blind into a ditch,' but the Word, keen of sight, penetrating into the secret places of the heart. Just as there cannot be a light that does not give light, nor a cause unless it produces some effect, nor a lover unless he loves, just so He can not be good unless He rendered us service and led us to salvation.

Let us, then, express our love for the commandments of the Lord by our actions. (Indeed, the Word Himself, when He became flesh in visible form, unceasingly showed not only the theory but also the practise of virtue.) Further, considering the Word as our law, let us see in His commandments and counsels direct and sure paths to eternity. For His precepts are filled with the spirit, not of fear, but of persuasion.

BOOK TWO

CHAPTER 1

In keeping with the purpose we have in mind, we must now select passages from the Scriptures that bear on education in the practical needs of life, and describe the sort of life he who is called a Christian should live throughout his life. We should begin with ourselves, and with the way we should regulate [our actions].

In the effort to maintain a proper proportion in this treatise, let us speak first of the way each should conduct himself in reference to his body, or, rather, of the manner in which he should exercise control over it. Now, whenever a man is drawn by reason away from external things and even from any further concern for his body to the realm of the understanding, and acquires a clear insight into the natural attributes of man, he will understand that he is not to be eager about external things, but is to purify that which is proper to man, the eye of his soul, and to sanctify even his body. For, if a man is completely purified and freed from the things that make him only dust, what could he have more serviceable for walking in the path that leads to the perception of God than his own self?

Other men, indeed, live that they may eat, just like unreasoning beasts; for them life is only their belly. But as for us, our Educator has given the command that we eat only to live. Eating is not our main occupation, nor is pleasure our chief ambition. Food is permitted us simply because of our stay in this world, which the Word is shaping for immortality by His education. Our food should be plain and ungarnished, in keeping with the truth, suitable to children who are plain and unpretentious, adapted to maintaining life, not self-indulgence.

Viewed in this sense, life depends upon two things only: health and strength. To satisfy these needs, all that is required is a disposition easily satisfied with any sort of food; it aids digestion and restricts the weight of the body. Thus, growth and health and strength will be fostered; not the unbalanced and unhealthy and miserable state of men such as athletes fed on an enforced diet. Surely, excessive variety in food must be avoided, for it gives rise to every kind of bad effect: indisposition of body, upset stomach, perversion of taste due to some misguided culinary adventure or foolish experiment in pastry cooking. Men have the nerve to style such self-indulgence nourishment, even though it degenerates into pleasures that only inflict harm. Antiphanes, the Delian physician, has said that rich variety in food is one of the causes of disease. Yet, there are those who grow dissatisfied with the truth in their restless ostentation, and reject simplicity of diet to engage in a frantic search for expensive menus that must be imported from across the seas.

I feel pity for their disease; but they themselves show no shame in flaunting their extravagances, going to no end of trouble to procure lampreys from the Sicilian straits and eels from Maeander, kids from Melos and mullets from Sciathos, Pelordian mussels and Abydean oysters, to say nothing of sprats from Lipara and Mantinean turnips and beets from Ascra. They anxiously search for Methymnian scallops, Attic turgots, laurel-thrushes, and the golden-brown figs for five thousand of which the notorious Persian sent to Greece. On top of all this, they buy fowl from Phasis, francolins from Egypt and peacocks from Medea. Gourmands that they are, they greedily yearn for these fowl and dress them up with sweet sauces, ravenously providing themselves with whatever the land and the depth of the sea and the vast expanse of the sky produce as food. Such grasping and excitable people seem to scour the world blunderingly for their costly pleasures, and make themselves heard for their 'sizzling frying-pans,' wasting the whole of their lives in hovering over mortar and pestle, omnivorous fellows who cling as close to matter as fire does. Why, they deprive even the stable food, bread, of its strength by sifting away the nourishing parts of wheat, turning a necessity of life into a dishonorable pleasure. There is no limit to the gluttony that these men practise. Truly, in ever inventing a multitude of new sweets and ever seeking recipes of every description, they are shipwrecked on pastries and honey-cakes and desserts.

To me, a man of this sort seems nothing more than one great mouth. 'Be not desirous,' Scripture says, 'of the meats of the rich. For these belong to a false and shameful life.' These men hug their delicacies to themselves, yet after a while they must yield them to the privy. As for us, who seek a heavenly food, we must restrain the belly and keep it under the control of heaven, and even more that which is made for the belly which 'God will destroy,' as the Apostle says, intending, no doubt, to curse gluttonous desires. 'Food is for the belly,' and the life of the body, belonging completely to this world and made for corruption, depends upon it.

If anyone dares mention the Agape with shameless tongue as he indulges in a dinner exhaling the odor of steaming meats and sauces, then he profanes the holy Agape, sublime and saving creation of the Lord, with his goblets and servings of soup; he desecrates its name by his drinking and self-indulgence and fragrant odors; he is deceiving himself completely, for he thinks he can buy off the commands of God with such a banquet. We can indulge in such gatherings for the sake of entertainment, and we would rightly call them banquets and dinners and receptions, but the Lord never called such feasts His Agape. He did say somewhere: 'When thou art invited to a wedding feast, do not recline in the first place, but when thou art invited, go and recline in the last place.' And somewhere else: 'When thou givest a dinner or a supper . . .' And again: 'But when thou givest a feast, invite the poor,' for whom a supper should be given more than for anyone else. And once more: 'A certain man gave a great supper and he invited many.'

No, I know where the beguiling lure of dinners originated: from 'the gullets and mad frequentation of the table,' in the words of the comic poet. 'There are many things for many people at a dinner'; never did they learn that God has provided food and drink for His creature, I mean man, not for his dissipation, but for his welfare. It is a natural law that the body is not benefitted by excessively rich food; quite the contrary, those who live on simpler foods are stronger and healthier and more alert, as servants are, for example, in comparison with their masters, or farmer-tenants in comparison with their landlords. It is not only that they are more robust; they are also sharper of mind than the wealthy, as the philosophers are, for they have not sated their minds with food nor seduced it with pleasure.

An Agape is in reality heavenly food, a banquet of the Word. The Agape, or charity, 'bears all things, endures all things, hopes all things; charity never fails.' 'Blessed is he who eats bread in the kingdom of God.' Surely, of all downfalls, the most unlikely is for charity, which faileth not, to be cast down from heaven to earth among all these dainty seasonings. Do you still imagine that I refer to a meal that is to be destroyed? 'If I distribute my goods to the poor and have not charity,' Scripture says, 'I am nothing.' On this charity depend the whole Law and the word. If you love the Lord thy God and thy neighbor, there will be a feast, a heavenly one, in heaven. The earthly feast, as we have proved from Scripture, is called a supper, one permeated with love, yet not identified with it, but an expression of mutual and generous good will.

'Let not then our good be reviled,' the Apostle says, 'for the kingdom of God does not consist in food and drink,' meaning the daily meal, 'but justice and peace and joy in the Holy Spirit.' Whoever eats of this feast is put in possession of the most wonderful of all things, the kingdom of God, and takes his place in the holy assembly of love, the heavenly Church. Certainly, love is pure, worthy of God, and its fruit is giving. 'The care of discipline is love,' Wisdom says, 'and love is the keeping of the laws.' Festive gatherings of themselves do contain some spark of love, for from food taken at a common table we become accustomed to the food of eternity. Assuredly, the dinner itself is not an Agape, yet let the feasting be rooted in love. 'Thy children, O Lord,' it is said, 'whom Thou lovest, know that it is not the growing of fruit that nourishest men, but Thy word preserves them that believe in Thee.' 'For it is not on bread that the just man will live.'

Let the meal be plain and restrained, of such sort that it will quicken the spirit. Let it be free of a too rich variety, and let not even such a meal be withdrawn from the guidance of the Educator. An Agape fosters communal living very well, for it supplies ample provisions for its journey, that is, self-sufficiency. Self-sufficiency, in dictating that food be limited to the proper amount, ministers to the health of the body, and, besides, can distribute some of its substance to its neighbor. But, if the diet overstep the limits of self-sufficiency, it harms man by dulling his mind and making his body susceptible to disease. Indeed, the pleasures of a luxurious table inflict untold damage: gluttony, squeamishness, gourmandizing, insatiability of appetite, voraciousness. Carrion flies and wheedling weasels and gladiators, as well as 'that wild tribe of parasites,' are of the same type, for the first have sacrificed reason, the second friendship, and the last life itself for the pleasures of the belly, creeping upon their bellies, beasts that merely resemble man, made to the likeness of their father, the ravening beast. Those who first called such men in Greek, *asótoi*, that is, abandoned and dissolute, suggested their end, I think, meaning, instead, *asóstoi*, with elision of the *sigma*, that is, beyond salvation. Are not such men who waste their lives on dishes and frivolous elaborate preparations of highly seasoned foods, whose minds have become base, are they not hidebound to earth, living for the passing moment as though they did not live at all?

The Holy Spirit complains of such men, in the words of Isaias, subtly refusing them the name of Agape, since their feast is contrary to reason: 'They made good cheer, killing calves and slaying rams, saying: Let us eat and drink, for tomorrow we die.' Because He considers such revelry a sin, He adds: 'And this iniquity shall not be forgiven till you die,' meaning, not that death, which will be unfelt, will be forgiveness for their sin, but that death to salvation will be its punishment. Wisdom says: 'Take no pleasure in luxury, be it ever so small.'

But let us turn our attention now to the food that is spoken of an 'idol-offered,' and to the command enjoining us to avoid it. These foods I consider a sacrilege and an abomination: from the blood of them fly 'the shades from out of Erybus now dead.' 'I would not have you become associates of devils,' the Apostle says. There are two sorts of food, one minstering to salvation, and the other proper to those who perish. We should abstain from his last sort, not out of fear (for there is no power in them), but to keep our consciences pure and to show our contempt for the devils to whom they have been dedicated. And another reason is the impressionability of those who interpret so many things in a way that harms themselves, 'whose conscience, being weak, is defiled. Now, food does not commend us to God,' 'nor does what goes into a man defile him, but what comes out of the mouth,' in the words of Scripture. The physical act of eating is indifferent. 'For neither do we suffer any loss if we eat,' Scripture continues, 'Nor if we do not eat shall we have any advantage.' But it is not right for those judged worthy of partaking of divine and spiritual food to share 'the table of devils.' 'Have we not a right,' the Apostle asks, 'to eat and drink and to take about with us a woman?' But it stands to reason that we forestall passion when we keep pleasures under control: 'Still, take care lest this right of yours become a stumbling-block to the weak.'

We ought not to misuse the gifts of the Father, then, acting the part of spendthrifts like the rich son in the Gospel; let us, rather, make use of them with detachment, keeping them under control. Surely we have been commanded to be the master and lord, not the slave, of food. It is an admirable thing indeed for a man to depend upon divine food in contemplation of the truth, and to be filled with the vision of that which really is, which is inexhaustible, tasting pleasure that is enduring and abiding and pure. Unquestionably, it is contrary to reason, utterly useless, and beneath human dignity for men to feed themselves like cattle being fattened for the slaughter, for those who come from the earth to keep looking down to the earth and ever bowed over their tables. Such men practise a life only of greed, by burying the good of this life in a way of life that will not last, and paying court only to their bellies, for whose sake they rate cooks more highly than they do those who work the soil. Not that we condemn conviviality, but we do suspect the danger lurking in banquets as unfortunate.

We must shun gluttony and partake of only a few things that are necessary. And if some unbeliever invites us to a banquet and we decide to accept—although it is well not to associate with the disorderly—[the Apostle] bids us eat what is set before us, 'asking no question for conscience' sake.' We do not need to abstain from rich foods completely, but we should not be anxious for them. We must partake of what is set before us, as

14

becomes a Christian, out of respect for him who has invited us and not to lessen or destroy the sociability of the gathering. We should consider the rich variety of dishes that are served as a matter of indifference, and despise delicacies as things that after a while will cease to be. 'Let not him who eats despise him who does not eat, and let not him who does not eat judge him who eats.' A little later [the Apostle] explains the reason for his command: 'He who eats,' he says, 'eats for the Lord and he gives thanks to God. And he who does not eat, abstains for the Lord and gives thanks to God.' We conclude, then, that the true food is thanksgiving. At any rate, he who always offers up thanks will not indulge excessively in pleasure.

But, if we would draw any of our fellow banqueters to virtue, we should refrain from these delicacies of the palate all the more, and make ourselves unmistakable examples of virtue, as Christ has done for us. 'For if any of these foods scandalize my brother, I will eat it no more for ever, lest I scandalize my brother,' that is, gaining the man by a little self-control. 'Have we not the right to eat and to drink?' 'We know the truth that there is no such thing as an idol in the world, and that there is no God but one, from whom are all things, and one Lord, Jesus Christ.' But he adds: 'through thy knowledge, the weak one will perish, the brother for whom Christ died. Now when you wound the conscience of your weak brother, you sin against Christ.' Therefore, the Apostle takes great pains to reach this decision with regard to these dinners of ours: 'Not to associate with one who is called a brother if he is immoral, or an adulterer, or an idolator; with such a one not even to take food,' neither the food of words nor that of meat, foreseeing the defilement of such contact, as with 'the table of devils.'

'It is good,' he says, 'not to eat meat and not to drink wine,' just as the Pythagoreans say. Eating and drinking is the occupation of animals, and the fumes rising from them, heavy and earth-laden, cast a shadow over the soul. But, if anyone does partake of them, he does not sin; only let him partake temperately, without being attached to them or dependent upon them, or greedy for any delicacy. A voice will whisper to him: 'Do not for the sake of food, destroy the work of God.'

Only a fool will hold his breath and gape at what is set before him at a public banquet, expressing his delight in words. But it is only a greater fool who will let his eyes become enslaved to these exotic delicacies, and allow self-control to be swept away, as it were, with the various dishes. Is it not utterly inane to keep leaning forward from one's couch, all but falling on one's nose into the dishes, as though, according to the common saying, one were leaning out from the nest of the couch to catch the escaping vapors with the nostrils? Is it not completely contrary to reason to keep dipping one's hands into these pastries or to be forever stretching them out for some dish, gorging oneself intemperately and boorishly, not like a person tasting a food, but like one taking it by storm? It is easy to consider such men swine or dogs rather than men, because of their voraciousness. They are in such a hurry to stuff themselves that both cheeks are puffed out at the same time, all the hollows of their face are filled out, and sweat even rolls down as they exert themselves to satisfy their insatiable appetite, wheezing from their intemperance, and cramming food into their stomachs with incredible energy, as though they were gathering a crop for storage rather than nourishment.

Lack of moderation, an evil wherever it is found, is particularly blameworthy in the matter of food. Gourmandising, at least, is nothing more than immoderate use of delicacies; gluttony is a mania for glutting the appetite, and belly-madness, as the name itself suggests, is lack of self-control with regard to food. The Apostle, in speaking of those who offend at a banquet, exclaims: 'For at the meal, each one takes first his own supper, and one is hungry, and another drinks overmuch. Have you not houses for your eating and drinking? Or do you despise the church of God and put to shame the needy?' If a person is wealthy, yet eats without restraint and shows himself insatiable, he disgraces himself in a special way and does wrong on two scores: first, he adds to the burden of those who do not have, and lays bare, before those who do have, his own lack of temperance. Little wonder, then, that the Apostle, after having taken to task those who were shamelessly lavish with their meals, and those who were voracious, never getting their fill, cried out a second time with an angry voice: 'Wherefore, my brethren, when you come together to eat, wait for one another. If anyone is hungry, let him eat at home, lest you come together unto judgment.'

Therefore, we must keep ourselves free of any suspicion of boorishness or of intemperance, by partaking of what is set before us politely, keeping our hands, as well as our chin and our couch, clean, and by preserving proper decorum of conduct, without twisting about or acting unmannerly while we are swallowing our food. Rather, we should put our hand out only in turn, from time to time; keep from speaking while eating, for speech is inarticulate and ill-mannered when the mouth is full, and the tongue, impeded by the food, cannot function properly but utters only indistinct sounds. It is not polite to eat and drink at the same time, either, because it indicates extreme intemperance to try to do two things together that need to be done separately.

'Whether you eat or drink,' the Apostle tells us, 'do all for the glory of God,' cultivating the frugality of truth. It seems to me that the Lord was teaching frugality when He blessed the loaves and fishes with which He fed the disciples, excellently illustrating indifference about food. Then, that other fish which Peter caught at the Lord's bidding is a good example of food easily gained, given by God, yet within the limits of self-restraint. In reality, Peter was commanded to rid those who rise to the bait of justice, from out the water, of all extravagance and love of money, just as he took the coin from the fish, in order to free them of vain ostentation; though he gave the stater to the tax-collector, rendering to Caesar what was Caesar's, he was commanded to keep for God what belonged to God. The stater could be explained in other ways, too, which would all be reasonable enough, but this is not the proper place to treat such explanations. It is enough to mention them in passing as we go on to ideas in keeping with our theme, ever keeping before ourselves the subject under discussion. This we have already done many times, drawing from the ever-useful fountain to irrigate the plants sown by our discussion for the main point at issue.

If it is true that 'it is lawful for me to partake of all things,' still, 'not all things are expedient.' For, they who take advantage of everything that is lawful rapidly deteriorate into doing what is not lawful. Just as justice is not acquired through covetousness, or temperance through licentiousness, so, too, the Christian way of life is not achieved by self-indulgence. Far from 'lust-exciting delicacies' is the table of truth. Even though all things have been created particularly for man, it is not well to make use of all things, nor to use them at all times. Surely, the occasion and the time, the manner and the motive, make some difference to one who is being educated [by Christ] to what is profitable. It is this goal that provides the strength we need to restrain ourselves from living lives centered about the table. Wealth chooses that sort of life, for its vision is blunted; it is an abundance that blinds in the matter of gluttony.

No one is destitute when it comes to the necessities of life, nor does any man need to look far for these. For, He who provides for the birds and the fish, and, in a word, for unreasoning beasts, is one God. They lack nothing, yet they are not anxious about their food. But we are better than they, because we are their masters, and are more akin to God, to the degree that we practise self-control. We have been created, not to eat and drink, but to come to the knowledge of God. 'The just man,' Scripture says, 'eateth and filleth his soul; but the belly of the wicked is ever in want,' ever hungry with a greed that cannot be quenched.

Lavishness is not capable of being enjoyed alone; it must be bestowed upon others. That is why we should shy away from foods that arouse the appetite and lead us to eat when we are not hungry. Even in moderate frugality, is there not a rich and wholesome variety? Roots, olives, all sorts of green vegetables, milk, cheese, fruits, and cooked vegetables of all sorts, but without the sauces. And should there be need for meat, boiled or dressed, let it be given. 'Have you anything here to eat?' the Lord asked His Apostles after His resurrection. 'And they offered Him a piece of broiled fish,' because He had taught them to practise frugality. 'And when He had finished eating, He said to them,' and Luke goes on to record all that He said. We should not overlook the fact, either, that they who dine according to reason, or, rather, according to the Word, are not required to leave sweetmeats and honey out of their fare. Surely,

18

of all the foods available, the most convenient are those which can be used immediately without being cooked. Inexpensive foods come next in order, since these are so accessible, as we have already said.

As long as those other fellows stay hunched over their groaning tables, catering to their lusts, the devil of gluttony leads them by the nose. I, for one, would not hesitate to call that devil the devil of the belly, the most wicked and deadly of them all. He is very much like the so-called *engastrimythos*, because he speaks, as it were, through his belly. It is far better to possess happiness than to have any daemon as a companion; happiness is the practise of the virtues.

Matthew the Apostle used to make his meal on seeds and nuts and herbs, without flesh meat; John, maintaining extreme self-restraint, 'ate locusts and wild-honey'; and Peter abstained from pork. But, 'he fell into an ecstasy,' it is written in the Acts of the Apostles, 'and saw heaven standing open and a certain vessel let down by the four corners to the earth; and in it were all the four-footed beasts and creeping things of the earth and birds of the air. And there came a voice to him: Arise and kill and eat. But Peter said: Far be it from me, Lord, for never did I eat anything common or unclean. And there came a voice a second time to him: What God has cleansed, do not thou call common.' The use of these foods is a matter of indifference for us, too, 'for not that which goes into the mouth defiles a man,' but the barren pursuit of wantonness. When God formed man, He said: 'All these things will be food for you.'

'Herbs with love rather than a fatted calf with deceit.' This is reminiscent of what we said before, that herbs are not the Agape, but that meals should be taken with charity. A middle course is good in all things, and no less so in serving a banquet. Extremes, in fact, are dangerous, but the mean is good, and all that avoids dire need is a mean. Natural desires have a limit set to them by self-sufficiency.

Among the Jews, frugality was made a matter of precept by a very wise dispensation of the Law. The Educator forbade them the use of innumerable things, and He explained the reasons, the spiritual ones hidden, the material ones obvious, but all of which they trusted. Some animals [were forbidden] because they were cloven-footed; others, because they did not ruminate their food; a third class, because they, alone among all the fish of the seas, had no scales; until, finally, there were only a few things left fit for food. And, even of those He permitted them to touch, He placed a prohibition on the ones found dead or offered to idols or strangled. They could not even touch them. He imposed upon them a contrary course of action until the inclination engendered by habits of easy living be broken, because it is difficult for one who indulges in pleasures to keep himself from returning to them.

Among men, pleasure generally gives rise to some sense of loss and of regret; overeating begets in the soul only pain and lethargy and shallow-mindedness. It is said, too, the bodies of the young in the period of their physical maturing are able to grow because they are somewhat lacking in nourishment; the life-principle which fosters growth is not encumbered—on the contrary, an excess of food would block the freedom of its course.

So it is that he who of all philosophers so praised truth, Plato, gave new life to the dying ember of Hebrew philosophy by condemning a life spent in revelry: 'When I arrived,' he said, 'what is here called a life of pleasure, filled with Italian and Syracusan meals, was very repulsive to me. It is a life in which one gorges oneself twice a day, sleeps not only during the night, and engages in all the pastimes that go with this sort of life. No one upon earth could ever become wise in this way, if from his youth he had followed such pursuits as these, nor would he ever attain in that way any reputation for an excellent physique.' Surely, Plato was not unacquainted with David, who, when he was settling the holy ark in the middle of the tabernacle of his city, made a feast for all his obedient subjects and 'before the face of the Lord, distributed to all the multitude of Israel, both men and women, to everyone, a cake of bread and baked bread and pan-cakes from the frying-pan.' This food sufficed, this food of Israel; that of the Gentiles is extravagance.

'You will never be able to become wise' if you indulge in such extravagance, burying your mind deep in your belly; you will resemble the so-called ass-fish which Aristotle claims is the only living thing which has its heart in its stomach, and which the comic poet Epicharmis entitles 'the huge-bellied.' Such are the men who trust in their belly, 'whose god is their belly, whose glory is their shame, who mind the things of earth.' For such men the Apostle makes a prediction foreboding nothing good, for he concludes: 'whose end is ruin.'

St. Hippolytus of Rome
170-236

The vision underlying Christian ethical teaching has been subject to a variety of expression throughout its twenty centuries. At times the expression is alive and fiery, at times dry and technical, at times highly poetic. The brief document known as the Letter to Diognetus, *composed during the late second or third century, is an unusually beautiful statement of the Christian view of life that serves as a basis for all human relationships and action. The letter consists of two parts, (paragraphs 1-10 and 11, 12), each written by a different person. Neither author is certainly known, though Hippolytus, who died a martyr in 236, is suggested as the author of the second part. Diognetus, to whom the letter is addressed, was the name of a tutor of Marcus Aurelius.*

The letter begins with a series of questions: Who are these Christians? Who is their God? Why do they care so little for the world, and even despise death? What is the character of their Christian love? One of the conditions fundmental to all ethical thinking is immediately established. In order to grasp the Christian vision, one must clear away all the prejudices that clutter the mind and begin by being a new man ready to give ear to a new story. This condition of openness, though highly attractive, is most rare. Yet, without it, one cannot approach or come to see why one acts the way he does.

Assuming that Diognetus can do this, the author moves on to the various questions mentioned above and leads Diognetus to an insight on the Christian way of life. Christians are no different from anyone else as regards nationality, speech or customs. "Yet the character of the culture they reveal is marvellous and, it must be admitted, unusual." They are at home everywhere and nowhere. They obey the laws of men but their lives are better than the laws. Christians live in the world but are not of the world. Their lives are anchored in God's gentleness, humility and love. Christians know that there is no real happiness in getting the better of a neighbor, in being rich, or in ordering others about. Christian faith makes it possible to see the world and everyone in it in a most extraordinary manner.

Obviously a life permeated with this outlook knows what to do in any situation and has the ability to respond to human needs with actions that are beyond the categories of good and evil. And this is what it means to live as a Christian.

The reader will find the Letter to Diognetus *a refreshing and invigorating composition. Oddly enough, it had little influence on writers of the early and medieval periods of Christianity. Perhaps its naked simplicity was too challenging for societies that needed what appeared to be more sophisticated and stricter statements of morality. The present effort of Christianity to shake off much of the unnecessary paraphernalia that has built up in the area of Christian ethical thinking, a statement such as the* Letter to Diognetus *might well serve to get Christians back to an unprejudiced hearing of the message of God's love.*

LETTER TO DIOGNETUS

MY DEAR DIOGNETUS: I see that you are eagerness itself to learn about the religion of the Christians. Your questions in regard to them have been drawn up with great clarity and care. You ask: In what God do they trust? How does their worship of Him help them—all of them—to care so little for the world and to despise death? Why do they neither esteem the gods that are considered as such by the Greeks nor keep the observances of the Jews? What is the character of the love that links them one with another? And, finally, why is it that this new group or institute has come into existence in our time and not earlier? I welcome this earnestness in you, and I pray to God who gives us power both to speak and to listen that I may be given the grace so to speak that you may profit by what you hear, and that you may be given the grace so to listen that, after I have spoken, I may not be disappointed.

The first thing, then, is to clear away all the prejudices that clutter your mind and to divest yourself of any habit of thought that is leading you into error. You must begin by being, as it were, a new man, ready, as you yourself put it, to give ear to a new story. You must take a look not only with your eyes, but with your mind, at what you call and consider gods, and ask: What substance or form can they really have? Is not this one made of stone, like the pavement under our feet, and that one of bronze, no better than what is in the pots and pans in daily use? Is not a third made of wood and already rotting, and a fourth of silver and in need of a custodian, lest it be stolen? Is not another made of iron that is corroded with rust, and still another of clay that is no more distinguished than what is made into a vessel for the lowliest use? Are not all of them perishable matter, or forged with iron and fire? Did not a sculptor make this one, a coppersmith that one, a silversmith a third, and a potter another of them? Is there any one of them that could not have been changed into any other shape before it was given this or that form by one or another of these arts? And, even now, given the right craftsmen, could not any of these utensils be turned into gods of the same material just like these? And could not any of these gods that are now worshipped by you be once more turned by man into pots and pans like the rest? Are they not all deaf and blind, without soul or sense or power to move? Are not all of them subject to rot and decay? You call these things gods; you serve them; you bow down before them; and, in the end, you become no better than they are. This is the reason why you hate the Christians—because they refuse to take these things for gods. But the fact is that you who now esteem and worship them despise them much more than the Christians do. When you leave the gods of stone and clay which you worship unguarded, while you lock up at night the gods of silver and gold, and set a guard over them by day, lest they be stolen, do you not mock and insult them much more than the Christians do? And so with the honors you imagine you pay them: If they are sensible of them, you insult them; if they are insensible, you convict them [of insensibility], while you are propitiating them with blood and fumes of fat. Imagine one of yourselves submitting to this, or allowing anything of the sort to happen to him! There is not a single human being who would willingly put up with such treatment—for the simple reason that he can feel and think. A stone endures it, because it feels nothing. And so, you disbelieve in its power of perception. There are many other things I might say on this matter of the Christians not being enslaved to such gods as these. But, if anyone finds what I have said, insufficient, it is useless, I think, to say more.

The next question, which I think you are very eager to have discussed, is why the Christians do not worship in the same way as the Jews. As for the Jews, in so far as they keep away from the service of idols I have just mentioned, they are right in claiming to revere one God and Lord over all; but, in so far as they worship God in ways like the ones already mentioned, they are in the wrong. If the Greeks offer a proof of their folly in making offerings to gods that can neither see nor hear, then the Jews, in making the same offerings to God, as though He were in need of them, should think this ridiculous rather than religious. For, He who made heaven and earth and all that is in them, and has provided us all with what we need, could not Himself have any need of the very things which He gives to those who think they are giving something to Him. As for those who think they can offer Him sacrifices with blood and fat and holocausts, and by such rites honor Him, they differ in nothing, so it seems to me, from those who show the same devotion to deaf idols. The latter think they can give to beings unable to take; the former to one who is in need of nothing.

But, now, as to certain ridiculous matters that call for no discussion—such as their scruples in regard to meat, their observance of the Sabbath days, their vain boasting about circumcision, and the hypocrisy connected with fasting and the feasts of the new moon—I do not suppose you need any instructions from me. For, how can it be other than irreligious to accept some of the things which God has created for men's use and to reject others, as though some were created to good purposes and others were useless and superfluous? And how can it be other than profane to lie against God, pretending that He has forbidden us to do a good deed on the Sabbath day? And is it not ridiculous to boast of a mutilation of the flesh as a sign of the chosen people, as though on account of this they were particularly loved by God? Take again their constant watching of the stars and the moon in order to make sure of the observance of months and days, and to commemorate the dispensations of God and the changes of the seasons according to their own whims, making this season a time of feasting and that one a time of fasting. Who would look on all this as evidence of religion and not, rather, as a sign of folly? And so, I hope I have said enough to show you how right the Christians are in keeping away from the plain silliness and error, the fussiness and vaunting of the Jews. But, as to the mystery of their own worship, you must not expect that any man fully instruct you.

Christians are not different from the rest of men in nationality, speech, or customs; they do not live in states of their own, nor do they use a special language, nor adopt a peculiar way of life. Their teaching is not the kind of thing that could be discovered by the wisdom or reflection of mere active-minded men; indeed, they are not outstanding in human learning as others are. Whether fortune has given them a home in a Greek or foreign city, they follow local custom in the matter of dress, food, and way of life; yet the character of the culture they reveal is marvellous and, it must be admitted, unusual. They live, each in his native land—but as though they were not really at home there. They share in all duties like citizens and suffer all hardships like strangers. Every foreign land is for them a fatherland and every fatherland a foreign land. They marry like the rest of men and beget children, but they do not abandon the babies that are born. They share a common board, but not a common bed. In the flesh as they are, they do not live according to the flesh. They dwell on earth, but they are citizens of heaven. They obey the laws that men make, but their lives are better than the laws. They love all men, but are persecuted by all. They are unknown, and yet they are condemned. They are put to death, yet are more alive than ever. They are paupers, but they make many rich. They lack all things, and yet in all things they abound. They are dishonored, yet glory in their dishonor. They are maligned, and yet are vindicated. They are reviled, and yet they bless. They suffer insult, yet they pay respect. They do good, yet are punished with the wicked. When they are punished, they rejoice, as though they were getting more of life. They are attacked by the Jews as Gentiles and are persecuted by the Greeks, yet those who hate them can give no reason for their hatred.

In a word, what the soul is to the body Christians are to the world. The soul is distributed in every member of the body, and Christians are scattered in every city in the world. The soul dwells in the body, and yet it is not of the body. So, Christians live in the world, but they are not of the world. The soul which is guarded in the visible body is not itself visible. And so, Christians who are in the world are known, but their worship remains unseen. The flesh hates the soul and acts like an unjust aggressor, because it is forbidden to indulge in pleasures. The world hates Christians—not that they have done it wrong, but because they oppose its pleasures. The soul loves the body and its members in spite of the hatred. So Christians love those who hate them. The soul is locked up in the body, yet it holds the body together. And so Christians are held in the world as in a prison, yet it is they who hold the world together. The immortal soul dwells in a mortal tabernacle. So Christians sojourn among perishable things, but their souls are set on immortality in heaven. When the soul is ill-treated in the matter of food and drink, it is improved. So, when Christians are persecuted, their numbers daily increase. Such is the assignment to which God has called them, and they have no right to shirk it.

For, as I said, it was no earthly discovery that was committed to them, nor is it mortal wisdom that they feel bound to guard so jealously, nor have they been entrusted with the dispensation of merely human mysteries. The truth is that the Almighty Creator of the Universe, the invisible God Himself, scattered from heaven among them the seed of truth and of holy thought which is higher than men's minds, and He made it take firm root in their hearts. He did not send a servant (whether angel or principality, whether of those that direct the affairs of earth or of those entrusted with arrangements in heaven), but He sent the very Artificer and Maker of the cosmos, by whom He created the heavens, Him by whom He enclosed the ocean in its proper bounds, Him whose mysterious laws all the elements faithfully observe, and by whom the measures of the length of days were given to the sun to guard, Him whom the moon obeys when it is bidden to shine by night and whom the stars obey when they follow the course of the moon, Him by whom all things are put in order and given their bounds and told to obey—the heavens and the things in heaven, the earth and the things in the earth, the sea and the things in the sea, fire and air and peace, the things in the heights and in the depths and those that are in between. To them He sent Him. Do you really think—as might be humanly possible—that He sent Him to impose His power with fear and terror? Certainly not. He came in gentleness and humility. He sent Him as a King would send a son and king; He sent Him as God for the sake of men. In sending Him, He acted as a Savior, appealing to persuasion and not to power—for it is not like God to use compulsion. He acted as one inviting, not as one pursuing; as a lover, not as a judge. Later on, indeed, He will send Him as a Judge; and then who will be able to withstand His coming? . . . . [Do you not see] them thrown to wild beasts to make them deny their Lord—and yet they are

not conquered? Do you not see that the more of them who are
punished, the more they grow in number? Such things do not
look like the works of men; they are the power of God; they
are signs of His coming.

Was there one among all mankind who knew what God
was before He came? Or, perhaps, you prefer to accept the
vacuous and silly professions of those specious philosophers?
One group of them said that God was fire—what they call God
is the place to which they are likely to go. Another group said
God was water; a third, one of the other elements that God
created. The trouble is that, if any one of these propositions
is acceptable, there is no reason why any one of the other
created things should not have an equal claim to be considered
God. The fact is that all this stuff is the sham and deceit of
tricksters. God showed Himself to men; not one of them has
seen or known Him. He revealed Himself by means of faith;
for by this alone it is possible to see God. For, God, the Lord
and Creator of all, who made all things and set them in order,
was not merely a lover of mankind, but was full of compassion.
Mild and good, calm and true—He always was and is and will be;
He alone is good. The great and ineffable Idea which He conceived He communicated to His Son alone. For a time, indeed,
He kept the plan of His wisdom to Himself and guarded it as a
mystery; and thus He seemed to have no care and thought for
us. But when, through His beloved Son, He removed the veil
and revealed what He had prepared from the beginning, He gave
us all at once—participation in His gifts, the graces of being able
to see and understand things beyond all our expectations.

In Himself and with His Son, His providence had all things
arranged. If, for a time before He came, He allowed us to be
carried along by our own whims and inordinate desires, to be
led astray by pleasures and lusts, it was in no sense because He
took any joy in our sins—He merely permitted them. He did
not approve of the period of our wickedness in the past; He
was merely preparing the present reign of grace. He wanted us
who, in times past, by our own sins, were convicted of being
unworthy, to become now, by the goodness of God, worthy
of life. He wanted us who proved that, by ourselves, we could
not enter into the kingdom of God, to become able, by the

power of God, to enter in. Once the measure of our sin had become full and overflowing, and it was perfectly clear that nothing but punishment and death could be expected as the wages of sin, the time came which God had foreordained. Henceforth He would reveal His goodness and grace—and Oh! how exceeding great is God's love and friendship for men. Instead of hating us and rejecting us and remembering our sins, He was compassionate and patient and took upon Himself our sins. He gave us His own Son for our redemption. For us who were sinful, He gave up the Holy One; for the wicked the Innocent One; the Just One for the unjust; the Incorruptible One for corruptible men; and for us mortals the Immortal One. For, what else but His righteousness could have concealed our sin? In whom, if not in the only Son of God, could we lawless and sinful men have been justified? What a sweet exchange! What an inexplicable achievement! What unexpected graces! that in One who was just the sin of many should be concealed, that the righteousness of One should justify many sinners. In the former time He proved the inability of our nature to obtain life, and now He has revealed a Savior capable of saving the incapable. For both these reasons He wanted us to believe in His goodness and to look upon Him as guardian, father, teacher, adviser, and physician, as our mind, light, honor, glory, strength, and life, and to have no solicitude about what we wear and eat.

This faith, if only you desire it, you can have, and, first of all, the knowledge of the Father. For, God loved men, and for their sake made the world and made all things on earth subject to them. He gave them their reason and their mind. Them alone He allowed to look up to heaven. He fashioned them in His own image. To them He sent His only-begotten Son. To them He promised the kingdom which is in heaven and He will give it to those who love Him. And with what joy do you think you will be filled when you come to know these things? And how you will love Him who first loved you so much! And, when you love Him, you will be an imitator of His goodness. And do not be surprised that a man may become an imitator of God. He can do so because God wills it. You know, there is no real happiness in getting the better of your neighbors, in wanting to have more than weaker men, in being rich and able to order your inferiors about. It is not in such ways that a man can imitate God, for these things are no part of His greatness. On the other hand, any man can be an imitator of God, if he takes on his own shoulders the burden of his neighbors, if he chooses to use his advantage to help another who is underprivileged, if he takes what he has received from God and gives to those who are in need—for such a man becomes God to those who are helped. When you have faith, you will see that God rules in heaven, even though you are on earth; you will begin to speak of the mysteries of God; you will love and admire men who suffer because they refuse to deny God; you will condemn the deceit and error of the world as soon as you realize that true life is in heaven, and despise the seeming death in this world, and fear the real death which is reserved for those who are to be condemned to eternal fire which shall torment forever those who are committed to it. When you have faith, you will admire those who, for the sake of what is right, bear the temporal fire, and you will think them blessed when you come to know that fire . . . .

* * * * *

I have no strange doctrines to preach, nor any queer questions to ask, but, having been a disciple of the Apostles, I have become a teacher of the Gentiles. To those who have become learners of the truth I try to be a worthy minister of the teaching that has been handed down. Is there any man who, once he has been properly taught and admitted as a friend of the Word, is not anxious to master as clearly as he can the lessons openly taught to the disciples by the Word? Unperceived by the unbelieving, but speaking at length to the disciples, the Word appeared and declared the truth, speaking freely of His mysteries. Further, those who were considered by Him to be faithful learned the mysteries of the Father. It was for this reason that He sent the Word, that He might appear to the world. Dishonored by the populace, He was preached by the Apostles and was believed in by the Gentiles. He was from the beginning. He appeared as new, but was found to be old and

32

ever young, when He is born in the hearts of the saints. He is the Eternal One, who in our day is accounted to be the Son. Through Him the Church is enriched, and in the saints His unfolded grace is multiplied. This grace gives understanding, makes mysteries clear, announces the acceptable times, rejoices over the faithful, is granted to those who seek, that is to say, to those by whom the promises to believe are not broken and the limits set down by the fathers are not overstepped. And so the fear of the Law is hymned, and the grace of the Prophets is acknowledged, and the faith of the Gospels is made firm, and the tradition of the Apostles is guarded, and the joy of the Church exults. If you do not reject this grace, you will understand what the Word says by the tongues of those whom He chooses, when He wills. We have been moved to utter with difficulty whatever it was the will of the Word to command us, and out of love of the things revealed to us we became sharers of them with you.

Now that you have come to know and have given earnest attention to these truths, you will learn how much God bestows on those who love Him properly. These men become a paradise of delight, a tree bearing every fruit and flower, growing up in themselves and adorned with various fruits. For, in this place there were planted a tree of knowledge and a tree of life. It is not the tree of knowledge, but disobedience, that kills. For, the Scriptures are not silent on how God from the beginning planted a tree of knowledge and a tree of life in the middle of Paradise, revealing life through knowledge. Those who did not use it properly in the beginning were made naked by the deceit of the serpent. For, there is neither life without knowledge, nor sound knowledge without true life. Hence, the one tree was planted near the other. The Apostle saw the force of this and, blaming the knowledge which is exercised without the truth of the command leading to life, he says: 'Knowledge only breeds self-conceit, it is charity that binds the building together.' For, the man who thinks he knows something, apart from the true knowledge to which witness is borne by life, knows nothing. He is deceived by the serpent, because he has not loved life. But, the man who with fear acknowledges and pursues life plants in hope and can expect fruit. Let your heart be knowledge and your life be true reason, properly understood. And so, bearing the tree of this truth and plucking the fruit, you will forever gather the harvest which God desires and which the serpent does not touch. Eve is not deceived nor destroyed by deception and is trusted as a virgin. Salvation is set forth and the Apostles are given understanding, and the Pasch of the Lord goes on, and the candles are brought together and arranged in order. In teaching the saints the Word is gladdened. Through Him the Father is glorified. To Him be glory forever. Amen.

Lactantius
250-320

The Edict of Milan, issued by Emperor Constantine in 313, was one of the major events in the history of early Christianity. The new religion, which for so long had known only official persecution and rejection, was not recognized as the religion of the empire. Among the Christian writers of the time, Lucius Caelius Firmianus, known as Lactantius, is of unusual importance. He was born between 250 and 260, most probably in Numidia, Africa. After receiving an excellent classical education, he taught Latin rehetoric at Nicomedia. Around the year 300, he was converted from paganism to Christianity. Lactantius was reduced to severe poverty when the school in which he taught was closed in 305/6. Life improved for him after the Edict of Milan. Due to his friendship with Emperor Constantine, he was commissioned to be the tutor for Cirspus, the Emperor's son. Little is known of his final years and death.

The major writing of Lactantius is The Divine Institutes, a portion of which is presented below. The book is an apology for the truth of Christianity and is directed against various pagan authors who, at the beginning of the fourth century, were writing bitter attacks against Christianity. It is important to note that Lactantius was more at home with the writings of Cicero, Vergil, the Epicureans and the Stoics than he was with the Sacred Scriptures. He wrote for a well educated audience and sought to defend

Christianity on their ground. As a result, while defending faith, he supports human reason. He did not fall into the trap of preferring one to the other. Lactantius's style is so perfect that he has been referred to as the Christian Cicero. He is certainly one of the early Christian writers who laid the foundations for Christian humanism. Though severely criticized at times by theologians who would prefer a bit more theology than philosophy in his writing, Lactantius had had influence on scholars from his own time to the present day.

The Divine Institutes are composed of seven books. The first three treat the false worship of the gods, the origin of error and the false wisdom of philosophers. Lactantius then turns to the positive task of blending wisdom and faith into the single and inseparable way to truth. He writes on justice, true worship and the happy life.

We have chosen his discussion of justice (Book V, chapters 5-23) for inclusion here. Lactantius's description of the human condition before the coming of Christ could serve to describe much of the twentieth century—the uncontrolled drive for wealth and power, the establishment of laws to protect the mighty minority from the masses, the almost complete lack of justice. But true justice, he contends, came with Christ. All men have knowledge of justice, he says, but most men reject it.

The tension between the concept of justice and realization of the concept in particular situations has not lessened since the fourth century. A meeting with Lactantius can at least make us aware of mankind's search for justice and provide a sense of oneness with the injustice of early Christianity.

THE DIVINE INSTITUTES

BOOK FIVE

CHAPTER 5

N ow we must set forth our proposed discussion about
justice: whether this is itself the greatest virtue or
whether it is the very source of virtue. Not only the
philosophers have sought this out, but the poets also who were
much earlier and were regarded as wise men before the name of
philosophy originated. They clearly understood that this justice
was far removed from human matters, and they depicted it
as, offended with the vices of men, having left the earth and
passed into the heavens. And in order to teach what it means to
live justly—for they used to give instructions in the round-about
manner of poetical disguise—they sought examples of justice
from the age of Saturn which they call 'golden,' and they
described the condition of human life when the world was in
that age. Indeed, this must not be regarded as poetical fiction,
but as truth. For while Saturn was reigning, and the cults of
the false gods had not yet been begun, and that people had not
as yet been given over to the idea of divinity, surely God was
worshiped. For this reason, then, there were no dissensions, nor
hatreds, nor wars. 'Fury had not yet unsheathed the maddened
swords,' as Caesar Germanicus says in the Aratean poem, 'nor
had discord among relatives become known.' In fact, there was
not any even among strangers, nor were there any swords which
would be bared. Who would have to take consideration about
his own protection, as long as justice were present and flour-
ishing, since no one would make any encroachments; or who
would contrive for the ruin of another, since no one would
covet anything?

'They preferred to live content with slight worship,' as
Cicero tells us in his poem of the same title which belongs to
our religious literature. 'It was not right even to mark off or

divide the fields with a measure; they sought from a central source,' for God had given the land in common to all, so that they might live a common life, not that grasping and raging greed might claim everything for itself, and that nothing would be lacking to anyone which came into existence for all. It is necessary that this saying of the poet be taken in such a way that we should not think that there was absolutely no private ownership at that time. Rather, we should interpret it as a poetic figure, that we may understand that men were so liberal that they did not exclude others from profits gained for themselves, nor did they in solitude brood upon hidden wealth, but they freely admitted the poor to a share of their proper work.

'Then the rivers were flowing with milk and with nectar.' And neither was this strange, since the facilities of the just were manifestly laid open to all; nor did avarice, intercepting the divine benefits, bring hunger and thirst upon the common people, but all enjoyed abundance equally, since those who had, gave bountifully and generously to those who had not.

But after Saturn was expelled by his son and brought into Latium, 'Fleeing the arms of Jove, and an exile deprived of his realm,' when the people had already ceased to worship God, either from fear of the new king, or depraved through their own fault, and had begun to regard the king as a god, although he himself, a near-parricide, was an example to the others for violating piety, 'The most just virgin speedily abandoned the earth,' but, it did not happen as Cicero says, that 'she tarried in the realm of Jupiter and in part of heaven.' For how could she tarry or reside in the kingdom of him who drove his father from his realm, persecuted him in war, and cast him out as an exile from the earth? 'That one added evil poison to the black snakes and bade the wolves to take prey,' that is, he inspired men with hatred and envy and deceit, so that they were as envenomed as snakes and rapacious as wolves. This is, indeed, what those people truly do who persecute those who are just and faithful to God, and who give to judges the power of raging furiously against the guiltless. Perhaps Jupiter did something of this sort for attacking and removing justice, and for this he is said to have made snakes savage and to have incited wolves to brutality. 'Then the fury of war and the love of possessing

38

followed,' and not without cause. For when the religion of God was taken away, they lost also the knowledge of good and evil. Thus community living perished among men, and the compact of human society was broken. Then, forces began to struggle against each other, and to plot, and gain glory for themselves at the price of human blood.

CHAPTER 6

The source of all of these evils was cupidity, and this certainly burst forth from the contempt of the true Majesty. For not only did they for whom there was some abundance not share with others, but they even took away the good of others, drawing in all things unto their own private gain, and the things which individuals were working on before for the use of all were conferred upon the homes of the few. In order to subject the rest to slavery, firstly, they began to steal away and pile up the necessities of life and keep them tightly closed up, so that they might keep the celestial benefits their own, not on account of their kindly human nature which was not in them at all, but to rake up all things as instruments of their greed and avarice. They also passed laws for themselves and sanctioned, under the name of justice, those most unfair and unjust measures by which they protected their thefts and avarice against the strength of the multitude. Therefore, they availed as much by authority as by strength or resources or evil.

Since there was in them not a vestige of justice, the offices of which are humanity, fairness, pity, now they were rejoicing in proud and swollen unfairness, and they put themselves higher than the rest of men because of the train of their satellites and weapons and distinctive garb. Hence, they discovered for themselves honors, and the purple and axes, so that they might rule over those they would strike with terror and fear, relying on the terrorizing power of their axes and swords as though upon the right of masters.

In this condition did that king constitute human life, who, after his sire had been defeated and put to flight, seized not a kingdom but an impious tyranny by force of armed men. He took away that golden and just age and forced men to become evil and wicked from this very fact, that he turned them from

God to adoring himself, which terror of most overweening power had wrung out from them. For who would not fear him whom arms encircles? Him whom the unusual flash of iron and swords surrounded? Or what stranger would he spare who had not even spared his own father? Whom would he fear who had overcome the strong, outstanding race of Titans in war, and had destroyed them by slaughtering them? Why is it strange if a whole multitude, oppressed with new fear, had yielded to the adulation of one? They venerated him. They conferred the greatest honor upon him. And since imitating the manners and vices of a king is judged to be a kind of flattery, they all cast aside reverence, lest they seem to reproach the king for his crimes if they lived reverently.

Thus, corrupted by this constant imitation, they abandoned the divine right and, little by little, the habit of evil living became the custom. And now nothing of the preceding age remained in its reverent and very fine condition, but justice having been exploded, took truth with it and left for men error, ignorance, and blindness. Not wisely, therefore, did the poets act who sang that justice fled to the kingdom of Jupiter. If justice was on the earth in that age which they call golden, then, surely, it was driven out by Jupiter who changed the golden age. Now the change of the golden age and the expulsion of justice must be considered, as I said, as nothing else than the desertion of the divine religion. For this alone brings it about that a man may hold his fellowman dear and know that he is bound to him with the bond of brotherhood, inasmuch as 'the same Father is God of all,' and that he may share the benefits of God, the common Father, with those who do not have them; that he may harm no one, oppress no one, not close his door to a guest-stranger, nor his ear to one entreating him; but that he may be 'bountiful, generous, liberal,' which Tully believed were 'kingly praises.' Actually, this is justice, and this the golden age, which was first corrupted in the reign of Jupiter, and then soon after, when he himself and all his progeny were consecrated by the worship of many gods which was then taken up, it had been entirely removed.

CHAPTER 7

But God, most indulgent parent that He is, when the end of time was drawing near, sent a messenger to lead back that old age and the justice that had been routed, so that the human race would not be thrown about by great and everlasting errors. The likeness of that golden time returned, therefore, and was given back to the earth, but justice was assigned only to a few. This justice is nothing else but a devoted and religious worship of the one God. Perhaps someone may be moved to ask why, if this is justice, it has not been given to the entire human race, and why all the people are not agreed upon it. This is a matter of great discussion; why separate selection was retained by God when He gave justice to the earth. I have brought this out in another place, and wherever it shall come up opportunely, it will be explained. Now it is sufficient to note this very briefly, that virtue is not able to be discerned unless there be contrary vices, nor is it perfected unless it be exercised by adversity. God wished this distinction of good and evil to exist, that we might know the quality of the good from evil, and, likewise, that of evil from good; and, if one is removed, the reason of the other cannot be understood.

So God did not exclude evil in order that the condition of virtue might be able to stand firm. For how could patience retain its force or its name, if there were nothing which we were forced to suffer? How could faith vowed to its God merit praise, unless there were someone who wished to turn it aside from God? Therefore, He permitted the unjust to be more powerful, that they could force men unto evil; and for this reason they are the more numerous, so that virtue would be precious because it is rare. Even Quintilian put this very briefly and in an outstanding manner in an obscure chapter: 'For what virtue would innocence be,' he said, 'unless its rare occurrence had given it praise? But since it has been so worked out by nature that hatred, desire, wrath toward something which they have come upon should drive men blind, it seems to be beyond man's nature to be free from fault. But if nature had given equal emotions to all, piety would be nothing.' How true this is the very demand of reason teaches. For if it is virtue to bravely

41

resist evils and vices, it is clear that without evil and vice there is no virtue. And in order that God might make this absolute and perfect, He kept that which was contrary to it, with which it could contend. For shaken by shattering evils it acquires stability, and as often as it is struck against, so much does it gain in strength. Without a doubt, then, this cause brings it about that, although justice has been conferred upon men, yet it is not said to be a golden age, for it has not endured evil to retain the opposite which alone holds the guaranty of a divine religion.

CHAPTER 8

Those who think that no one is just have justice before their eyes, but they do not want to perceive her. Why is it that they describe her in songs or in every speech, complaining of her absence, although it would be very easy for them to be good if they should wish? Why do you depict justice to yourselves as something inane, and why do you wish it to drop from the sky as though fashioned in some likeness? Behold, it is present before you. Take it up, if you can, and place it in the dwelling place of your heart, and do not think it difficult or foreign to these times. Be fair and good, and the justice which you seek will follow you of its own accord. Put aside from your hearts all evil designs, and immediately that golden time will return for you, which you cannot attain in any other way than by beginning to worship the true God. Your desire for justice on earth can in no way be realized as long as the cult of false gods remains. It could not have been even then, when you think, that when those gods did not exist whom you worship impiously, there must have been the worship of one God throughout the earth. It was the worship of Him, to be sure, who punishes evil and demands goodness; whose temple is not of stones or clay, but man himself who bears a likeness of God; and this temple is adorned, not with corruptible presents of gold and gems, but with the everlasting gifts of virtues.

Learn, then, if there is any mind left in you, that men are bad and unjust for this reason, that the false gods are worshiped. And, therefore, all the evils in human affairs grow daily more serious, because God, the Maker and Governor of this world, has been abandoned; because unholy religions have been embraced against that which is right; and, finally, because you allow God to be not worshiped at all even, or only by a few. For if God alone were worshiped, there would not be dissensions and wars. When men would know that they were sons of the one God and, therefore, bound together by a sacred, inviolable bond of divine relationship, no insidious plots would take place. When they knew what sort of punishments God was preparing for killers of souls, the God who sees through clandestine crimes and even thoughts themselves, there would not be frauds and rapine. If according to God's precept they had learned how to be content with what is their own and with a little, so that they might prefer firm and eternal things to those fragile and falling, there would not be crimes of adultery, and incest, and prostitution. If it were known to all that whatever is sought after beyond the desire of procreating is condemned by God, necessity would not force woman to violate her honor to seek a most disgraceful living for herself, when men also would restrain passion, and a loving and religious coming together of those who have would come to the aid of those who have not. There would not be, therefore, as I said, all these evils upon the earth if all were pledged to the law of God; if there were done by all men what this one people of ours does.

How blessed and how golden would be the condition of human affairs if, throughout the whole world, meekness and devotion and peace and innocence and fairness and temperance and faith should tarry! Finally, then there would not be need of so many and such various laws for ruling men, when the one law of God would suffice unto perfect innocence. Nor would there be need of prisons or the swords of guards and the terror of punishments, when the healthfulness of the heavenly precepts infused into human hearts would instruct men willingly to the works of justice.

Now the evil are those who are in ignorance of the right and the good. Indeed, Cicero saw this. When he was treating of law, he said: 'Just as by one and the same nature the world coheres and supports itself, all its parts fitting among themselves through depravity. And they do not understand that they are relatives and subjected under the one same tutelage.

But if this were grasped, men would surely live the life of the gods.' Therefore, all the evils with which the human race weakens itself in turn, have been brought on by the unjust and unholy worship of the false gods. For they could not retain piety who had denied as perfidious and rebel children the common Father of us all, God.

CHAPTER 9

Sometimes, however, they realize that they are evil, and they praise the condition of former times and infer that justice is not present because of their conduct and deserts. But even though it is before their eyes, they not only do not take it up, but they do not even acknowledge it; in fact, they even hate it violently and persecute it and strive to exterminate it. For a while now let us pretend that this is not justice which we seek. How, if that should come which they think is true, shall they receive it? Since, if the torturers and killers of men whom they confess to be imitators of the just, just because they do good and just works, killed only the evil, they would be worthy men to whom justice would not be coming, there was no other cause for justice to leave the earth than the shedding of human blood. How much more should this be so when they kill the reverent, and regard the very followers of justice as enemies, as more than enemies, I should say? Although they seek after their souls and their resources and their children with fire and sword, still they spare them when they are conquered, and there is place for clemency among their arms. Or if it please them to be merciless, then nothing more is done to them except that they are killed or carried off into slavery. This is unrecountable, however, because it is done against those who do not know how to do evil, and none are regarded as more harmful than those who are innocent of all harm.

The most wicked men, therefore, who surpass the wild beasts in their fierceness, who ravage the most placid flock of the Lord, 'wolves, or prowlers in the black darkness, who are driven blind by a wicked craving of their belly,' dare to make mention of justice. But, in truth, not a craving of the belly but of the heart has made them wild. They do not go about in the black darkness but in open plundering. Nor does a consciousness of crime ever call them back, lest they violate the sacred and holy name of justice with that mouth which drips, as if it were the gaping jaws of wild beasts, with the blood of the innocent.

Should we say most strongly that there is a cause for this hatred which is so great and so persistent? Is it that 'truth begets hatred,' as the poet says, filled as though with a divine inspiration? Or do they blush to be vile before the good and just? Or is it for both reasons? The truth is always hated for this reason, that he who sins wishes to have a free place for sinning, and he thinks that he can enjoy this delight of evildoers more securely in no other way than if there is no one to whom his crimes are not pleasing. Therefore, they strive to extirpate completely those witnesses of their crimes and malice and to remove those whom they think opposed to themselves as though their lives were proved guilty. For why are some good people unsuitable who make a loud outcry against corrupt public morals by living well? Why are not all equally evil, grasping, unchaste, adulterous, perjurious, greedy, fraudulent? Rather, let those be removed from us before whom it is a shame to live badly, men who strike the face of those who sin even though not with words, because they are silent, yet still reprove though not with words, because they are silent, yet still reprove them by their dissimilar kind of life. For whoever does not as if they do those things against men, since even against God Himself for the same reason the people rose up, a people also established in hope and not ignorant of God. The same inevitableness which violated the very author of justice follows the just. They harass, therefore, and torture with exquisite kinds of punishments, and hold it a slight thing to kill those whom they hate, except that the cruelty also ridicules and wastes their bodies. If there are some who through fear of pain or death, or through their own perfidy, turn away from the heavenly promise and show approval of those deadly sacrificial acts, they praise them and load them with honors, so that they might entice others by their example. But they overwhelm with all the powers of their murderousness, those who have valued their faith highly and have not denied that they were worshipers of God, just as though they thirst for blood, and they call them desperate because they do not spare their bodies at all, as though anything could be more desperate than to torture and hack him whom you know to be innocent. So there is no shame left in those from whom all humanity has gone, and arguments that fit themselves they twist against just men.

For they call impious those who are certainly pious and who keep away from human blood. If, however, they should consider their own actions and the actions which they condemn as impious, they would understand how deceitful their own are and how much more deserving of all those things which they say and do against the good. For not from our number, but from theirs, do those always arise who with arms block the roads; practice piracy on the seas; and if not permitted to go about openly, they mix poisons secretly; who kill their wives to gain their dowries, or their husbands to wed adulterers; who strangle their children when they are born, or if they are overly 'pious,' they expose them; who do not refrain from lust or incest either with a daughter or a sister or mother or a priestess; who conspire against their fellow-citizens and their country; who do not fear the sack; who, finally, commit sacrileges and despoil the temples of the gods whom they worship. And, that we may mention the deeds which are trivial and usual, they take inheritances, forge wills, take away or exclude just heirs. They are those who prostitute their bodies for pleasure; who, unmindful of why they have been born, contend with woman in submission to lust; who defile and profane the most sacred part of their bodies against all right; who measure their manliness with a sword; and what is more disgraceful that they may be high-priests of religion, they do not spare even their life, but sell their souls to be publicly extinguished. If they sit as judges, either they destroy the guiltless because they have been corrupted by bribe, or they let the guilty go unpunished. They also reach for the sky itself by their magic, as though the earth might not contain their malice. These crimes, I tell you, and more than these are done by those who worship the gods.

What is the place of justice among these, so many and such great crimes? And I gathered together a few from the many, not to make an accusation of them, but to illustrate my point. Whoever wishes to know them all may take in hand the books of Seneca, who was a very true describer and a very sharp railer of public habits and vices. But even Lucilius as well has circumscriptly and briefly depicted that shady life in these verses:

> Now in truth from morning until night, on feast
> day and the days before, the entire populace, and
> equally the patricians every day, all display themselves
> in the market place and never leave it. And they all
> devote themselves to the one same desire and skill:
> That they may give words cautiously, fight guilefully,
> strive with flattery, simulate that they are good men,
> and perform trickery, as if all were enemies to all.

What one of these can be cast against our people, whose whole religion is to live without crime and stain? When, therefore, they see that they and their own associates are doing those things which we mentioned, and that our people practice nothing else but what is fair and good, they would be able, if they had any sense, to learn from this that those who do these things are the pious, and that those who commit the crimes are the impious. For it is not possible that those who do not err in all the actions of their life should be mistaken in that which is most important, that is, in religion, which is the head of all. Impiety taken up in that which is the greatest concern would follow in all the rest. And it cannot justly be that those who err in all of life should not be deceived in religion also, since piety, keeping the rule in the highest matter, would preserve its tenor in the others. So it happens that in each way it is learned from the condition of the things which are done what sort of highest concern there is.

CHAPTER 10

It is worth attention to learn of their piety, that from those who act mercifully and reverently, it may be understood what kind of things are they which are done by them against the rights of piety. And so that I may not seem to be inclement in railing against anyone, I will take some poetic character, which may be even a very great example of piety. According to Maro, 'that king, than whom no other was more just, nor was anyone greater in piety, in war, and in arms,' showed us what examples of justice? 'He had bound behind their backs the hands of those whom he was to send to the shades below, about to sprinkle the flames with the blood of the slain.'

What can be more holy than this piety; what more clement than to immolate human victims to the dead and to feed the flame with the blood of men as though with oil?

But perhaps this was not his own vice, but that of the poet who defiled 'a man signed with piety' with the mark of crime. Where, the, poet, is that piety which you very often praise? Lo, reverent Aeneas 'seizes the four youths begotten of Sulmo, and just as many of those whom Ufens is bringing up; he takes them alive that he may immolate them to the shades and sprinkle the flames of the funeral pile with captive blood.' Why, then, did he say at that very same time in which he was sending bound men to immolation: 'Indeed, I would want to be yielding to the living,' when the living, whom he had in his power, he ordered to be slain in place of beasts?

But, this, as I said, was not his fault, who perhaps had not learned letters, but yours. For although you had been trained, you did not know what piety was, and that very thing which that hero did nefariously, detestably, you believed to be the function of piety. Of course, on this one score he is called 'pious,' that he loved his father. What of the fact that 'good Aeneas destroyed those praying for what was not to be despised'? Swearing by that same father and the 'hope of Iulus then growing up,' he spared not at all when 'stirred up by fury and wrath.' Will anyone think, therefore, that this man had any virtue in him, who burned with fury as though he were stubble, and who, forgetting the shade of his father through whom he was besought, could not bridle his wrath? He was 'pious,' then, in no way who killed not only those not resenting it, but even those making supplication to him.

Someone will say at this point: 'What, therefore, is piety, or where is it, or what sort of quality is it?' Surely, it rests with those who know not wars, who preserve harmony with all, who are friendly even to the unfriendly, who love all men as brothers, who know how to restrain wrath and to quell all fury of mind with tranquil moderation. How much smoke, and the clouds of how much darkness and error have darkened how many hearts of men who, when they think themselves especially pious, then, especially, do they become impious? The more religiously they do reverence to those earthly shrines, so much the more crime-laden do they rise up against the name of true Divinity. And so often in payment of their impiety they are vexed with even graver evils. Because they are not aware of their cause, the whole blame is ascribed to fortune, and the philosophy of Epicurus finds place, that nothing affects the gods as judges, that they are neither touched by favor nor moved by wrath, because they see their despisers are often the happy ones and their worshipers are miserable.

And this happens, since, when they seem to be religious and good by nature, they are believed to merit nothing comparable to what they often suffer. They console themselves, then, with the accusation against fortune, but they do not believe that, because if there were any fortune, she would never harm those devoted to her.

Rightly, therefore, does punishment follow piety of this sort, and divinity, offended with the evil crimes of falsely religious men, pursues them with dire calamity. Though these may live lives morally sound in the greatest faith and innocence, because, however, they worship false gods whose impious and profane rites the true God hates, they are alien to justice and the name of true piety.

Nor is it difficult to show why those worshipers of the gods cannot be good and just. For how will they abstain from blood who cherish those bloody gods, Mars and Bellona? How will they spare their parents who worship Jupiter, the expeller of his father; or how will they care for infants born of them who revere Saturn? How will they protect modesty who worship a nude goddess, an adulteress, and the prostitute, as it were, among the gods? How will they abstain from rapine and fraud who know that those who teach that the thefts of Mercury are not acts of fraud but of cleverness are deceiving? How will they restrain their concupiscence who venerate Jupiter, Hercules, Liber, Apollo, and the others whose adulteries and outrages upon men and women are known, not only to the learned, but are portrayed even in the theaters and sung about, so that they might become more known to all? Are men able to be just in the presence of these things, who, although they are good by nature, are, however, instructed unto injustice by the very gods? For it is necessary to please the god you worship with those things in which you know he takes joy and delight. Thus it happens that a god forms the life of his devotees according to the quality of his own deity, since imitation is the most religious form of worship.

CHAPTER 11

To those men, therefore, who conform to the customs of their gods, because it is serious and bitter justice, and who violently exercise against the just the same 'piety' which they use in other matters, not without reason has the name beasts been given by the prophets. Thus Marcus Tullius in an outstanding passage says: 'If there is no one who would not prefer to die rather than to be turned into some form of beast, even though he would hold the mind of man, how much more wretched is it to be in the shape of man with a mind that is wild? Indeed, it seems to me to be as much the worse evil as the soul is more noble than the body.' And so the bodies of beasts are spurned, by which those are more wild, and yet they are pleasing to themselves because they have been born men of whom they have nothing except the external features and the figure in general. For what Caucasus, what India, what Hyrcanian region ever sustained beasts so wild, so bloody? Because the madness of all the wild beasts rages only up to the satiety of their hunger, and when that has been abated, then immediately there is rest. That one, that is the true beast by whose one command 'Black blood is everywhere spilled, and everywhere cruel mourning, everywhere dread, and many an image of death.'

No one is able to describe rightly the wantonness of this so great monster which rages with its fierce fangs over the whole world though it lies in one place, and which not only scatters the limbs of men, but even reduces the very bones and grinds them to ashes, lest there be any place of burial. Just as though those who confess God were striving for this, that He should come to their sepulchres, and not that they come to God. What fierceness, then, is that, what fury, what madness to deny light to the living and earth to the dead? I say, therefore, that there is nothing more miserable than those men whom necessity has found or has made the ministers of another's fury, the satellites of an impious order. For that was not honor nor an advance in dignity, but the condemnation of a man to the work of execution, in fact, to the everlasting punishment of God. What those individuals have done throughout the whole world it is impossible to tell. What number of volumes will hold such infinite, such varied kinds of cruelty? For once power was gained, each one raged according to his own habits. Some, in the presence of excessive timidity, dared more than they were ordered; others gave vent to a personal hatred against the just; certain ones acted according to a natural wildness of spirit; some, to show favor and to fortify the way for themselves to higher offices by means of this one. Some stood out with a leaning to slaughter, as did the one in Phrygia who burned up an entire people along with the assembly itself.

But the more bitter one is, so much the more clement is he found: that is truly the worst kind which a false species of clemency flatters, and that one is the more severe; that one is the crueler executioner who has decided to kill no one. And so it cannot be said how great and what serious kinds of torments judges of this sort have contrived in order to attain an effect of their purpose. But they do these things, however, not only that they may boast that they have destroyed no innocent person—for I myself have heard some glorying in the fact that their ministry was bloodless in this regard—but also for the sake of envy, so that they themselves may not be overcome, or that the others may not attain to the glory of their virtue. So in thinking out the kinds of punishments, they think of nothing other than victory, for they know that it is a struggle and a fight. I saw in Bithynia a guard, marvelously elated with joy, as though he had subjected some barbarous nation, because one who had resisted with great courage for a period of two years seemed at last to be giving in.

They strive, therefore, to conquer, and they inflict exquisite pains on bodies, and they shun nothing other than that the tortured must not die, as though, indeed, the death alone would make them blessed and not the torments also, which the more serious they bring forth so much the greater glory of virtue. But they, stubborn in their foolishness, order care to be diligently applied to the tortured, so that their manners may be renewed for other torments and that new blood may be prepared for punishments. What can be done so pious, so beneficial, so human? They would not have cared so solicitously for those whom they loved. This is the training of their gods; for these works they instruct their worshipers; they desire these sacred rites. Why, even the most defiled homicides have heaped impious rights against the pious: for sacrilegious constitutions also and the disputations of those skilled in the law are read as unjust. Domitius, in the seventh book on the office of proconsul, collected the nefarious rescripts of princes in order to show with what punishments those who professed that they were worshipers of God should be punished.

CHAPTER 12

What would you do to those who call the butcheries of those ancient tyrants, raging madly against innocent people, a right? And although they are teachers of injustice and cruelty, yet they wish to seem just and prudent. They are blind and dull and ignorant of the truth of things. Is justice, then, so hateful to you, O depraved minds, that you equate it with the worst crime? Is innocence so lost among you that you judge it worthy, not even of a simple death, but that it is regarded beyond all crimes to admit no crime and to show a heart free from all contagion of evil? And since we are speaking in common with the worshipers of the false gods, it may be permitted by you to do something well with you. This is our law, this our work, this our religion. If we seem wise to you, imitate us; if fools, contemn us, or even ridicule if you wish. But our folly is of advantage to you. Why do you torture us, why afflict us? We do not envy your wisdom. We prefer this folly; we embrace it. We believe that this is for our benefit, that we love you and bestow all things upon you who hate. There is a place in Cicero not averse to the truth in that discussion which is delivered by Furius against justice: 'Suppose there are two, one of whom, a very fine man, very fair, of the highest justice, and singular faith, but the other of marked evil and daring, and that the state is in this error that it considers that good man evil, crime-laden, wicked; but on the other hand, he who is most evil it thinks possesses the most upright probity of morals and faith. And according to this opinion of all the citizens is that good man bothered and attacked, his hands taken from him, his eyes dug out. And it is thus that he is condemned, bound, consumed and left destitute and finally made to seem most wretched in the eyes of all even by strict right. And, then that evil man is praised, cultivated, loved by all. They confer all honors upon him, full commands, all resources, troops from all sides. Then shall he be judged by the opinion of all as the best man and most worthy of all good fortune. Who, then, will be so mad who would hesitate as to which of these he would prefer to be?' Surely, as though he were divining what evils were going to come about for us and in what way, he set forth this example. For our people suffer all these things because of the evil of those who are in error.

Indeed, the state, rather the whole world, is in the error to such a degree that it persecutes, tortures, condemns, and kills just men as though they were evil and impious. As to his saying that no one is so mad as to doubt what he prefers himself to be, indeed, that one, who was disputing about justice, realized this, that a wise man would prefer to be evil with a good reputation than good with an evil one. May this madness be far from us, to prefer the false to the true! Will the quality of our goodness depend on the errors of the people rather than upon our own consciences and the judgment of God? Or will any good fortune ever inveigle us into not choosing goodness with all evils rather than falsity with all its prosperity? 'Let kings have their realms and the rich their wealth,' as Plautus says, and let the prudent keep their prudence. Let them leave us our folly which, from the very fact that they envy us for it, is manifestly wisdom. Who would envy a fool unless he himself were a consummate fool? They, however, are not such fools as to envy fools, but from the fact that they carefully, zealously carry on the persecutions, they grant that we are not fools. Why would they rage so fiercely unless it were that they fear that, with justice growing stronger every day, they might be left with their precious gods? If, then, the adherents of those gods are wise and we the fools, why do they fear that the wise will be seduced by the fools?

CHAPTER 13

And since, then, our number is always increased from the worshipers of the false gods, never lessened, however, not even in persecution itself—because men can sin and be defiled by false worship, but cannot be turned away from God: for truth avails by its own power—who is so stupid and so blind but that he sees there is wisdom in each aspect? They are blinded by malice and fury, though, lest they see, and they think those fools who, although they have it in their power to escape punishments, prefer to be tortured and to die, when they are able to see from this very fact that that is no folly upon which so many thousands of men throughout the whole world are of unanimous opinion. For if women fall because of the weakness of their sex—sometimes they call it a 'womanly' or 'old womanish' superstition—certainly the men know what they are about. If children, if the young are improvident because of their age, surely the mature and the old have stable judgment. If one city loses sensibleness, innumerable others cannot certainly play the fool. If one province, one nation lacks prudence, all the rest of necessity must have knowledge of the right. Since, therefore, from the rising of the sun unto its going down, the divine law has been taken up and both sexes, every age and tribe and region serve God with one like spirit; and since everywhere there is the same patience, the same contempt of death, they had better understand that there is something of reason in that which is defended even unto death not without cause. They should realize that there is something of firmness and solidity which not only does not free that religion from injuries and vexation, but even increases it and makes it stronger by them. In this, too, their malice is refuted, because they think that they have completely overturned the religion of God if they have defiled men, although it is possible to make satisfaction to God and there is no one so bad a worshiper of God that, when the chance is given, he does not return to God's grace, and, indeed, with greater devotion. For the consciousness of sin and the fear of punishment make one more religious, and faith is always much stronger which repentance has recovered. If, then, they believe that their gods are placated by sacrifices and pleasant odors, when they think they are angry with them, why is it that they think our God so unyielding, so implacable, that one who has been forced against his will to offer sacrifices to their gods could no longer be a Christian? Unless, perhaps, they think that once men have been contaminated they will change their very souls so that they begin now to do of their own accord what they made them do under torments. Who would willingly execute that duty which started from an injury? When one sees the scars of his side, will he not hate the more those gods on account of whom he will bear everlasting marks of his punishments and scars branded on his body?

So it comes about that, when peace has been divinely restored, all those who have fled return and, on account of the miracle of virtue, another new people comes to the fold. For when the crowd sees men lacerated by various kinds of torments holding on to unconquered patience before executioners, they know that which is the fact, that the harmony and the patience of so many dying people is not vain, nor could the patience itself overcome such great suffering without God. Robbers and men of robust strength cannot endure lacerations of this sort; they cry out and groan; they are overcome with pain, because inspired patience is lacking to them. But among us—and I will not speak of the men—children even and frail women silently vanquish their torturers, nor was fire able to extract a groan from them. Let the Romans go and glory in a Mucius or a Regulus. The one handed himself over to the enemy to be killed because he was ashamed to live as a captive. The other, seized by the enemy, when he saw that he could not avoid death put his hand into the fire to satisfy for his crime to the enemy whom he wished to kill, and he gained thereby the pardon which he had not merited. Lo, the weak sex and fragile age suffer laceration of the whole body and burning, not of necessity, because they could avoid it if they wished, but of will, because they trust in God.

This is real courage which the philosophers also, glorying not in the thing but in vain words, boast of, prating that there is nothing so befitting the gravity and constancy of a wise man as to be able to be driven from his opinion and purpose by no terrors, and that it is of such great worth to be tortured and to die so as not to betray faith or leave a duty or do anything unjust through compulsion by fear of death or bitter pain. Or, perhaps, Flaccus seems to rant deliriously in those verses where he says: 'The just man and one tenacious of purpose not the ardor of the people ordering wicked things, not the expression of an insisting tyrant shakes from his firm belief. Nothing truer than this can be said, if this refers to those who refuse no tortures, no death, so that they may not swerve from faith and justice, who do not tremble at tyrannical orders, nor prison, nor the sword, provided that they keep true and lasting liberty in a constant mind, and it must be regarded by a wise man in his way alone. Who is so insolent, so lofty as to forbid me to raise my eyes to heaven, to impose on me the necessity either of worshiping what I do not want to or of not worshiping what I wish? What would be left to us further, if even this which must be done by will the desire of another wrenches from us? No one will bring about that if there is any virtue in us for despising death and pain.

If we hold this constancy, why are we judged fools who do those things which the philosophers praise? Rightly, then, does Seneca, throwing the charge of incongruence up to men, say: 'The highest virtue seems to them to be a great soul, and the same ones consider him who despises death as a lunatic, which is certainly an indication of the greatest perversity.'

But these adherents of false sects cast this up to us with the same folly with which they do not know the true God, people whom the Erythraean Sibyl calls 'light-minded' and 'unintelligent,' that is, thick and stupid, who neither hear nor perceive divine things, but who fear and adore the earth fashioned into images by their own fingers.

CHAPTER 14

There is a great reason—for they are not deceived in vain—why they consider those who are wise to be foolish, and we must carefully explain this, so that they may at last recognize their errors, if this is possible. Justice by its very nature bears

a certain likeness to folly, and I can confirm this by both
divine and human testimony. But perhaps we would do nothing with them unless we should show them from their own
authors that it is not possible for anyone to be just, which is
joined to true wisdom, unless the same man seem to be a fool.
Carneades was a philosopher of the sect of Academicians.
One who does not know the man's very work would understand what force, what eloquence, and what acumen in disputation was his from the praise of Cicero or Lucilius. In the
latter, Neptune, discussing a very difficult point, shows that it
cannot be explained, 'not if Orcus should send back Carneades
himself,' who, when he had been sent by the Athenians to
Rome, discussed justice fluently in the hearing of Galba and the
censorious Cato, then very great orators. But the same man on
the next day subverted his disputation by a contrary one, and
the justice which he had praised the day before, he took away,
not even with the gravity of a philosopher, whose opinions
ought to be firm and stable, but as though in a kind of ora-
torical exercise of taking both sides of a debate. He was accustomed to do that, to be able to refute others by taking any
particular stand. That discussion in which justice was overturned is recalled by Lucius Furius in Cicero. I suppose it was
because he was discussing the republic that he might bring in
its defense and praise, without which he believed the republic
could not be ruled. For Carneades, in order to disprove Aristotle
and Plato as patrons of justice, in the first disputation gathered
all those things which were said in behalf of justice, so that he
might be able to overturn it, as he did. For it was very easy for
justice to be made to fall since it did not have any base, because,
then, there was none on the earth, so that what it was, or of
what sort, was discerned by the philosophers. And would that
so many and such men had as much knowledge for fulfilling the
defense of the greatest virtue as of eloquence and spirit! The
origin of this virtue is in religion; its reason is in equity. Those
who do not know that first part could not even grasp the
second.

Now I want to first show what it is carefully and briefly,
so that it might be understood that the philosopher did not

know justice, and that they could not defend that which they did not know.

Although justice embraces all the virtues at the same time, there are two, the most important of all, which cannot be removed or separated from it: piety and equity. For faith, temperance, probity, innocence, integrity, and others of this sort can either by nature or by training of parents be in those men who do not know justice, just as they always have been. The old Romans who used to glory in justice, gloried certainly in those virtues which, as I said, can set out from justice and be separated from their very source. But piety and equity are its veins, as it were. In these two sources all justice rests: its head and origin in the first, in the second all its strength and reason.

Piety is nothing other than a getting acquainted with God, as Trismegistus defined it very truly, as we said before. If it is piety to know God, and this is the highest form of this acquaintance that you may cultivate, certainly he does not know justice who does not hold to the religion of God. For how can he know that itself who is ignorant of whence it comes to be? Plato said many things about the one God by whom he said the world was formed, but he said nothing about religion. He had dreamed about that God; he did not know Him. And if he or anyone else had wished to make a complete defense of justice, in the first place he ought to have overturned the religions of the false gods, because they are opposed to piety. Because Socrates tried to do just that, he was thrown into prison, so that it might then be clear what was going to happen to those men who began to defend true justice and serve the one God.

The other part of justice is equity. I do not speak of the equity of judging well, which is itself laudable in a just man, but I mean that of equalizing self with fellow-men, which Cicero calls equability. God who creates and inspires men wished them all to be fair, that is, equal. He set the same condition of living for all; He begot all unto wisdom; He promised immortality to all. No one is segregated from His heavenly benefits. Just as He divides His one light equally for all, lets His showers fall upon all, supplies food, grants the sweetest rest of sleep, so He bestows the virtue of equity upon all. With Him, no one is master, no one slave. For if He is the same Father to all, we are

58

all free by equal right. No one is a pauper with God except him who is in need of justice; no one rich, but him who is filled with the virtues; no one, finally, is distinguished except the one who has been good and innocent; no one very illustrious, unless he has done the works of mercy with largesse; no one quite perfect, unless he has completed all the steps of virtue. Wherefore, neither the Romans nor the Greeks could hold justice, because they had men distinguished by many grades, from the poor to the rich, from the lowly to the powerful, from private citizens even to the most sublime heights of kings. For when all are not equal, there is no equity, and inequality itself excludes justice, whose whole power is in this, that it makes equal those who came to the condition of this life by an equal lot.

CHAPTER 15

If those two sources of justice, then, are altered, all virtue and all truth is removed, and justice itself goes back into heaven. Therefore, it is not true that the good has been discovered by philosophers, since they did not know whence it came or what it accomplished. This has been revealed to our people and to no others. Someone will say: 'Are there not among you some poor, some rich, some slaves, some masters? Is there not something of concern to individuals?' Nothing. Nor is there any other reason why we take for ourselves the name of brother one to another, unless it is that we believe that we are equal. For since we measure all human things, not by the body, but by the spirit, and although the condition of the bodies may be diversified, there are not slaves among us, but we regard them and we speak of them as brothers in spirit and as fellow-slaves in religion. Riches do not make their possessors distinguished, except that they can make them more illustrious in good works. For they are rich, not because they have riches, but because they use them for works of justice. And those who seem poor are, however, rich in this, that they are not in need and they desire nothing. Since we who are free are equal to the slaves and the rich to the poor in lowliness of spirit, however, we are noted according to virtue in God's sight. One is the higher as he is more just. If it is justice to make oneself equal even with inferiors, although he excels in this very thing, that he coequates himself with inferiors; however, if he conducts himself, not only as an equal, but as an inferior, surely he will attain a much higher grade of dignity in the judgment of God.

Since in this wordly life all things are short and faltering, and men prefer themselves to others and strive over dignity, than which there is nothing more shameful, nothing more arrogant, nothing more removed from the way of wisdom, all those earthly things are opposed to those that are of heaven. Just as the wisdom of men is the height of foolishness with God, foolishness, as I explained, is the greatest wisdom, so he is lowly and despised with God who was conspicuous and lofty upon earth. But that I may be silent about the fact that these present goods of earth to which great honor is attributed are contrary to virtue and enervate the vigor of the mind, what nobility, then, can be firm, what wealth, what power, since God is able to make the very kings also inferior even to the lowest? And so, taking thought of us God especially fixed among the divine commands this one: 'Whoever exalts himself shall be humbled, and whoever humbles himself shall be exalted.' The healthfulness of this teaching shows that he who has made himself low among men and practiced humility will be regarded as outstanding and marked before God. Nor is that sentence in Euripides false which goes like this: 'What things are considered evil here, these are good in heaven.'

CHAPTER 16

I have set forth the reason why the philosophers could not discover justice nor defend it. Now I go back to that which I had intended. Carneades, therefore, because those things which were asserted by the philosophers were weak, took upon himself the boldness of refuting them, since he knew they could be refuted. This was the summation of his discussion: 'Men have sanctioned laws for themselves for utility, varied, obviously, according to customs, and often changed among the same people for a time. There is, however, no natural law. All men and other living creatures are driven toward their own advantage by the lead of nature. Accordingly, then, there is either no justice, or if there is some, it is the highest foolishness, since one would be harming himself by having consideration for another's advantage.' And he introduced these arguments. All people who flourished with power, even the Romans themselves, who were possessors of the whole world, if they should wish to be just, that is, if they make restitution of other people's goods, they would have to meet misfortune and be thrown in need and misery. Then, omitting the commonplaces, he came to individual things. 'A good man,' he said, 'if he have a fugitive slave, or an unwholesome and pestilential house, which fault he alone knows, and therefore advertizes their sale, shall he declare that he is selling a fugitive slave or a pestilential house, or shall he conceal this from his buyer? If he acknowledges it, he is indeed good because he does not deceive, but, however, he will be judged a fool, since he will sell at but a small price or not at all. If he conceals it, he will be indeed wise because he considers the matter, but the same man will be evil because he deceives. Again if one finds someone who thinks that he sells yellow copper, although that is gold, or lead, when it is silver, will he be silent so that he may purchase it as a small price, or will he make it known that it may cost him more? Surely it seems to be foolish to prefer the large price.' From this he wished it understood that both he who is just and good is a fool, and he who is wise, evil, and yet that this could be done without ruin, that men might be content with poverty.

Then, he passed on to greater matters in which no one could be just without peril of life. For he said: 'Surely, it is justice not to kill a man, absolutely, not to touch a stranger. What, then, shall a just man do, if perhaps he has suffered shipwreck and someone weaker in strength has taken his plank? Will not the plank overthrow that one so that he himself climbs up and leaning on it escapes, especially since there is no witness in the middle of the sea? If he is wise, he will do this; he must perish unless he does. But if that just man prefers to die now rather than bring force against another, he is a very fool who does not spare his own life while he spares another's. Likewise, if the enemy should begin to pursue, the battle line of their own side routed, and if a just man should come upon someone wounded on a horse, will he spare him and have himself killed, or will he throw him down from the horse, so that he himself may have a way to escape the enemy? If he does this, he is wise, but the same one is evil; if he does not do it, he is just, but at the same time he must be a fool.'

Thus, when he divided justice into two parts, saying that one was civil, the other natural, he subverted both, since there is a civil wisdom, indeed, but not justice; and that justice is, indeed, natural, but not wisdom. These are clearly sharp and envenomed points which Marcus Tullius could not refute. For when he makes Laelius answer Furius and speak for justice, he passed over these and left them unrefuted, as though they were a pit, so that the same Laelius seems to have defended, not natural justice which had come into the crime of foolishness, but that civil justice which Furius had conceded was wisdom, indeed, but injustice.

CHAPTER 17

Because it was pertinent to the previous discussion, I have showed how justice bears a resemblance to foolishness, in order that it may be clear that not without cause are they deceived who think that men of our faith are fools who are seen to do such things as that one proposed. Now I believe that it is further required of me to show why God has wished to take justice, enveloped in the likeness of folly, away from the eyes of men, if I shall have first answered Furius, because Laelius replied not at all fully. Though it be granted, surely, that he was wise, as he was called, however, he was not in any way able to uphold true justice, since he did not hold to the very head and source of justice. That defense is easier for us, though, to whom through the kindness of heaven justice is familiar and thoroughly understood, and who know it not merely by name but in actuality. Plato and Aristotle desired, truly with honest intention, to defend justice, and they would have accomplished something if the teachings of divine truths had aided their good attempts, their eloquence, the quality of their genius. So their work has lain vain and useless, nor have they been able to persuade any man to live by their prescription, because that teaching did not have a foundation from heaven.

It is necessary that our work be more certain, for God has taught us. They played around with words and imagined a justice which was not in sight, and they could not confirm with present examples the things which they asserted. For it could be answered by their hearers that it was not possible in the way they were prescribing in their discussion, for the reason that up to that time none had existed who followed that kind of life. We, however, show not merely by words, but by examples drawn from reality, that those things which we say are true. Carneades realized, therefore, what the nature of justice is, except that he did not perceive deeply that it was not folly, although I think I understand with what mind he did this. For he did not really believe that the man who is just is a fool, but although he knew that he was not, and yet did not grasp the reason why he seemed such, he wanted to show that the truth lay in hiding, in order that the principle of his teaching might be preserved. Its chief notion is that nothing can be perceived.

Let us see, then, whether or not justice can have any alliance with folly. He says that if a just man does not take away a horse from a wounded man or a plank from one shipwrecked in order to save his own life, he is a fool. First of all, I say that a chance of this sort can in no way befall a man who is, indeed, truly just, because a just man is not an enemy to anyone nor does he desire anything whatsoever that belongs to another. Why would he be sailing or what would he seek from another land whose own satisfies him? Why would he be waging war or involving himself in the rage of others in whose mind perpetual peace with men dwells? Actually, will he be delighted with foreign prizes and human blood who does not know how to acquire gain, whose manner of living suffices him, and who considers it wrong, not only for himself to commit murder, but even to be present and look on when others do it? But I pass by those things, because it can happen that even against his will a person may be forced to attend these affairs. Do you think, then, O Furius, or rather, you Carneades, for that whole speech was yours, that justice such as that is so inane, so superficial, and so contemptible to God, that it is of no avail and has nothing within itself which may be of value for its own protection? But, of course, those who do not know the pledge of man and, therefore, refer all things to this temporal life, are not able to know how much power there is in justice. For when they treat of virtue, although they know that it is very full of trials and miseries, they still say that it must be sought for its own sake, and its rewards, however, which are eternal and immortal, they see in no way. So, when all things are referred to this present life, clearly they reduce virtue to folly, inasmuch as it undertakes such great labors of this life in vain and inanely. But we will take this up more fully in another place; meanwhile, let us get back to justice as we began. Its power is so great that, when it raises its eyes to heaven, it merits all rewards from God. Rightly, then, did Flaccus say that the power of innocence was so great that it would need neither arms nor strength for its protection, wherever it might be. 'The man who is whole in life and free from crime has need of no Moorish darts, nor a quiver, no, Fuscus, nor of a case heavy with poisoned arrows, whether his way be through the burning Syrtes, or whether he will journey to the inhospitable Caucasus or the places which the fabulous Hydaspes washes.' It cannot but happen that amid the crises of tempests and battles heavenly protection will be with the just man, and also, even though he travel along with parricides and criminals, that he will be spared evils, so that one just and innocent soul may be freed, or certainly, that his alone will be saved, though others perish under them.

Let us grant that what the philosopher proposed can happen. What, then, will the just man do if he should find a wounded man on a horse or a shipwrecked one on a plank or raft? Not unwillingly I declare it. He will die rather than kill. And, therefore, justice, because it is the singular good of man, will not receive the name of folly. For what is better, what ought to be dearer to man than innocence? Surely, this must be so much the more perfect, as you have brought it to the extremity and have preferred to die lest anything of the purpose of innocence be lessened. It is foolishness, he says, to spare another's life at the ruin of one's own. Surely, you will not judge him a fool who dies for friendship, will you? Why, then, are those familiar Pythagorean philosophers praised by you, one of whom gave himself to the tyrant as death bail for the other, and that one at the appointed time, when his sponsor was already being led forth, made presentation of himself and by his intervention set him free? Their virtue, whereby one wished to die for his friend and the other for loyalty, would not be held in such great honor if they were thought fools. Finally, because of this very virtue the tyrant showed favor to them by saving them both, and the nature of a very cruel man was changed. It is said that he even besought them to receive him as the third into that friendship. He approached them, not as though they were fools, but as good and wise men. And so I do not see why, since it is thought to be the highest glory to die for friendship and faith, it is not also glorious for a man to die for innocence. Therefore, they are very foolish who charge us with crime for wishing to die for God, when those same people exalt to the sky with the highest praises him who wanted to die for a man.

And to conclude this discussion, then, reason itself shows that it is not possible for the same man to be just and a fool, for the same one to be wise and unjust. He who is a fool knows not what is just and good and, therefore, he always sins. He is led as though a captive by vices, and he is not able to resist in any way, since he lacks virtue which he does not know. The just man, however, restrains himself from sin, and he cannot act otherwise if he has the knowledge of right and wrong. But who can distinguish right from wrong unless he be wise? Thus it happens that he can never be just who is a fool, nor one who shall have been unjust ever wise. And if this is quite true, it is clear that he who has not taken a plank from a shipwrecked man or a horse from a wounded one is not a fool, since to do these things is a sin from which the wise man restrains himself. Still, he seems to be one, and I myself admit it, because of the error of those who are ignorant of the peculiar nature of each thing. So this whole question is solved not so much by arguments as by definition. Foolishness, therefore, is an erring in deeds and words through an ignorance of the right and good. So the foolish man is not he who does not spare himself even, so long as he does no harm to another, which is evil. This, in fact, both reason and truth itself prescribes for us. We see in all the animals who are without wisdom that nature is the cause of itself. They harm others, then, that they may advantage themselves, but they do not know that it is evil to do harm. Man, however, since he has the knowledge of good and evil, restrains himself from harming, even with inconvenience to himself, which an irrational animal is not able to do, and for this reason, innocence is numbered among the highest virtues of man.

From these things it is clear that he is very wise who prefers to die in order not to do harm, so that this may serve as the function by which he is distinguished from the dumb beasts. He who does not contradict the error of the salesman so that he may buy gold cheap, or the one who does not admit that the slave is a fugitive, or that he is selling a ruined house, because he is taking his own gain and advantage into consideration, is not wise, as Carneades wanted him to seem, but he is cunning and astute. Cunning and astuteness, though, are also present in the dumb animals, either when they lie in wait for others and take them by trickery in order to devour them, or when they mock the trickery of the others in various manners. Wisdom, however, applies to man alone. For wisdom is knowledge either for the doing of good and the right or for the refraining from wicked words and deeds. The wise man never desires gain, since he despises these earthly goods; nor does he suffer anyone to be deceived, because it is the duty of a good man to correct men's errors and to lead them back to the way of right, inasmuch as man's nature is social and kindly, by which means alone he has a relationship with God.

CHAPTER 18

But certainly this cause brings it about that he seems to be a fool who prefers to be in want or to die rather than to do harm or to take something from another, because they think that man is destroyed by death. From this conviction all errors arise, both those of the rank and file and those of the philosophers. If we are nothing after death, surely, only a very foolish man does not concern himself with this life, that it may last as long as possible and be full of all advantages. He who will be so concerned will necessarily depart from the rule of justice. But if there remains a life of man, better and longer, and we learn this from the arguments of the great philosophers and the responses of the seers and the divine words of the prophets, then it is the mark of a wise man to despise this present life with all its goods, every sacrifice of which is compensated for by immortality. In Cicero that same defender of justice, Laelius, says that 'virtue almost demands honor, and there is no other reward of virtue.' It is plainly and, indeed, most worthy of virtue, which you, Laelius, were never able to imagine, for you knew nothing of the divine writings. Then he continues: 'She easily, therefore, accepts this but does not bitterly exact it.' You are very much in error if you think that a reward could be paid to virtue by man, although you yourself said very truly in another place: 'What riches will you cast upon this man? What powers? What realms? He thinks those things human; he considers his own goods divine.' Who, then, would you a wise man, Laelius, when you contradict yourself, and a little while later take away from virtue that which you have just given it? But, of course, it is ignorance of the truth with an uncertain and wavering opinion. Then, what do you add? 'But if all the ungrateful or the many envious, or the unkind powerful ones despoil virtue of its rewards . . . .' How fragile, how empty a virtue you have brought in, if it can be despoiled of its own reward! If 'he judges his own goods as divine,' as you said, who can there be so ungrateful, so envious, so powerful as to be able to despoil virtue of those goods which were divinely conferred upon it?—'lest,' he says, 'she might delight herself with much solace and especially sustain herself with her beauty.' With what solace? What beauty? When she often comes into the charge of being crime, and when that beauty is turned into punishment. What if, as Furius said, she is 'seized, harassed, exterminated, put in want, her hands taken away, eyes dug out, condemned, bound, consumed, killed also in wretched ways,' shall virtue lose its reward then, or rather will she herself perish? By no means. She will still receive her reward, with God as judge, and she will live and will always flourish.

If you take this away, nothing in the life of men can seem to be so useless, so foolish as virtue, the natural goodness and uprightness of which can teach us that the soul is not mortal and that a divine reward has been constituted for it by God. For this reason God wished virtue itself to be concealed under the mask of folly, so that the mystery of His truth and religion might be secret; so that He might condemn of vanity and error these religions and that earthly wisdom which exalts itself too high and which gives much pleasure to itself; and so that, finally, when the difficulty has been determined, a very narrow path might lead the way to the reward of immortality on high.

I have disclosed, I think, why our people are regarded as foolish among fools. For to prefer to be tortured and killed rather than to put upon the fire the incense held by three finger tips seems as senseless as to care more for the life of another than for one's own. They do not know how wrong it is to adore anything else besides God, who established heaven and earth, who made human nature, inspired it, and gave it light. And if the most wicked of slaves, who abandoned his master by running away, is held, and that one is judged worthy of beatings and chains and the work-house and the cross and all evil, and if a son is believed in the same way depraved and impious, who has left his father so as not to obey him, and on account of this same reason is thought worthy to be disinherited and have his name blotted out from the family forever, how much more worthy of all this is he who deserts God to whom the two names of Lord and Father apply and are equally venerable? Does the man who buys a slave at a price confer any benefit upon him besides food, which he supplies to him for the sake of his own good? And he who begets a son does not have it in his own power that he be conceived, that he be born, that he live. From this it is clear that he is not a father but only a minister of generation. Of what punishments, then, is he deserving, who is a deserter of Him who is true Lord and Father except those which God Himself determined, who prepared eternal fire for the unjust spirits, because He Himself threatens the impious and rebellious through His prophets?

CHAPTER 19

Let those destroyers of souls, their own and those of others, learn, therefore, and admit how inexpiable is their crime; first, because they destroy themselves by serving the most depraved demons whom God has condemned to eternal punishments; then, because they do not allow God to be worshiped by others, but strive to avert men to deadly rites, and strain with the utmost diligence lest there be any soul unharmed on the earth which may gaze toward heaven, its condition being unimpaired. What else shall I say except that they are wretches who obey the instigations of their plunderers, whom they consider gods? They know neither their condition nor their origin nor their names nor their purpose, but by a common, inherent conviction, they gladly go astray with them and favor their folly. If you ask them the plan or purpose of this conviction, they can give none, but they take shelter in the decisions of their ancestors because they were wise, they approved of them, they knew what was best, and they despoil themselves of their senses, swear away from reason, while they believe the errors of others. Thus they are implicated by ignorance of all things, and they do not know themselves nor their gods. Would that they alone were in error, that they wished to be unwise by themselves! They drag others into the alliance of their evil, as though they would have comfort from the perdition of many. This very ignorance causes them to be so evil in following up the wise and to pretend that they are taking thought of them, that they wish to call them back to a good mind. They do not insist, do they, by this speech or some plan to cause those admissions? Never. But by force and torments. Strange, blind madness! An evil mind is thought to be in those who try to keep faith, but a good mind in torturers! Is an evil mind in those who are torn and lacerated against the right of humanity, against all justice, or is it rather in those things to the bodies of the innocent, which the most ravenous thieves have never done, nor the most angered enemies, nor the most savage barbarians? Do they not, therefore, lie to themselves, so that the names of good and evil are transferred and interchanged? Why, then, do they not call day, night, and the sunlight, darkness? Why, it is the same shamelessness to impose the name of the evil upon the good, that of fools upon the wise, that of the impious upon those who are just. And, furthermore, if they have any confidence either in philosophy or in eloquence, let them arm themselves and refute these tenets of ours, if they can. Let them come together and discuss the points singly.

It is fitting that they take up the defense of their gods, lest, if our arguments should become strengthened, as they are growing stronger daily, they be deserted along with their shrines and mockeries. And since they can effect nothing by force—for the religion of God is increased the more it is oppressed—they may succeed rather by speech and exhortations. Let their pontiffs come to the center, either the lesser ones or the greater, their flamens and augurers, likewise their sacrificial kings and those who are the priests and overseers of their religion. Let them invite us to the assembly. Let them urge the acceptance of the cults of their gods; let them persuade that there are many by whose power and providence all things are ruled; let them show the origins and the beginnings of their sacred rites and their gods and how these were handed down to mortals. Let them explain the source, what the reason is; let them put forth what gain there is in the religion, what penalty there is for its contempt; why they wish themselves to be reverenced by men; what human piety will confer upon them if they are blessed. Let them confirm all these points, not by their own personal assertion, for the authority of mortal man avails nothing, but by some divine testimony, just as we do. There is no need of force and injury, because religion cannot be forced. It is a matter that must be managed by words rather than by blows, so that it may be voluntary. Let them display a battle line of their geniuses. If their reason is true, it will be claimed. We are prepared to listen, if they should teach. Certainly, we believe nothing of those who are silent, just as we do not yield even to those who are in a rage. Let them imitate us, that they may expose the plan of the whole matter; for we do not entice that they may object to it, but we teach, we prove, we explain. And, therefore, no one is retained by us against his will—for he is useless to God who is without devotion and faith—and so no one departs while the truth itself is compelling.

Let them teach in this way if they have any assurance of truth. Let them speak, let them open their mouths; let them dare, I say, to discuss with us something of this sort, and then, indeed, their error and foolishness will be ridiculed by our 'little old women and children' whom they despise. For since they are very skilled and know the progeny of the gods and their deeds and powers and deaths and burials from books, and since they know that the very rites by which they were

70

initiated came to be from the actions of men or by chance or from the dead, it is incredible madness to think that they, who they do not dare to deny were mortals, are gods. Or if they should be so rash as to deny this, their writings and those of their own people would refute them; and finally, the very initiations of their sacred beliefs would convince them. They would know from this very fact how much difference there is between the true and the false, when they themselves, although they are eloquent, are not able to persuade, and the unskilled and untrained are able to, because the matter itself and the truth speaks.

Why, then, do they rage? That they may augment foolishness while they wish to lessen it. Poles apart are execution and piety, and truth cannot be joined with force nor justice with cruelty. But rightly do they not dare to teach anything about divine matters, lest they be mocked by our people and deserted by their own. For usually the common people whose judgment is simple and uncorrupted, if they should find out that those mysteries were established unto the memory of the dead, would condemn them and seek something else more true which they may revere. Hence, 'faithful silences in religious matters' have been instituted by clever men, so that the people may not know what they worship. But, since we are familiar with their teachings, why do they not believe us who know both, or why do they envy us who have preferred true ones to false? 'But the sacred rites which have been publicly embraced must be defended,' they say. How the poor things err, though their intention is honest! For they think that there is nothing in human affairs more important than religion and that it ought to be defended with the utmost strength, but as they are deceived in the very religion, so also are they in the manner of its defense. Religion ought to be defended, not by killing but by dying, not by fury but by patience, not by crime but by faith. The former action each time belongs to evil, the latter to good, and it is necessary that good be the practice of religion, not evil. If you wish, indeed, to defend religion by blood, if by torments, if by evil, then, it will not be defended, but it will be polluted and violated. There is nothing so voluntary as religion, and if the mind of the one sacrificing in a religious rite is turned aside, the act is now removed; there is no act of religion.

It is right reason, then, to defend religion by patience or death in which faith is preserved and is pleasing to God Himself, and it adds authority to religion. If someone, who in this earthly military service keeps faith toward his king by some outstanding deed, becomes more acceptable and dearer if he should live afterwards, and, if he should die, attains supreme glory because he met his death for his leader, how much more ought faith to be kept with the Commander of all, who is able to pay the reward of virtue, not only to the living, but also to the dead? Therefore, the worship of God, since it is a kind of heavenly military service, desires devotion and the greatest faith. For how will God love the one worshiping Him if He Himself is not loved by that man; or how will He grant whatever one praying should ask, when he comes to pray neither from his heart nor in a proper manner? When those others, however, come to do sacrifice, they offer nothing intimate, nothing personal to their gods; they have no uprightness of mind, no reverence, no fear. And when the empty sacrifices have been gone through, they leave all their religion in the temple and with the temple, just as they had found it, and they do not bring or take back with them anything from it.

Thence it is that religions of this sort cannot make people good, nor can these religions be firm and immutable. Men can easily be led astray by these, because in them nothing is learned for life, nothing for wisdom, nothing for faith. What, then, is the superstition of those gods? What is their power? What is their discipline? What origin have they? What reason? What foundation? What substance to their religion? Where does it tend, or what does it promise, so that it can be faithfully preserved and strongly defended by man? I see nothing else in it than a ritualistic act which pertains only to the fingers. Our religion, however, is firm and solid and immutable in this, that it teaches justice, that it is always with us, that it abides in one entire soul of the worshiper, that it has the mind itself for a sacrifice. In theirs, nothing else is required but the blood of beasts and smoke and a senseless libation; but in ours, a good mind, a pure heart, an innocent life. To the former there come

without any love shameless adulteresses, wanton bawds, indecent harlots; there come gladiators, thieves, robbers, poisoners,
and they pray for nothing else but that they may commit their
crimes with impunity. What would a sacrificing gladiator or
highwayman ask for except that they might kill? What would a
poisoner or wizard want except to deceive? What a harlot but
to sin more? What an adulteress except the death of her husband
or that she might conceal her impurities? What a seductress but
that she might divest many of their goods? What would a thief
desire except to pile up more? Here, however, there is no place
for false and common sin, and if anyone comes to the sacrifice
with a conscience not clear, he hears what God threatens, that
God who sees the hidden places of the heart, who is ever hostile
to sins, who exacts justice, who demands faith. What place is
there here for an evil mind or an evil prayer? But those unhappy
souls do not understand from their crimes how that which they
worship is evil, inasmuch as, defiled with all manner of outrages,
they come to pray and think that they have piously offered
sacrifice if they wash their skin, as if any rivers might wash or
any seas purify the wantonness enclosed in their hearts. How
much more wise it is rather to cleanse the mind which is defiled
by evil and to dispel all vices by the one washing of virtue and
faith! And whoever has done this, although he may have a
stained and sordid body, is sufficiently pure.

St. Augustine
354-430

The Confessions of St. Augustine is a source of great joy and encouragement to the Christian world. It is the story of the human spirit searching for God and of a specific human who sought and found that God. It assures the Christian of his human value, invites him to overcome the fears and anxieties that hold him prisoner, urges him on toward the freedom of love in God. Few books have had as great an impact on Christianity as the Confessions. Though written as a kind of spiritual autobriography by Augustine at the close of the fourth century, it is the common property of all mankind.

Augustine is one of those exceptional human beings who seem to be beyond the barriers of space and time. Yet his autobiography reveals a humanness that makes the reader feel at ease with him immediately. The general lines of his life are well known. He was born in 354, was well-educated, lived a life of sensual pleasures for several years, was constantly searching for truth and intellectual fulfillment, underwent a dramatic conversion process, and developed into the most influential theologian in the western Christian tradition. He died as Bishop of Hippo, Africa, in 430. His was a life that voyaged through darkness and light, that knew joy and sorrow, that drifted downward into the abyss of sin and soared up to unimaginable heights of graceful union with God. His brilliant intellect explored the depths of the human soul in an effort to capture its mysterious origin. This was the search that led him to exclaim, "You have made us for yourself, and our heart is restless until it rests in you." (Confessions, I.1)

God, transcendent yet ever present, was quite real to Augustine. He was the Source and Creator of all existing beings and the whole of existence was moving toward union with God through the God-man Jesus Christ. Meditation on the writings of St. Paul and St. John enabled Augustine to mature in this basic insight and to build his entire Christian life on it.

In the Confessions, one meets this life in a highly personal manner. Augustine is in dialogue with his God. He reviews before God his childhood and teenage years, his involvement with the Manichaean heresy, his experiences in Rome and Milan. He tells of his intellectual problems, of his struggle with belief and his conversion. The final books of the Confessions treat the themes of time and eternity, form and matter, and the creation of the world.

Book Eight of the Confessions, which is presented in its entirety below, is an incredible insight into the tension that the human soul experiences in its search for an eternal foundation for human action. Torn between flesh and spirit, the law of the inner man and the law of sin, darkness and light, tumult and peace, the soul must decide. And the decision is not an easy one. Augustine knew the frustration of knowing what must be done without having the capacity to do it. He was shaken in spirit when he saw that he was not entering into an agreement with the loving God who called to him. Then came his storm of tears and the question, "How much longer?" Then came the voice of a child, "Take and read." Then came the insight, "Put on the Lord Jesus Christ." Out of this death process came new life, a covenant with God which served as the starting point for all Christian action.

CONFESSIONS

BOOK EIGHT

CHAPTER 1

My God, may I recall and confess Thy mercies to me, in the act of giving thanks to Thee. Let my bones be bathed with Thy love and let them say: O Lord, 'who is like to Thee?' 'Thou hast broken my bonds: I will sacrifice to Thee the sacrifice of praise.' How Thou hast broken them I shall tell, and all men who worship Thee will say, when they hear these things: Blessed be the Lord in heaven and on earth; great and wonderful is His Name.

Thy words had clung tightly within the depths of my heart, and I was fenced in on all sides by Thee. I was certain concerning Thy eternal life, though I saw it 'in an obscure manner and as if through a mirror.' However, all doubt had been removed from me, concerning the incorruptible Substance, and that every substance sprang from it. I was desirous, not of greater certainty concerning Thee, but of becoming more steadfast in Thee. All the things in my temporal life were in a condition of uncertainty. My heart had to be cleansed of the 'old heaven.' The way itself, the Saviour, was pleasing, yet there was still some repugnance to walking His difficult ways.

Thou didst put the thought in my mind, and it seemed good in my view, to proceed to Simplicianus, who seemed to me to be a good servant of Thine, for Thy grace shone in him. I had heard, too, that he had lived from his youth in great devotion to Thee. And now, at this time, he had grown old, and he had a great deal of experience in his long life of following Thy way with such good zeal. It appeared to me that he was learned in many things, and truly he was. The desire came to me to discuss my troubles with him, so that he might indicate what was the proper method for a man, disposed as I was, to walk in Thy way.

I saw the Church with its full membership; one man proceeded in this way, another in that. The worldly activities in which I was engaged were not pleasing to me and had become quite a burden for me, now that my desires were not inflamed, as they had been, by the hope for honor and wealth to support such a heavy servitude. For, now, these things held no delight for me in comparison with Thy sweetness and the 'beauty of Thy house which I loved.' But, I was still firmly held in thralldom by women. Nor was I prohibited by the Apostle from marrying, though he did exhort to a better state, desiring greatly that all men live as he had. But, being weaker, I chose the easier place, and because of this one thing I was at sea in respect of everything else, enfeebled and consumed by exhausting cares, all because, having yielded and bound myself to the conjugal life, I was compelled to conform myself to it, even in some things that I was unwilling to undergo.

I had heard from the mouth of Truth that 'there are eunuchs who have made themselves so for the sake of the kingdom of heaven'; but, as is added, 'let him accept it who can.' 'Vain, indeed, are all men in whom there is not the knowledge of God, and who by these good things that are seen could not discover Him that is.' But, I was no longer in this condition of vanity. I had risen above it, and by the testimony of the whole of creation I had found Thee, our Creator, and Thy Word who is God along with Thee, and one God with Thee, through which Word Thou hast created all things.

And there is another kind of impious men, those who, 'knowing God, did not glorify Him as God or give thanks.' I had also fallen into this error, and Thy right hand took me, and, removing me from it, Thou didst place me where I could regain my health. For, Thou didst say to man: 'Behold, piety is wisdom,' and: 'Do not desire to appear wise, for while professing to be wise they have become fools.' And I had already found the 'precious pearl' and I should have bought it, selling all that I had, but I still hesitated.

CHAPTER 2

So, I went to Simplicianus, the spiritual father o Ambrose, who was then bishop, in his reception into grace, and loved by

Ambrose like a father. I told him the winding course of my error. When I mentioned that I had read some books of the Platonists, which Victorinus (at one time a rhetorician in the city of Rome, who had, I heard, died a Christian) had translated into Latin, he congratulated me that I had not happened on the writings of other philosophers, filled with errors and deceptions, according to the elements of this world, while in the writings of the Platonists God and His Word are indirectly introduced at every turn.

Then, in order to exhort me to the humility of Christ, which is hidden from the wise but revealed to the little ones, he recalled Victorinus himself, whom he had known as a very close friend when he was in Rome. And he told me a story about him, concerning which I shall not keep silent. It offers ample opportunity to praise Thy grace, which must be confessed unto Thee.

This very learned old man, skilled in all the liberal teachings, who had read and criticized so many works of the philosophers, the teacher of so many noble senators, a man who, as a mark of his distinguished career as a teacher, had deserved and received a statue in the Roman Forum (which the citizens of this world regarded as an outstanding honor), up to that time of his life a worshiper of idols and a participant in the sacrilegious mysteries whereby nearly all the Roman nobility were then puffed up, so that they breathed the cult of Osiris into the people, about 'every kind of God, monsters, and Anubis the barking god,' who at times battled against 'Neptune, Venus and Minerva,' and were beaten, but now Rome sought their help—these things the aged Victorinus had defended with the thundering of his frightening eloquence. Yet, he was not ashamed to be a slave of Thy Christ and a baby at Thy font, having bent his neck to the yoke of humility and submitted his forehead to the reproach of the Cross.

O Lord, Lord, who hast bowed down the heavens and descended, who hast touched the mountains and they gave forth smoke, by what means didst Thou work Thyself into that breast?

He read, as Simplicianus said, the holy Scripture and studied all the Christian writings with greatest care, examining them in detail. He used to say to Simplicianus, not openly, but in a private and friendly way: 'Do you know that I am already a Christian?' The latter would reply: 'I will not believe it, or reckon you among the Christians, unless I see you within the Church of Christ.' But, he would smile and say: 'So, do walls make men Christians?' He said this often, that he was already a Christian, and Simplicianus often gave the same reply, and the bantering remark about the walls was often repeated. For, he was afraid of offending his friends, proud worshipers of demons; he thought that their enmity would fall heavily upon him from the peak of their high position in Babylon, as from the cedars of Lebanon which the Lord had not yet broken down. But, afterwards, by reading and longing, he gained firmness of mind and became afraid to be denied by Christ before the holy angels, if he were fearful of confessing Him before men. By being ashamed of the mysteries of the humility of Thy Word and not being ashamed of the sacrilegious mysteries of proud demons which he had accepted as their proud follower, he appeared to himself to be guilty of a great crime. He put aside the shame arising from vanity and took on the shame arising from truth. Suddenly and unexpectedly, he said to Simplicianus (as the latter told the story): 'Let us go into the church; I wish to become a Christian.' The latter, overcome with joy, went along with him. Whereupon, he was introduced into the first mysteries of instruction and, shortly afterwards, he also gave in his name to be reborn through baptism, to the amazement of Rome and the joy of the Church. Proud men saw and grew angry; they gnashed their teeth and pined away. But, the Lord God was his hope, for Thy servant, and he regarded not vanities and lying follies.

At last, as the hour approached for the profession of faith (which at Rome was customarily uttered, by those who are about to enter into Thy grace, in set words learned and kept in memory, and from a prominent place in full view of the crowd of believers), an offer was made by the priests to Victorinus—Simplicianus said—to do it privately. It was customary to make this concession to such people as seemed likely to be frightened by embarrassment. However, he preferred to profess his salvation in the sight of the holy congregation. For, what he taught as a rhetorician was not productive of salvation, yet he had professed that in public. How much less, then, had he to fear Thy meek flock when he uttered Thy word, since he was not afraid of the crowds of madmen when uttering his own words?

Thus, when he got up to make his profession, everyone who knew him and all the people murmured his name among themselves, with a resounding exclamation of thanksgiving. Who was there who did not know him? From the mouths of all who shared the common joy, there resounded a moderated shout: 'Victorinus! Victorinus!' Quickly they cried out in exultation at seeing him, and quickly they fell into an intense silence in order to hear him. He proclaimed the true faith with admirable confidence, and all experienced the desire to snatch him to their hearts. This they did with love and joy, for these were the hands by which they caught him up.

CHAPTER 3

O good God, what is it that goes on in man, that he rejoices more at the salvation of a soul which has been despaired of and which has been delivered from a greater danger, than if hope had always been with it, or if the danger had been less? Thou too, O merciful Father, dost rejoice 'more over one sinner who repents, than over ninety-nine just who have no need of repentance.' And we listen with great joy, when we hear how the straying sheep is carried back on the exultant shoulders of the Shepherd, and how the drachma is returned to Thy treasury, her neighbors sharing in the joy of the woman who found it. And the festal joy of Thy house sheds tears when they read there of that younger son of Thine, that 'he was dead and has come to life again, he was lost and is found.' Indeed, Thou dost rejoice in us, and in Thy angels that are holy with a holy love. For, Thou art ever the same, who knowest always, and in the same manner, all things which are not forever in the same manner.

And so, what goes on in the soul, when there is more delight that things which it loves have been found or returned, than if it had always possessed them? Many other cases agree in attesting to this and all things are filled with evidence proclaiming: 'It is so.' The victorious commander triumphs, but he would not have conquered unless he had fought; the greater the danger was in battle, the greater is the joy in the triumph. A storm tosses sailors and threatens shipwreck; all grow pale at the thought of impending death: the sky and sea become peaceful, and, now, their joy knows no limits, for their fear was without limit. A loved one is sick and his pulse indicates the threat of danger; all those who desire to have him well grow sick at heart together with him. He gets better and walks again, though not yet with his former strength; still, there is already joy such as there never was when he walked well and strong before the illness. Men get these pleasures of human life, not just from unexpected and involuntary happenings, but from planned and voluntary hardships. There is no pleasure in eating and drinking unless they are preceded by the hardship of hunger and thirst. Drunkards eat salty foods, by which a disturbing thirst is produced; then a drink removes it and enjoyment is the result. It is an established practice for engaged girls not to be given immediately in marriage, lest the husband, when she is given, hold her in low esteem because he did not long for her during an extended engagement.

This is the case in shameful and blameworthy joy, in that which is permitted and legal, in that most honorable unrightness of friendship, in the case of the son who was dead and came back to life again, who was lost and is found: in all cases the greater joy is preceded by the greater hardship.

Why is this so, O Lord my God, since Thou, Thou Thyself, art Thine own eternal joy, and since certain beings made by Thee and dwelling near Thee experience everlasting joy—why is it that this our part of creation alternates between decline and progress, between affronts and reconciliations? Is this their mode of being, just what Thou didst grant, when from the highest heavens to the lowest parts of the earth, from the beginning unto the end of the ages, from the angelic being down to the worm, from the first movement until the last, Thou didst place all the kinds of good things and all Thy just works each in its proper location, and didst accomplish each in its own time? Ah me, how exalted art Thou in Thy heights, how deep in Thy depths! Thou dost never withdraw, yet we return to Thee only with great difficulty.

CHAPTER 4

O Lord, arouse us and recall us, enflame us and carry us off, make us ardent, attract us by Thy sweetness: let us love, let us run! Do not many men return to Thee from a deeper hell of blindness than Victorinus, approaching and being enlightened by the reception of the light, and, if they receive it, obtain from Thee the power to become Thy sons? However, if they are less well known to the people, then, even they who know them rejoice less over them. For, when one rejoices along with many people, then joy is increased in each person, because they warm themselves and are enkindled by each other. Then, too, those who are known to many people are of influence in the salvation of many, and, as they lead the way, many will follow. That is why there is much rejoicing for them even among those who have preceded them, for the rejoicing is not for them alone.

Far from me, of course, be the notion that in Thy tabernacle the rich should be more highly regarded than the poor, or the noble than the less well born, since Thou hast rather chosen the weak things of the world, to put to shame the strong, and Thou hast chosen the ignoble things of this world, and the despised things and those which are not, as if they were, to bring to naught the things that are. Yet this same man, 'the least of Thy apostles,' by whose tongue Thou didst pronounce these words, when Paul the proconsul, his pride conquered through this man's warfare, was sent to pass under the light yoke of Thy Christ to become an ordinary subject of the great King, this man, though previously known as Saul, was desirous of being called Paul, in testimony of so great a victory. For the Enemy is more completely vanquished in the case of a man over whom he holds fuller sway and through whom he holds sway over a larger number of other men. Now, he has greater power over the proud, because of the prestige of nobility, and through the proud over a larger number of other men by means of the authority of the former. When, therefore, Thy sons thought with satisfaction of the heart of Victorinus, which the Devil had occupied as an impregnable shelter, and of the tongue of Victorinus, which he had used as a great and sharp weapon to slay many, it was right that they should have rejoiced more abundantly because our King had bound the strong man, and they saw his vessels taken from him to be cleansed and made suitable for Thy honor, and to become 'useful to the Lord for every good work.'

CHAPTER 5

When Thy servant, Simplicianus, told me this story about Victorinus, I burned to imitate him. This, of course, was why he had told it. When he added that, in the time of the Emperor Julian, when Christians were prohibited by law from teaching literature and public speaking (Victorinus submitted willingly to this law, for he preferred to abandon the school of wordiness rather than Thy Word, by which Thou dost make eloquent the tongues of babes), his courage seemed to me not greater than his good fortune, for he thus found the opportunity to devote his time to Thee. This is what I was sighing for, being tied down not by irons outside myself, but by my own iron will. The Enemy had control of the power of my will and from it he had fashioned a chain for me and had bound me in it. For, lust is the product of perverse will, and when one obeys lust habit is produced, and when one offers no resistance to habit necessity is produced. By means, as it were, of these interconnected links—whence the chain I spoke of—I was held in the grip of a harsh bondage. But, the new will, which had begun to be in me, to serve Thee for Thy own sake and to desire to enjoy Thee, O God, the only sure Joyfulness, was not yet capable of overcoming the older will which was strengthened by age. Thus, my two voluntary inclinations, one old and the other new, one carnal and the other spiritual, were engaged in mutual combat and were tearing my soul apart in the conflict.

Thus I came to understand by personal experience the text which I had read, how the flesh 'lusts against the spirit and the spirit against the flesh.' Of course, I was on both sides, but I was more on the side of what I approved within myself than on the side of what I disapproved within myself. For, I was less identified with this latter side, since in great part I suffered it unwillingly rather than acted willingly. Still, the habit that opposed me with greater vigor had risen out of my very self, since I had willingly reached a state which I found to be against my will. And who could justly protest if a just punishment pursues the sinner? I no longer had the excuse which permitted me to think that the reason why I had not yet given up the world to serve Thee was that my perception of truth was uncertain; for, now, it also was certain. But, still earthbound, I refused to fight under Thy command and I feared as much to be freed of all my burdens, as one should fear to be hindered by them.

So, I was agreeably laden with a worldly burden, as in a dream, and the thoughts by which I meditated on Thee were like the endeavors of those who desire to waken themselves, but who sink back, overcome by a deep sleep. Yet, just as there is no one who wants to sleep all the time, and in the sound judgment of all men it is preferable to be awake, many a man nevertheless puts off the act of disrupting his sleep when there is a heavy lethargy in his bodily parts, and, though it is time to get up, he chooses to enjoy the sleep that is indeed not wholly pleasing. So was I sure that it was better to give myself over to Thy charity, rather than to give in to my own cupidity. But, while charity was attractive and was about to win its victory, cupidity was also alluring and held me in its fetters. There was no answer for me to give to Thee, when Thou didst say to me: 'Awake, sleeper, and arise from among the dead, and Christ will enlighten thee.' And, as Thou didst manifest from all sides the truth of Thy statements, there was not a thing for me to answer, being already convinced by the truth, but these slow and sleepy words: 'Later, just a bit later; wait a short time.' However, 'later and later' meant more than a bit, and 'wait a short time' lasted a long time. In vain was I delighted with that law of Thine according to the inner man, when the other law in my members was warring against the law of my mind and making me prisoner to the law of sin that was in my members. For, the law of sin is the force of habit by which the mind, though unwilling, is dragged and held tightly; rightly so, for the mind willingly slipped into this habit. Unhappy man that I was! Who should deliver me from the body of this death, except Thy grace through Jesus Christ, our Lord?

CHAPTER 6

I shall tell and confess unto Thy Name, O Lord, my Helper and my Redeemer, how Thou didst release me from the chains of desire for the pleasures of concubinage, by which I was most firmly bound, and from the bondage of worldly affairs.

I was living my usual life with increasing anxiety, sighing for Thee every day, going often to Thy church, whenever my work, under the weight of which I continued to groan, left me free. Alypius was with me, no longer engaged in the work of a legal consultant now that the third session of the assessor's court was over. He was looking for people to whom he could again sell his legal advice, just as I was selling skill in speaking, if this can be furnished by teaching. Nebridius, however, had yielded to the demands of our friendship and was teaching as an assistant to Verecundus, a very good friend of us all, a citizen and grammarian of Milan, who had urgently importuned and warmly begged, by virtue of this friendship, the trusted assistance of one of our group, which he greatly needed. Thus, it was not the desire of personal advantage which attracted Nebridius (he could have derived greater gains from his literary skill, had he desired), but, as a result of his courteous good will, this most lovable and gentle friend was unwilling to turn down our request. He worked most prudently at this task, guarding against becoming well known to personages who are important by this world's standards, and avoiding every mental disturbance by these measures, for he wished to keep his mind free and at liberty for as much time as possible, in order to pursue his own studies, to read or to hear something about wisdom.

So, on a certain day (I do not recall the reason why Nebridius was away), a man named Ponticianus came to visit myself and Alypius at our home. He was a compatriot of ours, in the sense that he was from Africa, and the holder of an important position at court. I do not know what he desired of us. We sat down together to have a talk. Just by chance, he noticed a book on the games table before us. He picked it up, opened it, and to his surprise, no doubt, discovered that it was the Apostle Paul. He had thought it one of the books which I was wearing myself out in teaching. He looked at me with a smile and expressed his felicitations and surprise at unexpectedly finding this work, and only this work, before my eyes. In fact, he was a Christian and a faithful one, accustomed to go on his knees before Thee, our God, in frequent and lengthy prayers in church. When I pointed out to him that I was devoting much attention to these writings, he began to tell the story of Anthony, the Egyptian monk, whose name shone very brilliantly among Thy servants, but was unknown to us up to that time. When he discovered this, he dwelt upon this point in his conversation, giving much information about this man to us who were ignorant, and expressing surprise at this ignorance of ours. We were amazed, of course, to hear of Thy miracles, of such recent memory and almost in our own times, which were well supported by testimony—miracles performed in the right faith and in the Catholic Church. We were all in a condition of wonder: we two, because these things were so important; he, because we had not heard of them.

From this, his conversation turned to the groups in the monasteries, to their manner of living, sweet with Thy odor, and to the populating of the waste spaces of the desert: of all this we knew nothing. There was even a monastery at Milan, outside the city walls, filled with good brothers under the patronage of Ambrose, and we did not know of it. He went right on speaking of his subject, while we remained silent and engrossed. Then, he happened to tell how he and three companions (I do not know at what time, but certainly it was at Treves), during the time of the afternoon that the emperor was attending the show in the circus, went out for a walk in the gardens beside the city walls. There, they happened to pair off, he taking one companion with him, and the other two wandering off likewise, but in another direction. This second pair, strolling along, happened upon a hut where were dwelling some of Thy servants who are 'poor in spirit, for of such is the kingdom of Heaven.' There, they found a book, in which the *Life of Anthony* had been written. One of them began to read it, and to wonder, and to catch the spark. As he read, he thought of embracing such a life and of giving up secular affairs to serve Thee. (They belonged to the group of officials called 'special agents.') Then, suddenly filled with a holy love and angry at himself with virtuous shame, he turned his eyes to his friend and said to him: 'Tell me, I beg of you, what goal do we hope to achieve with all these efforts of ours? What are we looking for? What reason have we for engaging in public service? Could our aspiration at the court be anything greater than to become "friends of Caesar"? And what is not unstable and full of danger in that position? Through how many dangers must one go to reach a greater danger? And when will one reach it? Now, if I wish, I can be a friend of God immediately.'

He said this and, in the throes of giving birth to a new life, he looked again at the text. As he read, he was changed within, in the part which Thou didst see. His mind withdrew from the world, as soon became evident. For, while he read and his heart surged up and down, he groaned at times as he made his decision. He decided in favor of the better, being now Thine, and said to his friend: 'I have just divorced myself from that ambition of ours and have determined to serve God. I shall begin this service from this hour and in this place. If you do not care to do likewise, do not speak in opposition.' The other man replied that he would cleave to his companion for so great a reward and so important a service. The two men then began building their tower for Thee, making the necessary outlay, leaving all their possessions and following Thee.

At this point, Ponticianus and his associate were walking in other parts of the garden and searching for the others. Arriving at the same place and finding them, they advised them to return, for the day was now drawing to a close. The others told about their decision and their resolution; how such a desire arose and became firmly established in them. They begged them not to offer any opposition, if they refused to join them. These two men were not changed from their former disposition, yet they wept for themselves (so Ponticianus said) and loyally felicitated the others, commending themselves to their prayers. With their hearts still dragging along on the earth, they went away to the imperial court, while their friends, with hearts fixed on heaven, remained in the hut.

Both men were engaged to be married. When their fiancées heard about this, they also dedicated their virginity to Thee.

CHAPTER 7

This was Ponticianus' story. Thou indeed, O Lord, didst
twist me back upon myself, while his words were being uttered,
taking me away from behind my own back, where I had placed
myself because I was unwilling to look at myself, and Thou
didst set me right in front of my own face so that I might see
how ugly I was, how deformed and vile, how defiled and
covered with sores. I saw and was filled with horror, yet there
was no place to flee from myself. If I attempted to turn my
gaze away from myself, he kept on telling his story, and Thou
didst again place me before myself, thrusting me up before my
eyes, so that I would discover my iniquity and detest it. I recognized it, but pretended not to: I thrust it from my sight and out
of my mind.

At this time, the more ardent was my approval of these
men (having heard of their salutary inclinations and how they
had given themselves entirely to Thee in order to be healed),
the more abhorrent was my condemnation of myself in comparison with them. For, many of my years (about twelve) had
flowed by since that period in my nineteenth year when, having
read the *Hortensius* of Cicero, I was aroused by the love of wisdom. I continued to put off the rejection of earthly happiness
whereby I might have been free to investigate that wisdom,
whose mere quest—not to speak of its discovery—should have
been preferred to the actual finding of treasures and kingdoms
among men, and to being surrounded by corporeal pleasures
at my beck and call. Yet, as a youth, I was quite unhappy,
unhappy in the beginning of the period of adolescence. I even
begged chastity of Thee, saying: 'Give me chastity and self-
restraint, but not just yet.' I was afraid that Thou wouldst
quickly heed my prayer, that Thou wouldst quickly cure me
from the disease of concupiscence, which I preferred to be
appeased rather than to be abolished. And I had walked the
crooked ways in sacrilegious superstition, not exactly certain
in it, but preferring it in a way to other teaching which I did not
search out with sincerity but which I fought against with
enmity.

I maintained the opinion that the reason why I was deferring from day to day the rejection of worldly ambition, in order to follow Thee alone, was because nothing by which I could direct my course seemed certain to me. But the day had come on which I was laid bare before myself. My conscience uttered this rebuke within me: 'Where is your tongue? Of course, you have been saying that you are unwilling to cast off the burden of vanity because the true is not certain. See, now it is certain, yet this burden still presses down upon you, while they, who have not been worn out in such a search and have not thought over these things for a decade or more, have taken wings on their less burdened shoulders.'

Thus was I gnawed from within and exceedingly troubled by a fearful shame, while Ponticianus spoke of such things. When he finished his conversation and the business for which he had come, he went his way, and I to myself. What did I not say within me? With what lashes of judgment did I not whip my soul so that it would follow me who yearned to follow Thee? Yet, it balked; it refused and made no effort to be excused. All arguments were used up and refuted. There remained only dumb fear. As if from death, my soul shrank back from being restrained from the flux of habit, in which it was wasting away unto death.

CHAPTER 8

Then, in that great struggle within my inner abode—which I had forcibly provoked with my soul in that little room of ours, my heart—being disturbed as much in my countenance as in my mind, I rush in upon Alypius and cry out: 'What is wrong with us? What does this mean, this story you heard? Unlearned men are rising up and storming heaven, while we with our teachings which have no heart in them, here we are tumbling about in flesh and blood! Is it because they have led the way that we are ashamed to follow, yet are not ashamed of the fact that we are not following?'

I said some such words, and then my mental agitation tore me away from him; while he kept silent, terrified as he looked upon me. Not even my voice sounded as usual. Forehead, cheeks, eyes, complexion, the way I spoke, gave more indication of my mental condition than did the words I uttered.

A little garden belonged to our residence, and we used it as we did the rest of the house, for our host, the landlord, did not live there. The tumult in my breast carried me out there, where no one could hinder the burning struggle which I had entered upon against myself; to what solution, Thou didst know, but I did not. Yet, my madness was healthful and my dying was life-giving; I was aware of the extent of my evil, but I was unaware of the extent of the good I would shortly attain.

So, I'withdrew to the garden, and Alypius followed in my footsteps. There was no lack of personal privacy for me when he was present. Moreover, how could he abandon me in such a frame of mind?

We sat down as far away from the building as possible. I was shaken in spirit, angered by a most violent indignation at the fact that I did not enter into an agreement and covenant with Thee, O my God, for all my bones cried out that I should make this step, and extolled it to the heavens with praises. Entry into this agreement did not require boats or chariots or movement of the feet; I did not even have to go as far as we had gone from the house to the place where we were sitting. For, not merely to go, but actually to reach that disposition, meant nothing else than to wish to go—strongly and completely of course, not just a half-wounded wish, turning now to this and now to that, nor a will threshing about in a struggle wherein, when one part rises up, another part is cast down.

At last, in these seething fevers of irresolution, I began to make many gesticulations, such as men wish to make at times, yet cannot, either because they have not the members, or because these members are bound in chains, or are undone by illness, or are hindered in some way. If it were a matter of pulling my hair, or striking my forehead, or grasping my knee with clenched fingers, I did it because I wished it. But, I could have wished and yet not done it, if the mobility of my members had not obeyed. Thus, I did so many things, in situations where willing was not identical with the power to act. Yet, I did not do the thing which was incomparably more attractive to me and which I was capable of executing just as soon as I had the will to act, for, as soon as I had willed it, then surely I willed it. In this case, the ability was identical with the will, and the act of willing was itself the performance. Yet, it was not done. It was easier for my body to obey the slightest wish of my soul, moving its members at a mere nod, than for my soul to obey itself for the carrying out, in the will alone, of a great act of will.

CHAPTER 9

What is the source of this monstrosity? What purpose does it serve? Let Thy mercy shine forth and let me ask the question, if perchance the mysteries of men's punishments and the darkest griefs of the sons of Adam can answer me. What is the source of this monstrosity? What purpose does it serve? The mind commands the body and is immediately obeyed; the mind commands itself and is resisted. The mind commands the hand to be moved and its readiness is so great that command can hardly be distinguished from enslavement. Yet, the mind is the mind, while the hand is the body. The mind commands the mind to will; it is not something else, yet it does not do it. What is the source of this monstrosity? What purpose does it serve? It commands, I say, that the will-act be performed, and it would not issue the command unless it willed it, yet its command is not carried out.

But, it does not will it completely, and so it does not command it completely. For, it commands to the extent that it wills; and what it commands it not done, to the extent that it does not will it, since the will commands that there be a will, not another will, but its very self. So, it does not command with its whole being; therefore, its command is not fulfilled. For, if it were whole, it would not command that it be done; it would already be done. Hence, it is not a monstrosity to will something in part and to oppose it in part; it is rather an illness of the mind, which, though lifted up by truth, is also weighed down heavily by habit; so it does not rise up unimpaired. And, thus, there are two voluntary inclinations, neither one of which is complete, and what is present in one is lacking in the other.

CHAPTER 10

Just as vain talkers and those who seduce the mind perish from before Thy presence, O God, so let those perish who, noticing the two voluntary tendencies in the process of deliberation, maintain that there are two natures belonging to two minds: the one a good nature; the other, bad. Truly, they themselves are evil when they entertain these bad opinions, and the same men will themselves become good if they form true opinions and give their assent to those that are true. As Thy Apostle says to them: 'You were once darkness, but now you are light in the Lord.' For, they wish to be light, not in the Lord but in themselves, being of the opinion that the nature of the soul is what God is. Thus, they have become denser darkness, since they have, with terrifying arrogance, departed farther from Thee—from Thee, the 'true Light which enlightens every man who comes into the world.' Give heed to what you say, be ye ashamed and come ye to Him and be enlightened, and your faces shall not be confounded.

When I was deliberating on the immediate act of becoming a servant of the Lord, my God, as I had intended for a long time, it was I myself who willed it, it was I who willed it not; it was I in both cases. Yet I neither willed it fully, nor refused wholly to will it. So, I struggled with myself and divided myself from myself. And this disintegration went on involuntarily within me, yet it did not demonstrate the nature of an alien mind but punishment of my own. Therefore, it was not I who did this work, but the sin that dwelt in me, arising from the punishment of a sin of a freer man, for I was a son of Adam.

Indeed, if there are as many opposed natures as there are voluntary inclinations which offer mutual resistance, then there will be not two wills, but many. If a person deliberates whether he will go to one of their meetings, or to the theatre, they cry out: 'See, two natures; the good one draws in this direction, the bad one draws away in that. Otherwise, whence come this hesitation of opposed wills within him?' But, I say they are both bad, both the one which draws the man to them and the one which draws him away to the theatre. But, they will not believe that there is anything but good in that which leads men to them. Suppose, now, one of our people deliberates and hovers within himself between two disputing inclinations of will, whether to go to the theatre or to our church, would they not themselves hesitate in giving an answer? For, either they will admit, against their will, that to go to our church is based on good will, just as they who go to church are initiated into and engaged in its mysteries, or else they will think that two bad natures and two bad minds are struggling within the one man, and their customary statement will then not be true: that there is one good and the other evil. Or else they will be converted to the truth and will not deny that, when a person deliberates, the one soul is agitated by contrary inclinations of will.

So, when they perceive that two wills are in conflict with themselves within one man, let them no longer say that two contrary minds arising from two contrary substances and from two contrary principles are fighting, one being good and the other evil. For, Thou, the truthful God, dost disprove them, dost refute and convict them: for instance, when both wills are bad, and someone deliberates whether to kill a man with poison or with steel; whether to steal this part or another part of another man's land, when he cannot steal both; whether to purchase sensual pleasure at extravagant cost or hoard his money with avarice; whether to go to the circus or the theatre, if both are having a performance on the same day—or (adding a third possibility) to go instead to rob another's house, the occasion presenting itself, or (with even a fourth) to set out to commit adultery, if at the same time the possibility of doing so presents itself. If all these possibilities come together in one instant of time, and all are simultaneously desired, but cannot be put into effect at the same time, then they tear the mind to pieces within itself by the opposing tendencies of four volitions, or even by a greater number, so numerous the things that can be desired; yet, the Manichees are not accustomed to claim that there is such a plurality of different substances.

The same is true in the case of good inclinations of will. For, I ask them whether it be good to take delight in the reading of the Apostle, and whether it be good to take delight in a solemn psalm, and whether it be good to discourse upon the Gospel. To each question they will answer: 'It is good.' What then? If they are all equally delightful at one and the same time, then are not contrary wills drawing the heart of man in various directions, while deliberation proceeds as to which action we should seize upon first? All these inclinations are good, yet they vie with each other until one action is chosen, whereto may be directed, one and entire, the will which before had been split into several tendencies.

Thus, too, when eternity delights from above and the sensual appeal of a temporal good pulls from below, it is the same soul which wishes the one or the other, but with a will that is not entire, and so the soul is torn apart with the weight of its vexation while truth causes it to prefer the former, but habit does not permit it to put aside the latter.

CHAPTER 11

So, I was sick at heart and suffered excruciating torture, accusing myself with a bitterness that far exceeded the customary. I twisted and turned in my chains, until they could be completely broken, for I was now held but weakly by them, but still held. And Thou didst urge from within my depths, O Lord, whipping me in the strictness of mercy with double scourges of fear and shame, lest I should again relapse and fail to break that weak and thin chain which remained, while it would become strong again and bind me more firmly.

Within myself, I kept saying: 'Here, do it now, do it now,' and, as I spoke, I was already progressing to the moment of decision. Now, I was almost ready to do it, yet I did not. I did not fall back into my previous state, but stood quite near and recovered my breath. I tried again and I was almost there—almost—I was practically grasping and holding it. Yet, I was not there; I neither grasped nor held it, hesitating to die unto death and to live unto life. Stronger within me was the accustomed worse than the unaccustomed better. The closer that point in time came, at which I would become a different being, the more terror did it strike within me; it did not force me back or turn me aside, it held me in suspense.

What held me were the trifles of trifles and vanities of vanities, my former mistresses, plucking softly at the garment of my flesh and whispering: 'Do you send us away?' and: 'From this moment unto eternity, we shall not be with you, and: 'From this moment unto eternity, this and that will not be permitted you.' What suggestiveness was there in that phrase, 'this and that'—O my God, what suggestiveness! May Thy mercy avert its gaze from the soul of Thy servant! What sordid things, what indecencies, did those words suggest! Yet, I far less half heard them now, for it was not as though they openly opposed me by going straight for me; rather, they murmured from behind me, furtively twitching, as it were, at me, as I moved to depart, so that I would look back. Yet, they did retard me, hesitant as I was to tear myself away and to cut myself off from them, and to make the leap to the position to which I was called, for, all-powerful custom said to me: 'Can you live without these things, do you think?'

But, it now was saying this very feebly. For, from the direction to which I had turned my face and to which I was afraid to pass, the chaste dignity of continence began to manifest itself: tranquil and joyful, but not in a lascivious way, inviting me in upright fashion to come ahead and not hesitate; stretching forth to receive and embrace me holy hands filled with a multitude of good examples. There, so many boys and girls; there, youth in great number; people of every age; venerable widows; women grown old in virginity—and in them all continence herself was in no way barren, but the fecund mother of children, of joys coming from espousal with Thee, O Lord.

With mocking encouragement, she mocked me, as if saying: 'Can you not live as these men and women do? In fact, do these men and women live by their own powers and not by the Lord their God? The Lord their God gave me to them. Why do you stand upon yourself and so have naught to stand on? Throw yourself upon Him, fear not; He will not pull Himself away and let you fall. Throw yourself confidently; He will take you up and heal you.' I was much ashamed, for I still heard the whisperings of those trifles, and hung as one in suspense. Again, she seemed to say: 'Turn a deaf ear to your unclean members on the earth, in order that they may be mortified.

They tell you a story of delights, but not as the Law of the Lord thy God.' This dispute within my heart was simply myself in opposition to myself. But Alypius kept right at my side and waited in silence for the outcome of my unaccustomed emotion.

CHAPTER 12

Now, when profound consideration had pulled out from the hidden depth and heaped together the whole of my wretchedness before the gaze of my heart, a mighty storm arose, bringing a mighty rain of tears. And, in order to shed the whole of it, with its accompanying groans, I stood up, away from Alypius (to me solitude seemed more fitting for the business of weeping), and I withdrew to a distance greater than that at which even his presence could be an annoyance to me. That is the way I felt then, and he perceived it; I suppose I said something or other, and my inflection revealed a voice weighted with tears, and so I had risen. Hence, he stayed where we had been sitting and was much astonished. I threw myself down under a fig tree, unconscious of my actions, and loosed the reins on my tears. They burst forth in rivers from my eyes, an acceptable sacrifice unto Thee. Not, indeed, in these words, but with this meaning, I said many things to Thee: 'And Thou, O Lord, how long? How long, O Lord, wilt Thou be angry unto the end? Remember not our former iniquities.' For I still felt that I was held by them and I uttered these wretched words: 'How much longer, how much longer? "Tomorrow" and "tomorrow"? Why not right now? Why not the end of my shame at this very hour?'

I kept saying these things and weeping with the bitterest sorrow of my heart. And, behold, I heard from a nearby house the voice of someone—whether boy or girl I know not—chanting, as it were, and repeating over and over: 'Take it, read it! Take it, read it!' And immediately, with a transformed countenance, I started to think with greatest concentration whether it was the usual thing for children to chant words such as this in any kind of game, and it did not occur to me that I had ever heard anything like it. Having stemmed the flow of my tears, I got up, taking it to mean that nothing else was divinely commanded me than that I should open a book and read the first passage that I should find. For I had heard about Anthony that he had been admonished from a reading of the Gospel on which he had come by chance, as if what was being read was said for him: 'Go, sell what thou hast, and give to the poor, and thou shalt have treasure in heaven; and come, follow me, and by such a revelation he was at once converted to Thee.

And so I went hurriedly back to the place where Alypius was sitting. I had placed there the copy of the Apostle, when I had got up from the place. Snatching it up, I opened it and read in silence the first passage on which my eyes fell: 'Not in revelry and drunkenness, not in debauchery and wantonness, not in strife and jealousy; but put on the Lord Jesus Christ, and as for the flesh, take no thought for its lusts.' No further did I desire to read, nor was there need. Indeed, immediately with the termination of this sentence, all the darknesses of doubt were dispersed, as if by a light of peace flooding into my heart.

Then, having marked it either with my finger or with some other sign, I closed the book and, with a now peaceful face, informed Alypius. Then, he gave an account of what was going on within him, of which I was in ignorance. He asked to see what I had read. I showed him and he paid attention even beyond that part which I had read. I did not know the section which followed. Actually, the continuation read: 'But him who is weak in faith, receive.' This, he applied to himself and he disclosed it to me. But he was strengthened by this admonition, in a decision and resolution which was good and most suitable to his moral qualities, in which he had far surpassed me for a long time, and he joined in without any trouble or delay.

After that, we went in to my mother and told her; she rejoiced. We gave her the story of what had happened; she was exultant, triumphant, and she blessed Thee, 'who art able to accomplish far more than we ask or understand.' She saw that much more in regard to me had been granted her by Thee than she was wont to ask with her unhappy and tearful laments. For Thou didst turn me unto Thee, so that I sought no wife or any ambition for this world, standing on that rule of faith where Thou hadst shown me in the revelation of so many years before. And 'Thou didst turn her mourning into joy,' much more abundant than she had desired, and much more fond and pure than she sought from any grandchildren of my flesh.

Anicius Manlius Severinus Boethius

480-524

True happiness, the ever elusive dream of mankind, is a central theme of ethics. What is its nature? Can it be experienced in this earthly life? Is it merely an illusion that will drive men mad till the end of time? Why is it that everything men seek in the name of happiness eventually withers and gives way to sadness?

One of the most beautiful and poetic statements on happiness in the history of Christian writers comes from Boethius, a most unusual man who lived at the end of the fifth and beginning of the sixth centuries. He was certainly a Christian. His studies in Athens brought him into contact with Greek philosophical traditions. Aristotle, particularly, influenced his thinking. After rising to a high magisterial office under Theodoric, King of the Ostrogoths, he was accused of treason, stripped of all his power and thrown into prison. He was executed in 524/5.

It was while in prison that this highly educated man, who is recognized as one of the major links between the ancient world and the middle ages, wrote The Consolation of Philosophy. While grieving of the tragic turn that his fortunes have taken, Lady Philosophy comes to console him. Because he is so totally wrapped up in his own misery, he does not at first recognize her. She gently rebukes him and gradually directs his attention to matters of much greater importance than his fortunes.

The work moves back and forth between prose and poetry. Boethius's knowledge of ancient literature is most obvious. He draws from the mythological as well as the philosophical literature of the Greeks. The Consolation of Philosophy *is divided into five books. Below we present Book III, which treats of true happiness.*

As Book III opens, Boethius is beginning to feel refreshed because of the strength of ideas and sweetness of music offered to him by Lady Philosophy. She tells him that she will now lead him into the realm of true happiness. But first he must learn to recognize false goods which humans so often mistake for happiness. Together they journey across riches, honor, power, fame and pleasure. These are commonly mistaken as the true good because of human error. None of them can ever be wholly satisfying, and in fact are often harmful. Philosophy leads Boethius to a recognition of false happiness and to the declaration that perfect happiness is that which makes a man self-sufficient, powerful, worthy of reverence and reknown, and joyful. Before revealing where to seek true happiness, Philosophy sings a song to the Father of all things without whose aid no beginning can be properly made. It is a beautiful poem (number 9) which evoked wide commentary during the Middle Ages. Philosophy then explains that the supreme good and highest happiness are found in God and, in fact, are God. God is One and the goal toward which all things tend; He rules the universe by his goodness; all created things obey Him. Evil appears in the closing lines of the book as a problem for Boethius. Its resolution is reserved for Book IV. The final poem, based on the fable of Orpheus and Eurydice, places the reader in the classical ethical tension between law and love, and presents the haunting question, "Who can give lovers a law?"

THE CONSOLATION
OF PHILOSOPHY

BOOK III

PROSE 1

Philosophy promises to lead Boethius to true happiness.

When her song was finished, its sweetness left me wondering and alert, eager to hear more. After a while I said, "You are the perfect comforter for weak spirits. I feel greatly refreshed by the strength of your ideas and the sweetness of your music; in fact, I think I may now be equal to the attacks of Fortune. And those remedies you spoke of earlier as being rather harsh—I not only do not fear them, I am quite eager to hear them."

Philosophy answered, "I knew it when I saw you so engrossed, so attentive to what I was saying. I waited for you to achieve this state of mind, or, to put it more truly, I led you to it. You will find what I have yet to say bitter to the taste, but, once you have digested it, it will seem sweet. Even though you say that you want to hear more, your eagerness would be even greater if you knew where I am about to lead you."

"Where?" said I.

"To true happiness, to the goal your mind has dreamed of. But your vision has been so clouded by false images you have not been able to reach it."

"Tell me then," I said. "Show me quickly what true happiness is."

"I will gladly, for your sake. But first I must try to make something else clear, something you know much more about. When you have understood that, you may turn your attention in the opposite direction and then you will be able to recognize the nature of true blessedness.

POEM 1

"The man who wants to sow a fertile field must first clear the ground of brush, then cut out the ferns and brambles with his sharp hook, so that the new grain may grow abundantly.

"Honey is sweeter to the taste if the mouth has first tried bitter flavors. Stars shine more brightly after Notus has stopped his rainy blasts. Only after Hesperus has driven away the darkness does the day drive forward his splendid horses.

"Just so, by first recognizing false goods, you begin to escape the burden of their influence; then afterwards true goods may gain possession of your spirit."

PROSE 2

Philosophy defines the supreme good and the perfect happiness to which all men naturally aspire. She then lists the kinds of false goods which men mistake for the true good.

Philosophy looked away for a moment, as though withdrawn into the sacred chamber of her mind; then she began to speak: "Mortal men laboriously pursue many different interests along many different paths, but all strive to reach the same goal of happiness. Now the good is defined as that which, once it is attained, relieves man of all further desires. This is the supreme good and contains within itself all other lesser goods. If it lacked anything at all, it could not be the highest good, because something would be missing, and this could still be desired. Clearly, then, perfect happiness is the perfect state in which all goods are possessed. And, as I said, all men try by various means to attain this state of happiness; for there is naturally implanted in the minds of men the desire for the true good, even though foolish error draws them toward false goods.

Some men, believing that the highest good is to have everything, exert themselves to become very rich. Others think that the highest good is to be found in the highest honors, and so they try to gain the esteem of their fellow citizens by acquiring various honors. Still others equate the highest good with the greatest personal power. Such men want to be rulers, or at least to associate themselves closely with those in power. Then there are those for whom fame seems the highest good and they labor to spread the glory of their names either in war or in practicing the arts of peace. Others measure the good in terms of gaiety and enjoyment; they think that the greatest happiness is found in pleasure. Finally, there are those who interchange the causes and results of these false goods: some desire riches in order to get power and pleasure; some desire power in order to get money or fame.

"Toward such false goods, and others like them, men direct their actions and desires; they want nobility and popularity, for example, because these seem to bring fame; or they want a wife and children because they regard them as sources of pleasure. With regard to friendship, the most sacred kind belongs to the goods of virtue, not of Fortune; all other kinds of friendship are sought out of a desire for power or pleasure. At this point it is a simple matter to evaluate the goods of the body in relation to those we have already discussed: size and strength seem to give power; beauty and speed bring fame; health gives pleasure. All this shows clearly that all men seek happiness; for whatever anyone desires beyond all else, he regards as the highest good. And, since we have defined the highest good as happiness, everyone thinks that the condition which he wants more than anything else must constitute happiness.

"You see here practically the whole range of human happiness: riches, honor, power, fame, and pleasure. Epicurus, who considered only these possibilities, held pleasure to be the highest good of them all, since the rest seem to bring joy to the soul.

"But let me return now to the goals men set for themselves. In spite of its hazy memory, the human soul seeks to return to its true good; but, like the drunken man who cannot find his way home, the soul no longer knows what its good is. Should we consider those men mistaken who try to have everything? Not at all, for nothing can so surely make a man happy as being in full possession of all good things, sufficient in himself and needing no one else. Nor are they mistaken who think that the best men are most worthy of honor, for nothing which nearly all men aspire to achieve can be despised as vile. Power, too, must be considered a good thing, for it would be ridiculous to regard as trivial an asset which can accomplish more than anything else. And what of fame; should we be scornful of it? Surely we must admit that great excellence always carries with it great fame. Finally, it goes without saying that happiness excludes sadness and anguish, that it implies freedom from grief and misery, since even in small things we desire whatever brings delight and enjoyment.

"These, then, are the things which men desire to have: riches, high rank, administrative authority, glory and pleasure, because they believe that these things will give them a good standard of living, honor, power, fame and joy. And whatever men strive for in so many ways must be the good. It is easy to show how strong and natural this striving is because, in spite of the variety and difference of opinion, still all men agree in loving and pursuing the goal of good.

POEM 2

"Now I will show you in graceful song, accompanied by pliant strings, how mighty Nature guides the reins of all things; how she providently governs the immense world by her laws; how she controls all things, binding them with unbreakable bonds.

"The Carthaginian lions endure their fair chains, are fed by hand, and fear the beatings they get from their masters; but if blood should smear their fierce mouths, their sluggish spirits revive, and with a roar they revert to their original nature. They shake off their chains and turn their mad fury on their masters, tearing them with bloody teeth.

"When the chattering bird, who sings in the high branches, is shut up in a narrow cage, she is not changed by the lavish care of the person who feeds her with sweet drink and tasty food. If she can escape from the cramped cage and see the cool shade of the wood, she will scatter the artificial food and fly with yearning to the trees where she will make the forest ring with her sweet voice.

A treetop bent down by heavy pressure will bow its head to the ground; but if the pressure is released, the tree looks back to heaven again. Phoebus sets at night beneath the Hesperian waves, but returning again along his secret path he drives his chariot to the place where it always rises.

"Thus all things seek again their proper courses, and rejoice when they return to them. The only stable order in things is that which connects the beginning to the end and keeps itself on a steady course.

PROSE 3

Nature inclines men toward the true good, but error deceives them with partial goods. Specifically, riches can never be wholly satisfying.

"You, too, who are creatures of earth, dream of your origin. However weak the vision of your dream may be, you have some vague idea of that goal of true happiness toward which you gaze. Nature leads you toward true good, but manifold error turns you away from it. Consider for a moment whether the things men think can give them happiness really bring them to the goal which nature planned for them. If money, or honor, or other goods of that kind really provide something which seems completely and perfectly good, then I too will admit that men can be happy by possessing them. But, if they not only cannot deliver what they promise, but are found to be gravely flawed in themselves, it is obvious that they have only the false appearance of happiness.

"First, then, since you recently were very rich, let me ask whether or not you were ever worried in spite of your abundant wealth."

"Yes," I answered, "I cannot recall a time when my mind was entirely free from worry."

"And wasn't it because you wanted something you did not have, or had something you did not want?"

"That is true," I answered.

"You wanted this, or didn't want that?"

"Yes."

"Then doesn't everyone lack something that he wants?"

"Yes, he does," I replied.

"And isn't the man who lacks something less than wholly self-sufficient?"

"That is true."

"And even you at the peak of your wealth felt this insufficiency?"

"Of course," I agreed.

"Then wealth cannot give a man everything and make him entirely self-sufficient, even though this is what money seems to promise. But I think it most important to observe that there is nothing in the nature of wealth to prevent its being taken from those who have it."

"That is quite true," I said.

"And why shouldn't you agree, since every day those who are powerful enough snatch it from those who are weaker. In fact, most lawsuits are concerned with efforts to recover money taken by violence or fraud."

I agreed that this was the case.

"Therefore, a man needs the help of others to protect his money."

"Of course."

"But he wouldn't need it, if he had no money to lose."

"There is no doubt about that."

"Well then, the situation is upside down; for riches, which are supposed to make men self-sufficient, actually make them dependent on the help of others.

"And now let us see whether riches really drive away need. Don't the wealthy become hungry and thirsty; don't they feel cold in the winter? You may argue that they have the means to satisfy their hunger and thirst, and to protect themselves against the cold. Nevertheless, the needs remain, and riches can only minimize them. For if needs are always present and making demands which must be met by spending money, clearly there will always be some need which is unsatisfied. And here I do not press the point that, although nature makes very modest demands, avarice is never satisfied. My present point is simply

106

this: if riches cannot eliminate need, but on the contrary create new demands, what makes you suppose that they can provide satisfaction?

POEM 3

"Though the rich man has a flowing torrent of gold, his avarice can never be fully satisfied. He may decorate his neck with oriental pearls, and plow his fertile lands with a hundred oxen, but biting care will not leave him during life, and when he dies his wealth cannot go with him.

PROSE 4

Honor is not the true good, nor is it the way to true happiness.

"But you may say that high public office makes the man who receives it honorable and worthy of reverence. Do you think that such offices have the power to make those who hold them virtuous and to free them from their vices? On the contrary, public honors usually reveal wickedness rather than correct it, and so we often complain that these honors are given to the worst men. Catullus, for example, called Nonius an ulcer, though he occupied high office. You can see, then, the disgrace that comes to evil men who receive honors. Their unworthiness would be less obvious without the publicity of public recognition. In your own case, could any threats of danger have persuaded you to share public office with Decoratus, once you had found him to be a scoundrel and a spy? We cannot judge men worthy of respect on account of the honors given them, if we find them unworthy of the honors they have received.

"But, if you found a man distinguished by his wisdom, could you think him unworthy of honor, or of the wisdom which is his?"

"Certainly not," I answered.

"For virtue has its own honor, and this honor is transferred to those who possess virtue. Since popular acclaim cannot accomplish this, clearly it does not have the beauty which is characteristic of true honor. More attention should be paid to this point, for if public contempt makes men abject, public acclaim makes wicked men even more despised since it cannot make them worthy of honor and it exposes them to the world. But public rank itself does not escape untouched, for unworthy men tarnish the offices which they hold by infecting them with their own disease.

"And, to prove further that true honor cannot be attained through these specious dignities, think what would happen if a man who had been many times consul should go to some uncivilized foreign countries. Would the honors which he held at home make him worthy of respect in those places? But, if veneration were a natural part of public honors, it would certainly be given in every nation, just as fire always gives heat wherever it is found in the world. But because popular respect is not a natural consequence of public office, but merely something which depends on untrustworthy public opinion, it vanishes when a man finds himself among those who do not regard his position in his home country as a special dignity.

"What I have said so far has to do with the attitudes of foreigners. Do you think that popular acclaim lasts forever among the citizens in the place where it had its origin? The office of praetor once had great power; now it is an empty name and a heavy burden on the treasury of the Senate. The man who in earlier times was responsible for food supply and distribution was counted a great man; now there is no office lower in public esteem. For, as I said before, whatever does not have its own honor in itself, but depends on public whim, is sometimes valued highly, sometimes not at all. Therefore, if public honors cannot make those who have them worthy of reverence, and if, in addition, they are often tainted by the touch of wicked men, and if their value deteriorates with the passage of time, and if they are contemptible in the eyes of foreigners, what desirable beauty do they have in themselves or give to others?

POEM 4

"Although proud Nero in his raging lust adorned himself in Tyrian purple and white pearls, he was hated by all his subjects. But this wicked man once assigned the tainted seats of consulship to venerable men. Who, then, can consider those men blessed who receive their honors from evil men?

PROSE 5

Power is not a guarantee of happiness.

"Can royal power, or familiarity with kings, make a man truly powerful? Perhaps, you may say, as long as his happy situation endures. But both the past and the present are full of examples of kings who have fallen from happiness to misery. How wonderful is power which is found incapable even of preserving itself! And even though political power is a cause of happiness, is it not also a cause of misery when it diminishes? Although some human empires extend very widely, there are always some nations which cannot be brought under control; and at the point where power, which makes rulers happy, ends, there the impotence, which makes them miserable, begins. For this reason, rulers have always more misery than happiness. A famous tyrant, who knew the dangers of his position, symbolized the fears of kingship by hanging a drawn sword over the head of a member of his court.

"What, then, is the nature of this power which cannot rid a man of gnawing anxieties nor save him from fear? Those who brag of their power want to live in security, but cannot. Do you consider a person powerful whom you see unable to have what he wants? Do you think a person mighty who is always surrounded by bodyguards, who is more afraid than those whom he intimidates, who puts himself in the hands of his servants in order to seem powerful?

"And what shall I say about the followers of men in power, when the power they attach themselves to is obviously so weak? They can be destroyed by the fall of their leader, or even by his whim while he is still in power. Nero forced his friend and teacher, Seneca, to choose his own manner of execution; Antoninus had Papinianus cut down by the swords of the soldiers, even though he had long been a power among the courtiers. Both of these unfortunate men wanted to give up their power; indeed, Seneca tried to give his wealth to Nero and retire. But both were destroyed by their very greatness and neither could have what he wanted.

"What, then, is the value of power which frightens those who have it, endangers those who want it, and irrevocably traps those who have it? Are those true friends whom we acquire by fortune rather than virtue? Misfortune will make an enemy of the man whom good fortune made a friend. And what scoundrel is more deadly than one who has been a friend?

POEM 5

"The man who wishes to be powerful must check his desires; he must not permit himself to be overcome by lust, or submit to its foul reins. For even though your rule extends so far that India trembles before you and Ultima Thule serves you, if you cannot withstand black care, and live without wretched moaning, you have no power.

PROSE 6

True happiness is not found in fame.

"As for glory, how deceptive it often is, and how shameful! The tragic playwright justly cries: 'Oh Fame, Fame, how many lives of worthless men you have exalted!' For many men have achieved a great name based on the false opinion of the masses; and what is more disgraceful than that? Those who are falsely praised must blush when they hear the applause. And, even if the praise is merited, what does it matter to the wise man who measures his virtue by the truth of his conscience, not by popular esteem. And if it seems a good thing to have widened one's fame, it follows that it must seem a bad thing not to have done so. But since, as I explained earlier, there will always be some countries to which a man's fame does not extend, it follows that the person you think famous will be unknown in some other part of the world.

"In this discussion of fame, I do not think mere popularity even worth mentioning since it does not rest on good judgment, nor has it any lasting life. Moreover, everyone knows that to be called noble is a stupid and worthless thing. If it has anything to do with fame, the fame belongs to others; for nobility appears to be a kind of praise which is really merited by parents. If praise makes a person famous, then those who receive praise are famous; therefore, the praise of others (in this case, of your parents) will not make you famous if you have no fame of your own. In my opinion, therefore, if there is anything to be said for nobility, it lies only in the necessity imposed on the nobility to carry on the virtues of their ancestors.

POEM 6

"The whole race of men on this earth springs from one stock. There is one Father of all things; One alone provides for all. He gave Phoebus his rays, the moon its horns. To the earth He gave men, to the sky the stars. He clothed with bodies the souls He brought from heaven.

"Thus, all men come from noble origin. Why then boast of your ancestors? If you consider your beginning, and God your Maker, no one is base unless he deserts his birthright and makes himself a slave to vice.

PROSE 7

Bodily pleasure cannot make men happy.

"What now shall I say about bodily pleasures? The appetite for them is full of worry, and the fulfillment full of remorse. What dreadful disease and intolerable sorrow, the fruits of wickedness, they bring to the bodies of those who enjoy them! What pleasure there may be in these appetites I do not know, but they end in misery as anyone knows who is willing to recall his own lusts. If they can produce happiness, then there is no reason why beasts should not be called happy, since their whole life is devoted to the fulfillment of bodily needs. The pleasure one finds in his wife and children ought to be a most wholesome thing, but the man who protested that he found his sons to be his torturers spoke what may too often be true. How terrible such a condition can be you must learn from me, since you have never experienced it at first hand, nor do you now suffer from it. In this matter I commend the opinion of Euripides who said that the childless man is happy by his misfortune.

POEM 7

"It is the nature of all bodily pleasure to punish those who enjoy it. Like the bee after its honey is given, it flies away, leaving its lingering sting in the hearts it has struck.

PROSE 8

Philosophy concludes that these limited goods are transitory and cannot bring happiness. On the contrary, they are often positively harmful.

"There is no doubt, therefore, that these are the wrong roads to happiness; they cannot take anyone to the destination which they promise. Let me briefly show you the evils within them. If you try to accumulate money, you must deprive someone else of it. If you want to cover yourself with honors, you will become indebted to those who can bestow them; and, by wishing to outdo others in honor, you will humiliate yourself by begging.

"If you want power, you risk the danger of your subjects' treachery. If you seek fame, you will become involved in difficulties and lose your security. If you seek a life of pleasure—but who would not spurn and avoid subjection to so vile and fragile a thing as his body? Indeed, those who boast of bodily goods are relying on weak and uncertain possessions. For you are not bigger than an elephant, nor stronger than a bull, nor as quick as a tiger.

"Fix your gaze on the extent, the stability, the swift motion of the heavens, and stop admiring base things. The heavens are not more remarkable in these qualities than in the reason by which they are governed. The beauty of your person passes swiftly away; it is more fleeting than spring flowers. And if, as Aristotle says, men had the eyes of Lynceus and could see through stone walls, would they not find the superficially beautiful body of Alcibiades to be most vile upon seeing his entrails? It is not your nature which makes you seem fair but the weak eyes of those who look at you. You may esteem your bodily qualities as highly as you like as long as you admit that these things you admire so much can be destroyed by the trifling heat of a three-day fever.

"All these arguments can be summed up in the truth that these limited goods, which cannot achieve what they promise, and are not perfect in embracing all that is good, are not man's path to happiness, nor can they make him happy in themselves.

POEM 8

"Alas, what ignorance drives miserable men along crooked paths! You do not look for gold in the green trees, nor for jewels hanging on the vine; you do not set your nets in the high mountains when you want a fish for dinner; nor, if you want to hunt deer, do you seek them along the Tyrenean seas. On the contrary, men are skilled in knowing the hidden caves in the sea, and in knowing where white pearls and scarlet dye are found; they know what beaches are rich in various kinds of fish.

"But, when it comes to the location of the good which they desire, they are blind and ignorant. They dig the earth in search of the good which soars above the star-filled heavens. What can I say to show what fools they are? Let them pursue their riches and honors and, when they have painfully accumulated their false goods, then they may come to recognize the true.

PROSE 9

Philosophy completes her discussion of false happiness and its causes. She then takes up the subject of true happiness and the supreme good.

"Up to this point," said Philosophy, "I have shown clearly enough the nature of false happiness, and, if you have understood it, I can now go on to speak of true happiness."

"I understand well enough," I answered, "that sufficiency is not attained by riches, nor power by ruling others, nor honor by public recognition, nor fame by public acclaim, nor joy by pleasures."

"But have you understood the reasons why this is so?"

"I think I have a vague idea," I said, "but I wish you would show me more plainly."

"The reasons are clear enough. What nature has made simple and indivisible, human error has divided and changed from true and perfect to false and imperfect. Would you say that one who lacks nothing stands in need of power?"

"Of course not."

"You are quite right; for whoever is deficient in any way needs outside help."

"That is true," I said.

"Therefore, sufficiency and power have one and the same nature."

"That seems to be true."

"And would you say that a thing which is perfectly self-sufficient and completely powerful should be scorned, or is it, on the contrary, worthy of honor?"

"Undoubtedly it is most worthy of honor."

"Then we may add reverence to sufficiency and power, and conclude that all three are really one."

"That is true."

"Next, would you think such a thing obscure and base, or rather, famous and renowned? Now think for a moment whether that which is conceded to be self-sufficient, all powerful, and worthy of great reverence can stand in need of any fame which it cannot give to itself, and therefore seem in some way defective."

"I confess that being what it is it must also be famous."

"It follows, then, that fame cannot be separated from the other three."

"That is true."

"Therefore, that which is self-sufficient, which can do everything by its own power, which is honored and famous, is not this also most pleasant and joyful?"

"I cannot imagine how anyone possessing all these attributes could be sad; and so, if the argument thus far is sound, I must confess that this thing must also be joyful."

"Then," Philosophy went on, "it must be granted that, although the names of sufficiency, power, fame, reverence, and joy are different, in substance all are one and the same thing."

"That must be granted," I agreed.

"Human depravity, then, has broken into fragments that which is by nature one and simple; men try to grasp part of a thing which has no parts and so get neither the part, which does not exist, nor the whole, which they do not seek."

"How is this?" I asked.

"The man who seeks wealth in order to avoid poverty is not interested in power; he would rather be obscure and weak and will even deprive himself of many natural pleasures so that he won't lose the money he has collected. But such a man does not even acquire sufficiency; he is powerless, plagued by trouble, held in contempt, and hidden in obscurity. Similarly, the man who seeks only power wastes his money, scorns pleasures and honors that carry with them no power, and thinks nothing of fame. But see how much he is missing: sometimes he is without the necessities of life, he is plagued by anxieties, and when he cannot overcome them he loses that which he wants most—he ceases to be powerful. Honors, fame, and pleasure can be shown to be equally defective; for each is connected with the others, and whoever seeks one without the others cannot get even the one he wants."

"What happens when someone tries to get them all at the same time?" I asked.

"He, indeed, reaches for the height of happiness, but can he find it in these things which, as I have shown, cannot deliver what they promise?"

"Of course not," I said.

"Happiness, then, is by no means to be sought in these things which are commonly thought to offer the parts of what is sought for."

"Nothing can be truer than this," I agreed.

"Now you have grasped the nature of false happiness and its causes. Now turn your mind's eye in the opposite direction and there you will see the true happiness which I promised to show you."

"But this is clear even to a blind man," I said, "and you revealed it a little while ago when you tried to explain the causes of false happiness. For, unless I am mistaken, true and perfect happiness is that which makes a man self-sufficient, powerful, worthy of reverence and renown, and joyful. And, to show that I have understood you, I acknowledge that whatever can truly provide any one of these must be true and perfect happiness, since all are one and the same."

"O, my scholar," Philosophy answered, "your observation is a happy one if you add just one thing."

"What is that?" I asked.

"Do you imagine that there is any mortal and frail thing which can bring about a condition of this kind?"

"Not at all," I said, "but I think you have proved that beyond any need for further discussion."

"Then these false causes of happiness are mere appearances of the true good and merely seem to give certain imperfect goods to mortal men; but they cannot give true and perfect good."

"I agree," I said.

"Now then, since you know what true happiness is, and the things that falsely seem to offer it, you must now learn where to look for true happiness."

"This," I answered, "is what I have eagerly looked forward to."

"But since, as Plato says in his *Timaeus,* we ought to implore divine help even in small things, what do you think is called for now if we are to gain access to the throne of the highest good?"

"We must invoke the Father of all things without whose aid no beginning can be properly made."

"You are right," said Philosophy, and she began to sing this song:

POEM 9

"Oh God, Maker of heaven and earth, Who govern the world with eternal reason, at your command time passes from the beginning. You place all things in motion, though You are yourself without

116

change. No external causes impelled You to make this work from chaotic matter. Rather it was the form of the highest good, existing within You without envy, which caused You to fashion all things according to the eternal exemplar. You who are most beautiful produce the beautiful world from your divine mind and, forming it in your image, You order the perfect parts in a perfect whole.

"You bind the elements in harmony so that cold and heat, dry and wet are joined, and the purer fire does not fly up through the air, nor the earth sink beneath the weight of water.

"You release the world-soul throughout the harmonious parts of the universe as your surrogate, threefold in its operations, to give motion to all things. That soul, thus divided, pursues its revolving course in two circles, and, returning to itself, embraces the profound mind and transforms heaven to its own image.

"In like manner You create souls and lesser living forms and, adapting them to their high flight in swift chariots, You scatter them through the earth and sky. And when they have turned again toward You, by your gracious law, You call them back like leaping flames.

"Grant, Oh Father, that my mind may rise to Thy sacred throne. Let it see the fountain of good; let it find light, so that the clear light of my soul may fix itself in Thee. Burn off the fogs and clouds of earth and shine through in Thy splendor. For Thou art the serenity, the tranquil peace of virtuous men. The sight of Thee is beginning and end; one guide, leader, path, and goal.

PROSE 10

Philosophy teaches Boethius that the supreme good and highest happiness are found in God and are God.

"Since you have seen the forms of imperfect and perfect good, I think it is now time to show where this perfection of happiness resides. First, we must ask whether a good of the kind you defined a short while ago can exist at all, so that we may not be deceived by an empty shadow of thought and thus be prevented from reaching the truth of our problem. Now, no one can deny that something exists which is a kind of fountain of all goodness; for everything which is found to be imperfect shows its imperfection by the lack of some perfection. It follows that if something is found to be imperfect in its kind, there must necessarily be something of that same kind which is perfect. For without a standard of perfection we cannot judge anything to be imperfect. Nature did not have its origins in the defective and incomplete but in the integral and absolute; it fell from such beginnings to its present meanness and weakness.

"But if, as I have just pointed out, there is a certain imperfect happiness in transitory goods, no one can doubt that there is a perfect and enduring happiness."

"That is firmly and truly established," I said.

"Now consider where this perfect happiness has its dwelling place. It is the common conception of the human mind that God, the ruler of all things, is good. For, since nothing can be thought of better than God, who can doubt that He is the good, other than whom nothing is better. And that God is good is demonstrated by reason in such a way as to convince us that He is the perfect good. If He were not, He could not be the ruler of all things; for there would be something better than He, something possessing perfect good, which would seem to be older and greater than He. For all perfect things have been shown to come before less perfect ones. And so, if we are to avoid progression *ad infinitum,* we must agree that the most high God is full of the highest and most perfect good. But we have already established that perfect good is true happiness; therefore it follows that true happiness has its dwelling in the most high God."

"I agree," I said. "Your argument cannot be contradicted."

"But observe," Philosophy continued, "how you may prove scrupulously and inviolably what I have just said, namely, that the most high God is full of the highest good."

"How?" I asked.

"By avoiding the notion that the Father of all things has received from others the highest good with which He is filled, or that He has it naturally in such a way that He and the happiness which He has may be said to differ in essence. For, if you should suppose that He receives it from someone else, you could think that the one who gives it is greater than the one who receives it; but we worthily confess that God is the most excellent of all beings. And if He has this happiness by nature, but differs from it, then someone else who can will have to explain how these diverse things are joined together, since we are speaking of God the Creator of all things. Finally, that which is different from anything cannot be the thing from which it differs; therefore, that which according to its nature differs from the highest good cannot be the highest good. But it is blasphemous to think this about One other than whom, as we know, nothing is greater. And surely there can be nothing better by nature than its source; therefore, I may conclude with certainty that whatever is the source of all things must be, in its substance, the highest good."

"I agree."

"And do you also agree that the highest good is happiness?"

"Yes."

"Then," said Philosophy, "you must agree that God is happiness."

"I found your earlier arguments unassailable, and I see that this conclusion follows from them."

"Then consider whether the same conclusion is not even more firmly established by this, that there cannot exist two highest goods which differ from one another. Clearly, when two goods differ, one cannot be the other; therefore, neither can be perfect since it lacks the other. But that which is not perfect certainly cannot be the highest good; therefore, those things which are the highest good cannot be diverse. But I have proved that happiness and God are the highest good; therefore, that must be the highest happiness which is the highest divinity."

"I can think of nothing truer, or more reasonable, or worthier of God," I said.

"From this conclusion, then, I will give you a kind of corollary, just as the geometricians infer from their demonstrated propositions things which they call deductions. Since men become happy by acquiring happiness, and since happiness is divinity itself, it follows that men become happy by acquiring divinity. For as men become just by acquiring integrity, and wise by acquiring wisdom, so they must in a similar way become gods by acquiring divinity. Thus everyone who is happy is a god and, although it is true that God is one by nature, still there may be many gods by participation."

"This is a beautiful and precious idea," I said, "whether you call it a corollary or a deduction."

"And there is nothing more beautiful," Philosophy went on, "than the truth which reason persuades us to add to this."

"What is that?" I asked.

"Since happiness seems composed of many things, would you say that all these are joined together in happiness, as a variety of parts in one body, or does one of the parts constitute the essence of happiness with all the rest complementing it?"

"I wish you would explain this point by recalling what is involved."

Philosophy then continued. "Do we not agree that happiness is good?"

"Indeed, it is the highest good," I replied.

"Then we must add this good to all the others; for happiness is considered the fullest sufficiency, the greatest power, honor, fame, and pleasure. Now are all these to be regarded as good in the sense that they are members of parts of happiness, or are they simply related to the good as to their crown?"

"I understand the problem now and am eager to have your answer."

"Here then is the solution. If all these goods were constituent parts of happiness, each would differ from the others; for it is the nature of parts to be different things constituting one body. But I have proved that all these goods are one and the same thing; therefore they cannot be parts. Otherwise, happiness would seem to be constituted of one part, which is a contradiction in terms."

"There is no doubt about that," I said, "but you have not yet given me the solution."

"Clearly, all the rest must be related to the good. For riches are sought because they are thought good, power because it is believed to be good, and the same is true of honor, fame, and pleasure. Therefore, the good is the cause and sum of all that is sought for; for if a thing has in it neither the substance nor the appearance of good, it is not sought or desired by men. On the other hand, things which are not truly good, but only seem to be, are sought after as if they were good. It follows, then, that goodness is rightly considered the sum, pivot, and cause of all that men desire. The most important object of desire is that for the sake of which something else is sought as a means; as, for example, if a person wishes to ride horseback in order to improve his health, he desires the effect of health more than the exercise of riding.

"Since, therefore, all things are sought on account of the good, it is the good itself, not the other things, which is desired by everyone. But, as we agreed earlier, all those other things are sought for the sake of happiness; therefore, happiness alone is the object of men's desires. It follows clearly from this that the good and happiness are one and the same thing."

"I cannot see how any one could disagree."

"But we have also proved that God and true happiness are one and the same."

"That is so."

"We can, therefore, safely conclude that the essence of God is to be found in the good, and nowhere else.

POEM 10

"Come, all you who are trapped and bound by the foul chains of that deceiving lust which occupies earth-bound souls. Here you will find rest from your labors, a haven of steady quiet, a refuge from misery.

"Nothing that the river Tagus with its golden shores can give, nor the Hermus with its jeweled

121

banks, the Indus of the torrid zone, gleaming with green and white stones, none of these can clear man's vision. Instead, they hide blind souls in their shadows.

"Whatever pleases and excites your mind here, Earth has prepared in her deep caves. The shining light which rules and animates the heavens avoids the dark ruins of the soul. Whoever can see this light will discount even the bright rays of Phoebus."

PROSE 11

Philosophy shows that God is One and that He is the goal toward which all things tend.

"I must agree, since your entire argument is established by sound reasons."

"Then," Philosophy continued, "how highly would you value it, if you could know what the absolute good is?"

"Such knowledge would be of infinite value," I said, "if I were also able to know God who is the absolute good."

"Well, I will show you this with certainty, if the conclusions we have arrived at so far are correct."

"They are indeed," I said.

"I have already proved that the things which most people want are not the true and perfect good since they differ from one another; and, since one or the other is always missing, they cannot provide full and perfect good. But I have also shown that they become the true good when they are gathered together as it were into a single form and operation, so that sufficiency becomes the same as power, honor, fame, and pleasure. And I have further shown that unless they are all one and the same, there is no reason to consider them desirable."

"You have proved this beyond doubt."

"Therefore, if these partial goods cannot be truly good if they are different, but are good if they become one, then clearly they become good by acquiring unity."

"This seems to be true," I said.

"But, if you also grant that every good is good by participating in the perfect good, then you should concede by a similar line of reasoning that the good and the one are the same. For things are of the same essence if their effects are of the same nature."

"I cannot deny that."

"And do you also understand that everything that is remains and subsists in being as long as it is one; but that when it ceases to be one it dies and corrupts?"

"How is this?"

"In the case of animals, when body and spirit are joined together in one being and remain so, that being is called a living thing; but when this unity is dissolved by the separation of body and soul, the being dies and is no longer a living animal. Even the body seems to be human as long as it remains one form in the union of its members; but, if this unity is broken by the separation and scattering of the body's members, it ceases to be what it was before. If we go on to examine other things we will see that each has its being as long as it is one, but when it begins to lose that oneness, it dies."

"On further consideration, I see that this is so."

"Is there anything, then, which acting naturally, gives up its desire to live and chooses to die and decay?"

"When I consider animals whose natures give them some choice, I know of none which gives up the will to live and of its own accord seeks death as long as it is free of external pressure. For every living being acts to preserve its life and to avoid death and injury. But, about plants and trees and inanimate objects, I simply do not know."

"You should not be in doubt about them, since you observe that trees and plants take root in suitable places and, to the extent made possible by their natures, do not wither and die. Some grow in the fields, some in the mountains, some in marshland, some in rocky places, some flourish in the sterile sands; but if any of these should be transplanted to some other place, they would die. Nature gives all things what they need and takes care that they live as long as they can. Why do all plants get their nourishment from roots, like a mouth drinking from the ground, and build up rugged bark over the pith? Why is the soft substance on the inside, while on the outside is the firm wood, and covering all is the bark, a rugged defender against harm, protecting the plant against storms? Note, too, how diligent nature is in propagating every species by multiplying the seed. Everyone knows that these natural processes are designed for the permanent preservation of the species as well as for the present life of individual plants.

"Even things believed to be inanimate do what is proper to their natures in much the same way. Why does lightness cause flames to rise and weight cause earth to settle, if not that these phenomena are appropriate to the things concerned? In addition, each thing is kept in being by that which is naturally proper to it, just as each thing is corrupted by that which is naturally opposed to it. Hard things, such as stones, resist fragmentation by the tough cohesion of their parts; but fluid things, such as air and water are easily parted, but then quickly flow together again; fire, however, cannot be cut at all. We are not concerned here with the voluntary motions of the intelligent soul, but only of those natural operations of which we are unconscious, such as, for example, digestion of food and breathing during sleep. Indeed, even in living beings, the desire to live comes not from the wishes of the will but from the principles of natures. For often the will is driven by powerful causes to seek death, though nature draws back from it. On the other hand, the work of generation, by which alone the continuation of mortal things is achieved, is sometimes restrained by the will, even though nature always desires it. Thus, this love for the self clearly comes from natural instinct and not from voluntary activity. Providence gave to his creatures this great urge for survival so that they would desire to live as long as they naturally could. Therefore you cannot possibly doubt that everything which exists naturally desires to continue in existence and to avoid harm."

"I now see clearly," I said, "what up to now seemed uncertain."

"Furthermore," Philosophy went on, "whatever seeks to exist and endure also desires to be one; for without unity existence itself cannot be sustained."

"That is true," I said.

"Then all things desire unity."

I agreed.

"But I have already shown that unity is the same as goodness."

"True," I said.

"Therefore, all things desire the good, so that we can define the good as that which is desired by all."

"That is perfectly correct," I agreed. "For either there is no one thing to which all other things are related, and therefore they wander without direction or goal, or, if there is something toward which all things hasten, it is the highest of all goods."

"I am greatly pleased with you, my pupil, for you have found the key to truth. And you also see clearly what a while ago you said you did not understand."

"What is that?" I asked.

"The end, or goal, of all things. For surely it is that which is desired by all; and, since we have identified that as the good, we must conclude that the good is the end toward which all things tend.

POEM 11

"The man who searches deeply for the truth and wishes to avoid being deceived by false leads, must turn the light of his inner vision upon himself. He must guide his soaring thoughts back again and teach his spirit that it possesses hidden among its own treasures whatever it seeks outside itself.

"Then all that was hidden by the dark cloud of error will shine more clearly than Phoebus; for the body, with its burden of forgetfulness, cannot drive all light from his mind. The seed of truth grows deep within and is roused to life by the breath of learning. For how can you answer questions truly unless the spark of truth glows deep in your heart? If Plato's Muse speaks truly, whatever is learned is a recollection of something forgotten."

PROSE 12

Philosophy shows that God rules the universe by his goodness and that all created things obey him.

"I agree fully with Plato," I said, "for this is the second time I have been reminded of these truths. I forgot them first under the oppressive influence of my body, then later when I was depressed by grief."

Philosophy replied, "If you consider carefully the conclusions you have so far granted, you will quickly remember something else which you said a while ago that you did not know."

"What is that?"

"The way the world is governed," she said.

"I do remember confessing my ignorance about that," I answered, "and, even though I can now anticipate your answer, I want to hear it plainly from you."

"Earlier in our discussion," Philosophy said, "you affirmed without any doubt that the world is ruled by God."

"I still have no doubt about it, and never will, for these reasons: this world could never have achieved its unity of form from such different and contrary parts unless there were One who could bring together such diverse things. And, once this union was effected, the very diversity of discordant and opposed natures would have ripped it apart and destroyed it, if there were not One who could sustain what He had made. Nor could the stable order of nature continue, nor its motions be so regular in place, time, causality, space and quality, unless there were One who could govern this variety of change while remaining immutable Himself. This power, whatever it may be, by which created things are sustained and kept in motion, I call by the name which all men use, God."

Philosophy answered, "Since this is your conviction, I think it will be easy to restore your happiness and bring you back safely to your own country. Now let us return to our task. Have we not already shown that sufficiency is among the attributes of happiness, and are we not agreed that God is absolute happiness?"

"That is right," I said.

"Then He needs no outside help in ruling the world; otherwise, if He were in need of anything He would not be completely self-sufficient."

"That is necessarily true," I said.

"Therefore He disposes all things by himself alone."

"I agree."

"Moreover, I have proved that God is absolute good."

"I remember that," I said.

"Then if He, whom we have agreed to be the good, rules all things by himself, He must dispose everything according to the good. He is, in a manner of speaking, the wheel and rudder by which the vessel of the world is kept stable and undamaged."

"I fully agree," I said, "and I saw in advance, though somewhat vaguely, that this is what you would say."

"I don't doubt it," Philosophy replied, "for I think that you are now looking more sharply for the truth. But what I am now going to tell you is equally clear."

"What is that?" I asked.

"Since God is rightly believed to govern all things with the rudder of goodness, and since all these things naturally move toward the good, as I said earlier, can you doubt that they willingly accept His rule and submit freely to His pleasure as subjects who are agreeable and obedient to their leader?"

"This must be so," I answered, "for no rule could be called happy if it were a bondage of willing slaves rather than one designed for the welfare of compliant citizens."

"Then there is nothing which, by following nature, strives to oppose God?"

"Nothing," I agreed.

"And, if anything should try to oppose Him, could it be at all successful against the One we have rightly shown to be the supreme power of happiness?"

"It would have no chance whatever," I said.

"Then there is nothing which has either the desire or the power to oppose this highest good?"

"Nothing."

"Then it is the supreme good which rules all things firmly and disposes all sweetly."

"I am delighted," I said, "not only by your powerful argument and its conclusion, but even more by the words you have used. And I am at last ashamed of the folly that so profoundly depressed me."

"You have read in the fables of the poets how giants made war on heaven; but this benign power overthrew them as they deserved. But now let us set our arguments against each other and perhaps from their opposition some special truth will emerge."

"As you wish," I said.

"No one can doubt that God is almighty," Philosophy began.

"Certainly not, unless he is mad," I answered.

"But nothing is impossible for one who is almighty."

"Nothing."

"Then can God do evil?"

"No, of course not."

"Then evil is nothing, since God, who can do all things, cannot do evil."

"You are playing with me," I said, "by weaving a labyrinthine argument from which I cannot escape. You seem to begin where you ended and to end where you began. Are you perhaps making a marvelous circle of the divine simplicity? A little while ago you began with happiness, declared it to be the highest good, and located its dwelling in almighty God. You said that God himself is the highest good and perfect happiness. From this you inferred that no one could be happy unless he too were a god. Then you went on to say that the very form of the good is the essence of God and of happiness; and you said further that unity is identical with the good which is sought by everything in nature. You also affirmed that God rules the universe by the exercise of His goodness, that all things willingly obey Him, and that there is no evil in nature. And you proved all this without outside assumptions and used only internal proofs which draw their force from one another."

Philosophy answered, "I have not mocked you at all. With the help of God whose aid we invoked we have reached the most important point of all. For it is the nature of the divine essence neither to pass to things outside itself nor to take any external thing to itself. As Parmenides puts it, the divine essence is 'in body like a sphere, perfectly rounded on all sides'; it rotates the moving orb of the universe while it remains unmoved itself. You ought not to be surprised that I have sought no outside proofs, but have used only those within the scope of our subject, since you have learned, on Plato's authority, that the language we use ought to be related to the subject of our discourse.

POEM 12

"Happy is he who can look into the shining spring of good; happy is he who can break the heavy chains of earth.

"Long ago the Thracian poet, Orpheus, mourned for his dead wife. With his sorrowful music he made the woodland dance and the rivers stand still. He made the fearful deer lie down bravely with the fierce lions, the rabbit no longer feared the dog quieted by his song.

"But as the sorrow within his breast burned more fiercely, that music which calmed all nature could not console its maker. Finding the gods unbending, he went to the regions of hell. There he sang sweet songs to the music of his harp, songs drawn from the noble fountains of his goddess mother, songs inspired by his powerless grief and the love which doubled his grief.

"Hell is moved to pity when, with his melodious prayer, he begs the favor of those shades. The three-headed guardian of the gate is paralyzed by that new song; and the Furies, avengers of crimes who torture guilty souls with fear, are touched and weep in pity. Ixion's head is not tormented by the swift wheel, and Tantalus, long maddened by this thirst, ignores the waters he now might drink. The vulture is filled by the melody and ignores the liver of Tityus.

"At last, the judge of souls, moved by pity, declares, 'We are conquered. We return to this man his wife, his companion, purchased by his song. But

129

our gift is bound by the condition that he must not look back until he has left hell.' But who can give lovers a law? Love is a stronger law unto itself. As they approached the edge of night. Orpheus looked back at Eurydice, lost her, and died.

"This fable applies to all of you who seek to raise your minds to sovereign day. For whoever is conquered and turns his eyes to the pit of hell, looking into the inferno, loses all the excellence he has gained."

Medieval Handbooks of Penance

Documents from the fifth through to the eighth century of the Christian era reveal interesting aspects of the moral codes by which people lived at that time. One set of such documents, from which portions are presented below, come from Ireland, Wales and Britain. The documents were written for the most part in Latin and were designed primarily for the use of the clergy who had to carry out the practical task of directing people's lives, evaluating their actions and assigning penances in proportion to sins committed. Though it is not possible to assign specific dates and certain authors to the documents, scholars can reasonably establish their authenticity as part of the early medieval period.

It is immediately obvious, upon reading the documents, that sin was taken quite seriously. The documents list penances to be administered for adultery, fornication, lust, homicide, theft, and magic. The penances were no joke. The two most common were a diet of nothing but bread and water for three years, and/or a diet without meat and wine for three years. Often these two penances were put together for a penance of six years plus a special seventh year. Physical punishment is rarely used. A beating with rods is directed for some crimes; the cutting off of a hand or foot is a proposed penance for correcting theft in a Church.

The principle of curing contrary by contrary is advocated. Thus covetousness is overcome by liberality and alms, wrathfulness by patience, envy by kindliness and love of God and neighbor, dejection by spiritual joy.

The penitentials contain an interesting approach to murder. The murderer is to go into exile for ten years of penance. Upon returning to his home country, he is to make satisfaction to the friends of the murdered. Should the murdered person's parents be alive, he is to place himself at their service in the stead of their lost son.

The language of the penitentials is clear and forthright. In dealing with specific actions under the theme of sin, the authors saw little room for discussion. They allowed that as long as a person was still alive, forgiveness and correction of one's life was possible. Their penances were designed to help the sinner toward true repentance and a firm decision never to sin again.

EARLY IRISH PENITENTIAL DOCUMENTS

CHAPTER 1

1. CANONS ATTRIBUTED TO ST. PATRICK

CANONS OF A SYNOD OF PATRICK, AUXILIUS, AND ISERNINUS

Here begins the Synod of the Bishops, that is, of Patrick, Auxilius, and Iserninus. We give thanks to God, the Father, the Son, and the Holy Spirit. To the presbyters, the deacons, and the whole clergy, Patrick, Auxilius, Iserninus, bishops, send greeting: It behoves us rather to admonish those who are negligent than to condemn the things that have been done, as Solomon says: "It is better to reprove than to be angry." Copies of our decision are written below, and begin thus:

1. If anyone for the redemption of a captive collects in the parish on his own authority, without permission, he deserves to be excommunicated.

2. Every reader shall become acquainted with the church in which he sings.

3. There shall be no wandering cleric in a parish.

4. If anyone receives permission, and the money has been collected, he shall not demand more than that which necessity requires.

5. If anything is left over, he shall place it on the altar of the priest that it may be given to some needy person.

6. If any cleric, from sexton to priest, is seen without a tunic, and does not cover the shame and nakedness of his body, and if his hair is not shaven according to the Roman custom, and if his wife goes about with her head unveiled, he shall be alike despised by laymen and separated from the Church.

7. Any cleric, who, having been commanded, on account of negligence does not come to the assemblies of matins or

vespers, shall be deemed a stranger, unless perchance he was detained in the yoke of servitude.

8. If a cleric becomes surety for a pagan in any amount, and it turns out (which is not strange), that through some craftiness that pagan fails the cleric, the cleric shall pay the debt with his own property; for if he fights with him in arms, he shall be justly reckoned to be outside the Church.

9. A monk and a virgin, the one from one place, the other from another, shall not dwell together in the same inn, nor travel in the same carriage from village to village, nor continually hold conversation with each other.

10. If anyone has shown the beginning of a good work in psalm singing and has now ceased, and lets his hair grow, he is to be excluded from the Church unless he restores himself to his former condition.

11. If any cleric has been excommunicated by someone, and another receives him, both shall alike exercise penance.

12. Alms shall not be accepted from any Christian who has been excommunicated.

13. It is not permitted to the Church to accept alms from pagans.

14. A Christian who slays, or commits fornication, or in the manner of the pagans consults a diviner, for each single offense shall do penance for a year. At the completion of a year of penance he shall come with witnesses and afterwards be absolved by the priest.

15. He who commits theft shall do penance for half a year, twenty days on bread [and water], and if it can be done, he shall restore the stolen goods; so shall he be denied [admission] into the Church.

16. A Christian who believes that there is a vampire in the world, that is to say, a witch, is to be anathematized; whoever lays that reputation upon a living being, shall not be received into the Church until he revokes with his own voice the crime that he has committed and accordingly does penance with all diligence.

17. A virgin who has taken the vow to God to remain chaste and afterwards marries a husband in the flesh shall be excommunicate until she is converted: if she has been converted

and desists from her adultery she shall do penance, and thereafter they shall not dwell in the same house or in the same
village.

18. If anyone is excommunicate he shall not enter a
church, not even on the eve of Easter, until he accepts a penance.

19. A Christian woman who takes a man in honorable
marriage and afterwards forsakes her first husband and is joined
to an adulterer—she who does this shall be excommunicate.

20. A Christian who defrauds anyone with respect to a
debt in the manner of the pagans, shall be excommunicated
until he pays the debt.

21. A Christian to whom someone has defaulted and who
brings him to judgment, not to the church so that the case may
there be investigated—whoever does this shall be an alien.

22. If anyone gives his daughter in honorable marriage, and
she loves another, and he yields to his daughter and receives the
marriage payment, both shall be shut out of the Church.

23. If anyone of the presbyters builds a church, he shall
not offer [the sacrifice in it] before he brings his bishop that he
may consecrate it; for this is proper.

24. If a new incumbent enters the parish he shall not
baptize, nor offer, nor consecrate, nor build a church until he
receives permission from the bishop; but whoever seeks permission from the tribesmen shall be an alien.

25. If any things have been given by religious men on those
days in which the bishop sojourns in the several churches, the
disposition of the pontifical gifts, as is the ancient custom, shall
appertain to the bishop, whether for necessary use or for
distribution to the poor, as the bishop himself may determine.

26. But if any cleric contravenes this and is caught seizing
the gifts, he shall be separated from the Church as one greedy of
filty lucre.

27. Any cleric who has recently entered the parish of a
bishop is not permitted to baptize and offer, nor to do anything:
if he does not act accordingly he shall be excommunicate.

28. If one of the clerics is excommunicate, he shall make
his prayer alone, not in the same house with his brethren, and

he may not offer or consecrate until he has corrected himself. If he does not act accordingly he shall be doubly punished.

29. If anyone of the brothers wishes to receive the grace of God, he shall not be baptized until he has done [penance for] a period of forty days.

30. Any bishop who passes from his own into another parish shall not presume to ordain, unless he receives permission from him who has authority there; however, on Sunday he may offer according to arrangement, and he shall be satisfied with compliance in this matter.

31. If one of two clerics who, as it happens, are in conflict over some disagreement hires an enemy who has offered himself to one of them to slay [the other], it is fitting that he be called a murderer. Such a cleric is to be held an alien to all righteous men.

32. If one of the clerics wishes to aid a captive he shall succour him with his own money; for if he delivers him by stealth many clerics are railed against on account of one thief. He who so acts shall be excommunicate.

33. A cleric who comes to us from the Britons without a certificate, even if he dwells in the parish, is not permitted to minister.

34. With us, likewise, a deacon who departs into another parish, not having consulted his abbot and without letters, ought not to distribute food, and he ought to be punished with penance by his own presbyter whom he has despised. And a monk who goes wandering without consulting his abbot ought to be punished.

Here end the determinations of the Synod.

CANONS OF THE ALLEGED SECOND SYNOD OF PATRICK

1. *Of dwelling with sinful brethren.*—Concerning what you have commanded with respect to dwelling among sinful brethren hearken unto the Apostle who says: "With such an one not so much as to eat." Thou shalt not partake of his food with him. Likewise if thou art an ox and treadest out the corn, that is, if thou art a teacher and teachest: "Thou shalt not muzzle the ox," and: "Thou art worthy of thy reward", but "Let not the

oil of the sinner fatten thy head." But thus far rebuke and chastise.

2. *Of their offerings.*—Be content with thy clothing and food; reject other things that are the gifts of the wicked since the lamp takes nothing but that by which it is fed.

3. *Of penance after fall.*—It is determined that the abbot give attention to the matter of those to whom he assigns the power of binding and loosing; but more fitting is pardon, according to the examples of the Scripture. If with weeping and lamentation and a garment of grief, under control, a short penance [is more desirable] than a long one, and a penance relaxed with moderation.

4. *Of the rejection of the excommunicated.*—Hearken unto the Lord when he saith: "If he will not hear thee let him be [to thee] as the heathen and the publican." Thou shalt not curse, but thou shalt reject an excommunicated person from communion and from the table and from the Mass and from the Pax; and if he is a heretic, after one admonition avoid him.

5. *Of suspected cases.*—Hearken unto the Lord when he saith: "Suffer both to grow until the harvest," that is, "until he cometh who will make manifest the counsels of the hearts," that thou make not judgment before the Day of Judgment. Behold Judas at the table of the Lord, and the thief in paradise.

6. *Of the punishments of the Church.*—Hearken again unto the Lord when he saith, "Whosoever shall shed innocent blood, his blood shall be shed:" but [it is to be shed] by him who carries the sword; moreover, the chief magistrate is held innocent in punishment. Of others, however, [the matter is determined] by the evangelical law, from that place in which it says: "And of him that taketh away thy goods, ask them not again." But, if he restores anything, gladly receive it in humility.

7. *Of questions concerning baptism.*—They determine that those who have received the tradition of the symbol be not rebaptized, from whomsoever they have received it, since the seed is not defiled by the wickedness of the sower. But if they have not received it, it is not rebaptism, but baptism. We believe that those who have lapsed from the faith are not to be absolved unless they are received with imposition of hands.

8. *Of accused persons taken from a church.*—A church is not made for the defense of accused persons; but judges ought to be persuaded that they would slay with spiritual death those who flee to the bosom of mother Church.

9. *Of those who have fallen after attaining to clerical rank.*— Hearken to the canonical institutes. Whoever falls when he has clerical rank shall arise without rank. Content with the name [of cleric] alone, he shall lose his ministry; except that when he sins in the sight of God alone, he does not withdraw [from his ministry].

[No. 10 is lacking.]

11. *Of the separation of the sexes after fall.*—Each one shall consider in his conscience whether the love and desire of sin have ceased, since a dead body does not harm another dead body; if this is not the case they shall be separated.

12. *Of offering for the dead.*—Hearken unto the Apostle when he saith: "There is a sin unto death, for that I say not that any man ask." And [to] the Lord: "Give not that which is holy to dogs." For he who did not in his life deserve to receive the sacrifice, how shall it be able to help him after death?

13. *Of the sacrifice.*—On the eve of Easter, [even] if it is permissible to carry it outside, it is not to be carried outside, but brought down to the faithful. What else signifies it that the Lamb is taken in one house, but that Christ is believed and communicated under one roof of faith?

14. *Of votive or legal abstinence from food.*—It is established that after the coming of Christ the Bridegroom, he shall set forth no fixed laws of fasting. But the difference between the Novationists and the Christians is that whereas a Novationist abstains continually, a Christian does so for a time only, that place, time, and person should in all things be regarded.

15. *Of leaving or of teaching one's own country.*—One's country is first to be taught, after the example of Christ; and afterwards if it does not make progress, it is to be abandoned, according to the example of the Apostle. But he who is able to do it may take the risk, teach and show himself everywhere; he who is not able, let him be silent and depart. One, you recall, is sent by Jesus to his own house; another is commanded to follow Him.

16. *Of false bishops.*—He who is not chosen by another bishop, according to the Apostle, is to be condemned; thereafter he is to be deposed and degraded to [the status of] the rest of the people.

17. *Of the provost of the monks.*—There are monks who dwell as solitaries without worldly resources, under the power of a bishop or an abbot. But they are not [really] monks, only pretenders to philosophy, that is, despisers of the world. Each one ought to be drawn to the perfect life in mature age, that is, from twenty years, not in witnessing to, but in fulfilling, his vow: as saith this [passage], "Let each do as he hath purposed in his heart," and, "That I shall render my vows in the sight of the Lord," and so forth. With whatever vow he is bound, the location of places limits it, if excess is to be avoided in all things in life; for they are called in cold and nakedness, in hunger and thirst, in vigils and fasts.

18. *Of the three seeds of the Gospels.*—The "hundredfold" are the bishops and teachers, who are all things to all men. The "sixtyfold" are the clergy and widows who are continent. The "thirtyfold" the lay folk who are faithful, who perfectly believe in the Trinity. Beyond these there is nought in the harvest of the Lord. Monks and virgins we combine with the "hundredfold."

19. *Of the proper age for baptism.*—On the eighth day they are catechumens; thereafter they are baptized in the solemn feast days of the Lord, that is at Easter, Pentecost, and Epiphany.

20. *Of parishes.*—We are not to speak with the monks whose wickedness is unusual, we who not improperly maintain the unity of the parish.

21. *Of monks to be retained or dismissed.*—Let every one enjoy his fruit in the church in which he has been instructed, unless the cause of greater success requires that he bear to another's [church] the permit of his abbot (?). If, indeed, there appears a weightier cause, it shall be said with blessing: "Behold the Lamb of God," each one seeking not the things that are his own but those which are Jesus Christ's. But they do not permit their subjects to run about on the claim of a vocation.

22. *Of taking the Eucharist after a fall.*—After a proving of the flesh it is to be taken, but especially on the eve of Easter; for he who does not communicate at that time is not a believer. Therefore short and limited are the seasons for such persons, lest the faithful soul perish, famished by so long a time of correction, for the Lord saith: "Except you eat the flesh of the Son of Man, you shall not have life in you."

23. *Of taking an oath.*—"Swear not at all." Following from this, the series of the lection teaches that no other creature is to be sworn by, none but the Creator, as is the custom of the prophet: "The Lord liveth," and "My soul liveth," and "The Lord liveth in whose sight I stand." But there is "an end of controversy" unless [the oath is] by the Lord. For by all that a man loves, by this does he make oath.

24. *Of the contention of two without witnesses.*—They determine that before he takes communion he who is being approved shall testify by the four holy gospels, and then he shall be left to the judgment of fire.

25. *Of the bed of a dead brother.*—Hear the decree of the synod: "A surviving brother shall not enter the bed of a dead brother." For the Lord saith: "and they shall be two in one flesh": therefore the wife of thy brother is thy sister.

26. *Of a prostitute wife.*—Hearken unto the Lord when he saith: "He who is joined to a harlot is made one body." Also, "An adulteress shall be stoned; that is, she shall die for this fault, that she may cease to increase who does not cease to commit adultery. Further, if a woman has become corrupted, does she return to her former husband? Moreover, it is not permitted to a man to put away his wife, except because of fornication—and if he says it is for that reason: hence, if he marries another, as if after death of the former, [authorities] do not forbid it.

27. *Of the will of the maiden or of the father in marriage.*—What the father wishes, the maiden shall do, since the head of the woman is the man. But the will of the maiden is to be inquired after by the father, since "God left man in the hand of his own counsel."

28. *Of the first or the second vows.*—First vows and first marriages are to be observed in the same way, that the first be

not made void for the second, unless they have been stained with adultery.

29. *Of consanguinity in marriage.*—Understand what the Law saith, not less nor more: but what is observed among us, that they be separated by four degrees, they say they have neither seen nor read.

30. *Of the assertion of customs.*—What is never forbidden is permitted. Truly the laws of the Jubilee are to be observed, that is, the fifty years, that a doubtful method be not established in the change of time. And therefore every business transaction is confirmed by subscription.

31. *Of the pagans who believe before baptism: how they receive penance.*—The sins of all are indeed remitted in baptism; but he who with a believing conscience lives for a time as an unbeliever is to be judged as a believing sinner.

Here ends the Synod of Patrick.

2. THE PENITENTIAL OF FINNIAN

In the name of the Father and of the Son and of the Holy Ghost.

1. If anyone has sinned in the thoughts of his heart and immediately repents, he shall beat his breast and seek pardon from God and make satisfaction, that he may be whole.

2. But if he has frequently entertained [evil] thoughts and hesitated to act on them, whether he has mastered them or been mastered by them, he shall seek pardon from God by prayer and fasting day and night until the evil thought departs and he is whole.

3. If anyone has thought evil and intended to do it, but opportunity has failed him, it is the same sin but not the same penalty; for example, if he intended fornication or murder, since the deed did not complete the intention he has, to be sure, sinned in his heart, but if he quickly does penance, he can be helped. This penance of his is half a year on an allowance, and he shall abstain from wine and meats for a whole year.

4. If anyone has sinned in word by an inadvertence and immediately repented, and has not said any such thing of set purpose, he ought to submit to penance, but he shall keep

a special fast; moreover, thereafter let him be on his guard throughout his life, lest he commit further sin.

5. If one of the clerics or ministers of God makes strife, he shall do penance for a week with bread and water and seek pardon from God and his neighbor, with full confession and humility; and thus can he be reconciled to God and his neighbor.

6. If anyone has started a quarrel and plotted in his heart to strike or kill his neighbor, if [the offender] is a cleric, he shall do penance for half a year with an allowance of bread and water and for a whole year abstain from wine and meats, and thus he will be reconciled to the altar.

7. But if he is a layman, he shall do penance for a week, since he is a man of this world and his guilt is lighter in this world and his reward less in the world to come.

8. But if he is a cleric and strikes his brother or his neighbor or sheds blood, it is the same as if he had killed him, but the penance is not the same. He shall do penance with bread and water and be deprived of his clerical office for an entire year, and he must pray for himself with weeping and tears, that he may obtain mercy of God, since the Scripture says: "Whosoever hateth his brother is a murderer," how much more he who strikes him.

9. But if he is a laymen, he shall do penance forty days and give some money to him whom he struck, according as some priest or judge determines. A cleric, however, ought not to give money, either to the one or to the other (?).

10. But if one who is a cleric falls miserably through fornication he shall lose his place of honor, and if it happens once [only] and it is concealed from men but known before God, he shall do penance for an entire year with an allowance of bread and water and for two years abstain from wine and meats, but he shall not lose his clerical office. For, we say, sins are to be absolved in secret by penance and by very diligent devotion of heart and body.

11. If, however, he has long been in the habit of sin and it has not come to the notice of men, he shall do penance for three years with bread and water and lose his clerical office, and

for three years more he shall abstain from wine and meats, since it is not a smaller thing to sin before God than before men.

12. But if one of the clerical order falls to the depths of ruin and begets a son and kills him, great is the crime of fornication with homicide, but it can be expiated through penance and mercy. He shall do penance three years with an allowance of bread and water, in weeping and tears, and prayers by day and night, and shall implore the mercy of the Lord, if he may perchance have remission of sins; and he shall abstain for three years from wine and meats, deprived of the services of the clergy, and for a forty-day period in the last three years he shall fast with bread and water; and [he shall] be an exile in his own country, until a period of seven years is completed. And so by the judgment of a bishop or a priest he shall be restored to his office.

13. If, however, he has not killed the child, the sin is less, but the penance is the same.

14. But if one of the clerical order is on familiar terms with any woman and he has himself done no evil with her, neither by cohabiting with her nor by lascivious embraces, this is his penance: For such time as he has done this he shall withdraw from the communion of the altar and do penance for forty days and nights with bread and water and cast out of his heart his fellowship with the woman, and so be restored to the altar.

15. If however he is on familiar terms with many women and has given himself to association with them and to their lascivious embraces, but has, as he says, preserved himself from ruin, he shall do penance for half a year with an allowance of bread and water, and for another half year he shall abstain from wine and meats and he shall not surrender his clerical office; and after an entire year of penance, he shall join himself to the altar.

16. If any cleric lusts after a virgin or any woman in his heart but does not utter [his wish] with the lips, if he sins thus but once he ought to do penance for seven days with an allowance of bread and water.

17. But if he continually lusts and is unable to indulge his desire, since the woman does not permit him or since he is

ashamed to speak, still he has committed adultery with her in his heart. It is the same sin though it be in the heart and not in the body; yet the penance is not the same. This is his penance: let him do penance for forty days with bread and water.

18. If any cleric or woman who practices magic misleads anyone by the magic, it is a monstrous sin, but [a sin that] can be expiated by penance. Such an offender shall do penance for six years, three years on an allowance of bread and water, and during the remaining years he shall abstain from wine and meats.

19. If, however, such a person does not mislead anyone but gives [a potion] for the sake of wanton love to some one, he shall do penance for an entire year on an allowance of bread and water.

20. If some woman by her magic misleads any woman with respect to the birth of a child, she shall do penance for half a year with an allowance of bread and water and abstain for two years from wine and meats and fast for six forty-day periods with bread and water.

21. But if, as we have said, she bears a child and her sin is manifest, she shall do penance for six years with bread and water (as is the judgment in the case of a cleric) and in the seventh year she shall be joined to the altar; and then we say her honor can be restored and she should don a white robe and be pronounced a virgin. So a cleric who has fallen ought likewise to receive the clerical office in the seventh year after the labor of penance, as saith the Scripture: "Seven times a just man falleth and ariseth," that is, after seven years of penance he who fell can be called "just," and in the eighth year evil shall not lay hold on him. But for the remainder [of his life] let him preserve himself carefully lest he fall; since, as Solomon saith, as a dog returning to his vomit becomes odious, so is he who through his own negligence reverts to his son.

22. But if one has sworn a false oath, great is the crime, and it can hardly, if at all, be expiated; but none the less it is better to do penance and not to despair: great is the mercy of God. This is his penance: first, he must never in his life take an oath, since a man who swears much will not be justified and "the scourge shall not depart from his house." But the medicine

of immediate penance in the present time is needful to prevent perpetual pains in the future; and [it is needful] to do penance for seven years and for the rest of one's life to do right, not to take oaths, and to set free one's maidservant or manservant or to give the value of one [servant] to the poor or needy.

23. If any cleric commits murder and kills his neighbor and he is dead, he must beome an exile for ten years and do penance seven years in another region. He shall do penance for three years of this time on an allowance of bread and water, and he shall fast three forty-day periods on an allowance of bread and water and for four years abstain from wine and meats; and having thus completed the ten years, if he has done well and is approved by testimonial of the abbot or priest to whom he was committed, he shall be received into his own country and make satisfaction to the friends of him whom he slew, and he shall render to his father or mother, if they are still in the flesh, compensation for the filial piety and obedience [of the murdered man] and say: "Lo, I will do for you whatever you ask, in the place of your son." But if he has not done enough he shall not be received back forever.

24. But if he killed him suddenly and not from hatred—the two having formerly been friends—but by the prompting of the devil, through an inadvertence, he shall do penance for three years on an allowance of bread and water, and for three more years he shall abstain from wine and meats; but he shall not remain in his own country.

25. If a cleric commits theft once or twice, that is, steals his neighbor's sheep or hog or any animal, he shall do penance an entire year on an allowance of bread and water and shall restore fourfold to his neighbor.

26. If, however, he does it, not once or twice, but of long habit, he shall do penance for three years.

27. If anyone who formerly was a layman, has become a cleric, a deacon, or one of any rank, and if he lives with his sons and daughters and with his own concubine, and if he returns to carnal desire and begets a son with his concubine, or says he has, let him know that he has fallen to the depths of ruin; his sin is not less than it would be if he had been a cleric from his youth and sinned with a strange girl, since they have sinned

after his vow and after they were consecrated to God, and then they have made the vow void. He shall do penance for three years on an allowance of bread and water and shall abstain for three years more from wine and meats, not together, but separately, and then in the seventh year [such clerical offenders] shall be joined [to the altar] and shall receive their rank.

28. But if a cleric is covetous, this is a great offense; covetousness is pronounced idolatry, but it can be corrected by liberality and alms. This is the penance for his offense, that he cure and correct contraries by contraries.

29. If a cleric is wrathful or envious or backbiting, gloomy or greedy, great and capital sins are these; and they slay the soul and cast it down to the depth of hell. But there is this penance for them, until they are plucked forth and eradicated from our hearts: through the help of the Lord and through our own zeal and activity let us seek the mercy of the Lord and victory in these things; and we shall continue in weeping and tears day and night so long as these things are turned over in our heart. But by contraries, as we said, let us make haste to cure contraries and to cleanse away the faults from our hearts and introduce virtues in their places. Patience must arise for wrathfulness; kindliness, or the love of God and of one's neighbor, for envy; for detraction, restraint of heart and tongue; for dejection, spiritual joy; for greed, liberality; as saith the Scripture: "The anger of man worketh not the justice of God"; and envy is judged as leprosy by the law. Detraction is anathematized in the Scriptures; "He that detracteth his brother" shall be cast out of the land of the living. Gloom devours or consumes the soul. Covetousness is "the root of all evil," as saith the Apostle.

30. If any cleric under the false pretense of the redemption of captives is found out and proved to be despoiling churches and monasteries, until he is confounded, if he has been a "conversus," he shall do penance for an entire year on an allowance of bread and water and all the goods which were found with him of those things which he had gathered shall be paid out and lent to the poor: for two years he shall abstain from wine and meat.

31. We require and encourage contributing for the redemption of captives; by the teaching of the Church, money is to be lent to the poor and needy.

32. But if he has been a "conversus" he is to be excommunicated and be anathema to all Christians and be driven from the bounds of his country and beaten with rods until he is converted,—if he has compunction.

33. We are obliged to serve the churches of the saints as we have ability and to suffer with all who are placed in necessity. Pilgrims are to be received into our houses, as the Lord has written; the infirm are to be visited; those who are cast into chains are to be ministered to; and all things commanded of Christ as to be performed, from the greatest unto the least.

34. If any man or woman is nigh unto death, although he (or she) has been a sinner and pleads for the communion of Christ we say that it is not to be denied to him if he promise to take the vow, and let him do well and he shall be received by Him. If he becomes a novice let him fulfill in this world that which he has vowed to God. But if he does not fulfill the vow which he has vowed to God, [the consequences] will be on his own head. As for us, we will not refuse what we owe to him: we are not to cease to snatch prey from the mouth of the lion or the dragon, that is of the devil, who ceases not to snatch at the prey of our souls; we may follow up ard strive [for his soul] at the very end of a man's life.

35. If one of the laity is converted from his evil-doing unto the Lord, and if he has previously wrought every evil deed, that is, the committing of fornication and the shedding of blood, he shall do penance for three years and go unarmed except for a staff in his hand, and shall not live with his wife. But in the first year he shall do penance on an allowance of bread and water and not live with his wife. After a penance of three years he shall give money for the redemption of his soul and the fruit of repentance into the hand of the priest and make a feast for the servants of God, and in the feast [his penance] shall be ended; and he shall be received to communion and shall resume relations with his wife after an entire and complete penance, and if it is satisfactory he shall be joined to the altar.

147

36. If any layman defiles his neighbor's wife or virgin daughter, he shall do penance for an entire year on an allowance of bread and water, and he shall not have intercourse with his own wife; after a year of penance he shall be received to communion, and shall give alms for his soul. So long as he is in the body, he shall not go in to commit fornication again with a strange woman; or if [he defiles] a virgin two years shall be his penance, the first with bread and water. In the other [year] he shall fast for forty days, abstain from wine and meat, and give alms to the poor and the fruit of his penitence into the hands of his priest.

37. If anyone has defiled a vowed virgin and lost his honor and begotten a child by her, let such an one, being a layman, do penance for three years; but in the first year he shall go on an allowance of bread and water and unarmed and shall not have intercourse with his own wife, and for two years more he shall abstain from wine and meats and shall not have intercourse with his wife.

38. If, however, he does not beget a child, but nevertheless defiles the virgin, [he shall do penance for] an entire year on an allowance of bread and water, and for half a year he shall abstain from wine and meats, and he shall not have intercourse with his wife until his penance is completed.

39. If any layman with a wife of his own has intercourse with his female slave, the procedure is this: the female slave is to be sold, and he himself shall not have intercourse with his own wife for an entire year.

40. But if he begets by this female slave one, two, or three children, he is to set her free, and if he wishes to sell her it shall not be permitted to him, but they shall be separated from each other, and he shall do penance an entire year on an allowance of bread and water and shall have no further intercourse with his concubine but be joined to his own wife.

41. If anyone has a barren wife, he shall not put away his wife because of her barrenness, but they shall both dwell in continence and be blessed if they persevere in chastity of body until God pronounces a true and just judgment upon them. For I believe that if they shall be as Abraham and Sarah were, or Isaac and Rebecca, or Anna the mother of Samuel, or Elizabeth

the mother of John, it will come out well for them at the last.
For the Apostle saith: "And let those that have wives be as if
they had none, for the fashion of this world passeth away."
But if we remain faithful we shall receive what God hath given
whether unto prosperity or unto adversity, always with joy.

42. We declare against separating a wife from her husband;
but if she has left him, [we declare] that she remain unmarried
or be reconciled to her husband according to the Apostle.

43. If a man's wife commits fornication and cohabits with
another man, he ought not to take another wife while his wife is
alive.

44. If perchance she is converted to penance, it is becoming
to receive her, if she has fully and freely sought this, but he
shall not give her a dowry, and she shall go into service to her
former husband; as long as he is in the body she shall make
amends in the place of a male or a female slave, in all piety and
subjection.

45. So also a woman, if she has been sent away by her
husband, must not mate with another man so long as her former
husband is in the body; but she should wait for him, unmarried,
in all patient chastity, in the hope that God may perchance put
patience in the heart of her husband. But the penance of these
persons is this—that is, of a man or woman who has committed
fornication: they shall do penance for an entire year on an
allowance of bread and water separately and shall not sleep in
the same bed.

46. We advise and exhort that there be continence in
marriage, since marriage without continence is not lawful, but
sin, and [marriage] is permitted by the authority of God not
for lust but for the sake of children, as it is written, "And the
two shall be in one flesh," that is, in unity of the flesh for the
generation of children, not for the lustful concupiscence of the
flesh. Married people, then, must mutually abstain during three
forty-day periods in each single year, by consent for a time, that
they may be able to have time for prayer for the salvation of
their souls; and on Sunday night or Saturday night they shall
mutually abstain, and after the wife has conceived he shall not
have intercourse with her until she has borne her child, and they
shall come together again for this purpose, as saith the Apostle.

149

But if they shall fulfill this instruction, then they are worthy of the body of Christ, as by good works they fulfill matrimony, that is, with alms and by fulfilling the commands of God and expelling their faults, and in the life to come they shall reign with Christ, with holy Abraham, Isaac, Jacob, Job, Noah, all the saints; and there they shall receive the thirtyfold fruit which as the Savior relates in the Gospel, he has also plucked for married people.

47. If the child of anyone departs without baptism and perishes through negligence, great is the crime of occasioning the loss of a soul; but its expiation through penance is possible, since there is no crime which cannot be expiated through penance so long as we are in this body. The parents shall do penance for an entire year with bread and water and not sleep in the same bed.

48. But if a cleric does not receive a child [to baptism], if it is a child of the same parish he shall do penance for a year on bread and water.

49. He is not to be called a cleric or a deacon who is not able to baptize and to receive the dignity of a cleric or a deacon in the Church.

50. Monks, however, are not to baptize, nor to receive alms; if, then, they do receive alms, why shall they not baptize?

51. If there is anyone whose wife commits fornication with another man, he ought not to hold intercourse with her until she does penance according to the penalty which we laid down above, that is, after an entire year of penance. So also a woman is not to hold intercourse with her husband, if he has committed fornication with another woman, until he performs a corresponding penance.

52. If anyone loses a consecrated object or a blessing of God, he shall do penance for seven days.

53. He shall not go to the altar until his penance has been completed. Here endeth: thanks be to God.

Dearly beloved brethren, according to the determination of Scripture or the opinion of some very learned men I have tried to write these few things concerning the remedies of penance, impelled by love of you, beyond my ability and authority. There are still other authoritative materials, concerning either the remedies or the variety of those who are to be treated, which now by reason of brevity, or the situation of a place, or from poverty of talent, I am not permitted to set down. But if anyone who has searched out the divine Scripture should himself make larger discoveries, or if he will produce or write better things, we will both agree with him and follow him.

Here endeth this little work which Finnian adapted to the sons of his bowels, by occasion of affection or of religion, overflowing with the graces of Scripture, that by all means all the evil deeds of men might be destroyed.

6. FROM AN IRISH COLLECTION OF CANONS

Lib. II, cap. 25. Of the Time in Which the Priests Ought to Be Absent from a Church, and of Their Penance If They Are Absent beyond the Time

a. An Irish synod has decreed that a priest shall be absent from his church only one day; if he is absent two days, he shall do penance for seven days with bread and water; moreover, if a dead man is brought to the church and [the priest] is absent, he ought to do penance, since he is answerable for the man's penalty.

b. If he is absent from the church one Sunday, he shall do a penance of twenty days on bread and water; but if for two or three days, he is to be deposed from the honor of his rank.

XXVIII, 5. Of the Penance for Homicide Committed Unintentionally

A Roman treatise declares: "First definition: he who shedding blood takes flight, forfeits all; chiefly he shall be absolved by reconciliation with the next of kin of the slain man. Second definition: he shall be condemned to a pilgrimage of seven years or else remain in the bosom of the protecting church unto the end of his life."

XXVIII, 10. Of Diverse Penances of Murderers Who Slay Intentionally

b. An Irish synod says, All murderers, if they are converted with all their heart, shall perform a penance of seven years strictly under the rule of a monastery.

XXIX, 6. Of Theft Committed in a Church

An Irish synod has decreed: A first theft committed in a church is, however, to be compensated for, and penance is to be done according to the judgment of a priest; and he makes this [judgment] in accordance with the clemency of the church. But if it is done a second time, double or quadruple restitution is to be made. But if the goods of a man of the world are carried off, and the church is catholic and free from all obligation, the damage shall be made good to the owner, and the interest of it shall go to the church. If indeed the church is under obligation to the king, the same damage shall be made good to the owner, and the interest shall go to the king and the church.

XXIX, 7. Of the Penance of One Who Steals in a Church

Patrick says: He who has stolen treasure either from a holy church or within the city where martyrs and the bodies of the saints sleep—the lot shall be cast on three things: either his hand or his foot shall be cut off; or he shall be committed to prison, to fast for such time as the seniors shall determine and restore entire what he carried off; or he shall be sent forth on pilgrimage and restore double, and shall swear that he will not return until he has completed the penance and [that] after the penance he will be a monk.

XXXVII, 27. Of the Penance of One Who Rails against a Good Prince

Patrick says: He who murmurs words of railing against a good prince through hatred or envy, shall do penance for seven days on bread and water, as did Mary for murmuring against Moses.

XLII, 22. Of What Punishment They Deserve Who Desert Infants in a Church of God

The Irish synod: Persons who unknown to the abbot desert infants in a church of God, if there are bishops buried in it or if [bishops] are present, shall do penance for three years and a half. If they commit murder in it, they shall do penance for seven years. This is because the bishop has seven grades and

152

the church is septiform. If they have no bishops and the church is small, they shall do penance for a year and a half.

XLIV, 8. Of a Decree of Irishmen on the Violation of Relics

Whoever violates the relics of bishops or martyrs by murder, shall do penance for seven years as a pilgrim. If by theft for three years. But if he slays on the bounds of a holy place in which laymen are given hospitality, one year. Let us concede to later times [by saying] fifty days, since that is not to be called a holy place into which murderers with their despoilings, thieves with their thefts, adulterers, perjurers, hawkers, and wizards have entrance. Not only ought every holy place to be cleansed within, but also its bounds, which have been consecrated, ought to be clean.

Peter Abelard
1079-1142

The twelfth century of western Europe was one of creative intellectual development. Notably in France, centers of learning attracted brilliant scholars from all over Europe, scholars who energetically pursued theological and biblical studies. One of the most outstanding and exciting personalities of the century was Peter Abelard, logician and theologian. His life is unusually well known because of the fact that he wrote his autobiography, The History of My Troubles.

Abelard was born near Nantes, France. He was well educated, especially in rhetoric. His love for intellectual combat and harsh treatment of his opponents won for him both a following of students and the bitter criticism of theologians. His love affair with Heloise, full of passion and tragedy, revealed human qualities that tempered and clouded his intellectual life. Though he sought the peace and calm of several monasteries, Abelard's stormy temperament often led to rejection and loneliness. Though twice he was condemned, he ended his days as an exemplary monk at Cluny.

Anyone who entered the arenas of logic and theology in the twelfth century certainly had to deal with Peter Abelard, either verbally or through his writings. The Ethics, *from which the reading below is taken, serves as a valuable introduction to the moral issues of twelfth century Christianity and to the theological response to those issues. The century was torn by ethical questions similar to those of the twentieth century. How can violence and corruption exist within a society that professes itself to be Christian? How does one guide moral formation? What is good and evil as lived by a society? Can a society establish moral concepts and a moral language that can serve as a sound measure for the actions of individuals within the society?*

Abelard entitled his book on ethics Know Thyself *(Scito te ipsum). The title reveals his concern for the person who acts as distinct from the nature of the action performed. Abelard seeks to clarify the role of intention in human activity and grapples with the difficult problem of whether an action is right or wrong because of one's intention to do good or evil. He argues that actions, in themselves, are morally indifferent and are called good or evil only because of the agent's intention. Furthermore, God considers not what is done, but the intention of the doer; thus merit and blame are due to intention, not the action. Abelard saves himself from falling into a simple subjectivism by subscribing to the thesis that out beyond the person who performs an action there exist the standards of divine law which ultimately determine right and wrong.*

One can see the importance of self knowledge in such an approach to morality. A person has the responsibility to know his abilities, his strengths and weaknesses, his capacity to act in accordance with divine law.

The reader will find Abelard's discussion of sin, penance, confession, absolution and satisfaction rather challenging. It was during the twelfth century that the practice of private confession came into being. Abelard was one of the first to realize that a healthy development of his practice would require a thorough understanding of the psychology of the penitent. His provocative insights and examples illustrate the tension that any thinking person encounters when trying to understand human action as right or wrong, good or evil.

ETHICS

W e consider morals to be the vices or virtues of the mind which make us prone to bad or good works. However, there are vices or goods not only of the mind but also of the body, such as bodily weakness or the fortitude which we call strength, sluggishness or swiftness, limpness or being upright, blindness or vision. Hence to distinguish these, when we said 'vices' we added 'of the mind'. Now these vices, that is of the mind, are contrary to the virtues, as injustice is to justice, sloth to constancy, intemperance to temperance.

Of vice of the mind which concerns morals

There are also, however, some vices or good things of the mind which are separate from morals and do not make human life worthy of blame or praise, such as dullness of mind or quickness of thinking, forgetfulness or a good memory, ignorance or learning. Since all these befall the wicked and the good alike, they do not in fact belong to the composition of morality nor do they make life base or honourable. Hence rightly when above we presented 'vices of the mind' we added, in order to exclude such things, 'which make us prone to bad works', that is, incline the will to something which is not at all fitting to be done or to be forsaken.

The difference between sin and vice inclining to evil

Mental vice of this kind is not, however, the same as sin nor is sin the same as a bad action. For example, to be irascible, that is, prone or ready for the emotion of anger, is a vice and inclines the mind impetuously or unreasonably to do something which is not at all suitable. However, this vice is in the soul, so that in fact it is ready to be angry even when it is not moved to anger, just as the limpness for which a man is said to be lame is in him even when he is not walking limply, because the vice is present even though the action is not. So too nature itself or the constitution of the body makes many prone to luxury just as it does to anger, yet they do not sin in this because that is how they are, but through this they have the material for a struggle so that triumphing over themselves through the virtue of temperance they may obtain a crown. As Solomon said: 'The patient man is better than the valiant: and he that ruleth his spirit than he that taketh cities.' For religion does not consider it base to be beaten by man but by vice. The former happens in fact to good men too; in the latter we turn away from good things. The Apostle commends this victory to us, saying: 'He will not be crowned except he strive lawfully.' Strive, I say, in resisting vices rather than men, lest they entice us into wrongful consent; even if men cease, vices do not cease to assault us, and their attack is so much more dangerous for being more constant and victory is so much more brilliant for being more difficult. But however much men prevail over, us, they bring no turpitude into our lives unless after the manner of the vices and having, as it were, converted us to vices they submit us to a shameful consent. When they command our bodies, so long as the mind remains free, true freedom is not in peril and we do not fall into an indecent subjection. For it is shameful to serve vice, not man; subjection to vices soils the soul, bodily servitude does not. For whatever is common to good and bad men alike is of no importance to virtue or vice.

What is mental vice and what is properly said to be sin

And so vice is that by which we are made prone to sin, that is, are inclined to consent to what is not fitting so that we either do it or forsake it. Now this consent we properly call sin, that is, the fault of the soul by which it earns damnation or is made guilty before God. For what is that consent unless it is contempt of God and an offence against him? For God cannot be offended against through harm but through contempt. He indeed is that supreme power who is not impaired by any harm but who avenges contempt of himself. And so our sin is contempt of the Creator and to sin is to hold the Creator in contempt, that is, to do by no means on his account what we believe we ought to do for him, or not to forsake on his account what we believe we ought to forsake. So, by defining sin negatively, that is to say, as not doing or not forsaking what is fitting, we plainly show there is no substance of sin; it subsists as not being rather than being, just as if in defining darkness we say it is the absence of light where light used to be.

But perhaps you will say that the will to do a bad deed is also sin and makes us guilty before God, even as the will to do a good deed makes us just, so that just as virtue consists in a good will, so sin consists in a bad will and not only in not being but also, and like virtue, in being. For just as we please God by willing to do what we believe to please him, so we displease him by willing to do what we believe to displease him and we seem to offend him or hold him in contempt. But I say that if we consider this more carefully, our conclusion should be very different from what it seems. For since we sometimes sin without any bad will and since that bad will when restrained but not extinguished procures a prize for those who resist it and brings the material for a struggle and a crown of glory, it ought not to be called sin so much as a weakness which is now necessary. For consider: there is an innocent man whose cruel lord is so burning with rage against him that with a naked sword he chases him for his life. For long that man flees and as far as he can he avoids his own murder; in the end and unwillingly he is forced to kill him lest he be killed by him. Tell me, whoever you are, what bad will he had in doing this. If he wanted to escape death, he wanted to save his own life. But surely this was not a bad will? You say: not this, I think, but the will he had to kill the lord who was chasing him. I reply: that is well and cleverly said if you can show a will in what you claim. But, as has already been said, he did this unwillingly and under compulsion; as far as he could he deferred injury to life; he was also aware that by this killing he would put his own life in danger. So how did he do willingly what he committed with danger to his own life as well?

If you reply that that too was done out of will, since it is agreed that he was led to this out of a will to avoid death, not to kill his lord, we do not confute that at all but, as has already been said, that will is in no way to be derided as bad through which he, as you say, wanted to evade death, not to kill the lord. And yet although he was constrained by fear of death, he did do wrong in consenting to an unjust killing which he should have undergone rather than have inflicted. In fact he took the sword himself; no power had handed it to him. Whence Truth says: 'All that take the sword shall perish by the sword.' 'He who takes the sword', he says, by presumption, not he to whom it has been granted for the purpose of administering vengeance, 'shall perish by the sword', that is, he incurs by this rashness damnation and the killing of his own soul. And so he wanted, as has been said, to avoid death, not to kill the lord. But because he consented to a killing to which he ought not to have consented, thus unjust consent of his which preceded the killing was a sin.

If perhaps someone says that he wanted to kill his lord for the sake of avoiding death, he cannot therefore simply infer that he wanted to kill him. For example, if I were to say to someone: 'I want you to have my cap for this reason, that you give me five *solidi*' or 'I gladly want it to become yours at that price', I do not therefore concede that I want it to be yours. Moreover if anyone held in prison wants to put his son there in his place so that he may seek his own ransom, surely we do not therefore simply concede that he wants to put his own son in prison—something which he is driven to endure with floods of tears and with many sighs? At any rate such a will which consists in great grief of mind is not, I would say, to be called will but rather suffering. That he wills this on account of that is the equivalent of saying that he endures what he does not will on account of the other things which he desires. Thus the sick man is said to want a cauterization or an operation in order to be healed and martyrs to suffer in order to come to Christ or Christ himself in order that we may be saved by his suffering. Yet we are not therefore compelled to concede simply that they want this. On no occasion can there be suffering except where something is done against will nor does anyone suffer where he fulfils his will and gains delight in doing so. Certainly the Apostle who says: 'I desire to be dissolved and to be with Christ', that is, to die for the purpose of coming to him, himself observes elsewhere: 'We would not be unclothed but clothed upon, that that which is mortal may be swallowed up by life.' The blessed Augustine also remembers this thought which the Lord expressed when he said to Peter: 'Thou shalt stretch forth thy hands, and another shall gird thee and lead thee whither thou wouldest not.' In the weakness which he had assumed of human nature the Lord also said to the Father: 'If it be possible, let this chalice pass from me. Nevertheless, not as I will but as thou wilt.' His soul naturally dreaded the great suffering of death and what he knew to be painful could not be voluntary for him. Although it is written of him elsewhere: 'He was offered because it was his own will', this is either to be understood according to the nature of the divinity in whose will it was that the assumed man should suffer, or 'it was his will' means 'it was his plan' as it does when the Psalmist says: 'He hath done all things whatsoever he would.' So it is evident that sometimes sin is committed entirely without bad will; it is therefore clear from this that what is sin is not to be called will.

Certainly, you will say, that is so where we sin under constraint, but not where we do so willingly, as for instance if we want to commit something which we know should not be done by us at all. There indeed that bad will and the sin seem to be the same. For example, someone sees a woman and falls into concupiscence and his mind is affected by the pleasure of the flesh, so that he is incited to the baseness of sexual intercourse. Therefore, you say, what else is this will and base desire than sin?

I answer that if that will is restrained by the virtue of temperance but is not extinguished, it remains for a fight and persists in struggling and does not give up even when overcome. For where is the fight if the material for fighting is lacking? Or whence comes the great reward if what we endure is not hard? When the struggle is over, it no longer remains to fight but to receive the reward. Here, however, we strive by fighting, so that elsewhere as winners of the struggle we may receive a crown. But in order that that there be a fight, it is evident that there must be an enemy who resists, not one who actually gives up. This surely is our bad will, over which we triumph when we subdue it to the divine will, but we do not really extinguish it, so that we always have it to fight against.

Indeed, what great thing do we for God if we support nothing against our will but rather discharge what we will?

And who has thanks for us if in what we say we are doing for him we fulfil our own will? But what, you will say, do we gain before God out of what we do whether willingly or unwillingly? I reply: nothing, certainly, since he considers the mind rather than the action when it comes to a reward, and an action adds nothing to merit whether it proceeds from a good or a bad will, as we shall later show. But when we put his will before our own so as to follow his rather than ours, we obtain great merit with him according to that perfectness of Truth: 'I came not to do my own will but the will of him that sent me.' Exhorting us to this he says: 'If any man come to me and hate not his father and mother, yea and his own life also, he is not worthy of me', that is, if he does not renounce their suggestions or his own will and subject himself completely to my precepts. If therefore we are ordered to hate but not to destroy a father, so too our will; we are not to follow it but neither are we to destroy it completely. For he who said: 'Go not after thy lusts: but turn away from thy own will', taught us not to fulfil our lusts, but not to be entirely without them. The former is vicious, but the latter is not possible for our weakness. So sin is not lusting for a woman but consenting to lust; the consent of the will is damnable, but not the will for intercourse.

What we have said with repsect to luxury, let us consider with respect also to gluttony. Someone passes through another man's garden and seeing delightful fruits he falls into longing for them; however, he does not consent to his longing so as to remove something from there by theft or robbery, even though his mind has been incited to great desire by the pleasure of food. But where desire is, there undoubtedly is will. And so he desires to eat of that fruit in which he is certain there is pleasure. In fact by the very nature of his infirmity he is compelled to desire what he is not allowed to take without the knowledge or the permission of the lord. He represses his desire; he does not extinguish it, but because he is not drawn to consent, he does not incur sin.

Now where does this lead us? It shows in short that in such things also the will itself or the desire to do what is unlawful is by no means to be called sin, but rather, as we have stated, the consent itself. The time when we consent to what is unlaw-

ful is in fact when we in no way draw back from its accomplish-
ment and are inwardly ready, if given the chance, to do it. Anyone who is found in this disposition incurs the fullness of guilt;
the addition of the performance of the deed adds nothing to
increase the sin. On the contrary, before God the man who to
the extent of his power endeavours to achieve this is as guilty
as the man who as far as he is able does achieve it—just as if,
so the blessed Augustine reminds us, he too had also been
caught in the act.

Now, although will is not sin and, as we have said, we
sometimes commit sins unwillingly, yet some say that every sin
is voluntary, and they find a certain difference between sin and
will, since will is said to be one thing and what is voluntary
is said to be something different, that is, will is one thing but
what is committed through the will is another. But if we call sin
what we have previously said is properly called sin, that is,
contempt of God or consent to that which we believe should be
forsaken on God's account, how do we say that sin is voluntary,
that is, our own willing to offer the contempt of God which is
sin or to become worse or to be made worthy of damnation?
For although we may want to do that which we know ought to
be punished of for which we may deserve to be punished, we
do not, however, want to be punished. Obviously we are wicked
in this, that we want to do what is wicked, yet we do not want
to submit to the fairness of a just punishment. The punishment
which is just is displeasing; the action which is unjust is pleasing.
Moreover, it often happens that when we want to lie with a
woman whom we know to be married and whose looks have
enticed us, yet we by no means want to be adulterous with
her—we would prefer that she was unmarried. There are, on the
other hand, many men who for their own renown desire the
wives of the mighty more keenly because they are married to
such men than they would if they were unmarried; they want to
commit adultery rather than fornication, that is, to transgress
by more rather than by less. There are people who are wholly
ashamed to be drawn into consent to lust or into a bad will and
are forced out of the weakness of the flesh to want what
they by no means want to want. Therefore I certainly do not
see how this consent which we do not want to have may be

called voluntary with the result, as has been said, that we should, according to some, call every sin voluntary, unless we understand voluntary to exclude the element of necessity, since clearly no sin is unavoidable, or unless we call voluntary that which proceeds from will. For even if he who killed his lord under constraint did not have the will to kill, yet he did it out of will, since in fact he wanted to avoid or to defer death.

There are people who may be considerably disturbed when they hear us say that the doing of sin adds nothing to guilt or to damnation before God. They object that in the action of sin a certain pleasure may follow which increases the sin, as in sexual intercourse, or in that eating which we mentioned. They would not in fact say this absurdly if they were to prove that carnal pleasure of this sort is sin and that such a thing cannot be committed except by sinning. If they really admit this, it is definitely not lawful for anyone to have this fleshly pleasure. Therefore, spouses are not immune from sin when they unite in this carnal pleasure allowed to them, nor is he who enjoys the pleasurable consumption of his own fruit. Also, all invalids would be at fault who relish sweeter foods to refresh themselves and to recover from illness; they certainly do not take these without pleasure or if they did so, they would not benefit. And lastly the Lord, the creator of foods as well as of bodies, would not be beyond fault if he put into them such flavours as would necessarily compel to sin those who eat them with pleasure. For how would he produce such things for our eating or allow their eating if it were impossible for us to eat them without sin? And how can sin be said to be committed in that which is allowed? For what were at one time unlawful and prohibited acts, if they are later allowed and thus become lawful, are now committed wholly without sin, for example the eating of swine's flesh and many other things formerly forbidden to Jews but now permitted to us. And so when we see Jews converted to Christ also freely eating foods of this sort which the Law had forbidden but now conceded to them the concession itself excuses sin and removes the contempt of God, who will say that anyone sins in that which a divine concession has made lawful to him? If therefore to lie with a wife or even to eat delicious food has been allowed to us since the first day of our creation which was lived in Paradise without sin, who will accuse us of sin in this if we do not exceed the limit of the concession?

Yet again they say that marital intercourse and the eating of delicious food are in fact conceded in such a way that the pleasure itself is not conceded; they should be performed wholly without pleasure. But assuredly if this is so, they are allowed to be done in a way in which they cannot be done at all and it was an unreasonable permission which allowed them to be done in a way in which it is certain that they cannot be done. Besides, by what reason did the law once prescribe marriage so that everyone should leave his seed in Israel or the Apostle urge spouses to pay their debt to one another, if these cannot be done at all without sin? In what way does he speak here of debt where now necessarily there is sin? Or how is one to be compelled to do what in sinning will offend God? It is clear, I think, from all this that no natural pleasure of the flesh should be imputed to sin nor should it be considered a fault for us to have pleasure in something in which when it has happened the feeling of pleasure is unavoidable. For example, if someone compels a religious who is bound in chains to lie between women and if he is brought to pleasure, not to consent, by the softness of the bed and through the contact of the women beside him, who may presume to call this pleasure, made necessary by nature, a fault?

But if you object that, as it seems to some, carnal pleasure in legitimate intercourse is also to be considered a sin, since David says: 'For, behold, I was conceived in iniquities', and since the Apostle when he said: 'Return together again, lest Satan tempt you for your incontinency' adds: 'But I speak this by indulgence, not by commandment', the pressure upon us to say that this carnal pleasure itself is sin seems to come from authority rather than from reason. For it is known that David had been conceived not in fornication but in matrimony and, as they say, indulgence, that is, pardon, does not occur where fault is wholly absent. In my view, however, David's statement that he had been conceived in iniquities or in sins—he did not add whose they were—represents the general curse of original sin by which everyone is subjected to damnation because of the fault of his parents, in accordance with what is written elsewhere: 'No one is free from uncleanness nor is the one-day-old child if he is alive upon earth.' For as the blessed Jerome has mentioned, and as manifest reason holds, as long as the soul exists in the age of infancy it lacks sin. If therefore it is clean from sin, how is it soiled with the uncleanness of sin unless the former is to be understood with respect to fault, the latter with respect to punishment? One who does not yet see through reason what he should do has no fault arising from contempt of God, but he is not free of the stain of earlier parents and thence he already contracts punishment, but not fault, and he sustains in his punishment what they committed in their fault. So when David says he was conceived in iniquities or in sins, he saw that he was subjected to a general sentence of damnation by virtue of the fault of his own parents and he referred these crimes back less to his immediate parents than to earlier ones.

However, what the Apostle calls indulgence is not to be interpreted, as they want, as if he had meant this indulgence of permission to be the pardon of a sin. In fact what he says, 'by indulgence, not by commandment', means 'by permission, not by compulsion'. For if spouses want and have decided with equal consent, they can abstain altogether from carnal relations and they should not be driven into them by authority. But if they have not taken this decision, they have the indulgence, that is, the permission to turn aside from the more perfect life into the practice of a laxer life. In this place, therefore, the Apostle did not mean by indulgence pardon for sin but permission for a laxer life for the sake of avoiding fornication, so that a lower life might prevent a magnitude of sin and one might be smaller in merits lest one become greater in sins.

Now we have mentioned this lest anyone, wishing perhaps every carnal pleasure to be sin, should say that sin itself is increased by action when one carries the consent given by the mind into the commission of an act and is polluted not only by shameful consent but also by the blemishes of an action—as if an exterior and corporeal act could contaminate the soul. The doing of deeds has no bearing upon an increase of sin and nothing pollutes the soul except what is of the soul, that is, the consent which alone we have called sin, not the will which precedes it nor the doing of the deed which follows. For even though we will or do what is not fitting, we do not therefore sin, since these things often happen without sin, just as conversely consent occurs without them. This we have already partly shown for the will which lacks consent, in the case of the man who fell into longing for a woman he had seen or for fruit which did not belong to him and yet is not brought to consent, and for evil consent without evil will, in the case of him who killed his lord unwillingly.

Moreover, I think everyone knows how often things that should not be done are done without sin, when, that is, they are committed under coercion or through ignorance, as for example if a woman is forced to lie with another woman's husband or if a man who has been tricked in some way or other sleeps with a woman whom he thought to be his wife or kills in error a man whom he believed he, as a judge, should kill. And so it is not a sin to lust after another's wife or to lie with her but rather to consent to this lust or action. This consent to covetousness the Law calls covetousness when it says: 'Thou shall not covet.' In fact, what had to be forbidden was not the coveting of what we cannot avoid or in which, as had been said, we do not sin, but the assenting to that. What the Lord said has similarly to be understood: 'Whosoever shall look on a woman to lust after her', that is, whosoever shall look in such a way as to fall into consent to lust, 'hath already committed adultery in his heart', although he has not committed the deed of adultery, that is, he is already guilty of sin although he is still without its outcome.

If we carefully consider also all the occasions where actions seem to come under a commandment or a prohibition, these must be taken to refer to the will or to consent to actions rather than to the actions themselves, otherwise nothing relating to merit would be put under a commandment and what is less within our power is less worthy of being commanded. There are in fact many things by which we are restrained from action yet we always have dominion over our will and consent. Behold, the Lord says: 'Thou shalt not kill', 'Thou shall not bear false witness.' If, following the sound of the words, we take these to refer only to the deed, guilt is by no means forbidden nor is fault thereby, but the action of a fault is prohibited. Truly, it is not a sin to kill a man nor to lie with another's wife; these sometimes can be committed without sin. If a prohibition of this kind is understood, according to the sound of the words, to refer to the deed, he who wants to bear false witness or even consents to speaking it, as long as he does not speak it, whatever the reason for his silence, does not become guilty according to the Law. For it was not said that we should not want to bear false witness or that we should not consent to speaking it, but only that we should not speak it. The Law forbids us to take our sisters or to commingle with them, but there is no one who can keep this ordinance, since one is often unable to recognize one's sisters—no one, I mean, if the prohibition refers to the act rather than to consent. And so when it happens that someone through ignorance takes his sister, he is not surely the transgressor of an ordinance because he does what the Law has forbidden him to do? He is not a transgressor, you will say, because in acting ignorantly he did not consent to transgression. Therefore, just as he is not to be called a transgressor who does what is forbidden, but he who consents to that which it is evident has been prohibited, so the prohibition is not to be applied to the deed but to the consent, so that when it is said 'do not do this or that' the meaning is 'do not consent to do this or that', just as if it were said 'do not venture this knowingly'. The blessed Augustine carefully considered this and reduced every commandment or prohibition to charity or cupidity rather than to deeds, saying: 'The Law ordains nothing except charity and prohibits nothing except cupidity.' Hence also the Apostle says: 'All the Law is fulfilled in one word: Thou shalt love thy neighbour as thyself.' And again: 'Love is the fulfilling of the Law.' It does not in fact matter to merit whether you give alms to the needy; charity may make you ready to give and the will may be there when the opportunity is missing and you no longer remain able to do so, whatever the cause preventing you. It is indeed obvious that works which it is or is not at all fitting to do may be performed as much by good as by bad men who are separated by their intention alone. In fact, as the same Doctor has observed, in the same deed in which we see God the Father and the Lord Jesus Christ we also see Judas the betrayer. The giving up of the Son was certainly done by God the Father; and it was done by the Son and it was done by that betrayer, since both the Father delivered up the Son and the Son delivered up himself, as the Apostle observed, and Judas delivered up the Master. So the betrayer did what God also did, but surely he did not do it well? For although what was done was good, it certainly was not well done nor should it have benefited him. For God thinks not of what is done but in what mind it may be done, and the merit or glory of the doer lies in the intention, not in the deed. In fact the same thing is often done by different people, justly by one and wickedly by another, as for example if two men hang a convict, that one out of zeal for justice, this one out of a hatred arising from an old enmity, and although it is the same act of hanging and although they certainly do what it is good to do and what justice requires, yet, through the diversity of their intention, the same thing is done by diverse men, by one badly, by the other well.

Who, finally, may be unaware that the devil himself does nothing except what he is allowed by God to do, when either he punishes a wicked man for his faults or is allowed to strike a just man in order to purge him or to provide an example of patience? But because on the prompting of his own wickedness he does what God allows him to do, so his power is said to be good or even just, while his will is always unjust. For he receives the former from God; the latter he holds of himself. Moreover, in respect of works, who among the elect can be compared with hypocrites? Who endures or does out of love of God as much as they do out of greed for human praise? Who lastly may not know that what God forbids to be done is sometimes rightly performed or should be done, just as conversely he sometimes ordains some things which, however, it is not at all fitting to do? For consider, we know of some miracles of his that when by them he healed illnesses, he forbade that they should be revealed, as an example, that is, of humility, lest someone who had a similar grace granted to him should perhaps seek prestige. None the less they who had received those benefits did not stop publicizing them in honour, of course, for him who had both worked them and had prohibited their revelation. Of such it was written: 'The more he charged them that they should not tell, so much the more did they publish it', etc. Surely you will

not judge such men guilty of transgression for acting contrary
to the command which they had received and for even doing
this knowingly? What will excuse them from transgression if not
the fact that they did nothing through contempt of him who
commanded; they decided to do this in honour of him. Tell me,
I ask you, if Christ ordained what should not have been ordained
or if they repudiated what should have been kept? What was
good to be commanded was not good to be done. You at any
rate will reproach the Lord in the case of Abraham, whom at
first he commanded to sacrifice his son and later checked from
doing so. Surely God did not command well a deed which it
was not good to do? For if it was good, how was it later forbidden? If, moreover, the same thing was both good to be commanded and good to be prohibited—for God allows nothing to
be done without reasonable cause nor yet consents to do it—
you see that the intention of the command alone, not the
execution of the deed, excuses God, since he did well to command what is not a good thing to be done. For God did not
urge or command this to be done in order that Abraham should
sacrifice his son but in order that out of this his obedience and
the constancy of his faith or love for him should be very greatly
tested and remain to us as an example. And this indeed the
Lord himself subsequently avowed openly when he said: 'Now
I know that thou fearest the Lord', as if he were saying ex-
pressly: the reason why I instructed you to do what you showed
you were ready to do was so that I should make known to
others what I myself had known of you before the ages. This
intention of God was right in an act which was not right, and
similarly, in the things which we mentioned, his prohibition
was right which prohibited for this reason, not so that the
prohibition should be upheld but so that examples might be
given to us weaklings of avoiding vainglory. And so God enjoined
what was not good to be done, just as conversely he prohibited
what was good to be done; and just as the intention excuses
him in the one case, so too in this case it excuses those who
have not fulfilled the command in practice. They knew indeed
that he had not made the command on this account, that it
should be observed, but so that the example that has been
mentioned should be set forth. While not violating the will of

him who commands, they did not offer contempt to him to whose will they understood that they were not opposed.

If therefore we think of deeds rather than the intention, we shall not only see that sometimes there is a will to do something against God's commandment but also that it is done and knowingly so without any guilt of sin. So, when the intention of him to whom the command is made does not differ from the will of the commander, one should not speak of an evil will or an evil action simply because God's commandment is not kept in a deed. Just as intention excuses the commander who commands to be done what is however not at all fitting to be done, so also the intention of charity excuses him to whom the command is made.

To bring the above together in a brief conclusion, there are four things which we have put forward in order carefully to distinguish them from each other, namely the vice of the mind which makes us prone to sinning and then the sin itself which we fixed in consent to evil or contempt of God, next the will for evil and the doing of evil. Just as, indeed, to will and to fulfil the will are not the same, so to sin and to perform the sin are not the same. We should understand the former to relate to the consent of the mind by which we sin, the latter to the performance of the action when we fulfil in a deed what we have previously consented to. When we say that sin or temptation occurs in three ways, namely in suggestion, pleasure, and consent, it should be understood in this sense, that we are often led through these three to the doing of sin. This was the case with our first parents. Persuasion by the devil came first, when he promised immortality for tasting the forbidden tree. Pleasure followed, when the woman, seeing the beautiful fruit and understanding it to be sweet to eat, was seized with what she believed would be the pleasure of the food and kindled a longing for it. Since she ought to have checked her longing in order to keep the command, in consenting she was drawn into sin. And although she ought to have corrected the sin through repentance in order to deserve pardon, she finally completed it in deed. And so she proceeded to carry through the sin in three stages. Likewise we also frequently arrive by these same steps not at sinning but at the carrying through of sin, namely by suggestion, that is, by the encouragement of someone who incites us externally to do something which is not fitting. And if we know that doing this is pleasurable, even before the deed our mind is seized with the pleasure of the deed itself and in the very thought we are tempted through pleasure. When in fact we assent to this pleasure through consent, we sin. By these three we come at last to the execution of the sin.

* * * * *

That a work is good by reason of a good intention

In fact we say that an intention is good, that is, right in itself, but that an action does not bear anything good in itself but proceeds from a good intention. Whence when the same thing is done by the same man at different times, by the diversity of his intention, however, his action is now said to be good, now bad, and so it seems to fluctuate around the good and the bad, just as this proposition 'Socrates is seated' or the idea of it fluctuates around the true and the false, Socrates being at one time seated, at another standing. Aristotle says that the way in which this change in fluctuating around the true and the false happens here is not that what changes between being true and being false undergoes anything by this change, but that the subject, that is Socrates, himself moves from sitting to standing or vice versa.

Whence an intention should be said to be good

There are those who think that an intention is good or right whenever someone believes he is acting well and that what he does is pleasing to God, like the persecutors of the martyrs mentioned by Truth in the Gospel: 'The hour cometh that whosoever killeth you will think that he doth a service to God.' The Apostle had compassion for the ignorance of such as these when he said: 'I bear them witness that they have a zeal for God, but not according to knowledge', that is, they have great fervour and desire in doing what they believe to be pleasing to God. But because they are led astray in this by the zeal or the eagerness of their minds, their intention is in error and the eye of their heart is not simple, so it cannot see clearly, that is,

172

guard itself against error. And so the Lord, in distinguishing works according to right or wrong intention, carefully called the mind's eye, that is, the intention, sound and, as it were, free of dirt so that it can see clearly; or, conversely, dark when he said: 'If thy eye be sound thy whole body shall be full of light', that is, if the intention was right, the whole mass of works coming from it, which like physical things can be seen, will be worthy of the light, that is, good; conversely also. And so an intention should not be called good because it seems to be good but because in addition it is just as it is thought to be, that is, when, believing that one's objective is pleasing to God, one is in no way deceived in one's own estimation. Otherwise even the unbelievers themselves would have good works just like ourselves, since they too, no less than we, believe they will be saved or will please God through their works.

That there is no sin unless it is against conscience

However, if one asks whether those persecutors of the martyrs or of Christ sinned in what they believed to be pleasing to God, or whether they could without sin have forsaken what they thought should definitely not be forsaken, assuredly, according to our earlier description of sin as contempt of God or consenting to what one believes should not be consented to, we cannot say that they have sinned in this, nor is anyone's ignorance a sin or even the unbelief with which no one can be saved. For those who do not know Christ and therefore reject the Christian faith because they believe it to be contrary to God, what contempt of God have they in what they do for God's sake and therefore think they do well—especially since the Apostle says: 'If our heart do not reprehend us, we have confidence towards God'? As if to say: where we do not presume against our conscience our fear of being judged guilty of fault before God is groundless; alternatively, if the ignorance of such men is not to be imputed to sin at all, how does the Lord pray for his crucifiers, saying: 'Father, forgive them, for they know not what they do', or Stephen, taught by this example, say in prayer for those stoning him: 'Lord, lay not this sin to their charge'? For there seems no need to pardon where there was no prior fault; nor is pardon usually said to be anything other than the remission of a punishment earned by a fault. Moreover, Stephen manifestly calls sin that which came from ignorance.

* * * * *

Whether every sin is forbidden

It is furthermore asked whether God forbids every sin in us. If we admit this, he seems to do it unreasonably, since this life can by no means be spent without at least venial sins. If in fact he has commanded us to guard against all sins, we nevertheless cannot guard against them all; at any rate he does not lay on us, as he himself promised, a sweet yoke and a light burden but one which far exceeds our strength and which we cannot bear at all, just as the Apostle Peter professed in respect of the yoke of the Law. For who can always be on his guard against even an idle word, so that never exceeding in this he maintains that perfection of which James says: 'If any man offend not in word, the same is a perfect man'? Since he had also said: 'in many things we all offend' and since another Apostle of great perfection says: 'If we say that we have no sin we deceive ourselves and the truth is not in us', how difficult, nay impossible, it seems for our weakness to stay wholly free from sin is, I imagine, hidden from no one. So I say, if we take the word 'sin' broadly, as we said, we shall also call sins whatever we do unfittingly. If, however, understanding sin properly we say that sin is only contempt of God, this life can truly be passed without it, although with very great difficulty. Nor, as we have mentioned above, is anything prohibited to us by God except the consent to evil by which we offer contempt to God, even when a command seems to be made about a deed, as we showed above, where we also showed that otherwise his commands could not be kept by us at all.

Some sins are said to be venial and, as it were, light, others damnable or grave. Again, some damnable sins are said to be criminal and are capable of making a person infamous or criminous if they come to the hearing of other people, but some are not in the least. Sins are venial or light when we consent to what we know should not be consented to, but when, however, what we know does not occur to our memory. We know many things even when asleep or when we do not remember them. For we do not lay aside our knowledge or become foolish when sleeping or become wise when awake. And so sometimes we consent either to boasting or to excessive eating or drinking, yet we know this should by no means be done, but we do not remember then that it should not be done. So such consents as we fall into through forgetfulness are said to be venial or light sins, that is, not to be corrected with a penalty of great satisfaction such as being punished on account of them by being put outside the church or being burdened with a heavy abstinence. Indeed to have such carelessness forgiven by repenting, we frequently resort to the words of the daily confession in which mention should by no means be made of graver faults, but only of lighter ones. For we should not say there: I have sinned in perjury, in murder, in adultery, and such like, which are said to be damnable and weightier sins. We do not incur these like the others through forgetfulness, but commit them with assiduity, as it were, and with deliberation, and are made abominable to God also, according to the Psalmist: 'They are become abominable in their ways', as if execrable and exceedingly hateful for what they have knowingly presumed. Others of these sins are called criminal which, known through their effect, blot a man with the mole of a great fault and greatly detract from his reputation; such are consent to perjury, murder, adultery which greatly scandalize the church. But when we indulge in food beyond what is necessary or in vanity adorn ourselves with immoderate dress, even if we presume this knowingly, these are not classed as crime and among many receive more praise than blame.

* * * * *

Of the reconciliation of sins

And since we have displayed the soul's wound, let us strive to show the medicine which heals. Whence Jerome says: 'Doctor, if you are skilful, just as you have stated the cause of the disease, so also show that of health!' Although therefore we offend God by sinning, there remain ways by which we can be reconciled to him. And so there are three things in the reconciliation of the sinner to God, namely repentance, confession, satisfaction.

What may be said properly to be repentance

Now, repentance is properly called the sorrow of the mind over what it has done wrong, when, namely, someone is ashamed at having gone too far in something. However, this repentance at one time happens out of love of God and is fruitful, at another because of some penalty with which we do not want to be burdened; such is that repentance of the damned of whom it has been written: 'These seeing it shall be troubled with terrible fright, and shall be amazed at the suddenness of their unexpected salvation, saying within themselves, repenting and groaning for anguish of spirit: These are they whom we had some time in derision', etc. And we read the repentance of Judas for having betrayed the Lord. We believe this happened not so much on account of the fault of a sin as on account of the vileness of him who felt himself damned in everyone's judgement. For when a man who is corrupted by money or by some other means has betrayed another man into perdition, he is considered a traitor who is vile to no one more than to this man, and no one trusts him less than he who has a specially full experience of his faithlessness. Daily indeed we see many about to depart from this life repenting of their shameful accomplishments and groaning with great compunction, not so much out of love of God whom they have offended or out of hatred of the sin which they have committed as out of fear of the punishment into which they are afraid of being hurled. Moreover, they remain wicked because the wickedness of their fault does not displease them as much as the just severity of the punishment and they do not hate what they have done because it was wrong so much as the just judgement of God which they fear in the form of punishment, hating equity rather than iniquity. Having long been blinded and called upon to turn away from their wickedness, divine justice at last delivers them up to a base mind, and having struck them with blindness absolutely casts them away from his face, so that they should not have knowledge of wholesome repentance nor be able to observe how satisfaction should be made.

How very many indeed do we daily see dying, groaning deeply, reproaching themselves greatly for usuries, plunderings, oppressions of the poor, and all kinds of injuries which they have committed, and consulting a priest to free them from these faults. If, as is proper, the first advice given to them is this, that selling all they have, they restore to others what they have taken—in accordance with Augustine: 'If something which belongs to another is not returned when it can be returned, repentance is not done but is feigned'—instantly by their reply they declare how hollow is their repentance for these things. How then, they say, could my household live? What might I leave to my sons, what to my wife? How could they support themselves? That rebuke of the Lord for the first time occurs to them: 'Thou fool, this night do they require thy soul of thee; and whose shall those things be which thou hast provided?' Such a wretch, whoever you are, nay, most wretched of all wretches and most foolish of fools, you are not attending to what you will keep for yourself but to what you will hoard for others. With what presumption do you offend God, to whose dreaded judgement you will be snatched, in order to propitiate your relatives, whom you enrich with plunder from the poor? Who would not laugh at you if he heard you hoped to make others more kindly to you than you were yourself? You trust in the alms of your relatives whom, because you believe you have successors, you make alike heirs to your wickedness, and you leave to them the property of other people to hold through plunder. You snatch life away from the poor, by taking from them their sustenance, and in them you contrive to kill Christ again, in accordance with what he himself said: 'What you did to one of the least of mine, you did it to me.' So what do you, who are wrongly loyal to your relatives and cruel to yourself as much as to God, expect from the just judge to whom, whether you want to or not, you are hastening to be judged and who demands a reason not only for plunder but even for an idle word? He has steadfastly shown in the punishment of earlier men how severe is his vengeance. Adam sinned but once and by comparison with our own, as the blessed Jerome has observed, his sin was very slight. He oppressed none with violence and he took nothing away from anyone; he partook but once of the fruit which could have been restored. In this very slight transgression, which also recoiled through its punishment upon all posterity, the Lord decided to point out what would be done with greater faults. The rich man, who the Lord says descended into hell, not because he had seized the possessions of others but because he did not share his own with the needy Lazarus and ate them as if this were lawful, plainly shows what punishment will strike those who seize other people's goods, if he, who did not give away his own goods, was thus damned and buried in hell. Once your memory was buried with you and their tears which you had at your funeral had quickly dried— according to the rhetor Apollonius, 'nothing dries quicker than a tear'—your wife next prepared herself for a new wedding to devote herself to the pleasures of a new husband with the aid of the plunder which you bequeathed to her, and she will warm with another body the bed in which your body has been hitherto, while you will smart wretchedly in the flames of hell at those pleasures. And the same should be expected from your children. If perhaps someone asks why in remembering you they are not propitious to you with their alms, they seem able to excuse themselves on many grounds. For they would reply thus: 'Since he refused to be kind to himself, how foolish was it for him to hope others would be kind to him and to commit to others the salvation of his soul for which he definitely should himself have provided! Who did he believe would be kinder to him than he himself? He was cruel to himself: in whose mercy did he trust?' And then they can bring forward his avarice as an excuse and say: 'We know moreover that what he left to us is not meant to be used by us as alms.' All will laugh and ought to laugh who hear these things. But the wretch who in his time reduced to weeping the poor whom he plundered shall weep there for ever. Some who wish to hide their negligence from men, not from God, say, to make excuses in sins, that they have plundered so many that they are quite unable to identify or trace them. Since they assume no concern for this they incur that judgement of apostolic opinion: 'And if any man know not, he shall not be known.' They do not find them because they do not look; the right hand of God to whom they showed contempt will find them. It has also been written of this: 'Thy right hand will find out all them that hate thee.' The same Prophet who said this feared it exceedingly and, thinking there was no place of escape, said elsewhere: 'Whither shall I go from thy spirit? And whither shall I flee from thy face? If I ascend into heaven, thou art there: if I descend into hell, thou art present.' And because often the greed of the priest is no less than that of the people—according to the Prophet: 'And as the people so shall the priests be'—the cupidity of priests seduces many of the dying by promising them a false security if they offer their property in sacrifices and buy Masses which they would certainly not get free. In this trade they clearly have a fixed price, namely one denarius for a Mass and five solidi for Masses and all the hours for thirty years and sixty for once a year. They do not advise the dying to restore their plunderings but to offer them in sacrifice, although it is written against this: 'He that offereth sacrifice of the goods of the poor is as one that sacrificeth the son in the presence of his father.' For the killing of a son hurts a father more when done in his own presence than if he did not see it. And it is as if a son were killed by immolation when the goods of the poor, in which their livelihood consists, are put into a sacrifice. And Truth, preferring mercy to sacrifice, says: 'Go, learn what this meaneth: I will have mercy and not sacrifice.' Furthermore, it is worse to retain plunder than not to give mercy, that is, to take from the poor what belongs to them rather than not to give our own, as we mentioned above in the damnation of the rich man.

Of fruitful repentance

Because we have spoken of unfruitful repentance, let us consider fruitful repentance all the more carefully because it is more beneficial. The Apostle invites to it all who are stubborn and do not take thought for the dreadful judgement of God, saying: 'Or despisest thou the riches of his goodness and patience and longsuffering? Knowest thou not that the benignity of God leadeth thee to penance?' With these words he plainly declares what is wholesome repentance, proceeding from the love of

God rather than from fear, with the result that we are sorry to have offended or to have shown contempt of God because he is good rather than because he is just. For the longer we show contempt of himself (just as conversely secular princes do who, when they are offended, do not know how to spare or how to postpone the avenging of injuries to themselves), the more justly therefore he inflicts a heavier punishment for contempt of himself and is more severe in vengeance according as he was more patient in waiting. The same Apostle later showed this saying: 'But according to thy hardness and impenitent heart thou treasurest up to thyself wrath, against the day of wrath.' Then indeed wrath, now mildness, because vengeance then, patience now. Demanding justice there he will avenge contempt of himself all the more heavily the less he should have been held in contempt and the longer he endured it. We are afraid to offend men, and when we do not flee in fear from those we offend we avoid them in shame. We seek a hiding-place when we fornicate lest we be seen by men and we cannot then endure to be seen even by one man. We know that God is present, from whom nothing can be concealed. We would be thrown into confusion at the sight of one little man, but we do not blush to be seen in this act of shame by him and by the whole court of heaven. We are very greatly afraid to presume anything in front of an earthly judge by whom we know we shall be sentenced with only a temporal, not an eternal, penalty. Carnal desire makes us do or endure many things, spiritual desire few. Would that we would do or endure as much for God to whom we owe all as for our wife or children or any mistress!

With what penalty, I pray, should this wrong be condemned whereby we put a mistress before him? He himself complains through the Prophet that love is not shown to him as a father nor fear as to a master. 'The son', he says, 'honoureth the father and the servant fears his master. If I be a father, where is my honour? And if I be a master, where is my fear?' He complains that a father or a master is preferred to him. Consider, therefore, how indignant he is that a mistress too is put before him and that he is held in greater contempt for the supreme patience of his goodness for which he ought to be loved the more. These who repent healthily, considering this goodness and the forbearance of his patience, are moved to compunction less by fear of penalties than by love of him, in accordance with the exhortation of the Apostle mentioned above. Here he carefully described healthy repentance by saying conversely: 'Or the riches of his goodness', that is, the rich and copious goodness or the overflowing benignity of his forbearing patience with which he endures you for so long, 'despisest thou', because, that is, he does not punish quickly, 'not knowing', that is, not considering, 'that his benignity is such' that in itself 'it leads thee to penance', that is, brings it about that through considering it you ought to be converted to repentance because you showed contempt for one who is so kind? And this indeed is truly fruitful repentance for sin, since this sorrow and contrition of mind proceeds from love of God, whom we consider to be so kind, rather than from fear of punishments.

Moreover, with this sigh and contrition of heart which we call true repentance sin does not remain, that is, the contempt of God or consent to evil, because the charity of God which inspires this sigh does not put up with fault. In this sigh we are instantly reconciled to God and we gain pardon for the preceding sin, according to the Prophet: 'In what hour soever the sinner shall sigh, he shall be saved', that is, he will be made worthy of the salvation of his soul. He did not say: in what year or in what month or in what week or on what day, but in what hour, so as to show that he is worthy of pardon without delay, and that eternal punishment, in which the condemnation of sin consists, is not owing to him. For although he may be prevented by some necessity from having an opportunity of coming to confession or of performing satisfaction, he by no means meets with hell on leaving this life sighing thus. This is God's pardon for sin, namely, making him what he is not yet worthy of being, just as previously because of the preceding sin he could be eternally punished by God. For when God pardons penitents their sin, he does not forgive them every penalty but only the eternal one. For many penitents who, prevented by death, have not performed the satisfaction of penance in this life are detained for purgatory, not damnatory, punishments in the future. Whence it is uncertain how long a time the supreme day of judgement will last, on which many of the faithful are to be suddenly punished, although the resurrection will occur 'in a moment, in the twinkling of an eye', with the result, that is, that there, as far as God shall determine, they will render satisfaction for faults for which they have deferred, or have not been permitted to make, satisfaction.

* * * * *

Of confession

It is incumbent upon us to deal now with confession of sins. The Apostle James urged us to this, saying: 'Confess your sins one to another; and pray one for another, that you may be saved. For the continual prayer of a just man availeth much.' There are people who think that confession should be made to God alone—a view which some attribute to the Greeks. But I do not see what confession avails with God who knows all, or what indulgence our tongue obtains for us, although the Prophet says: 'I have acknowledged my sin to thee: and my injustice I have not concealed.' For many reasons the faithful confess their sins to one another, in accordance with the above quotation from the Apostle, both, that is, for the reason mentioned, that we may be more helped by the prayers of those to whom we confess, and also because in the humility of confession a large part of satisfaction is performed and we obtain a greater indulgence in the relaxation of our penance, as was written of David, who replied, when accused by the Prophet Nathan: 'I have sinned'; immediately he heard a reply from the same Prophet: 'The Lord also hath taken away thy sin.' For the greater the sublimity of the king, the more acceptable was his humility in confessing to God. Lastly, priests, to whom have been committed the souls of those who confess, have to impose satisfactions of penance upon them, so that those who have used their judgement wrongly and proudly by showing contempt of God may be corrected by the judgement of another power, and that they may attend more safely to this the better they follow, by obeying their prelates, the will of these rather than their own. If perhaps these have not instructed rightly when he was ready to obey, that should be imputed to them rather than to him. 'For we are not ignorant', says the Apostle, 'of Satan's devices', and we must not here pass over his wickedness by which he impels us to sin and draws us back from confession. In fact, in inciting us to sin he divests us of fear as well as of shame, so that now nothing remains which may call us back from sin. For there are many things we dare not to do for fear of punishment; we are ashamed to undertake many things because of damage to our reputation, even though we could do it with impunity. So anyone unimpeded by these two tethers, as it were, will become strongly inclined to commit any kind of sin. By this means the same things which he earlier took away from him so that he should commit sin, he later restores to him to call him away from confession. Then he is afraid or is ashamed to confess; when first he should have done so, he was not afraid nor was he ashamed. He fears lest by perhaps becoming known through confession he, who did not fear to be punished by God, be punished by men. He is ashamed that men should know what he was not ashamed to commit before God. But he who seeks medicine for a wound, however foul it is, however smelly, must show it to a doctor so that an effective cure may be applied. The priest in fact occupies the place of a doctor and he, as we have said, must establish the satisfaction.

That sometimes confession may be dispensed with

However, it should be known that sometimes by a wholesome dispensation confession can be avoided, as we believe was true of Peter, whose tears over his denial we know, although we do not read of other satisfaction or of confession. Whence Ambrose on Luke says of this very denial by Peter and of his weeping: 'I do not find what he said; I find that he wept. I read of his tears; I do not read of his satisfaction. Tears wipe away a wrong which it is disgraceful to confess with one's vice and weeping guarantees pardon and shame. Tears declare the fault without dread, they confess without prejudicing shame. Tears do not request pardon but deserve it. I find why Peter was silent, namely lest by asking for pardon so soon he should offend more.' We must ascertain what in fact is this shame or awe of confession whereby Peter satisfied by weeping rather than by confessing. For if he felt ashamed to confess for this single reason lest, if his sin became known, he be thought of as viler, surely he was proud and was providing for the renown of his honour rather than for the salvation of his soul. But if what was being protected was the shame of the Church rather than his own, this should not be derided. He perhaps foresaw that the Lord would establish him as leader over the Lord's people, and he feared lest, if this triple denial of his quickly became public knowledge through his confession, the Church would be gravely scandalized by it and shaken in might embarrassment that the Lord had placed over it one so ready to deny and so pusillanimous. So if he put off confessing less to safeguard his own position than on account of this general embarrassment of the Church, he did it with foresight, not from pride. His fear of damage to the Church rather than of loss of his own reputation was also reasonably caused. He knew indeed that the Church had been specially committed to him by the Lord, when he said to him: 'And thou, being once converted, confirm thy brethren.' So if, convicted by his own confession, this very dreadful lapse of his were to reach the ears of the Church, who would not swiftly say: 'We will not have this man to reign over us', and would not readily censure the Lord's judgement which chose to strengthen the brethren the one who was first to fail? And by this forethought many could put off confession, or completely dispense with it, without sin, if they believed confession would do them more harm than good, because we incur no offence against God by fault where we in no way offer contempt of him. Since Peter was still tender in faith and the Church was weak, he put off confessing his sin until his virtue had been proved by his preaching or miracles. Later, however, when this was at last evident, the same Peter, without any commotion in the Church against the desperation of those who lapse, was able to confess this, with the result, moreover, that a written account was left by the Evangelists.

There are perhaps people to whom it may seem that Peter, who was set over all the others and did not have a superior to whom his soul had been committed, had no necessity at all to confess his sin to a man, as if satisfaction should be arranged by him and he should obey his command as that of a superior. But if he need not have had to confess to someone in order that satisfaction should be imposed, he could have done so without incongruity for the sake of obtaining the help of prayer. Indeed, when it was said: 'Confess your sins one to another', there followed: 'and pray one for another that you may be saved.' Moreover, nothing prevents prelates from choosing subjects in order to make confession or to receive satisfaction, so that what is done may be made more acceptable to God the more humbly they carry it out. And who will forbid anyone to choose in such matters a more religious or more discreet person, to whose judgement he may entrust his satisfaction and by whose prayers he may be very greatly helped? Whence, although it was first said: 'and pray one for another that you may be saved', there was added immediately: 'for the continual prayer of a just man availeth much.' For just as many become unskilful doctors to whom it is dangerous or useless for the sick to be entrusted, so too many are found among the prelates of the Church who are neither religious nor discreet, and are moreover liable to disclose the sins of those who confess, so that to confess to them seems not only useless but also ruinous. Such indeed neither intend to pray nor deserve to be heard in their prayers, and since they do not know the canonical rules nor know how to arrange the fixing of satisfactions, frequently they promise in such things false security and with a worthless hope deceive those who confess, according to the Truth: 'They are blind and leaders of the blind', and again: 'If the blind lead the blind, both fall into the pit.' And since, as we have said, they lightly reveal confessions which they receive, they rouse penitents to indignation, and they, who should have healed sins, inflict new wounds of sin and frighten those who hear them away from confession.

Sometimes also by revealing sins either in anger or in levity, they gravely scandalize the Church and place those who have confessed in great dangers. Whence they, who have decided on account of these disadvantages to avoid their prelates and to choose in such matters others whom they believe to be more suitable for them, should by no means be condemned but rather approved of for turning to a more expert doctor. However, if in doing so they can obtain the assent of their prelates to direct them to others, they act so much more suitably the more humbly they do this in obedience. But if proud prelates forbid this to them, as if considering that, if better doctors are required, they must themselves be rather vile, none the less the sick man anxious for his health may seek with greater anxiety what he believes is better medicine and may give greatest preference to better advice. For no one should follow into the ditch a leader whom someone has granted to him if he discovers he is blind; and it is better to choose him who sees, so that one arrives where one is going, than to follow wrongly to the precipice a leader who has been wrongly assigned to one. Indeed, the man who has assigned to him such a leader, so as to show him the way, has either done this knowingly through malice or innocently through ignorance. If through malice, one should have been on one's guard lest his malice be implemented; if through ignorance, by no means is it to go against his will if we do not follow into danger him who had been given to us as a leader. However, it is useful first to consult those to whom we know our souls are committed and, having heard their advice, not to forsake their wholesome medicine if it is what we hope for, especially when we believe that they are ignorant of the law and are not just unconcerned about what they should do, but unaware of what they should deplore; they should be considered worse than they of whom Truth says: 'The Scribes and the Pharisees have sitten on the chair of Moses. All things therefore whatsoever they shall say to you, observe and do; but according to their works do ye not.' As if to say: such obtain a mastership of the law whose deeds, since they are bad, are for this reason to be rejected, yet the words of God which they utter from the chair of Moses, that is, from the mastership of the law, are to be accepted, so that we should simultaneously reject the actions which are their own and retain the words which are of God.

So the teaching of such men is not to be held in contempt; they preach well although they live badly, and they instruct in the word although they do not edify in example, and they show the way which they refuse to follow; they should be condemned less for the blindness of ignorance than for the fault of negligence. But in the case of those who are not capable of showing the way to their subjects, who should commit themselves to their leadership and seek a lesson from them who know not how to teach? Yet subjects should not despair of the mercy of God when, wholly ready for satisfaction, they deliver themselves to the judgement of their prelates, although they are blind, and in obedience diligently perform what they in error inadequately determine. For the error of prelates does not damn their subjects, nor does their vice reproach them, nor does there now remain in their subjects any fault in which they may die; repentance had already beforehand, as we have said, reconciled them to God, that is, before they came to confession or got their satisfaction determined. However, if any part of the penalty of satisfaction is determined as less than it should be, God, who forgives no sin without punishment and punishes each as much as he should, upholds the fairness of satisfaction according to the amount of the sin, not, that is, by reserving those penitents for eternal torture, but by afflicting them in this life or in the future with purgatorial punishments, if we, I say, have been negligent in our satisfaction. Whence the Apostle says: 'If we would judge ourselves, we should not be judged.' Which is to say: if we would ourselves punish or correct our own sins, they would not be punished by him more severely at all. Surely God's mercy is great when he forgives us on the basis of our own sentencing in order not to punish us more severely. Now these penalties of our present life with which we make satisfaction for sins, by fasting or praying, by keeping vigil, or by whatever means macerating the flesh, or by distributing to the needy what we forgo ourselves, these we call satisfaction. We know they are called by another name in the Gospel, 'the fruits of penance', that is, where it is said: 'Bring forth fruits worthy of penance', as if to say openly: by correcting what you have done wrong with a fitting satisfaction, be thus reconciled to God here, so that in turn he may by no means find what he himself would punish, and prevent severer penalties by means of milder ones. For as the blessed Augustine states: 'The penalties of the future life, although they are purgatorial, are graver than all these of the present life.' And so great caution should be shown concerning them and great care should be taken, so that, according to the rules of the holy Fathers, such satisfaction should be undertaken here that nothing remains to be purged there. So when priests who do not know these canonical rules have been unwise, with the result that they impose less satisfaction than they should, penitents thereby incur a great disadvantage since, having wrongly trusted in them, they are later punished with heavier penalties for that for which they could have made satisfaction here by means of lighter penalties.

There are some priests who deceive their subjects less through error than through greed, so that for an offering of denarii they pardon or relax the penalties of an imposed satisfaction, not considering so much the will of the Lord as the power of money. Of these the Lord himself complained through the Prophet, saying: 'My priests did not say: Where is the Lord?' as if to say: where, then, is the money? And not only priests but even the very leaders of priests, the bishops that is, are, we know, so shamelessly ablaze with this greed that when, at dedications of churches or consecrations of altars or blessings of cemeteries or at any solemnities, they have gatherings of people from which they expect a plentiful offering, they are prodigal in relaxing penances, remitting to all in common now a third, now a fourth, part of their penance under some pretext of charity of course, but really of the highest cupidity. They extol themselves for their power which they received, they say, in Peter or the apostles when the Lord said to them: 'Whose sins you shall forgive, they will be forgiven them' or: 'Whatsoever you shall loose upon earth shall be loosed also in heaven'; then especially do they boast what they can do when they impart this kindness to their subjects. And would that they at least did it for them, not for money, so that it seemed a sort of kindness rather than greed. But surely if this is to be taken as commendation of their kindness that they relax a third or fourth part of a penance, their piety will be much more amply proclaimed if they remit a half or a whole penance altogether, just as they avow that it is lawful and has been granted to them by the Lord and that the heavens, as it were, had been put in their hands in accordance with the testimonies given above concerning the forgiveness or absolution of sins. Finally, and on the other hand, it seems they should be accused of great impiety, for the reason that they do not absolve all their subjects from all their sins and allow none of them to be damned, if, I say, it has thus been placed in their power to forgive or to retain what sins they will, or to open or shut the heavens to those whom they choose. At any rate they would be proclaimed most blessed if they could, when they wanted to, open these for themselves. But if in fact they cannot or do not know how to, certainly to my thinking they fall under that poetic saying: 'The arts which benefit all do not benefit the lord.' Anyone, not I, may seek that power by which he can benefit others rather than himself, as if he had it in his own power to save other souls rather than his own; on the other hand, anyone who is discerning may think the opposite.

St. Thomas Aquinas
1225-1274

Among the great thinkers and writers of the Christian theological tradition, St. Thomas Aquinas is one of the very few whose influence is too vast to measure. His philosophy and theology have been central to Catholic teaching for seven centuries. He was born in Italy in 1225. He was schooled as a child in the Benedictine Monastery of Montecassino, studied at the University of Naples and continued his studies in Paris and Cologne. From 1252 through to the end of his life, he was dedicated to teaching, though he also found time to preach. He was a member of the Dominican Order. He died at the age of 49.

Thomas lived during a period of tremendous intellectual ferment. The philosophies of Plato and Aristotle were being explored vigorously by the theologians of the thirteenth century. Thomas contributed his abilities generously. The result was the creation of a philosophico-theological structure which incorporated not only the best in Plato and Aristotle but the major elements of the Christian theological tradition as well.

No doubt, Thomas is best known for his Summa Theologiae, *though he wrote much more than that. The* Summa *is an exhaustive and systematic treatment of all the significant themes of theology, such as, God, creation, Man—his nature, purpose, knowledge, actions, habits, law, and grace.*

A few words of caution are in order. Thomas wrote in the style of the schoolmen of his time. He used the question—response methodology. It is a slow, steady, unusually logical method, designed to analyze the question at hand, to arrive at sound conclusions and to offer good reasons for the conclusions. The twentieth century reader may find this approach somewhat tedious. Further, in order to appreciate Thomas' insights for what they are worth, one must have some introduction to the technical terms used in philosophy and theology during the thirteenth century.

The second major portion of the Summa Theologiae *concentrates on the process by which the rational creature advances toward God. Carefully, Thomas examines the purpose of man, the nature of human acts, passions, habits in general, virtues and vices, law and grace. Rising up from this study is one of the most complete ethical systems ever developed. It is by his activity that man either unites himself with or separates himself from God. By the life of virtue, in faith, hope, charity, prudence, justice, fortitude and temperance, man fulfills the purpose for which he was created. Within Thomas' Christian perspective, this entire movement of the human toward God is perfected in the mystery of Christ.*

We have included here a selection from Thomas' treatment of charity. Should man love God more than his neighbor or himself? Should he love one neighbor more than another, a blood relative more than other relatives, father more than son, mother more than father? These and other questions are answered by Thomas as he probes the greatest of all virtues, charity.

SUMMA THEOLOGICA
ON THE ORDER OF CHARITY

QUESTION XXVI

(In Thirteen Articles.)

We must now consider the order of charity, under which head there are thirteen points of inquiry: (1) Whether there is an order in charity? (2) Whether man ought to love God more than his neighbour? (3) Whether more than himself? (4) Whether he ought to love himself more than his neighbour? (5) Whether man ought to love his neighbour more than his own body? (6) Whether he ought to love one neighbour more than another? (7) Whether he ought to love more, a neighbour who is better, or one who is more closely united to him? (8) Whether he ought to love more, one who is akin to him by blood, or one who is united to him by other ties? (9) Whether, out of charity, a man ought to love his son more than his father? (10) Whether he ought to love his mother more than his father? (11) Whether he ought to love his wife more than his father or mother? (12) Whether we ought to love those who are kind to us more than those whom we are kind to? (13) Whether the order of charity endures in heaven?

FIRST ARTICLE

WHETHER THERE IS ORDER IN CHARITY?

We Proceed thus to the First Article:—

Objection 1. It would seem that there is no order in charity. For charity is a virtue. But no order is assigned to the other virtues. Neither, therefore, should any order be assigned to charity.

Obj. 2. Further, Just as the object of faith is the First Truth, so is the object of charity the Sovereign Good. Now no order is appointed for faith, but all things are believed equally. Neither, therefore, ought there to be any order in charity.

Obj. 3. Further, Charity is in the will: whereas ordering belongs, not to the will, but to the reason. Therefore no order should be ascribed to charity.

On the contrary, It is written (Cant. ii. 4): *He brought me into the cellar of wine, he set in order charity in me.*

I answer that, As the Philosopher says (*Metaph.* v., text. 16), the terms *before* and *after* are used in reference to some principle. Now order implies that certain things are, in some way, before or after. Hence wherever there is a principle, there must needs be also order of some kind. But it has been said above (Q. XXIII., A. 1: Q. XXV., A. 12) that the love of charity tends to God as to the principle of happiness, on the fellowship of which the friendship of charity is based. Consequently there must needs be some order in things loved out of charity, which order is in reference to the first principle of that love, which is God.

Reply Obj. 1. Charity tends towards the last end considered as last end: and this does not apply to any other virtue, as stated above (Q. XXIII., A. 6). Now the end has the character of principle in matters of appetite and action, as was shown above (Q. XXIII., A. 7, *ad* 2: I.-II., A. 1, *ad* 1). Wherefore charity, above all, implies relation to the First Principle, and consequently, in charity above all, we find an order in reference to the First Principle.

Reply Obj. 2. Faith pertains to the cognitive power, whose operation depends on the thing known being in the knower. On the other hand, charity is in an appetitive power, whose operation consists in the soul tending to things themselves. Now order is to be found in things themselves, and flows from them into our knowledge. Hence order is more appropriate to charity than to faith.

And yet there is a certain order in faith, in so far as it is chiefly about God, and secondarily about things referred to God.

Reply Obj. 3. Order belongs to reason as the faculty that orders, and to the appetitive power as to the faculty which is ordered. It is in this way that order is stated to be in charity.

WHETHER GOD OUGHT TO BE LOVED MORE THAN OUR NEIGHBOUR?

We proceed thus to the Second Article:—

Objection 1. It would seem that God ought not to be loved more than our neighbour. For it is written (1 Jo. iv. 20): *He that loveth not his brother whom he seeth, how can he love God, Whom he seeth not?* Whence it seems to follow that the more a thing is visible the more lovable it is, since loving begins with seeing, according to *Ethic.* ix. 5, 12. Now God is less visible than our neighbour. Therefore He is less lovable, out of charity, than our neighbour.

Obj. 2. Further, Likeness causes love, according to Ecclus. xiii. 19: *Every beast loveth its like.* Now man bears more likeness to his neighbour than to God. Therefore man loves his neighbour, out of charity, more than he loves God.

Obj. 3. Further, What charity loves in a neighbour, is God, according to Augustine (*De Doctr. Christ.* i. 22, 27). Now God is not greater in Himself than He is in our neighbour. Therefore He is not more to be loved in Himself than in our neighbour. Therefore we ought not to love God more than our neighbour.

On the contrary, A thing ought to be loved more, if others ought to be hated on its account. Now we ought to hate our neighbour for God's sake, if, to wit, he leads us astray from God, according to Luke xiv. 26: *If any man come to Me and hate not his father, and mother, and wife, and children, and brethren, and sisters . . . he cannot be My disciple.* Therefore we ought to love God, out of charity, more than our neighbour.

I answer that, Each kind of friendship regards chiefly the subject in which we chiefly find the good on the fellowship of which that friendship is based: thus civil friendship regards chiefly the ruler of the state, on whom the entire common good of the state depends; hence to him before all the citizens own fidelity and obedience. Now the friendship of charity is based on the fellowship of happiness, which consists essentially in God, as the First Principle, whence it flows to all who are capable of happiness.

Therefore God ought to be loved chiefly and before all out of charity: for He is loved as the cause of happiness, whereas our neighbour is loved as receiving together with us a share of happiness from Him.

Reply Obj. 1. A thing is a cause of love in two ways: first, as being the reason for loving. In this way good is the cause of love, since each thing is loved according to its measure of goodness. Secondly, a thing causes love, as being a way to acquire love. It is in this way that seeing is the cause of loving, not as though a thing were lovable according as it is visible, but because by seeing a thing we are led to love it. Hence it does not follow that what is more visible is more lovable, but that as an object of love we meet with it before others: and that is the sense of the Apostle's argument. For, since our neighbour is more visible to us, he is the first lovable object we meet with, because *the soul learns, from those things it knows, to love what it knows not,* as Gregory says in a homily (*In Evang.* xi.). Hence it can be argued that, if any man loves not his neighbour, neither does he love God, not because his neighbour is more lovable, but because he is the first thing to demand our love: and God is more lovable by reason of His greater goodness.

Reply Obj. 2. The likeness we have to God precedes and causes the likeness we have to our neighbour: because from the very fact that we share along with our neighbour in something received from God, we become like to our neighbour. Hence by reason of this likeness we ought to love God more than we love our neighbour.

Reply Obj. 3. Considered in His substance, God is equally in all, in whomsoever He may be, for He is not lessened by being in anything. And yet our neighbour does not possess God's goodness equally with God, for God has it essentially, and our neighbour by participation.

THIRD ARTICLE

WHETHER, OUT OF CHARITY, MAN IS BOUND TO LOVE GOD MORE THAN HIMSELF?

We proceed thus to the Third Article:—

Objection 1. It would seem that man is not bound, out of charity, to love God more than himself. For the Philosopher says (*Ethic.* ix. 8) that *a man's friendly relations with others arise from his friendly relations with himself.* Now the cause is stronger than its effect. Therefore man's friendship towards himself is greater than his friendship for anyone else. Therefore he ought to love himself more than God.

Obj. 2. Further, One loves a thing in so far as it is one's own good. Now the reason for loving a thing is more loved than the thing itself which is loved for that reason, even as the principles which are the reason for knowing a thing are more known. Therefore man loves himself more than any other good loved by him. Therefore he does not love God more than himself.

Obj. 3. Further, A man loves God as much as he loves to enjoy God. But a man loves himself as much as he loves to enjoy God; since this is the highest good a man can wish for himself. Therefore man is not bound, out of charity, to love God more than himself.

On the contrary, Augustine says (*De Doctr. Christ.* i. 22): *If thou oughtest to love thyself, not for thy own sake, but for the sake of Him in Whom is the rightest end of thy love, let no other man take offence if him also thou lovest for God's sake.* Now *the cause of a thing being such is yet more so.* Therefore man ought to love God more than himself.

I answer that, The good we receive from God is twofold, the good of nature, and the good of grace. Now the fellowship of natural goods bestowed on us by God is the foundation of natural love, in virtue of which not only man, so long as his nature remains unimpaired, loves God above all things and more than himself, but also every single creature, each in its own way, i.e. either by an intellectual, or by a rational, or by an animal, or at least by a natural love, as stones do, for instance, and other things bereft of knowledge, because each part naturally loves the common good of the whole more than its own particular good. This is evidenced by its operation, since the principal inclination of each part is towards common action conducive to the good of the whole. It may also be seen in civic virtues whereby sometimes the citizens suffer damage even to their own property and persons for the sake of the common good. Wherefore much more is this realized with regard to the friendship of charity which is based on the fellowship of the gifts of grace.

Therefore man ought, out of charity, to love God, Who is the common good of all, more than himself: since happiness is in God as in the universal and fountain principle of all who are able to have a share of that happiness.

Reply Obj. 1. The Philosopher is speaking of friendly relations towards another person in whom the good, which is the object of friendship, resides in some restricted way; and not of friendly relations with another in whom the aforesaid good resides in totality.

Reply Obj. 2. The part does indeed love the good of the whole, as becomes a part, not however so as to refer the good of the whole to itself, but rather itself to the good of the whole.

Reply Obj. 3. That a man wishes to enjoy God pertains to that love of God which is love of concupiscence. Now we love God with the love of friendship more than with the love of concupiscence, because the Divine good is greater in itself, than our share of good in enjoying Him. Hence, out of charity, man simply loves God more than himself.

FOURTH ARTICLE

WHETHER OUT OF CHARITY, MAN OUGHT TO LOVE
HIMSELF MORE THAN HIS NEIGHBOUR?

We proceed thus to the Fourth Article:—

Objection 1. It would seem that a man ought not, out of charity, to love himself more than his neighbour. For the principal object of charity is God, as stated above (A. 2: Q. XXV., AA. 1, 12). Now sometimes our neighbour is more closely united to God than we are ourselves. Therefore we ought to love such a one more than ourselves.

Obj. 2. Further, The more we love a person, the more we avoid injuring him. Now a man, out of charity, submits to injury for his neighbour's sake, according to Prov. xii. 26: *He that neglecteth a loss for the sake of a friend, is just.* Therefore a man ought, out of charity, to love his neighbour more than himself.

Obj. 3. Further, It is written (I Cor. xiii. 5) that *charity seeketh not its own.* Now the thing we love most is the one

198

whose good we seek most. Therefore a man does not, out of charity, love himself more than his neighbour.

On the contrary, It is written (Lev. xix. 18, Matth. xxii. 39): *Thou shalt love thy neighbour* (Lev. *loc. cit.,—friend*) *as thyself.* Whence it seems to follow that man's love for himself is the model of his love for another. But the model exceeds the copy. Therefore, out of charity, a man ought to love himself more than his neighbour.

I answer that, There are two things in man, his spiritual nature and his corporeal nature. And a man is said to love himself by reason of his loving himself with regard to his spiritual nature, as stated above (Q. XXV., A. 7): so that accordingly, a man ought, out of charity, to love himself more than he loves any other person.

This is evident from the very reason for loving: since, as stated above (Q. XXV., AA. 1, 12), God is loved as the principle of good, on which the love of charity is founded; while man, out of charity, loves himself by reason of his being a partaker of the aforesaid good, and loves his neighbour by reason of his fellowship in that good. Now fellowship is a reason for love according to a certain union in relation to God. Wherefore just as unity surpasses union, the fact that man himself has a share of the Divine good, is a more potent reason for loving than that another should be a partner with him in that share. Therefore man, out of charity, ought to love himself more than his neighbour: in sign whereof, a man ought not to give way to any evil of sin, which counteracts his share of happiness, not even that he may free his neighbour from sin.

Reply Obj. 1. The love of charity takes its quantity not only from its object which is God, but also from the lover, who is the man that has charity, even as the quantity of any action depends in some way on the subject. Wherefore, though a better neighbour is nearer to God, yet because he is not as near to the man who has charity, as this man is to himself, it does not follow that a man is bound to love his neighbour more than himself.

Reply Obj. 2. A man ought to bear bodily injury for his friend's sake, and precisely in so doing he loves himself more as regards his spiritual mind, because it pertains to the perfection of virtue, which is a good of the mind. In spiritual matters, however, man ought not to suffer injury by sinning, in order to free his neighbour from sin, as stated above.

Reply Obj. 3. As Augustine says in his Rule (*Ep.* ccxi.), the saying, '*charity seeks not her own,*' means that it prefers the common to the private good. Now the common good is always more lovable to the individual than his private good, even as the good of the whole is more lovable to the part, than the latter's own partial good, as stated above (A.3).

FIFTH ARTICLE

WHETHER A MAN OUGHT TO LOVE HIS NEIGHBOUR
MORE THAN HIS OWN BODY?

We proceed thus to the Fifth Article:—

Objection 1. It would seem that a man is not bound to love his neighbour more than his own body. For his neighbour includes his neighbour's body. If therefore a man ought to love his neighbour more than his own body, it follows that he ought to love his neighbour's body more than his own.

Obj. 2. Further, A man ought to love his own soul more than his neighbour's, as stated above (A. 4). Now a man's own body is nearer to his soul than his neighbour. Therefore we ought to love our body more than our neighbour.

Obj. 3. Further, A man imperils that which he loves less for the sake of what he loves more. Now every man is not bound to imperil his own body for his neighbour's safety: this belongs to the perfect, according to Jo. xv. 13: *Greater love than this no man hath, that a man lay down his life for his friends.* Therefore a man is not bound, out of charity, to love his neighbour more than his own body.

On the contrary, Augustine says (*De Doctr. Christ.* i. 27) that *we ought to love our neighbour more than our own body.*

I answer that, Out of charity we ought to love more that which has more fully the reason for being loved out of charity, as stated above (A. 2: Q. XXV., A. 12). Now fellowship in the participation of happiness which is the reason for loving one's neighbour, is a greater reason for loving, than the participation of happiness by way of overflow, which is the reason for loving one's own body. Therefore, as regards the welfare of the soul we ought to love our neighbour more than our own body.

Reply Obj. 1. According to the Philosopher (*Ethic.* ix. 8) *a thing seems to be that which is predominant in it:* so that when we say that we ought to love our neighbour more than our own body, this refers to his soul, which is his predominant part.

Reply Obj. 2. Our body is nearer to our soul than our neighbour, as regards the constitution of our own nature: but as regards the participation of happiness, our neighbour's soul is more closely associated with our own soul, than even our own body is.

Reply Obj. 3. Every man is immediately concerned with the care of his own body, but not with his neighbour's welfare, except perhaps in cases of urgency: wherefore charity does not necessarily require a man to imperil his own body for his neighbour's welfare, except in a case where he is under obligation to do so; and if a man of his own accord offer himself for that purpose, this belongs to the perfection of charity.

SIXTH ARTICLE

WHETHER WE OUGHT TO LOVE ONE NEIGHBOUR MORE THAN ANOTHER?

We proceed thus to the Sixth Article:—

Objection 1. It would seem that we ought not to love one neighbour more than another. For Augustine says (*De Doctr. Christ.* i. 28): *One ought to love all men equally. Since, however, one cannot do good to all, we ought to consider those chiefly who by reason of place, time or any other circumstance, by a kind of chance, are more closely united to us.* Therefore one neighbour ought not to be loved more than another.

Obj. 2. Further, Where there is one and the same reason for loving several, there should be no inequality of love. Now there is one and the same reason for loving all one's neighbours, which reason is God, as Augustine states (*De Doctr. Christ.* i. 27). Therefore we ought to love all our neighbours equally.

Obj. 3. Further, To love a man is to wish him good things, as the Philosopher states (*Rhet.* ii. 4). Now to all our neighbours we wish an equal good, viz. everlasting life. Therefore we ought to love all our neighbours equally.

On the contrary, One's obligation to love a person is proportionate to the gravity of the sin one commits in acting against that love. Now it is a more grievous sin to act against the love of certain neighbours, than against the love of others. Hence the commandment (Lev. xx. 9),—*He that curseth his father or mother, dying let him die,* which does not apply to those who cursed others than the above. Therefore we ought to love neighbours more than others.

I answer that, There have been two opinions on this question: for some have said that we ought, out of charity, to love all our neighbours equally, as regards our affection, but not as regards the outward effect. They held that the order of love is to be understood as applying to outward favours, which we ought to confer on those who are connected with us in preference to those who are unconnected, and not to the inward affection, which ought to be given equally to all including our enemies.

But this is unreasonable. For the affection of charity, which is the inclination of grace, is not less orderly than the natural appetite, which is the inclination of nature, for both inclinations flow from Divine wisdom. Now we observe in the physical order that the natural inclination in each thing is proportionate to the act or movement that is becoming to the nature of that thing: thus in earth the inclination of gravity is greater than in water, because it is becoming of earth to be beneath water. Consequently the inclination also of grace which is the effect of charity, must needs be proportionate to those actions which have to be performed outwardly, so that, to wit, the affection of our charity be more intense towards those to whom we ought to behave with greater kindness.

We must, therefore, say that, even as regards the affection we ought to love one neighbour more than another. The reason is that, since the principle of love is God, and the person who loves, it must needs be that the affection of love increases in proportion to the nearness to one or the other of those principles. For as we stated above (A. 1), wherever we find a principle, order depends on relation to that principle.

Reply Obj. 1. Love can be unequal in two ways: first
on the part of the good we wish our friend. In this respect we
love all men equally out of charity: because we wish them all
one same generic good, namely everlasting happiness. Secondly love is said to be greater through its action being more intense: and in this way we ought not to love all equally.

Or we may reply that we have unequal love for certain
persons in two ways: first, through our loving some and not
loving others. As regards beneficence we are bound to observe
this inequality, because we cannot do good to all: but as regards
benevolence, love ought not to be thus unequal. The other
inequality arises from our loving some more than others: and
Augustine does not mean to exclude the latter inequality, but
the former, as is evident from what he says of beneficence.

Reply Obj. 2. Our neighbours are not all equally related
to God; some are nearer to Him, by reason of their greater
goodness, and those we ought, out of charity, to love more
than those who are not so near to Him.

Reply Obj. 3. This argument considers the quantity of
love on the part of the good which we wish our friends.

SEVENTH ARTICLE

WHETHER WE OUGHT TO LOVE THOSE WHO ARE
BETTER MORE THAN THOSE WHO ARE MORE
CLOSELY UNITED TO US?

We proceed thus to the Seventh Article:—

Objection 1. It would seem that we ought to love those
who are better more than those who are more closely united to
us. For that which is in no way hateful seems more lovable than
that which is hateful for some reason: just as a thing is all the
whiter for having less black mixed with it. Now those who are
connected with us are hateful for some reason, according to
Luke xiv. 26: *If any man come to Me, and hate not his father,*
etc. On the other hand good men are not hateful for any reason.
Therefore it seems that we ought to love those who are better
more than those who are more closely connected with us.

Obj. 2. Further, By charity above all, man is likened to
God. But God loves more the better man. Therefore man also,

out of charity, ought to love the better man more than one who is more closely united to him.

Obj. 3. Further, In every friendship that ought to be loved most which has most to do with the foundation of that friendship: for, by natural friendship we love most those who are connected with us by nature, our parents for instance, or our children. Now the friendship of charity is founded upon the fellowship of happiness, which has more to do with better men than with those who are more closely united to us. Therefore, out of charity, we ought to love better men more than those who are more closely connected with us.

On the contrary, It is written (I Tim. v. 8): *If any man have not care of his own, and especially of those of his house, he hath denied the faith, and is worse than an infidel.* Now the inward affection of charity ought to correspond to the outward effect. Therefore charity regards those who are nearer to us before those who are better.

I answer that, Every act should be proportionate both to its object and to the agent. But from its object it takes its species, while, from the power of the agent it takes the mode of its intensity: thus movement has its species from the term to which it tends, while the intensity of its speed arises from the disposition of the thing moved and the power of the mover. Accordingly love takes its species from its object, but its intensity is due to the lover.

Now the object of charity's love is God, and man is the lover. Therefore the specific diversity of the love which is in accordance with charity, as regards the love of our neighbour, depends on his relation to God, so that, out of charity, we should wish a greater good to one who is nearer to God; for though the good which charity wishes to all, viz. everlasting happiness, is one in itself, yet it has various degrees according to various shares of happiness, and it belongs to charity to wish God's justice to be maintained, in accordance with which better men have a fuller share of happiness. And this regards the species of love; for there are different species of love according to the different goods that we wish for those whom we love.

On the other hand, the intensity of love is measured with regard to the man who loves, and accordingly man loves those who are more closely united to him, with more intense affection as to the good he wishes for them, than he loves those who are better as to the greater good he wishes for them.

Again a further difference must be observed here: for some neighbours are connected with us by their natural origin, a connection which cannot be severed, since that origin makes them to be what they are. But the goodness of virtue, wherein some are close to God, can come and go, increase and decrease, as was shown above (Q. XXIV., AA. 4, 10, 11). Hence it is possible for one, out of charity, to wish this man who is more closely united to one, to be better than another, and so reach a higher degree of happiness.

Moreover there is yet another reason for which, out of charity, we love more those who are more nearly connected with us, since we love them in more ways. For, towards those who are not connected with us we have no other friendship than charity, whereas for those who are connected with us, we have certain other friendships, according to the way in which they are connected. Now since the good on which every other friendship of the virtuous is based, is directed, as to its end, to the good on which charity is based, it follows that charity commands each act of another friendship, even as the art which is about the end commands the art which is about the means. Consequently this very act of loving someone because he is akin or connected with us, or because he is a fellow-countryman or for any like reason that is referable to the end of charity, can be commanded by charity, so that, out of charity both eliciting and commanding, we love in more ways those who are more nearly connected with us.

Reply Obj. 1. We are commanded to hate, in our kindred, not their kinship, but only the fact of their being an obstacle between us and God. In this respect they are not akin but hostile to us, according to Mich. vii. 6: *A man's enemies are they of his own household.*

Reply Obj. 2. Charity conforms man to God proportionately, by making man comport himself towards what is his, as God does towards what is His. For we may, out of charity, will certain things as becoming to us which God does not will, because it becomes Him not to will them, as stated above (I.-II.,

Q. XIX., A. 10), when we were treating of the goodness of the will.

Reply Obj. 3. Charity elicits the act of love not only as regards the object, but also as regards the lover, as stated above. The result is that the man who is more nearly united to us is more loved.

EIGHTH ARTICLE

WHETHER WE OUGHT TO LOVE MORE THOSE WHO ARE
CONNECTED WITH US BY TIES OF BLOOD?

We proceed thus to the Eighth Article:—

Objection 1. It would seem that we ought not to love more those who are more closely united to us by ties of blood. For it is written (Prov. xviii. 24): *A man amiable in society, shall be more friendly than a brother.* Again, Valerius Maximus says (*Fact. et Dict. Memor.* iv. 7): *The ties of friendship are most strong and in no way yield to the ties of blood. Moreover it is quite certain and undeniable, that as to the latter, the lot of birth is fortuitous, whereas we contract the former by an untrammelled will, and a solid pledge.* Therefore we ought not to love more than others those who are united to us by ties of blood.

Obj. 2. Further, Ambrose says (*De Officiis* i. 7): *I love not less you whom I have begotten in the Gospel, than if I had begotten you in wedlock, for nature is no more eager to love than grace. Surely we ought to love those whom we expect to be with us for ever more than those who will be with us only in this world.* Therefore we should not love our kindred more than those who are otherwise connected with us.

Obj. 3. Further, *Love is proved by deeds,* as Gregory states (*Hom. in Ev.* xxx.). Now we are bound to do acts of love to others than our kindred: thus in the army a man must obey his officer rather than his father. Therefore we are not bound to love our kindred most of all.

On the contrary, The commandments of the decalogue contain a special precept about the honour due to our parents (Exod. xx. 12). Therefore we ought to love more specially those who are united to us by ties of blood.

I answer that, As stated above (A. 7), we ought out of charity to love those who are more closely united to us more, both because our love for them is more intense, and because there are more reasons for loving them. Now intensity of love arises from the union of lover and beloved: and therefore we should measure the love of different persons according to the different kinds of union, so that a man is more loved in matters touching that particular union in respect of which he is loved. And, again, in comparing love to love we should compare one union with another.

Accordingly we must say that friendship among blood relations is based upon their connection by natural origin, the friendship of fellow-citizens on their civic fellowship, and the friendship of those who are fighting side by side on the comradeship of battle. Wherefore in matters pertaining to nature we should love our kindred most, in matters concerning relations between citizens, we should prefer our fellow-citizens, and on the battlefield our fellow-soldiers. Hence the Philosopher says (*Ethic.* ix. 2) that *it is our duty to render to each class of people such respect as is natural and appropriate. This is in fact the principle upon which we seem to act, for we invite our relations to a wedding. . . . It would seem to be a special duty to afford our parents the means of living . . . and to honour them.*

The same applies to other kinds of friendship.

If however we compare union with union, it is evident that the union arising from natural origin is prior to, and more stable than, all others, because it is something affecting the very substance, whereas other unions supervene and may cease altogether. Therefore the friendship of kindred is more stable, while other friendships may be stronger in respect of that which is proper to each of them.

Reply Obj. 1. In as much as the friendship of comrades originates through their own choice, love of this kind takes precedence of the love of kindred in matters where we are free to do as we choose, for instance in matters of action. Yet the friendship of kindred is more stable, since it is more natural, and preponderates over others in matters touching nature: consequently we are more beholden to them in the providing of necessaries.

Reply Obj. 2. Ambrose is speaking of love with regard to favours respecting the fellowship of grace, namely, moral instruction. For in this matter, a man ought to provide for his spiritual children whom he has begotten spiritually, more than for the sons of his body, whom he is bound to support in bodily sustenance.

Reply Obj. 3. The fact that in the battle a man obeys his officer rather than his father proves, that he loves his father less, not simply but relatively, i.e. as regards the love which is based on fellowship in battle.

NINTH ARTICLE

WHETHER A MAN OUGHT, OUT OF CHARITY , TO LOVE HIS CHILDREN MORE THAN HIS FATHER?

We proceed thus to the Ninth Article:—

Objection 1. It seems that a man ought, out of charity, to love his children more than his father. For we ought to love those more to whom we are more bound to do good. Now we are more bound to do good to our children than to our parents, since the Apostle says (2 Cor. xii. 14): *Neither ought the children to lay up for the parents, but the parents for the children.* Therefore a man ought to love his children more than his parents.

Obj. 2. Further, Grace perfects nature. But parents naturally love their children more than these love them, as the Philosopher states (*Ethic.* viii. 12). Therefore a man ought to love his children more than his parents.

Obj. 3. Further, Man's affections are conformed to God by charity. But God loves His children more than they love Him. Therefore we also ought to love our children more than our parents.

On the contrary, Ambrose says: *We ought to love God first, then our parents, then our children, and lastly those of our household.*

I answer that, As stated above (A. 4, *ad* 1, A. 7), the degrees of love may be measured from two standpoints. First, from that of the object. In this respect the better a thing is, and the more like to God, the more is it to be loved: and in this way a man ought to love his father more than his children, because, to wit, he loves his father as his principle, in which respect he is a more exalted good and more like God.

Secondly, the degrees of love may be measured from the standpoint of the lover, and in this respect a man loves more that which is more closely connected with him, in which way a man's children are move lovable to him than his father, as the Philosopher states (*Ethic.* viii.). First, because parents love their children as being part of themselves, whereas the father is not part of his son, so that the love of a father for his children, is more like a man's love for himself. Secondly, because parents know better that so and so is their child than vice versa. Thirdly, because children are nearer to their parents, as being part of them, than their parents are to them to whom they stand in the relation of a principle. Fourthly, because parents have loved longer, for the father begins to love his child at once, whereas the child begins to love his father after a lapse of time; and the longer love lasts, the stronger it is, according to Ecclus. ix. 14: *Forsake not an old friend, for the new will not be like to him.*

Reply Obj. 1. The debt due to a principle is submission of respect and honour, whereas that due to the effect is one of influence and care. Hence the duty of children to their parents consists chiefly in honour: while that of parents to their children is especially one of care.

Reply Obj. 2. It is natural for a man as father to love his children more, if we consider them as closely connected with him: but if we consider which is the more exalted good, the son naturally loves his father more.

Reply Obj. 3. As Augustine says (*De Doctr. Christ.* i. 32), *God loves us for our good and for His honour.* Wherefore since our father is related to us as principle, even as God is, it belongs properly to the father to receive honour from his children, and to the children to be provided by their parents with what is good for them. Nevertheless in cases of necessity the child is bound out of the favours received to provide for his parents before all.

TENTH ARTICLE

WHETHER A MAN OUGHT TO LOVE HIS MOTHER
MORE THAN HIS FATHER?

We proceed thus to the Tenth Article:—

Objection 1. It would seem that a man ought to love his mother more than his father. For, as the Philosopher says (*De Gener. Animal.* i. 20), *the female produces the body in generation.* Now man receives his soul, not from his father, but from God by creation, as stated in the First Part (Q. XC., A. 2: Q. CXVIII.). Therefore a man receives more from his mother than from his father: and consequently he ought to love her more than him.

Obj. 2. Further, Where greater love is given, greater love is due. Now a mother loves her child more than the father does: for the Philosopher says (*Ethic.* ix. 7) that *mothers have greater love for their children. For the mother labours more in child-bearing, and she knows more surely than the father who are her children.*

Obj. 3. Further, Love should be more fond towards those who have laboured for us more, according to Rom. xvi. 6: *Salute Mary, who hath laboured much among you.* Now the mother labours more than the father in giving birth and education to her child; wherefore it is written (Ecclus. vii. 29): *Forget not the groanings of thy mother.* Therefore a man ought to love his mother more than his father.

On the contrary, Jerome says on Ezech. xliv. 25 that *man ought to love God the Father of all, and then his own father,* and mentions the mother afterwards.

I answer that, In making such comparisons as this, we must take the answer in the strict sense, so that the present question is whether the father as father, ought to be loved more than the mother as mother. The reason is that virtue and vice may make such a difference in suchlike matters, that friendship may be diminished or destroyed, as the Philosopher remarks (*Ethic.* viii. 7). Hence Ambrose says: *Good servants should be preferred to wicked children.*

Strictly speaking, however, the father should be loved more than the mother. For father and mother are loved as principles of our natural origin. Now the father is principle in a more excellent way than the mother, because he is the active principle, while the mother is a passive and material principle. Consequently, strictly speaking, the father is to be loved more.

Reply Obj. 1. In the begetting of man, the mother supplies the formless matter of the body; and the latter receives its form through the formative power that is in the semen of the father. And though this power cannot create the rational soul, yet it disposes the matter of the body to receive that form.

Reply Obj. 2. This applies to another kind of love. For the friendship between lover and lover differs specifically from the friendship between child and parent: while the friendship we are speaking of here, is that which a man owes his father and mother through being begotten of them.

The *Reply* to the *Third Objection* is evident.

ELEVENTH ARTICLE

WHETHER A MAN OUGHT TO LOVE HIS WIFE MORE THAN HIS FATHER AND MOTHER?

We proceed thus to the Eleventh Article:—

Objection 1. It would seem that a man ought to love his wife more than his father and mother. For no man leaves a thing for another unless he love the latter more. Now it is written (Gen. ii. 24) that *a man shall leave father and mother* on account of his wife. Therefore a man ought to love his wife more than his father and mother.

Obj. 2. Further, The Apostle says (Eph. v. 33) that a husband should *love his wife as himself.* Now a man ought to love himself more than his parents. Therefore he ought to love his wife also more than his parents.

Obj. 3. Further, Love should be greater where there are more reasons for loving. Now there are more reasons for love in the friendship of a man towards his wife. For the Philosopher says (*Ethic.* viii. 12) that *in this friendship there are the motives of utility, pleasure, and also of virtue, if husband and wife are virtuous.* Therefore a man's love for his wife ought to be greater than his love for his parents.

On the contrary, According to Eph. v. 28, *men ought to love their wives as their own bodies.* Now a man ought to love his body less than his neighbour, as stated above (A. 5): and among his neighbours he should love his parents most. Therefore he ought to love his parents more than his wife.

I answer that, As stated above (A. 9), the degrees of love may be taken from the good (which is loved), or from the union between those who love. On the part of the good, which is the object loved, a man should love his parents more than his wife, because he loves them as his principles and considered as a more exalted good.

But on the part of the union, the wife ought to be loved more, because she is united to her husband, as one flesh, according to Matth. xix. 6: *Therefore now they are not two, but one flesh.* Consequently a man loves his wife more intensely, but his parents with greater reverence.

Reply Obj. 1. A man does not in all respects leave his father and mother for the sake of his wife: for in certain cases a man ought to succour his parents rather than his wife. He does however leave all his kinsfolk, and cleaves to his wife as regards the union of carnal connection and cohabitation.

Reply Obj. 2. The words of the Apostle do not mean that a man ought to love his wife equally with himself, but that a man's love for himself is the reason for his love of his wife, since she is one with him.

Reply Obj. 3. There are also several reasons for a man's love for his father; and these, in a certain respect, namely, as regards good, are more weighty than those for which a man loves his wife; although the latter outweigh the former as regards the closeness of union.

As to the argument in the contrary sense, it must be observed that in the words quoted, the particle *as* denotes not equality of love but the motive of love. For the principal reason why a man loves his wife is her being united to him in the flesh.

TWELFTH ARTICLE

WHETHER A MAN OUGHT TO LOVE MORE HIS
BENEFACTOR THAN ONE HE HAS BENEFITED?

We proceed thus to the Twelfth Article:—

Objection 1. It would seem that a man ought to love his benefactor more than one he has benefited. For Augustine says

(*De Catech. Rud.* iv.): *Nothing will incite another more to love you than that you love him first: for he must have a hard heart indeed, who not only refuses to love, but declines to return love already given.* Now a man's benefactor forestalls him in the kindly deeds of charity. Therefore we ought to love our benefactors above all.

Obj. 2. Further, The more grievously we sin by ceasing to love a man or by working against him, the more ought we to love him. Now it is a more grievous sin to cease loving a benefactor or to work against him, than to cease loving one to whom one has hitherto done kindly actions. Therefore we ought to love our benefactors more than those to whom we are kind.

Obj. 3. Further, Of all things lovable, God is to be loved most, and then one's father, as Jerome says. Now these are our greatest benefactors. Therefore a benefactor should be loved above all others.

On the contrary, The Philosopher says (*Ethic.* ix. 7), that *benefactors seem to love the recipients of their benefactions, rather than vice versa.*

I answer that, As stated above (AA. 9, 11), a thing is loved more in two ways: first because it has the character of a more excellent good, secondly by reason of a close connection. In the first way we ought to love our benefactor most, because, since he is a principle of good to the man he has benefited, he has the character of a more excellent good, as stated above with regard to one's father (A. 9).

In the second way, however, we love those more who have received benefactions from us, as the Philosopher proves (*Ethic.* ix. 7) by four arguments. First because the recipient of benefactions is the handiwork of the benefactor, so that we are wont to say of a man: *He was made by so and so.* Now it is natural to a man to love his own work (thus it is to be observed that poets love their own poems): and the reason is that we love *to be* and *to live,* and these are made manifest in our *action.* Secondly, because we all naturally love that in which we see our own good. Now it is true that the benefactor has some good of his in the recipient of his benefaction, and the recipient some good in the benefactor; but the benefactor sees his virtuous good in the recipient, while the recipient sees his useful good in the benefactor. Now it gives more pleasure to see one's virtuous good than one's useful good, both because it is more enduring,—for usefulness quickly flits by, and the pleasure of calling a thing to mind is not like the pleasure of having it present,—and because it is more pleasant to recall virtuous goods than the profit we have derived from others. Thirdly, because it is the lover's part to act, since he wills and works the good of the beloved, while the beloved takes a passive part in receiving good, so that to love surpasses being loved, for which reason the greater love is on the part of the benefactor. Fourthly because it is more difficult to give than to receive favours: and we are most fond of this which have cost us most trouble, while we almost despise what comes easy to us.

Reply Obj. 1. It is something in the benefactor that incites the recipient to love him: whereas the benefactor loves the recipient, not through being incited by him, but through being moved thereto of his own accord: and what we do of our own accord surpasses what we do through another.

Reply Obj. 2. The love of the beneficiary for the benefactor is more of a duty, wherefore the contrary is the greater sin. On the other hand, the love of the benefactor for the beneficiary is more spontaneous, wherefore it is quicker to act.

Reply Obj. 3. God also loves us more than we love Him, and parents love their children more than these love them.

Yet it does not follow that we love all who have received good from us, more than any of our benefactors. For we prefer such benefactors as God and our parents, from whom we have received the greatest favours, to those on whom we have bestowed lesser benefits.

THIRTEENTH ARTICLE

WHETHER THE ORDER OF CHARITY ENDURES IN HEAVEN?

We proceed thus to the Thirteenth Article:—

Objection 1. It would seem that the order of charity does not endure in heaven. For Augustine says (*De Vera Relig.* xlviii.): *Perfect charity consists in loving greater goods more, and lesser goods less.* Now charity will be perfect in heaven.

Therefore a man will love those who are better more than either himself or those who are connected with him.

Obj. 2. Further, We love more him to whom we wish a greater good. Now each one in heaven wishes a greater good for those who have more good, else his will would not be conformed in all things to God's will: and there to be better is to have more good. Therefore in heaven each one loves more those who are better, and consequently he loves others more than himself, and one who is not connected with him, more than one who is.

Obj. 3. Further, In heaven love will be entirely for God's sake, for then will be fulfilled the words of I Cor. xv. 28: *That God may be all in all.* Therefore he who is nearer God will be loved more, so that a man will love a better man more than himself, and one who is not connected with him, more than one who is.

On the contrary, Nature is not done away, but perfected, by glory. Now the order of charity given above (AA. 2, 3, 4) is derived from nature: since all things naturally love themselves more than others. Therefore this order of charity will endure in heaven.

I answer that, The order of charity must needs remain in heaven, as regards the love of God above all things. For this will be realized simply when man shall enjoy God perfectly. But, as regards the order between man himself and other men, a distinction would seem to be necessary, because, as we stated above (AA. 7, 9), the degrees of love may be distinguished either in respect of the good which a man desires for another, or according to the intensity of love itself. In the first way a man will love better men more than himself, and those who are less good, less than himself: because, by reason of the perfect conformity of the human to the Divine will, each of the blessed will desire everyone to have what is due to him according to Divine justice. Nor will that be a time for advancing by means of merit to a yet greater reward, as happens now while it is possible for a man to desire both the virtue and the reward of a better man, whereas then the will of each one will rest within the limits determined by God.—But in the second way a man will love himself more than even his better neighbours, because the intensity of the act of love arises on the part of the person who loves, as stated above (AA. 7, 9). Moreover it is for this that the gift of charity is bestowed by God on each one, namely, that he may first of all direct his mind to God, and this pertains to a man's love for himself, and that, in the second place, he may wish other things to be directed to God, and even work for that end according to his capacity.

As to the order to be observed among our neighbours, a man will simply love those who are better, according to the love of charity. Because the entire life of the blessed consists in directing their minds to God, wherefore the entire ordering of their love will be ruled with respect to God, so that each one will love more and reckon to be nearer to himself those who are nearer to God. For then one man will no longer succour another, as he needs to in the present life, wherein each man has to succour those who are closely connected with him rather than those who are not, no matter what be the nature of their distress: hence it is that in this life, a man, by the inclination of charity, loves more those who are more closely united to him, for he is under a greater obligation to bestow on them the effect of charity. It will however be possible in heaven for a man to love in several ways one who is connected with him, since the causes of virtuous love will not be banished from the mind of the blessed. Yet all these reasons are incomparably surpassed by that which is taken from nighness to God.

Reply Obj. 1. This argument should be granted as to those who are connected together; but as regards man himself, he ought to love himself so much the more than others, as his charity is more perfect, since perfect charity directs man to God perfectly, and this belongs to love of oneself, as stated above.

Reply Obj. 2. This argument considers the order of charity in respect of the degree of good one wills the person one loves.

Reply Obj. 3. God will be to each one the entire reason of his love, for God is man's entire good. For if we make the impossible supposition that God were not man's good, He would not be man's reason for loving. Hence it is that in the order of love man should love himself more than all else after God.

QUESTION XXVII

OF THE PRINCIPAL ACT OF CHARITY, WHICH IS TO LOVE

(In Eight Articles.)

We must now consider the act of charity, and (1) the principal act of charity, which is to love, (2) the other acts or effects which follow from that act.

Under the first head there are eight points of inquiry: (1) Which is the more proper to charity, to love or to be loved? (2) Whether to love considered as an act of charity is the same as goodwill? (3) Whether God should be loved for His own sake? (4) Whether God can be loved immediately in this life? (5) Whether God can be loved wholly? (6) Whether the love of God is according to measure? (7) Which is the better, to love one's friend, or one's enemy? (8) Which is the better, to love God, or one's neighbour?

FIRST ARTICLE

WHETHER TO BE LOVED IS MORE PROPER TO CHARITY THAN TO LOVE?

We proceed thus to the First Article:—

Objection 1. It would seem that it is more proper to charity to be loved than to love. For the better charity is to be found in those who are themselves better. But those who are better should be more loved. Therefore to be loved is more proper to charity.

Obj. 2. Further, That which is to be found in more subjects seems to be more in keeping with nature, and, for that reason, better. Now, as the Philosopher says (*Ethic.* viii. 8), *many would rather be loved than love, and lovers of flattery always abound.* Therefore it is better to be loved than to love, and consequently it is more in keeping with charity.

Obj. 3. Further, *The cause of anything being such is yet more so.* Now men love because they are loved, for Augustine says (*De Catech. Rud.* iv.) that *nothing incites another more to*

love you than that you love him first. Therefore charity consists
in being loved rather than in loving.

On the contrary, The Philosopher says (*Ethic.* viii. 8) that
friendship consists in loving rather than in being loved. Now
charity is a kind of friendship. Therefore it consists in loving
rather than in being loved.

I answer that, To love belongs to charity as charity. For,
since charity is a virtue, by its very essence it has an inclination
to its proper act. Now to be loved is not the act of the charity
of the person loved; for this act is to love: and to be loved is
competent to him as coming under the common notion of
good, in so far as another tends towards his good by an act of
charity. Hence it is clear that to love is more proper to charity
than to be loved: for that which befits a thing by reason of itself and its essence is more competent to it than that which is
befitting to it by reason of something else. This can be exempli-
fied in two ways. First, in the fact that friends are more com-
mended for loving than for being loved, indeed, if they be
loved and yet love not, they are blamed. Secondly, because a
mother, whose love is the greatest, seeks rather to love than to
be loved: for *some women,* as the Philosopher observes (*ibid.*)
*entrust their children to a nurse; they do love them indeed, yet
seek not to be loved in return, if they happen not to be loved.*

Reply Obj. 1. A better man, through being better, is more
lovable; but through having more perfect charity, loves more.
He loves more, however, in proportion to the person he loves.
For a better man does not love that which is beneath him less
than it ought to be loved: whereas he who is less good fails to
love one who is better, as much as he ought to be loved.

Reply Obj. 2. As the Philosopher says (*ibid.*), *men wish
to be loved in as much as they wish to be honoured.* For just as
honour is bestowed on a man in order to bear witness to the
good which is in him, so by being loved a man is shown to have
some good, since good alone is lovable. Accordingly men seek
to be loved and to be honoured, for the sake of something else,
viz. to make known the good which is in the person loved. On
the other hand, those who have charity seek to love for the sake
of loving, as though this were itself the good of charity, even

as the act of any virtue is that virtue's good. Hence it is more proper to charity to wish to love than to wish to be loved.

Reply Obj. 3. Some love on account of being loved, not so that to be loved is the end of their loving, but because it is a kind of way leading a man to love.

SECOND ARTICLE

WHETHER TO LOVE CONSIDERED AS AN ACT OF
CHARITY IS THE SAME AS GOODWILL?

We proceed thus to the Second Article:—

Objection 1. It would seem that to love, considered as an act of charity, is nothing else than goodwill. For the Philosopher says (*Rhet.* ii. 4) that *to love is to wish a person well;* and this is goodwill. Therefore the act of charity is nothing but goodwill.

Obj. 2. Further, The act belongs to the same subject as the habit. Now the habit of charity is in the power of the will, as stated above (Q. XXIV., A. 1). Therefore the act of charity is also an act of the will. But it tends to good only, and this is goodwill. Therefore the act of charity is nothing else than goodwill.

Obj. 3. Further, The Philosopher reckons five things pertaining to friendship (*Ethic.* ix. 4), the first of which is that a man should wish his friend well; the second, that he should wish him to be and to live; the third, that he should take pleasure in his company; the fourth, that he should make choice of the same things; the fifth, that he should grieve and rejoice with him. Now the first two pertain to goodwill. Therefore goodwill is the first act of charity.

On the contrary, The Philosopher says (*ibid.,* 5) that *goodwill is neither friendship nor love, but the beginning of friendship.* Now charity is friendship, as stated above (Q. XXIII., A. 1). Therefore goodwill is not the same as to love considered as an act of charity.

I answer that, Goodwill properly speaking is that act of the will whereby we wish well to another. Now this act of the will differs from actual love, considered not only as being in the sensitive appetite but also as being in the intellective appetite or will. For the love which is in the sensitive appetite is a passion. Now every passion seeks its object with a certain eagerness. And the passion of love is not aroused suddenly, but is born of an earnest consideration of the object loved; wherefore the Philosopher, showing the difference between goodwill and the love which is a passion, says (*Ethic.* ix. 5) that *goodwill does not imply impetuosity or desire,* that is to say, has not an eager inclination, because it is by the sole judgment of his reason that one man wishes another well. Again suchlike love arises from previous acquaintance, whereas goodwill sometimes arises suddenly, as happens to us if we look on at a boxing-match, and we wish one of the boxers to win. But the love, which is in the intellective appetite, also differs from goodwill, because it denotes a certain union of affections between the lover and the beloved, in as much as the lover deems the beloved as somewhat united to him, or belonging to him, and so tends towards him. On the other hand, goodwill is a simple act of the will, whereby we wish a person well, even without presupposing the aforesaid union of the affections with him.

Accordingly, to love, considered as an act of charity, includes goodwill, but such dilection or love adds union of affections, wherefore the Philosopher says *(ibid.)* that *goodwill is a beginning of friendship.*

Reply Obj. 1. The Philosopher, by thus defining *to love,* does not describe it fully, but mentions only that part of its definition in which the act of love is chiefly manifested.

Reply Obj. 2. To love is indeed an act of the will tending to the good, but it adds a certain union with the beloved, which union is not denoted by goodwill.

Reply Obj. 3. These things mentioned by the Philosopher belong to friendship because they arise from a man's love for himself, as he says in the same passage, in so far as a man does all these things in respect of his friend, even as he does them to himself: and this belongs to the aforesaid union of the affections.

THIRD ARTICLE

WHETHER OUT OF CHARITY GOD OUGHT TO BE LOVED FOR HIMSELF?

We proceed thus to the Third Article:—

Objection 1. It would seem that God is loved out of charity, not for Himself but for the sake of something else. For Gregory says in a homily (*In Evang.* xi.): *The soul learns from the things it knows, to love those it knows not,* where by things unknown he means the intelligible and the Divine, and by things known he indicates the objects of the senses. Therefore God is to be loved for the sake of something else.

Obj. 2. Further, Love follows knowledge. But God is known through something else, according to Rom. i. 20: *The invisible things of God are clearly seen, being understood by the things that are made.* Therefore He is also loved on account of something else and not for Himself.

Obj. 3. Further, *Hope begets charity* as a gloss says on Matth. i. 1, and *fear leads to charity,* according to Augustine in his commentary on the First Canonical Epistle of John (*In prim. canon. Joan., Tract.* ix.). Now hope looks forward to obtain something from God, while fear shuns something which can be inflicted by God. Therefore it seems that God is to be loved on account of some good we hope for, or some evil to be feared. Therefore He is not to be loved for Himself.

On the contrary, According to Augustine (*De Doctr. Christ.* i.), *to enjoy is to cleave to something for its own sake.* Now *God is to be enjoyed* as he says in the same book. Therefore God is to be loved for Himself.

I answer that, The preposition *for* denotes a relation of causality. Now there are four kinds of cause, viz. final, formal, efficient, and material, to which a material disposition also is to be reduced, though it is not a cause simply but relatively. According to these four different causes one thing is said to be loved for another. In respect of the final cause, we love medicine, for instance, for health; in respect of the formal cause, we love a man for his virtue, because, to wit, by his virtue he is formally good and therefore lovable; in respect of the efficient cause, we love certain men because, for instance, they are the sons of such and such a father; and in respect of the disposition which is reducible to the genus of a material cause, we speak of loving something for that which disposed us to love it, e.g. we love a man for the favours received from him, although after we have begun to love our friend, we no longer love him for his favours, but for his virtue.

Accordingly, as regards the first three ways, we love God, not for anything else, but for Himself. For He is not directed to anything else as to an end, but is Himself the last end of all things; nor does He require to receive any form in order to be good, for His very substance is His goodness, which is itself the exemplar of all other good things; nor again does goodness accrue to Him from aught else, but from Him to all other things.

In the fourth way, however, He can be loved for something else, because we are disposed by certain things to advance in His love, for instance, by favours bestowed by Him, by the rewards we hope to receive from Him, or even by the punishments which we are minded to avoid through Him.

Reply Obj. 1. *From the things it knows the soul learns to love what it knows not,* not as though the things it knows were the reason for its loving things it knows not, through being the formal, final, or efficient cause of this love, but because this knowledge disposes man to love the unknown.

Reply Obj. 2. Knowledge of God is indeed acquired through other things, but after He is known, He is no longer known through them, but through Himself, according to Jo. iv. 42: *We now believe, not for thy saying: for we ourselves have heard Him, and know that this is indeed the Saviour of the world.*

Reply Obj. 3. Hope and fear lead to charity by way of a certain disposition, as was shown above (Q. XVII., A. 8: Q. XIX., AA. 4, 7, 10).

FOURTH ARTICLE

WHETHER GOD CAN BE LOVED IMMEDIATELY IN THIS LIFE?

We proceed thus to the Fourth Article:—

Objection 1. It would seem that God cannot be loved immediately in this life. For the *unknown cannot be loved*

222

as Augustine says (*De Trin.* x. 1). Now we do not know God immediately in this life, since *we see now through a glass, in a dark manner* (I Cor. xiii. 12). Neither, therefore, do we love Him immediately.

Obj. 2. Further, He who cannot do what is less, cannot do what is more. Now it is more to love God than to know Him, since *he who is joined* to God by love, *is one spirit* with him (I Cor. vi. 17). But man cannot know God immediately. Therefore much less can he love Him immediately.

Obj. 3. Further, Man is severed from God by sin, according to Isa. lix. 2: *Your iniquities have divided between you and your God.* Now sin is in the will rather than in the intellect. Therefore man is less able to love God immediately than to know Him immediately.

On the contrary, Knowledge of God, through being mediate, is said to be *enigmatic,* and *falls away* in heaven, as stated in I Cor. xiii. 12. But charity *does not fall* away as stated in the same passage (*verse* 8). Therefore the charity of the way adheres to God immediately.

I answer that, As stated above (P. I., Q. LXXXII., A. 3: Q. LXXXIV., A. 7), the act of a cognitive power is completed by the thing known being in the knower, whereas the act of an appetitive power consists in the appetite being inclined towards the thing in itself. Hence it follows that the movement of the appetitive power is towards things in respect of their own condition, whereas the act of a cognitive power follows the mode of the knower.

Now in itself the very order of things is such, that God is knowable and lovable for Himself, since He is essentially truth and goodness itself, whereby other things are known and loved: but with regard to us, since our knowledge is derived through the senses, those things are knowable first, which are nearer to our senses, and the last term of knowledge is that which is most remote from our senses.

Accordingly, we must assert that to love which is an act of the appetitive power, even in this state of life, tends to God first, and flows on from Him to other things, and in this sense charity loves God immediately, and other things through God. On the other hand, with regard to knowledge, it is the reverse, since we know God through other things, either as a cause through its effects, or by way of pre-eminence or negation as Dionysius states (*Div. Nom.* i. cf. P. I., Q. XII., A. 12).

Reply Obj. 1. Although the unknown cannot be loved, it does not follow that the order of knowledge is the same as the order of love, since love is the term of knowledge, and consequently, love can begin at once where knowledge ends, namely in the thing itself which is known through another thing.

Reply Obj. 2. Since to love God is something greater than to know Him, especially in this state of life, it follows that love of God presupposes knowledge of God. And because this knowledge does not rest in creatures, but, through them, tends to something else, love begins there, and thence goes on to other things by a circular movement so to speak; for knowledge begins from creatures, tends to God, and love begins with God as the last end, and passes on to creatures.

Reply Obj. 3. Aversion from God, which is brought about by sin, is removed by charity, but not by knowledge alone: hence charity, by loving God, unites the soul immediately to Him with a chain of spiritual union.

FIFTH ARTICLE

WHETHER GOD CAN BE LOVED WHOLLY?

We proceed thus to the Fifth Article:—

Objection 1. It would seem that God cannot be loved wholly. For love follows knowledge. Now God cannot be wholly known by us, since this would imply comprehension of Him. Therefore He cannot be wholly loved by us.

Obj. 2. Further, Love is a kind of union, as Dionysius shows (*Div. Nom.* iv.). But the heart of man cannot be wholly united to God, because *God is greater than our heart* (I Jo. iii. 20). Therefore God cannot be loved wholly.

Obj. 3. Further, God loves Himself wholly. If therefore He be loved wholly by another, this one will love Him as much as God loves Himself. But this is unreasonable. Therefore God cannot be wholly loved by a creature.

On the contrary, It is written (Deut. vi. 5): *Thou shalt love the Lord thy God with thy whole heart.*

I answer that, Since love may be considered as something between lover and beloved, when we ask whether God can be wholly loved, the question may be understood in three ways, first so that the qualification *wholly* be referred to the thing loved, and thus God is to be loved wholly, since man should love all that pertains to God.

Secondly, it may be understood as though *wholly* qualified the lover: and thus again God ought to be loved wholly, since man ought to love God with all his might, and to refer all he has to the love of God, according to Deut. vi. 5: *Thou shalt love the Lord thy God with thy whole heart.*

Thirdly, it may be understood by way of comparison of the lover to the thing loved, so that the mode of the lover equal the mode of the thing loved. This is impossible: for, since a thing is lovable in proportion to its goodness, God is infinitely lovable, since His goodness is infinite. Now no creature can love God infinitely, because all power of creatures, whether it be natural or infused, is finite.

This suffices for the *Replies* to the *Objections,* because the first three objections consider the question in this third sense, while the last takes it in the second sense.

SIXTH ARTICLE

WHETHER IN LOVING GOD WE OUGHT TO OBSERVE ANY MODE?

We proceed thus to the Sixth Article:—

Objection 1. It would seem that we ought to observe some mode in loving God. For the notion of good consists in mode, species and order, as Augustine states (*De Nat. Boni* iii., iv.). Now the love of God is the best thing in man, according to Coloss. iii. 14: *Above all . . . things, have charity.* Therefore there ought to be a mode of the love of God.

Obj. 2. Further, Augustine says (*De Morib. Eccl.* viii.): *Prithee, tell me which is the mode of love. For I fear lest I burn with the desire and love of my Lord, more or less than I ought.* But it would be useless to seek the mode of the Divine love, unless there were one. Therefore there is a mode of the love of God.

Obj. 3. Further, As Augustine says (*Gen. ad lit.* iv. 3), *the measure which nature appoints to a thing, is its mode.* Now the measure of the human will, as also of external action, is the reason. Therefore just as it is necessary for the reason to appoint a mode to the exterior effect of charity, according to Rom. xii. 1: *Your reasonable service,* so also the interior love of God requires a mode.

On the contrary, Bernard says (*De Dilig. Deum,* 1) that *God is the cause of our loving God; the measure is to love Him without measure.*

I answer that, As appears from the words of Augustine quoted above (*Obj.* 3) mode signifies a determination of measure; which determination is to be found both in the measure and in the thing measured, but not in the same way. For it is found in the measure essentially, because a measure is of itself the determining and modifying rule of other things; whereas in the things measured, it is found relatively, that is in so far as they attain to the measure. Hence there can be nothing unmodified if it fails to attain to the measure, whether by deficiency or by excess.

Now in all matters of appetite and action the measure is the end, because the proper reason for all that we desire or do should be taken from the end, as the Philosopher proves (*Phys.* ii. 9). Therefore the end has a mode by itself, while the means take their mode from being proportionate to the end. Hence, according to the Philosopher (*Polit.* i. 3), *in every art, the desire for the end is endless and unlimited,* whereas there is a limit to the means: thus the physician does not put limits to health, but makes it as perfect as he possibly can; but he puts a limit to medicine, for he does not give as much medicine as he can, but according as health demands, so that if he give too much or too little, the medicine would be immoderate.

Again, the end of all human actions and affections is the love of God, whereby principally we attain to our last end, as stated above (Q. XXIII., A. 6), wherefore the mode in the love of God, must not be taken as in a thing measured where we find too much or too little, but as in the measure itself, where there cannot be excess, and where the more the rule is attained the better it is, so that the more we love God the better our love is.

Reply Obj. 1. That which is so by its essence takes precedence of that which is so through another, wherefore the goodness of the measure which has the mode essentially, takes precedence of the goodness of the thing measured, which has its mode through something else; and so too, charity, which has a mode as a measure has, stands before the other virtues, which have a mode through being measured.

Reply Obj. 2. As Augustine adds in the same passage, *the measure of our love for God, is to love Him with our whole heart,* that is, to love Him as much as He can be loved, and this belongs to the mode which is proper to the measure.

Reply Obj. 3. An affection, whose object is subject to reason's judgment, should be measured by reason. But the object of the Divine love which is God surpasses the judgment of reason, wherefore it is not measured by reason but transcends it. Nor is there parity between the interior act and external acts of charity. For the interior act of charity has the character of an end, since man's ultimate good consists in his soul cleaving to God, according to Ps. lxxii. 28: *It is good for me to adhere to my God;* whereas the exterior acts are as means to the end, and so have to be measured both according to charity and according to reason.

SEVENTH ARTICLE

WHETHER IT IS MORE MERITORIOUS TO LOVE AN ENEMY THAN TO LOVE A FRIEND?

We proceed thus to the Seventh Article:—

Objection 1. It would seem more meritorious to love an enemy than to love a friend. For it is written (Matth. v. 46): *If you love them that love you, what reward shall you have?* Therefore it is not deserving of reward to love one's friend: whereas, as the same passage proves, to love one's enemy is deserving of a reward. Therefore it is more meritorious to love one's enemy than to love one's friend.

Obj. 2. Further, An act is the more meritorious through proceeding from a greater charity. But it belongs to the perfect children of God to love their enemies, whereas those also who have imperfect charity love their friends. Therefore it is more meritorious to love one's enemy than to love one's friend.

Obj. 3. Further, Where there is more effort for good, there seems to be more merit, since *every man shall receive his own reward according to his own labour* (I Cor. iii. 8). Now a man has to make a greater effort to love his enemy than to love his friend, because it is more difficult. Therefore it seems more meritorious to love one's enemy than to love one's friend.

Obj. 4. *On the contrary,* The better an action is, the more meritorious it is. Now it is better to love one's friend, since it is better to love a better man, and the friend who loves you is better than the enemy who hates you. Therefore it is more meritorious to love one's friend than to love one's enemy.

I answer that, God is the reason for our loving our neighbour out of charity, as stated above (Q. XXV., A. 1). When therefore it is asked which is better or more meritorious, to love one's friend or one's enemy, these two loves may be compared in two ways, first, on the part of our neighbour whom we love, secondly, on the part of the reason for which we love him.

In the first way, love of one's friend surpasses love of one's enemy, because a friend is both better and more closely united to us, so that he is a more suitable matter of love, and consequently the act of love that passes over this matter, is better, and therefore its opposite is worse, for it is worse to hate a friend than an enemy.

In the second way, however, it is better to love one's enemy than one's friend, and this for two reasons. First, because it is possible to love one's friend for another reason than God, whereas God is the only reason for loving one's enemy. Secondly, because if we suppose that both are loved for God, our love for God is proved to be all the stronger through carrying a man's affections to things which are furthest from him, namely, to the love of his enemies, even as the power of a furnace is proved to be the stronger, according as it throws its heat to more distant objects. Hence our love for God is proved to be so much the stronger, as the more difficult are the things we accomplish for its sake, just as the power of fire is so much the stronger, as it is able to set fire to a less inflammable matter.

Yet just as the same fire acts with greater force on what is near than on what is distant, so too, charity loves with greater fervour those who are united to us than those who are far removed; and in this respect the love of friends, considered in itself, is more ardent and better than the love of one's enemy.

Reply Obj. 1. The words of Our Lord must be taken in their strict sense: because the love of one's friends is not meritorious in God's sight when we love them merely because they are our friends: and this would seem to be the case when we love our friends in such a way that we love not our enemies. On the other hand the love of our friends is meritorious, if we love them for God's sake, and not merely because they are our friends.

The *Reply* to the other *objections* is evident from what has been said in the article, because the two arguments that follow consider the reason for loving, while the last considers the question on the part of those who are loved.

EIGHTH ARTICLE

WHETHER IT IS MORE MERITORIOUS TO LOVE
ONE'S NEIGHBOUR THAN TO LOVE GOD?

We proceed thus to the Eighth Article:—

Objection 1. It would seem that it is more meritorious to love one's neighbour than to love God. For the more meritorious thing would seem to be what the Apostle preferred. Now the Apostle preferred the love of our neighbour to the love of God, according to Rom. ix. 3: *I wished myself to be an anathema from Christ, for my brethren.* Therefore it is more meritorious to love one's neighbour than to love God.

Obj. 2. Further, In a certain sense it seems to be less meritorious to love one's friend, as stated above (A. 7). Now God is our chief friend, since *He hath first loved us* (I John iv. 10). Therefore it seems less meritorious to love God.

Obj. 3. Further, Whatever is more difficult seems to be more virtuous and meritorious, since *virtue is about that which is difficult and good* (*Ethic.* ii. 3). Now it is easier to love God than to love one's neighbour, both because all things love God naturally, and because there is nothing unlovable in God, and this cannot be said of one's neighbour. Therefore it is more meritorious to love one's neighbour than to love God.

On the contrary, That on account of which a thing is such, is yet more so. Now the love of one's neighbour is not meritorious, except by reason of his being loved for God's sake. Therefore the love of God is more meritorious than the love of our neighbour.

I answer that, This comparison may be taken in two ways. First, by considering both loves separately: and then, without doubt, the love of God is the more meritorious, because a reward is due to it for its own sake, since the ultimate reward is the enjoyment of God, to Whom the movement of the Divine love tends: hence a reward is promised to him that loves God (Jo. xiv. 21): *He that loveth Me, shall be loved of My Father, and I will . . . manifest Myself to him.* Secondly, the comparison may be understood to be between the love of God alone on the one side, and the love of one's neighbour for God's sake, on the other. In this way love of our neighbour includes love of God, while love of God does not include love of our neighbour. Hence the comparison will be between perfect love of God, extending also to our neighbour, and inadequate and imperfect love of God, for *this commandment we have from God, that he, who loveth God, love also his brother* (I Jo. iv. 21).

Reply Obj. 1. According to one gloss, the Apostle did not desire this, viz. to be severed from Christ for his brethren, when he was in a state of grace, but had formerly desired it when he was in a state of unbelief, so that we should not imitate him in this respect.

We may also reply, with Chrysostom (*De Compunct.* i. 8) that this does not prove the Apostle to have loved his neighbour more than God, but that he loved God more than himself. For he wished to be deprived for a time of the Divine fruition which pertains to love of oneself, in order that God might be honoured in his neighbour, which pertains to the love of God.

Reply Obj. 2. A man's love for his friends is sometimes less meritorious in so far as he loves them for their sake, so as to fall short of the true reason for the friendship of charity, which is God. Hence that God be loved for His own sake does not diminish the merit, but is the entire reason for merit.

Reply Obj. 3. The *good* has, more than the *difficult,* to do with the reason of merit and virtue. Therefore it does not follow that whatever is more difficult is more meritorious, but only what is more difficult, and at the same time better.

Desiderius Erasmus
1466-1536

Desiderius Erasmus was one of the great humanists of the early sixteenth century. He was born in Rotterdam, Holland in 1466 and received his early education in that country. As an adult he studied and travelled in England, France, Italy, Switzerland and the Low Countries. One of his closest friends was Thomas More, to whom Erasmus dedicated what is perhaps his best known writing, Praise of Folly *(1509). His rich background in the classics, philosophy, Scripture and the Fathers of the Church prepared him to produce writings that spread his fame across the whole of Europe.*

Some of his writings harshly criticized abuses in the church and called for a restoration of early Christian piety. Martin Luther, one of his readers, hoped that Erasmus would support him in his efforts at reform. Erasmus did not and, in fact, clearly repudiated the writings of Luther.

Erasmus remained faithful throughout his entire lifetime to his ideal of the Christian humanist. He was totally dedicated to study and writing and based his life on the message of the gospel. In resolving disagreements, he preferred intelligent persuasion to force. Unfortunately, this wonderful humanist's plea for harmony and peace among Christians went unheard in a world that had committed itself to war and factions. He died in Basel, Switzerland, in 1535.

Perhaps the atmosphere of the times in which he lived made it logical for Erasmus to speak and write of the Christian life as a type of continual warfare. In 1503, he published The Handbook of the Militant Christian, *a brief guide for spiritual living which could help the reader "attain those virtues of mind that should characterize him who is truly Christian." The influence of the Greek philosophers and Fathers of the Church, as well as his commitment to sacred scripture, is most evident. The reading below is taken from the early chapters of the book.*

Erasmus begins by observing that the majority of people are easily deceived and dwell in a sense of victory and false security. The truth is that we are surrounded by vices. Indulgence in pleasure rather than hard work is the most common norm. The Christian should not forget that he is pledged to Christ and is indebted to Him. Among the signs of the diseased soul are a nauseous feeling at hearing the Word of God, reluctance to perform works of piety, anger at losing money, lack of feeling upon seeing one's brother suffering indignities. The weapons of the Christian are prayer, knowledge, dedication to the scriptures. The Philosophy and the classics may be used, if one feels that they are a help. The crown of wisdom is true self-knowledge. Plato's influence on Erasmus is quite obvious in his discussion of the complexity of man. The human soul may be likened to the divine, the body to a dumb beast. Tragically, the majority of those who call themselves Christian are dumb beasts, slaves of bodily senses. The true Christian enters the struggle courageously. He overcomes temptation, crucifies the flesh and finds true peace and tranquility.

This model of the Christian life has continued to have an impact on ethical thinking right down to the present century.

THE HANDBOOK OF
THE MILITANT CHRISTIAN

I

Y ou have requested, my dearly beloved in Christ, that I
compose for you a kind of compendium, or guide for
spiritual living, so that being instructed by it you may
attain those virtues of mind that should characterize him who is
truly Christian. In this request you have also indicated that your
preoccupation with mundane affairs has forced you to perceive
the need you have of abandoning worldly pursuits and turning
your efforts rather to the attainment of virtue. Our own close
friendship only adds to the joy with which I undertake this proposal, and I sincerely hope that He who is solely responsible for
your decision will aid me in this endeavor. So that what I have
to write will not in the end prove fruitless, let us begin by calling
upon the kindly spirit of Jesus so that He will fill my mind with
words of salvation, and that what I write will be for you a source
of strength and determination.

1. In this life it is necessary that we be on our guard

To begin with we must be constantly aware of the fact that
life here below is best described as being a type of continual
warfare. This is a fact that Job, that undefeated soldier of vast
experience, tells us so plainly. Yet in this manner the great majority of mankind is often deceived, for the world, like some
deceitful magician, captivates their minds with seductive blan-
dishments, and as a result most individuals behave as if there had
been a cessation of hostilities. They celebrate as if they were
assured of victory when, as a matter of fact, genuine peace could
never be further away. It is amazing to see in what false security
these people live and in what a complacent manner they close
their minds to reality. In the meantime the vices, our armored
enemies, attack us unceasingly; we are entrapped by their espi-
onage and assaulted by their endless deceptions. If you but look

around, you will see that regardless of where you go they are observing you. They are prepared to attack us with a thousand stratagems and, evil demons that they are, they concentrate on wounding our minds with inflammable and poisonous weapons. Unless we ward them off with the impenetrable shield of faith, they will prove to wield weapons of certain death. Nor is there any slackening in the manner of their attack, as it comes from all sides.

This is that world that St. John describes so well as being constituted entirely of vice. It is a world that is both contrary and hateful to Christ. It must be pointed out that the type of warfare it wages is anything but simple and straightforward. From time to time, especially in adverse circumstances, this raging world shakes the very walls of the mind. At other times it incites the mind to betrayal with vain promises. Or again, whenever it finds us unaware, in idle and false security, it unexpectedly and with secret contrivances captures the mind. Most important of all, that slimy snake, the first betrayer of our peace and the father of restlessness, never ceases to watch and lie in wait beneath the heel of woman, whom he once poisoned. By "woman" we mean, of course, the carnal or sensual part of man. For this is our Eve, through whom the crafty serpent entices and lures our minds to deadly pleasures. And yet, as if it were not enough that he threatens us from all directions on the outside, he also penetrates into the inner recesses of our minds. This is the ancient and earthly Adam, more intimate than our closest companions and more zealous than our deadliest enemy, since he cannot be contained by entrenchment or expelled with an army. He must be watched, then, with a hundred eyes, lest he expose God's fortress to demons.

Since it is quite plain that all of us are engaged in a major and difficult effort against an enemy who is numerically superior, better armed and more experienced than we are, are we not insane if we fail to take up arms against him? Are we not extremely foolish if we do not stand continually on our guard and hold all things suspect? The fact of the matter is, however that we slumber complacently through the whole siege. Indulgence in pleasure rather than hard work seems to be the norm. The self-interest we display would convince one that we are living in peaceful times. It seems that life is a drinking bout rather than a war. We clothe ourselves with boudoir trappings rather than armor. Ease and self-indulgence are everywhere preferred to the rigors of military preparedness. We practice on the peaceful harp rather than on the weapons of warfare, unaware that this sort of peace is the most terrible of all wars.

Anyone who concludes a treaty with vice violates the agreement made with God in baptism. You foolishly cry, "peace, peace," and at the same time treat as an enemy God, who alone is peace and the author of peace. He Himself has made it quite plain through His prophet: "There is no peace for the wicked." The condition that He lays down for peace is that we fight in the garrison of the body against all of our vices. If we compromise, if we consort with vice, we will make a foe of Him who alone, as a friend, is able to bless us, but who as an enemy will surely damn us. He will be our enemy for two reasons. First of all we will be siding with those vices that are diametrically opposed to the divine, for how can light and darkness be in agreement? In the second place, in so doing we ungratefully fail to abide by the pledge that we have made to Him, violating what we have solemnized with sacred ceremonies. Perhaps you are now aware, O Christian soldier, that when you were initiated into the mysteries of life-giving Baptism, you gave yourself by name to Christ as your leader. That is the reason you are doubly indebted to Him. He not only gave you life in the first place but He also restored it. You owe Him more than you could ever owe to yourself. If you break this contract, does it not occur to you that you are violating a pledge to such a kindly leader? Does it become quite plain to you that you have dedicated yourself in this sacrament to His most noble cause? Why did He see to it that you were signed on the brow with the sign of the cross unless He intended that you fight under His banner during this life? For what purpose were you anointed with sacred oils except to take up arms in this struggle against vice? What could be more shameful, more degrading, than to separate yourself from this princely leader? Is there any reason why you should hold Christ the King in derision? Does not the fact that He is God at least instill you with fear? Are you not moved by the love of Him who for your sake became man? Has no one ever warned you of the promise you once laid before Him? Will you actually betray Him who once redeemed you with the price of His blood?

Certainly you show the greatest impudence if you dare raise a hostile standard against a King who gave His life for your sake. He Himself has told us clearly that He who does not stand for Him stands against Him, and he who does not gather with Him, scatters. Not only do you fight under a disgraceful banner, but consider for a moment what your reward will be. St. Paul, the standard-bearer of Christian warfare, tells us "the wages of sin is death." Would anyone engage in warfare if death were the only reward? Death of the soul is hardly a reward. Look at the actual condition of misery that accompanies human warfare. What motivates the soldiers to endure such hardships and deprivation? Is it not the promise of booty, the dread of loss, and the fear of being accused of cowardice? If all they get is the praise of their officers or the hope of a little more pay, that is not much of a reward. Our motives can be neither the fear of shame nor the hope of reward. The same Person witnesses our struggle who will one day reward us. Our reward is that which "neither eye has seen, nor ear heard, nor has entered into the heart of man." I think this in itself ought to be of great consolation as we carry on the battle, for it is eternal happiness that will be ours.

In all earthly engagements a reputation for bravery is the goal, and even the material rewards are handed out by lot. With us in our struggle against vice the case is not quite the same. We do not fight for praise but for Life itself. And the very highest reward will go to him who perseveres, just as the most severe punishment will be meted out to him who deserts. Heaven itself is the promise we seek, and certainly the very hope of such a prize ought to encourage our efforts, especially when it is promised by Him who can neither deceive nor be deceived. Then, too, our struggle takes place before the all-seeing eye of God and is witnessed by the entire populace of heaven. The shame of defeat in the presence of such an audience ought at least to help inspire us to bravery. He will praise our effort whose mere approval alone is the equivalent of the greatest happiness. If the tepid mind is not aroused by the prospect of reward, it must be admitted that fear of punishment can awaken even the most indolent.

In ancient times it was customary in war to violate the corpses of the enemy. It was considered a great calamity if the body were separated by the sword from the soul. This enemy of ours is not only determined to destroy the body but he intends to cast both the body and the soul into hell. For this is actually what occurs when life, which is God Himself, is taken away from the soul. We know well enough that it is the nature of the body eventually to perish because, even though no one attempts to kill it, it cannot live on forever. But for the soul to die is another matter, one of extreme misfortune. I do not have to point out to you the great care and solicitude we exercise in caring for the wounds of the body; we doctor them with the greatest of concern. And yet at the same time we woefully neglect the wounds of the soul. All of us are horrified at the sight of a dying body because we are able to witness it with our bodily eyes. Yet, since the death of the soul is something we cannot witness, there are very few who believe in it and even fewer who are actually frightened at the thought of it. I might point out that the death of the soul is certainly more frightful than the death of the body. This is evident enough from the fact that the soul is something far greater than the body, and God, whose loss it entails, is greater than the soul.

Let me give you some signs, some evidence, whereby you can determine whether or not your soul is diseased or perhaps even dead. If you are troubled with indigestion, if it is difficult to retain food, it is quite apparent that there is something physically wrong with your body. Now the Word of God has been referred to as the food of the soul. If it is unpalatable, if it nauseates you, there can be little doubt that the palate of your soul is infected with diseases. If food is not retained, if it does not proceed along the digestive tract, it is pretty clear that your soul is sick. When your knees totter and it is only with difficulty that you drag your ailing limbs about, it is quite evident that you have an ailing body. Now you must certainly have a disease of the soul when the performance of an act of piety is done with great reluctance and hesitancy, when you have no strength to bear up under a slight rebuke, or when the loss of a few pennies makes you troubled and angry. There can be no doubt that after the sight leaves the body, when the ears fail to hear and the whole body loses its sensitivity, then the soul has departed. When the eyes of the heart are so obscured that you cannot perceive the brightest light (that is, truth), when you are no longer aware with your inner ears of the divine voice, do you think your soul is really alive? You see your brother suffering indignities. Provided your own affairs are not endangered, your mind is not in the least moved. Why at this point does your soul feel absolutely nothing? It certainly must be because it is dead. Why dead? Because God, its very life, is not present. Where God is, there is charity, for God is charity. Otherwise, if you are a living member, how can any part of the body be in pain without your feeling anything?

Let me give you another sign that is even more certain. Supposing that you have deceived a friend, or that you have committed adultery; in other words, you should have received a major wound, and yet not only are you unaware of any pain, but you actually take pleasure in recalling your wickedness. Can there be any doubt that your soul is dead? We generally assume that the body is not alive if it is insensible to the prick of a pin. Can a soul be considered alive if it is unfeeling in this matter? Let us take another example. You happen to be in the company of someone who is using filthy language, who is raging in anger against his neighbor. If you think that his soul is alive, you are deceiving yourself. It is more like a stinking corpse whose foulness infects all who come near it. Christ referred to the Pharisees as whitened sepulchers. Why? Because they carried their dead souls about within themselves. The bodies of holy people are temples of the Holy Spirit. The bodies of evil men are sepulchers of dead corpses. No cadaver is so dead as that soul that has been abandoned by God. And certainly no corpse offends the nostrils of men to the extent that the evil odor of the buried soul offends the sensibility of the heavenly court. When dying words proceed from the heart, we can assume that a dead soul lies within. For, according to the saying of the Gospel, "the mouth speaks from the abundance of the heart," and if God, the life of the soul, is present, the soul will speak divine words.

If we read the Gospel, we find that the disciples once asked our Lord, "Whither shall we go? You have the words of life."

238

Why "words of life"? The only answer to be found is the fact that these words flowed from a soul that was never for a moment separated from the divinity and that alone restores us to everlasting life. It is not a rare thing that pious men have recalled a dead body to life. But we must never forget that God does not revive a dead soul except by an extraordinary and gratuitious power, and certainly He does not resuscitate it if it is already dead when it leaves the body. I think that we can agree that the sensation of death in the body is very slight or, at least, very brief. The sensation of death in the case of the soul is entirely different; it is more than death itself, because it is everlasting.

With these remarks in mind need I point out further the tremendous powers of our adversary? It would be sheer stupidity not to be aroused to this fearful danger and to take the necessary precautions against it. On the other hand you must avoid the pitfalls of losing courage or feeling unable to cope with the situation. For we must never forget that regardless of the strength of the enemy we have an ever-present and an all-powerful auxiliary. "If God is for us, who is against us?" If He sustains us, what can be lacking? We must be ever inflamed with the hope and conviction of final victory. Let us not forget that our encounter is not with an undefeated enemy but with one who was once broken and who many years ago was overthrown, despoiled, and led captive by Christ our Head. This same Christ will unquestionably subdue him again in us. If we but remember to whose Body we belong, we will triumph in the strength of our Head. No man is strong in his own strength. In Him alone will we find our real worth.

This is the reason why I reiterate that the outcome of this war is not in the least to be doubted. Victory is not something that depends upon chance; it is entirely in the hands of God and, through Him, also in our hands. Anyone who has failed in this struggle was simply lacking in a will to conquer. The kindness of our Leader has never failed anyone. If you but listen to His call and do your part, you will be assured of victory, for not only will He fight alongside you, but His very liberality will be imputed to you as merit. At the same time you must thank Him alone for the victory. He alone is immune from sin and He alone first oppressed its tyranny. Yet this victory will not come without your own effort and diligence, for He who said, "Have confidence, I have conquered the world," does not want your confidence to be a matter of complacency. Profiting by His example, we will fight as He fought. We must steer a middle course between Scylla and Charybdis, neither acting too presumptuously because we rely too much on divine grace, nor surrendering in despair because we are disheartened by the difficulties of war.

2. The weapons of Christian warfare

I think we can truthfully say that nothing is more important in military training than a thorough knowledge of the weapons to be employed and the nature of the enemy to be encountered. I would add to this that the need for preparedness, of having the weapons close at hand, is also of the utmost importance. In ordinary warfare it is customary that leave of absence or actual retirement to winter quarters brings about a cessation of hostilities from time to time. This is certainly not the case in the kind of warfare we are describing. We can never permit ourselves to be even a finger's length from our weapons. Since our enemy is incessant in his attacks, we must be constantly on the battle line, constantly in a state of preparedness. As a matter of fact, our enemy, when he appears peaceful, when he feigns flight or a truce, can at that very moment be assumed to be preparing for an attack. He is most dangerous when he appears peaceful, and it is during his violent attacks that we can actually feel most secure. It is for this reason that our primary concern must be to keep the mind armed. Our enemies are armed for no other purpose than to destroy us; surely we should not be ashamed to take up arms so as not to perish.

We will speak about Christian armor more in detail when we treat that subject later on. Meanwhile I would like to point out briefly two weapons that we should prepare to use in combating the chief vices. These weapons are prayer and knowledge. St. Paul clearly expresses the desire that men be continually armed when he commands us to pray without ceasing. Pure prayer directed to heaven is able to subdue passion, for it is, as it were, a citadel inaccessible to the enemy. Knowledge, or learning, fortifies the mind with salutary precepts and keeps virtue ever before us. These two are inseparable, the former imploring but the latter suggesting what should be prayed for. St. James tells us that we should pray always for faith and hope, seeking the things of salvation in Jesus' name. We may recall that Christ asked the sons of Zebedee if they really knew what they were praying for. We must always emphasize the dual necessity of both prayer and knowledge. In your flight from sin imitate Aaron as a model of prayer and Moses as an example of knowledge of the law. Neither allow your knowledge to lessen nor your prayer to become sterile.

Listen for a moment to what Christ has to say in Matthew's Gospel: "But in praying, do not multiply words, as the Gentiles do; for they think that by saying a great deal, they will be heard. So do not be like them; for your Father knows what you need before you ask Him." And St. Paul condemns ten thousand words spoken with the lips in favor of five uttered in understanding. Moses spoke nothing yet he heard the words, "Why do you call after me?" It is not the loud sound of the mouth, but rather the pleas of an ardent soul that reach the divine ear. Try to let this be a practice with you: When the enemy assaults you and the other vices give you trouble, lift up your mind to heaven and in your faith do not fail to raise up your hands also. Perhaps the best remedy in this matter is to be continually occupied with works of piety so that you will revert, not to wordly affairs, but to Christ.

You must believe me when I say that there is really no attack from the enemy, no temptation so violent, that a sincere resort to Holy Writ will not easily get rid of it. There is no misfortune so sad that a reading of the Scripture does not render bearable. Therefore, if you will but dedicate yourself entirely to the study of the Scriptures, if you meditate day and night on the divine law, nothing will ever terrorize you and you will be prepared against any attack of the enemy.

I might also add that a sensible reading of the pagan poets and philosophers is a good preparation for the Christian life. We have the example of St. Basil, who recommends the ancient poets for their natural goodness. Both St. Augustine and St. Jerome followed this method. St. Cyprian has worked wonders in adorning the Scriptures with the literary beauty of the ancients. Of course it is not my intention that you imbibe the bad morals of the pagans along with their literary excellence. I am sure that you will nonetheless find many examples in the classics that are conducive to right living. Many of these writers were, of course, very good teachers of ethics. We have the example of Moses, who did not spur the advice of Jethro. These readings mature us and constitute a wonderful preparation for an understanding of the Scriptures. I feel this is quite important, because to break in upon these sacred writings without this preparation is almost sacrilegious. St. Jerome assails the presumption of those who, even though they may be learned in other fields, presume to expatiate on the Bible. You can imagine the audacity of those who, having no preparation whatsoever, try to do the same thing.

We must not persist in clinging to the letter, and the reading of Homer and Virgil will be of no use unless we look to its allegorical side. If you like the classics, then you will understand what I mean. If the obscene passages in the ancients bother you, then by all means refrain from reading them. Of all the philosophical writings I would recommend the Platonists most highly. For not only their ideas but their very mode of expression approaches that of the Gospels. Of course they should be read in a cursory manner, and whatever is of real value in them should be applied and referred to Christ. If to the pure of heart all things are clean, then to the impure everything appears to be unclean. Whenever the reading of secular selections arouses your baser appetites, then leave them alone.

Reading the Scriptures with a clean heart is a basic rule. It prevents what is intended to be medicinal from becoming noxious. You must maintain at all times a high regard for the revealed word. It is genuine because it has its origin in the very mind of God. If you approach the Scriptures in all humility and with regulated caution, you will perceive that you have been breathed upon by the Holy Will. It will bring about a transformation that is impossible to describe. You will perceive the delights of the Blessed Bridegroom; you will see the riches of Solomon. The hidden treasures of eternal wisdom will be yours. Yet I would caution you. The entrance to this abode of wisdom is narrow. The doorway is low, and there is danger in not stooping when you enter. There is nothing that you can believe with greater certitude than what you read in these writings. The senses themselves cannot offer greater certainty. Divine revelation has made it clear that heaven and earth will not pass away before all that is contained therein is fulfilled. Man may lie and make mistakes; the truth of God neither deceives nor is deceived.

Let me mention another requirement for a better understanding of Holy Scripture. I would suggest that you read those commentators who do not stick so closely to the literal sense. The ones I would recommend most highly after St. Paul himself are Origen, Ambrose, Jerome, and Augustine. Too many of our modern theologians are prone to a literal interpretation, which they subtly misconstrue. They do not delve into the mysteries, and they act as if St. Paul were not speaking the truth when he says that our law is spiritual. There are some of these theologians who are so completely taken up with these human commentators that they relegate what the Fathers had to say to the realm of dreams. They are so entranced with the writings of Duns Scotus that, without ever having read the Scriptures, they believe themselves to be competent theologians. I care not how subtle their distinctions are; they are certainly not the final word on what pertains to the Holy Spirit.

If your interest in sacred doctrine revolves more about what is vital and dynamic rather than merely dialectical, if you incline more toward what moves the inner man than to what leads to empty arguments, then read the Fathers. Their deep piety has withstood the test of time. Their very thoughts constitute a prayerful meditation, and they penetrate into the very depths of the mysteries they propound. I do not mean to condemn modern theologians; I am merely pointing out that in view of our purpose, namely, a more practical piety, they are hardly to be recommended. Let us not forget that the Divine Spirit has its own manner of speaking and its own figures of speech. Learn these from the very outset. The Divine Wisdom speaks to us and, like an attentive mother, adjusts Her language to our infancy. For the tiny infants She provides milk and for the sick, herbs. To receive solid food you must grow up spiritually. She lowers Herself to your humility. You must raise yourself to Her sublimity. To remain like an infant is unfortunate. Unending illness reprehensible. Pluck the marrow from the broken bone: meditation upon a single verse gives more nourishment, brings more wisdom, than continued verbal repetition of the whole psalm.

I warn you with the more diligence because I know that this error has confused, not merely the crowd, but also those who in name and in garb claim perfect religion. These people believe the greatest piety is repeating as many psalms as possible every day, though they scarcely understand them. On every side monastic piety grows cold, languishes, and disappears because the monks grow old and gray in the letter of the Scriptures rather than maturing to a spiritual understanding. They fail to hear Christ proclaiming in the Gospel, "The flesh profits nothing, it is the spirit that gives life." We know the law is spiritual. Spiritual things should not be made carnal. In times past the Father was worshipped in the mountains. Now He wants to be worshipped in the spirit.

I do not want to be misunderstood. I by no means despise the weakness of those who, from feebleness of mind, do the only things they are able to do. Certain words in magic rituals are thought efficacious even when those who pronounce them do so without understanding them. Likewise, divine words, though little understood, should be believed beneficial for those who speak or hear them in sincere faith and pure affection. The angels who are present bring assistance. Nor, indeed, does Paul condemn those who sing in the spirit or those who speak in tongues. But he does urge a fuller use of graces. Of course there is no shame for those prevented from better things by vice, not of the mind, but of nature. As St. Paul has said, "Let not him who eats despise him who does not eat; and let not him who does not eat judge him who eats."

However, I do not want you who are better endowed to remain content with the barren letter. Rather, I want you to pass on to the more profound mysteries. Strengthen yourself with frequent prayer, until He who holds the key of David, who closes and no one opens, will open for you the book sealed with the seven seals—the secrets of the Father, which no one knows except the Son and he to whom the Son deigns to reveal them.

But how should you pray? I intended to describe a way of life, not a method of learning. Yet I deviated a bit to point out an arsenal of weapons that you could profitably use in this new type of warfare. So pick out from pagan books whatever is best. In studying the ancients follow the example of the bee flying about the garden. Like the bee, suck out only what is wholesome and sweet; reject what is useless and poisonous. Follow this rule, and your mind will be better clothed. Then you will enter into the battle of daily life better armed. Nonetheless, whenever you find truth and virtue, refer it to Christ. If you wish to consult the treasure house of Paul, that valiant captain, there you will discover "that the weapons of our warfare are not of the flesh, but are mighty before God for the destruction of fortifications, destroying counsels and every height that tends to bar the knowledge of God." You will find the weapons of God by which you can endure an evil day. On your right you will find the arms of justice, on your left the armor of truth, the breastplate of justice, and the shield of faith, a shield with which you can ward off the fiery darts of the devil. You will find also the helmet of salvation and the sword of the spirit, which is the word of God. Carefully fortified with these weapons, a man can fearlessly utter those courageous words of Paul: "Who shall separate us from the love of Christ? Shall tribulation, or distress, or famine, or peril, or persecution, or the sword?" See the many enemies the devil directs and how frightened they are at everything. But hear something stronger. Paul adds, "But in all these things we conquer because of Him who has loved us. For I am sure that neither death, nor life, nor angels, nor principalities, nor powers, nor things present, nor any other creatures shall be able to separate us from the love of God which is in Christ Jesus." What a happy confidence the arms of light give to Paul, an insignificant man who called himself a castoff of the world!

But to return to our original purpose. We must forge a handy weapon, an *enchiridion,* a dagger, that you can always carry with you. You must be on guard when you eat or sleep, even when you travel in the course of worldly concerns and perhaps become weary of bearing this righteous armor. Never allow yourself to be totally disarmed, even for a moment, lest your wily foe oppress you. Do not be ashamed to carry this little sword with you. For it is neither a hardship to bear nor useless in defending yourself. Though it is a small weapon, it will enable you, if you use it skillfully, to withstand the enemy's tumultuous assaults quite easily and avoid a deadly wound. Now is the time for us to teach ourselves a kind of "manual of arms." I

promise that, if you diligently train yourself in it, our sovereign
Lord, Jesus Christ, will transfer you, rejoicing and victorious,
from this garrison to the city of Jerusalem, where there is neither
tumult nor war at all, but everlasting peace and perfect tranquillity. Meanwhile all hope of safety should be placed in your arms
and your armor.

3. The crown of wisdom is that you know yourself; and of the two sorts of wisdom, false and true

Peace is the highest good to which even the lovers of the
world turn all their efforts. As has been said, however, their
peace is a false one. It is this same sort of peace that the philosophers promise to those who follow their teachings. Christ alone
grants that peace that the world cannot give. There is but one
way to attain it; we must wage war with ourselves. We must contend fiercely with our vices. God, our peace, is separated from
these enemeies by an implacable hatred. His nature is virtue itself.
He is the parent and author of all virtue. The dregs drawn from
every kind of vice are called folly by the staunchest defenders
of virtue, the Stoics. Scripture labels this folly malice. Among
all these writers absolute probity is called wisdom. Does not the
oracle of the wise man say "wisdom conquers malice"? The father and prince of malice is that ruler of darkness, Belial. Anyone
who follows his leadership, walking in the night, hastens to eternal
night. On the contrary, the author of wisdom, and Himself Wisdom, Christ Jesus, who is the true Light, alone shatters the night
of earthly folly. He is the Splendor of paternal glory, who, as
He was made the redemption and justification for us reborn in
Him, so also was made Wisdom, as Paul testifies: "We preach
Christ crucified, to the Jews a stumbling block, and to the Gentiles foolishness; but to them that are called, both Jews and
Greeks, Christ is the Power of God and the Wisdom of God."
Through this Wisdom, by His example, we are able to triumph
over the malice of the enemy. If we are wise in Him, in Him also
shall we conquer. Make the most of this Wisdom. Embrace it!
You must set at naught the wisdom of the world, which bears a
false title and shows itself only to fools. For St. Paul there is no
greater foolishness in the sight of God than worldly wisdom; it
must be forgotten by him who would be truly wise. If any man

among you seems to be wise in this world, let him be known as a fool, for the wisdom of this world is foolishness with God. It is written, "I will destroy the wisdom of the wise, and the prudence of the prudent I will reprove." Where is the wise man, where is the subtle lawyer, where is the searcher of this world? Has not God made the wisdom of this world foolishness?

I doubt not that these wise fools now trouble you hatefully. These blind leaders of the blind shout that you are raving mad. They become hysterical because you are preparing to go over to Christ's side. Merely in the name are they Christians. In all other respects they are first mockers and then attackers of Christ's teachings. Beware lest you be swayed by the blindness of those whose blindness ought to be pitied and deplored rather than imitated. For what is this preposterous kind of wisdom that is so cautious and skillful in worthless things and nothingness? Indeed, it is employed for wicked ends. Furthermore, it is no wiser than a dumb beast in those things that alone pertain to our salvation. Paul wishes us to be wise, but in what is good; simple in what is evil. These are wise that they may act evilly; they know not how to be good.

The eloquent Greek poet Hesiod judges those who, though they lack wisdom themselves, still refuse to accept good advice to be useless. In what class must we place those who, despite the fact that they are perniciously foolish themselves, never cease to disturb, to mock, and to hinder those who have recovered their senses? But shall not the mockers be mocked? He who dwells in the heavens shall mock them, and our Lord shall laugh them to scorn. We read in the Book of Wisdom, "They shall see and shall despise him, but God shall mock them." To be mocked by evil men is, as it were, to be praised. Their worldly wisdom leads inevitably to false presumption, which is followed by blindness of the mind, slavery to base appetites, and all other species of vice. The bad habits developed in this manner produce a dullness or insensibility of the mind, and the victim no longer considers himself a sinner. The climax of this gradual process of degradation is a sudden and unprovided-for death, which is followed by death everlasting.

But of the wisdom of Christ, which the world considers foolishness, we read, "All good things came to me together with her, and innumerable honors came to me through her hands. And I rejoiced in all of these for this wisdom went before me and I knew not that she was the mother of them all." She brings as her companions modesty and gentleness. Gentleness enables you to receive the divine Spirit, for the Spirit rejoices to rest upon a humble and gentle person. While there, it will imbue your minds with its sevenfold grace; it will produce an abundant crop of virtues that will bear blessed fruits—especially that inner or secret joy that is known only to those who have experienced it and that, in the end, neither vanishes nor is destroyed, but is gathered up into eternal joy. My brother, you ought, in accordance with James' admonition, to seek this wisdom from God with the most ardent intentions and, according to a certain wise man, to "dig it out" from the veins of Divine Scripture "like treasures."

The crown of this God-given wisdom is to know yourself, a maxim that the ancients belived sent from heaven and in which the great authors took enormous delight, holding it to epitomize the fullness of wisdom. However, let even this have little weight among you if it does not agree with Scripture. The mystical lover in Canticles threatens his bride, ordering her to depart unless she know herself: "If you know not yourself, O beautiful among women, go forth and follow after the sheep of your flock." No one should hold the fantastic opinion that he knows himself well enough. Might I not also question whether anyone knows his body completely or, indeed, whether anyone will truly recognize a habit of mind? Even Paul, whom God so loved that He revealed to him the mysteries of the third heaven, dared not to judge himself. He would undoubtedly have done so had he known himself well enough. If such a man, a man so spiritual that he could judge all things without himself being judged by anyone, knew himself so little, in what are we carnal folk to put our faith? Surely a soldier who knows neither his own forces nor those of the enemy is quite useless. Yet our war is not between man and man, but within ourselves: The hostile battle lines spring forth in opposition to us from our very flesh itself. A friend is distinguished from an enemy by such a fine line that there is great danger of inadvertently defending an enemy as a friend, or attacking a friend thinking him to be an enemy. Our notorious enemy always takes on the appearance of an angel of light. We need always ask, "Are you one of ours or one of our adversaries?" Since you must war with yourself and since the first hope of victory lies in whether you know yourself as much as possible, I shall not put before you a kind of likeness of yourself so that you may plainly know what is within and what is merely skin-deep.

4. Of the outer and inner man

Man is a very complex creature composed of several contending parts: a soul, which may be likened to a sort of divine will, and a body, comparable to a dumb beast. Insofar as the body is concerned we do not surpass the dumb beasts; indeed, we are inferior to them in every bodily endowment. In regard to the soul we are capable of divinity, that is, we may climb in flight above the minds of the very angels themselves and become one with God. If you did not possess a body, you would be but a spirit; if you were not endowed with a mind, you would be but a beast. The greatest craftsman of all has joined together in happy concord these two diverse natures, but the serpent, hating peace, has split them in unhappy discord. Now they can neither be separated without the greatest suffering nor live together without constant war. Either of these natures might well say to the other, "I cannot live either with you or without you." They contend with one another to such an extent that one would think that they were utterly incompatible, but they are, in reality, one. Inasmuch as the body is itself visible, it delights in things visible; inasmuch as it is mortal, it follows things temporal; inasmuch as it is heavy, it sinks downward. On the contrary, the soul, mindful of its celestial nature, struggles strenuously against the weight of the earthly body to press upward. It distrusts things seen because it knows such things to be transient. It seeks only those things that are true and everlasting. The immortal loves things immortal; the heavenly, things heavenly. Like takes to like unless it be too deeply immersed in the sordid things of the body. The resulting contagion may cause it to lose its natural gentleness. Neither the fabled Prometheus nor nature itself has implanted this discord, but sin, evilly corrupting what has been well founded, has sown the poisonous seeds of dissension between these two natures that formerly dwelt together in peace. In the past the mind commanded the body without trouble, and the body obeyed freely and willingly. Now, with the natural order of things disturbed, the passions of the body seek to override the reason, and reason is compelled, in a sense, to forsake its direction.

Man, hampered as he is by this perplexing division, may be compared to an unruly state. Such a state is composed of various sorts of men whose dissensions create frequent disturbances and factions. To prevent strife the greatest power must be given to one supreme authority, and this authority must be of such a nature that it commands nothing that is not for the welfare of the state. To this end it is necessary for him who is wiser to govern, while he who is less wise ought to obey. No one is more lacking in sense than the lower classes, and for this reason they should obey the magistrate and not hold office themselves. The king, it is true, should consult the nobility, or the greater by birth, but the final decision must remain in his hands. He should sometimes be warned, but he should never allow himself to be forced or led.

In man, reason discharges the office of king. His nobles may be considered to be certain bodily, but not brute, affections. These include: true piety toward parents, charity toward brothers, benevolence toward friends, compassion for those who are afflicted, fear of dishonor, desire for an honest reputation, and like qualities. Consider the dregs of the lower classes to be those affections or passions that dissent as much as possible from the decrees of reason and that are least humble. These are lust, lechery, envy, and similar diseases of the mind, which we ought to resist as overseers restrain dirty, vile slaves so as to ensure that they perform the tasks assigned them by the master, or, at least, so as to prevent them from doing harm. The divinely inspired Plato wrote of all these things in his *Timaeus*.

The proper endowments of kings are: first, that they be as wise as possible so that they do not go amiss through error or lack of knowledge; then, that they do only those things they know to be good and right and that they do not will, falsely and corruptly, anything contrary to the dictates of reason. Whoever lacks either of these two qualities judge to be not a king but a usurper.

5. Of the diversity of passions

Though our king, reason, may at times be oppressed, he cannot be corrupted without protesting. He will be able to recover because of the eternal law that has been divinely engraven upon him. If the rest of the common people will obey him, he will do nothing either pernicious or that should be repented. He will do all things with the greatest moderation and the greatest calmness. While the Stoics and Peripatetics disagree on the subject of the affections, they both agree that we should be guided by reason rather than by passion. The Stoics believe that, when those passions that are most closely connected with the senses have educated you to the point of being able to discriminate between what is to be avoided and what is to be sought, then those passions are to be discarded. They not only regard them as useless for the further pursuit of knowledge, but they consider them to be actually pernicious. For this reason they contend that the truly wise man must be free of all passions of this sort as diseases of the mind. Indeed, they scarcely wish to concede to the perfectly wise man those primary and more human impulses which precede the reason and which they call fantasies. On this point the Peripatetics disagree: they teach that the passions are not to be completely destroyed but merely subdued, for they consider them to be of value as incentive to virtue. Thus they regard anger as the incentive to fortitude and envy as the incentive to industry. Socrates, in the *Phaedo* of Plato, appears to agree with the Stoics when he says that philosophy is nothing more than a meditation upon death, that is, a withdrawal of the mind, as much as possible, from corporal and sensible things, and a dedication to those things that can be perceived only by reason.

Therefore, it is fitting, first, that we come to recognize the inclinations of the mind, and then that we realize that none of them is so violent that it cannot be restrained by reason or redirected toward virtue. Everywhere I hear the harmful opinion that men are compelled to vice. And there are others who, because of their ignorance of their own natures, follow those passions believing them to be the precepts of reason. Because anger or envy has prompted them, they think they have acted from zeal for God. As one state is more strife-ridden than another, so, too, is one person more prone to virtue than another. However, this difference proceeds, not from any mental differences, but either from the influence of heavenly bodies, or from their ancestors, or from their upbringing, or from the complexion of the body itself. Socrates' fable of the good and bad charioteers and the good and bad horses is no old wives' tale. There are some who are born with such a moderate temper and who are so easy to get along with that they incline toward virtue without any virtue at all. They even seem to hurry on of their own accord without any prodding whatsoever. For others the rebellious body can scarcely be subdued with the roughest rein, goad, or spur, so like to a ferocious, untamed, bucking horse is it. If such happens to be your lot, do not immediately abandon the struggle, but persevere with greater determination. Convince yourself, not that the path of virtue is closed to you, but that a richer means of virtue has been offered you. If, instead, you are endowed with a gentle mind, do not consider yourself to be better than another. You are merely more fortunate, and more fortunate in such a way that you are under greater obligation. Furthermore, who is so fortunate in disposition that there are not a great many things in which he needs to struggle?

Therefore, reason must especially guard that in which one feels most vulnerable. Certain vices appear to be most characteristic of certain nations. Thus deceit is a common vice among some people, gluttony among others, and lechery among still others. These vices accompany certain bodily habits, as for example, effeminacy and love of pleasure with the sanguine; anger, ferocity, and evil tongues with the quick-tempered; inactivity and sluggishness with the phlegmatic; envy, sadness, and bitterness with the melancholic. Some of these passions either slacken or increase with age. For example, in youth there is lust, prodigality, and rashness, while in old age there is niggardliness, moroseness, and avarice. There are also passions that seem to be related to sex. For example, men are characterized by ferocity; women by vanity and desire for revenge. Meanwhile, nature, as if to make amends, compensates certain diseases of the mind with certain virtues. Thus this person is prone to pleasure, but at the same time he is not at all irascible or envious; another person is of uncorrupted modesty, but is prouder, more irascible, and more worldly. Nor is there any lack of those who are troubled by such great and fatal vices as theft, sacrilege, and homicide. Every effort must be made to combat these, and a firm wall of definite purpose must be built against their exertions. On the other hand there are certain passions that are so similar to virtue that there is danger lest we be deceived by the doubtful distinction between them. These ought to be corrected in such a manner as to turn them toward the nearby virtue. To give an example, a person who is quite irascible should throw a rein over his mind, and he will be eager, not the least bit sluggish, and he will walk erect. He will be free and simple. Another person is somewhat grasping; let him exercise his reason and he will be frugal. Let him who is inflexible become constant. Let him who is sad become serious-minded. Let him who is tactless become courteous. Other light diseases of the mind should be directed to similar ends. We must be on our guard, however, lest we cloak a vice of nature with the name of a virtue, calling sadness gravity, harshness justice, envy zeal, niggardliness thrift, adulation friendship, scurrility urbanity.

This then is the only road to happiness: first, know yourself; do not allow yourself to be led by the passions, but submit all things to the judgment of the reason. Be sane and let reason be wise, that is, let it gaze upon decent things.

You say that it is difficult to put this advice into practice. Who denies it? Plato has a fitting saying: "Those things which are beautiful are also difficult." Nothing is harder than for a man to conquer himself, but there is no greater reward or blessing. St. Jerome expresses this thought very clearly, just as he does all others. No one is happier than the Christian to whom is promised the Kingdom of Heaven. No one is more burdened than he who must fear for his life every day. No one is stronger than he who conquers the devil. No one is weaker than he who is overcome by the desires of the flesh. If you carefully weigh your own strength, you will say that there is nothing more difficult than to subject the flesh to the spirit; but if you are mindful of God as your helper, there is nothing easier. Assume a perfect life as your goal; having done so, pursue it in a spirit of determination. The human mind has never strongly commanded itself to do anything it has failed to accomplish. One of the most essential elements of Christianity is a willingness to be and to act as a Christian. This rule of conduct may appear to be too difficult to accomplish at first, but in the process of time it will become easy and, with persistence, actually a pleasure. As the poet Hesiod declares, "The way of virtue is difficult at first, but after you have arrived at the summit there is perfect tranquillity." There is no beast so ferocious that he cannot be tamed by human effort. Can it be that there is no power to tame that agent that is the tamer of all things? In order to train the body you are able to abstain from overindulgence in drink and to give up the company of women for certain periods of time. Why, then, can you not sacrifice a few months to gain control of your evil inclinations? You must do all things necessary to save your body, as well as your soul, from eternal death.

6. Of the inner and outer man and his two parts as found in Holy Scripture

It is always a great source of embarrassment to me to realize that the great majority of those who bear the name Christian act for the most part as if they were dumb beasts. Most of them are such slaves to their baser appetites that in this spiritual combat they are unable to distinguish between the dictates of reason and the promptings of passion. They actually believe that they are behaving in a reasonable manner so long as they act upon what they feel or see. In fact, they consider that alone to have existence which is perceptible to the senses. Their only criterion for right or wong is that which appeals to their desires. What they mean by peace is in reality a deplorable state of servitude. Entirely bereft of reason, they follow heedlessly wherever their selfish interests lead. This is that false and unhappy peace that Christ, the Author of peace, who will one day reward us, has come to do away with. He accomplishes this by stirring up a wholesome war between father and son, husband and wife, and between those things that weak arguments have attempted to reconcile.

I think it is agreed that the authority of the philosophers rests upon the fact that they state what is contained in a different manner in the Scriptures. What the philosophers term "reason" St. Paul calls either "the spirit" or "the inner man" or occasionally the "law of the mind." What they refer to as the "passions" he calls "the flesh," "the body," "the outer man," or "the law of the members." He says, for example, "Walk in the Spirit, and you shall not fulfill the lusts of the flesh. For the flesh lusts against the flesh . . . so that you do not the things you would." And again: "If you live according to the flesh you will die; if, however, you mortify the flesh by the spirit, you will live." Certainly this is a new order of things; to seek peace in war, war in peace, life in death, death in life, freedom in slavery, slavery in freedom. Listen to what Paul says of freedom: "But if you are led by the Spirit, you are not under the law. We have not received the spirit of adoption, as sons of God." We read also in St. Paul concerning "the outer man who is corrupt and the inner man who is renewed from day to day." Plato distinguished two souls in one man. In the same way, Paul describes two men so joined in one that both of them will be together in eternal glory or eternal damnation. They cannot be separated. The death of one cannot be the life of the other. What Paul writes to the Corinthians is, I believe, also pertinent: "The first came from the earth and is terrestrial. The second came from heaven and is celestial." And to make this even more clear he applies this duality not only to Christ and to Adam but to ourselves as well. "As was the earthy man, such also are the earthy; and as is the heavenly man, such also are the heavenly. Therefore, even as we have borne the likeness of the earthy, let us bear also the likeness of the heavenly. This I say, brethren, because flesh and blood can obtain no part of the kingdom of God, neither will corruption have any part in incorruption."

I think you can see how evident it is that Paul, who elsewhere spoke of the "flesh" and the "outer or corruptible man," here calls him the "earthy Adam." This is certainly the "body of death" about which Paul so frequently speaks. "Unhappy man that I am, who will deliver me from the body of this death?" Pointing out a far different fruit of the flesh and spirit, he writes elsewhere: "For he who sows in the flesh will also reap corruption but he who sows in the Spirit will reap life everlasting." We know that a messenger of Satan came to trouble Paul in the flesh. When the tempter refused to leave him, God gave him this answer: "Paul, my grace is sufficient for thee." For strength is made perfect in weakness. This certainly is a new sort of remedy.

Lest Paul be proud, he is tempted by pride. That he might be made firm in Christ, he is forced to be infirm. For he carried the treasure of heavenly revelations in a vessel of clay, that the sublimity might reflect the power of God, and not his own power. There are, of course, many other examples in the writings of St. Paul that indicate how we are to overcome temptation. Our first recourse in any kind of temptation is to implore the assistance of Almighty God. In fact, those who are well advanced on the road to perfection will actually welcome these temptations, for they guard virtue and, especially, form a bulwark against the danger of vanity that often lurks in the midst of the virtues. We might compare this vanity to the Herculean hydra because it is so difficult to destroy. Let us follow the example of the holy patriarch Jacob in this struggle against sin. He teaches us to persevere during the dark night of struggle until the dawn of divine assistance shines forth. Like him, let us say to God, "I will not let go until you bless me. . . ." The reward that this great wrestler with evil obtained contains a message for all of us. In the first place God blessed him on the very spot. This shows that after we overcome a temptation graces are immediately granted us so that we can resist the next attack. Furthermore, we read that God and the angel then smote Jacob so that henceforth he was lame in one foot. This was, of course, to show that God curses those who attempt to serve two masters. From that time Jacob walked only on the right root, that is to say, he walked in the spirit. Even his name was changed, and from a highly active person he was transformed into a contemplative. In like manner, after you have overcome temptation and crucified your flesh with its evil desires, you will find true peace and tranquillity, and you will see that the Lord is sweet. God is never perceived in the midst of temptation, but once the tempest subsides, we will bask in the sunshine of spiritual consolation. Examine yourself in all honesty. If you are flesh alone, you will not see God, you will not be saved. Make it your determined effort, then, to become spiritual.

Fulton John Sheen
1895-

The name of Fulton J. Sheen has been well known to
Americans, Catholic, Protestant and Jew, for several decades.
His popular weekly television program served as a powerful
vehicle to present religious concepts to a vast audience throughout the nation. And long before the era of television, his books
were already well received, particularly in Catholic circles.

Sheen's talent for presenting traditional ideas in an imagi-
native and attractive style won him a large following among
both clergy and laity. His excellent education, which included a
Doctorate of Philosophy from the University of Louvain in
Belgium, exposed him not only to the intellectual tradition of
Thomas Aquinas but to the writings of contemporary philosophers as well.

Underlying his popular writing and speaking style one
detects a deep devotion to the Thomistic tradition of philosophy
and theology. While admitting that there is some good to be
found in contemporary ideas, he tends to be critical of modern
movements in philosophy and theology.

During the several decades preceding the Second Vatican
Council, it made sense to the majority of Catholics to insist on
holding to the old way of things and on looking askance at what
could be tagged modern. Within this atmosphere, Sheen's
approach to moral questions was quite natural. The eternal

principles were sound, mankind had only to get a clear knowledge of them and then live them out. Moral theories suggesting that man can create his own moral codes were obviously inaccurate. The new thinking and the new morality would come and go; the old doctrine would remain unshaken.

Perhaps this approach was too close to the discovery of the magnificent theories of evolution and relativity to realize that these discoveries called for a radical review of all human morality, that one could no longer appeal to the intellectual structures of previous centuries, that it would not suffice to dress the old tradition in new garments, and that man had entered a new epoch in history. Perhaps it was too close also to the two great wars that shattered forever the foundations of western morality and put twentieth century man in the position, not of rebuilding the old morality, but of creating an entirely new one.

We have selected passages from Sheen's Old Errors and New Labels, *which was published in 1931. It will give the reader an idea of the outlook common among Catholic teachers toward the realm of morals. Awareness of this outlook makes it possible to understand why, during the 1960s, Catholicism experienced panic and threat when Pope John XXIII opened the windows of the Church to the modern world.*

OLD ERRORS AND NEW LABELS

ETHICS FOR THE UNETHICAL

There should be a vacation for certain overworked words, and in particular the word "crisis." What "service" is to a Kiwanis booster, the words "crisis" is to moralists. This latter class have used it so often as to prove without doubt that Stevenson was right in saying that not by bread alone do men live but principally by catchwords. It is hardly possible to pick up a magazine to-day without reading an article by some self-styled ethicist on "The Crisis in Morals."

The repeated use of the word "crisis" in reference to morals is interesting, for it reveals a tendency on the part of many modern writers to blame the abstract when the concrete is really at fault. They speak, for example, of the problem of crime, rather than of the criminal; of the problem of poverty, rather than of the poor; and of the "crisis in morals," when really the crisis is amongst men who are not living morally. The crisis is not in ethics but in the unethical. The failure is not in the law, but in the law-breakers. The truth of this observation is borne out by the failure of such writers to distinguish between the problem of making men conform to standards and that of making standards conform to men. Instead of urging men to pass the test, they alter the test. Instead of inspiring them to hold to their ideals, they change the ideals. In accordance with this logic, they urge that morals be changed to suit those who cannot live morally, and that ethics be changed to please those who cannot live ethically. All this takes place in accordance with the democratic principle of certain philosophers, who are prepared to construct any kind of philosophy that man desires. If men want ghosts, the democratic philosophers, who know the will of the populace, will write a philosophy justifying ghosts; if the man in the street wants to follow the line of least moral resistance, philosophers will develop for him the justifying philosophy of "self-expression"; if the man of affairs has no time for the thoughts of eternity, then philosophers develop for him the philosophy of "space-time."

There are ultimately only two possible adjustments in life: one is to suit our lives to principles; the other is to suit principles to our lives. "If we do not live as we think, we soon begin to think as we live." The method of adjusting moral principles to the way men live is just such a perversion of the due order of things. Just suppose this logic were applied in the class-room. Boys and girls find it difficult to spell "knapsack" and "pneumonia," because the spelling of these words is not in the line of least phonetic resistance. Others, too, find it very hard to learn the multiplication table. Many a budding liberal mathematician cannot crush the urge to say that three times three equals six. Now here is a real "crisis" in spelling and mathematics, a kind of intellectual anarchy much akin to the moral anarchy described by our intelligentsia. How meet the "crisis"? One way to meet it is the way to meet any crisis, that is, by criticism; the other way to meet it is to write a new speller and a new mathematics entitled "A Preface to Spelling" or "Crisis in Mathematics." This is precisely what has taken place in the field of morals. Instead of making men conform to principles of morality, they change the principles. This kind of philosophy would never have permitted the Prodigal Son to return to his father's house. It would have settled the "crisis" by finding a new and handsome name for the husks he was throwing to the swine, and called it "progress away from antiquated modes of morality."

All the books and articles on "the crisis in morality" touch on three points: the nature of morality, its origin, and its test. In discussing the general nature of morality, most authors reduce it to convention or tastes. But before arriving at that conclusion they seem to sense the inadequacy of the very solution they propose, and one of them makes this rather excellent observation: "Social conventions change: the particular actions calculated to suit them change with them, as, e.g., if the rule of the road were changed in England we should drive on the right instead of the left. But the quality required for the right action does not change. It is just as important to drive carefully and considerately whatever the law of the road may be. The driver who says, 'First they say "left," then they say "right"; it is all a mess and I am free to be a road-hog' is indulging in a false argument."

So far, so good. But he immediately falls into the very logical pitfall he had asked others to avoid, for he makes two diametrically opposed moral principles akin to the convention of driving on the right or left side of the road. He writes: "So monogamy and polygamy are social conventions." In other words, for him there is no more difference between a moral system that permits a man to have many wives, than there is between a traffic system that permits vehicles to drive on the right and another that permits vehicles to drive on the left. Now this is very poor logic. The difference between monogamy and polygamy is not the difference between the right side of the road and the left side of the road; it is a question of different roads, for monogamy is a one-road marriage, and polygamy is a boulevard. One could still be traveling in the proper direction whether he drove to the right as in America or to the left as in England. But he would not be doing so if he took an entirely different road, or a wrong road. Such is polygamy in relation to morality.

We agree with this philosopher in saying that this conclusion is false: "First they say 'left,' then they say 'right'; it is all a mess and I am free to be a road-hog." Why, then, does he, who makes morality a convention, consent to make man a wife-hog, for such he does when he makes polygamy a matter of taste? If traffic laws and marriage laws are both conventions, why say the road-hog is wrong in one instance and not the wife-hog in the other instance? For the life of me, I cannot see why, if it is wrong to take up more than one half the road, it is not also wrong or more wrong to take up more than one better-half. Such authors' moral traffic needs regulation, and needs it badly.

Morality is evolutionary in its origin, according to this school of writers. This point is made in the following typical lines: "The point is that man, who has risen from the ape, has apparently done so by the help and guidance of this inward spirit which reject filth and denies it. It is not Victorian prudery, it is not Christian asceticism, it is not even the Hellenic tradition, which dislikes uncleanness, physical and moral; it is something that springs eternal in the nature of man."

There are enough errors in these two statements to make a comedy of errors. Space will permit us to indicate only a few. If man "has risen from the ape," he has certainly done so in time, and not in eternity. How then can the author in the very next sentence speak of something "that springs eternal in the nature of man"? If there is something eternal in the nature of man, then man was always man, and did not come from the ape. If he did come from the ape, how could there be any eternal springs in his nature as man? Man, it is said, has apparently risen from the ape by the "inward spirit." Now, if man arose from the beast by this "inward spirit," then the "inward spirit" was already in man before he sprang from the ape, and he was man before he was an ape. The spring that enables jack-in-the-box to come from the box is already there, and we cannot say that the spring evolved from the box. Such philosophy puts the rabbit in the silk hat and pulls it out by evolution. Granting evolution, how account for the origin of morality from the ape? Imagine two apes fighting or prepared to fight in accordance with the evolutionary law of the survival of the fittest. Call one ape A, the other B. When locked in a death struggle, ape B is suddenly seized by an "inward spirit" of charity and a brotherly feeling for his fellow-ape. The dawning of reason tells him that ape A has a right to life, liberty, and the pursuit of happiness. And so ape B, in accordance with this first flash of morality, desists from the combat. Ape A wins the struggle; ape B goes to the grave with his "inward spirit." The first moral idea is lost to the world, and what happened to ape B would happen to every other ape in ape-land, for feelings of charity could never survive in an animal kingdom where might is right. The animal with the "higher urge to morality" would always succumb, and thus it would be impossible for such ideas ever to enter humanity through animality.

The great difficulty with evolutionary morals is to account for the "inward spirit" of morality. If it comes from the animal, then the animal should act like man; then man can always be expected to act like an ape because he came from one. If the "inward spirit" comes from above, that is, from God, then man can always be expected to act like God, because made to His own image and likeness. It seems very far-fetched for any moralist to become concerned about a "crisis in morals" when his first principle is that man is only a glorified ape. The real crisis is not in morals but in logic—the logic that expects the amoral to produce the moral, and the monkey to produce the organ-grinder.

Finally, the new philosophy of morality offers æsthetics or "fastidiousness" as the test of morality. "As far as I can analyze my own feelings," one writes, "I should say that the motive which keeps me from a bad action is a feeling that as I contemplate it I do not like the look of it or the smell of it. I feel it to be ugly or foul or not decent—not the sort of thing with which I want to be associated. And, similarly, the thing that nerves me towards a good but difficult action is a feeling that it seems beautiful or fine, the sort of thing that I love as I look at it and would like to have for my own."

Here there is the false equation between feeling good and being good, and between feeling bad and being bad. What is wrong is not considered wrong but ugly, and what is right is not considered right but beautiful. The Scholastics were fond of saying that there is no disputing about tastes. The new morality would make taste the ground and foundation of morality. But the test of "fastidiousness" and "æsthetics" for morality leaves no basis for obligation. How apply it to debts? Will the bills at the end of the month be paid according to the principles of æsthetics or the principles of justice? Will only those statements printed on beautiful parchment receive our attention, while those printed on yellow fools-cap are left unpaid? Will the thief of the new moral generation be exonerated because he looks like John Gilbert or be condemned because he looks like Ben Turpin? Will it be wrong for a future Volsteadian generation to drink rye because it is colorless and right to drink creme de menthe because of its beautiful emerald color?

Suppose this test of morality were applied to international conflicts. According to its principles, it would be wrong to go to war with Turkey because one does not "like the looks of it," but it would be right to go to war with Switzerland because its Alpine heights are "beautiful." By the same æsthetic test, adultery would be wrong if Mr. Smith's wife has lost her "school-girl complexion," but would be right if she had the "skin you love to touch." Murder would be wrong only for the man who, "analyzing his feelings," admits he does not like "the smell of it," but it would be right for the one who reduced it to a fine art. What the new morality resolves itself into is this: You are wrong if you do a thing you do not feel like doing; and you are right if you do a thing you feel like doing. Such a morality is based not only on "fastidiousness," but on "facetiousness." The standard of morality then becomes the individual feeling of what is beautiful, instead of the rational estimate of what is right.

The "smell of a thing" may be a good test for garlic, but is not a good test for morality. "The sort of a thing that I love as I look at it" may be a good test for a sunset, but there can be no end to moral confusion worse confounded if it is going to justify a violation of the ninth commandment, "Thou shalt not covet thy neighbor's wife"—with Protestants part of the tenth commandment. In a word, the fundamental difficulty with this system of morals is that it is impossible to be wrong—unless, perchance, one disagrees with its æsthetics. A little less of æstheticism and a trifle more of asceticism would have made a happier morality. These moralists begin their search for a standard or test of morality with "human experience," or the "facts of life." In this they are right. Both Aristotle and St. Thomas Aquinas began their moral philosophy with both feet on the ground. First of all, they studied the way men lived and sought out their fundamental tendencies and aspirations. Thus far the French moralists of the Durkheim and Lévy-Bruhl school and the moralists under consideration are in agreement. Next, Aristotle and St. Thomas stated that these natural tendencies, such as the preservation of life, the propagation of life, and the self-expansion that results in private ownership, must be considered in relationship to the nature of man. But the nature of man is rational or intellectual. Here the modern moralists stop—they refuse to follow reason; "feelings" alone constitute the standard.

If the nature of a man is rational, then these tendencies must be judged rationally. But to judge anything rationally is to judge it in relation to the end or purpose for which it was created. A pen is to be judged by its capacity for writing, but that is why it was made; an eye is to be judged by its powers of vision, for that is the reason of its being. Man was made for a perfect fruition of his desire and striving for Life, Truth, and Love, which is God. Man, therefore, is to be judged in relation to this end, that is, in his submission to or rebellion against it. In other words, man has duties to God and God is entitled to them, for the same reason that every author is entitled to royalties on his books, because they are his creation. This fulfilment of our duties to God, this obedience to His will, which is synonymous with the perfect development of our whole nature, is the ground and basis of morality. Morality, then, is order in relation to an end. And that all things might tend to their own proper destiny, Almighty God has placed in the various hierarchies of creation an immanent law to guide them. The laws of nature, such as gravitation, chemical affinity, and the like direct the chemicals to the fulfilment of their natures. The laws of life, such as metabolism, guide plants to the perfection of their destiny. Instincts guide animals, and reason directs man. The practical reason of man that enables him to fit particular cases under the general principles touching his final destiny is conscience.

So, first, morality means a conscious relation between the nature of man and the goal of his being; and secondly, it entails an immanent principle of guidance in the work, which is conscience. The immanent law in creation below man is unconscious and necessary. Hence, an acorn works out its destiny naturally: it grows to be an oak. Man, however, is free to stunt his growth, and to choose another end than the efflorescence of his faculties in union with Perfect Love. If man chooses, he need not grow up to be an oak; he can remain a poor sapling or just a "poor sap." And that is what this new school of morality would make of each of us.

A PRE-FACE TO MORALS

When one has read one book on morals by any "new" thinker of our day, he has read them all. Two dominant ideas run through each of them: the first is the decay of old traditions through the advance of modern culture; the second is a plea for a new morality suitable to the way men live to-day. The first argument is generally couched in some such language as this: "We do not live in a patriarchal society. We do not live in a world that disposes us to believe in a theocratic government. And therefore in so far as moral wisdom is entangled with the promises of a theocracy, it is unreal to me. It is the unconscious assumption that we are related to God as creatures to a creator, as vassals to a king, as children to a father, that the acids of modernity have eaten away." All these things have ceased to be consistent with our normal experience of ordinary affairs. Men no longer believe seriously that they are governed from Heaven, and anarchy will result from all this confusion unless by conscious effort they find ways of governing themselves.

The second part of these books is generally consecrated to the elevation of Humanism to a system of morals. Starting with the premise that the history of every man is a history of his progress from infantilism to maturity, they conclude that a goal for moral effort can be found in the notion of maturity. "To replace the conception of man as the subject of a heavenly king, which dominates the ancestral order of life, humanism takes as its dominant pattern the progress of the individual from helpless infancy to self-governing maturity."

Maturity, then, is the goal of morals, and a successful passage from childhood to maturity means a breaking up and reconstruction of those habits which were appropriate only to our earliest experience. For example, when a childish disposition is carried over into an adult environment the result is a false valuation of that environment. The child-pattern is not the ideal. All this is another way of saying that when we become men we put away the things of a child. An infant knows neither vice nor virtue because it can respond only to that which touches it immediately. A man has virtue in so far as he can respond to a larger situation. "To have virtue then is to respond to larger situations and to longer stretches of time and without much interest in their immediate result in convenience or pleasure. It is to overcome the impulses of immaturity, to detach oneself from objects that preoccupy it and from one's own preoccupations." Morality, then, for the individual will be procured by working for society or the commonwealth. Each man will be supposed to adjust his will to the will of others instead of trusting to custom and organic loyalties. The individual will learn to crush his selfish nature by looking to the good of humanity, of which he is a part.

As the ideal of maturity as the goal of morals unfolds itself, new labels are found, such as "maturity," "detachment," and "disinterestedness," all names for the goal of Humanistic morality or "high religion," which "will untangle the moral confusion of the ego and make plain what we are really driving at in our manifold activity."

What is to be thought of this type of book? Two general criticisms occur to us, one referring to the section that deals with the "modernity" of the modern mind, the other referring to the second section, which treats of the new morals of "disinterestedness" or "maturity." We should say that the first part on the modern mind is too unmodern, and of the second part, that on the morals of "maturity," that it is too immature and the morals of "disinterestedness" are too selfish. When it is argued that the modern man can no longer live under the ancestral morality and the theocratic religions, and that a new morality must be found for him, one is really stating something very old and ancient. There are new men in the world, but there is still the "old man," in the sense that human nature has not changed. All such an author has done is to develop a man's lip-worship, or better still, to reburnish the Golden Calf.

Once upon a time, long before there were twentieth-century Modernists, Moses went up into the mountain to pray, and there he remained forty days and nights conversing with God. Now the people who were below—the really progressive people, who knew the thrill of fleshpots—became impatient with the authority of Moses and the ancestral idea of a Sovereign God, and so they besought Aaron, saying: "Make us gods that may go before us. For as to this Moses, the man that brought us out of the land of Egypt, we know not what has befallen him." This is the first part of the modern plea expressed in different words. What difference is there, except that of language? What difference is there between saying, "We know not what has befallen him" and, "The acids of modernity have melted away ancestral morality"? But to continue the story.

And so the people brought together their earrings and precious stones, and Aaron made for them a Golden Calf before which they fell down adoring, saying: "These are thy gods, O Israel, that have brought thee out of the land of Egypt," and they began in their maturity to become "disinterested" and "detached" from the God of Moses and wedded to the calf of Apis. Again, I must say there is little difference between Aaron's gathering a gold ring here and a gold earring there and melting them into a calf, and a modern Aaron's gathering a fragment from a psychologist here and a lesser fragment from a Freudian there, and fusing them into a modern Golden Calf called, say, "A Preface to Morals," and saying, "These are the gods that will bring us out of the darkness of old faiths and older creeds."

This reflection is passed apart from the intrinsic worth of the new morals advocated, which we shall pass on later. It is stated only to emphasize the truth that there are no "acids of modernity"; acids are what they were from the beginning of the world, whether they be sulphuric acid or the acid of skepticism. There is no such thing as modernity in thought; there is only antiquity with new labels, like new advertisements. Modernity belongs only to the world of mechanics, but there is nothing new in the world of morals. From the fall of the angels up until the crack of doom there have been and will be only two moral systems possible: one is to live the way we think, the other is to think the way we live. The latter has always been called the "modern" and the other the "ancient" or "ancestral," but the modernity is only a matter of new tags and new labels and not one of new enthusiasms. Speaking of tags, singular is the new label entitled "high religion." We have had "high adventures," "high hats," "high Anglicanism," "high-balls"—now we have "high religion." Metaphors from Alpine climbers only becloud the issue. If writers who use such metaphors cared for directness, honesty, and outspokenness, they would not say that "ancestral morality" is too antiquated; they would say it is too hard! Such complaints against traditional morality have done nothing new except give the complaint against Moses a "new complexion" in the sense that modern beauty-specialists advertise, "Which complexion will you wear to-day?" But they have not given it a new face—they have merely given a new label

268

to an old error. That is probably why such a work should be entitled "A Pre-face to Morals."

There is one fundamental criticism we would make of the morality of "maturity," and that is its immaturity; and one criticism of the morality of "disinterestedness," and that is its selfishness. It is well to remember that there are two kinds of maturity: physical maturity and spiritual maturity. Physical maturity is the full-orbed development of either the human organism or the body corporate in its material goings and comings. Spiritual maturity, however, is the perfection of spiritual faculties and the realization of all their tendencies and inclinations. The new morals provide for physical maturity in the sense that man, in his social relation with other men, is equipped with a principle that will enable him to reduce conflict, discord, and friction with other men to a minimum. Petty desires, which sometimes spoil the devoted scientist, selfish interests, which endanger social intercourse—all these are fairly well taken care of by a maturity of disinterestedness. But this is only a maturity of the material things round about us—men, affairs, business, social life. It is not a maturity about the things of the mind.

What provision does such a system make for the maturing of a mind which desires a love that does not end when a cold clod falls upon the object loved, but a love that is abiding and eternal; what provision does it make for the maturing of a mind that desires a truth which is not fragmentary like one found at the lower end of a microscope or the upper end of a telescope, but a truth that is pregnant with the intelligibility of the mysteries of life and death; what provision does it make for the maturing of a mind which craves for a life that never passes the last embrace from friend to friend, or crumbles the last cake at life's great feast, but a life ever throbbing and aglow with eternal heart-beats? No morality is moral that matures man only in his social relations and in his physical wants and leaves unnourished and underfed and embryonic those ideals which differentiate him from the animals and the stars. It tells us how we may grow mature physically, but it has left us as unguided children so far as spiritual maturity is concerned. It is a morality for the finite reaches of our body, but not for the spiritual reaches of our soul; it supplies a maturity for the man who goes to bed, eats, drinks, plays golf, attends conferences, reads newspapers, buys and sells, but it does not supply a maturity for the man who thinks thoughts beyond these things, who has remorse of conscience, who wonders what is beyond the stars, and who sits up nights pondering on truth and justice.

The goal of this morality is the clock and the calendar. It is the maturity that leads to overripeness, then mellowness, then death, then dissolution. And the most striking proof that it has not given a thought to the maturity of the spirit is that it applies the notion of maturity of the body only to the Standard Oil Company, the Senate, and sex—business, government, and marriage. In the cold pedestrian language of everyday life, that kind of morals can be summed up in this injunction: "Unless you become as old men, you cannot enter into the Kingdom of Heaven." It might have been well for it to have considered more at length a Man Who gave a religion and a morality based upon the paradox of the maturity of infancy, and which startled men out of physical maturity when He said: "Unless you become as little children, you cannot enter the Kingdom of Heaven."

Finally, the morals of "disinterestedness" are too selfish. By salvaging from the wreck of Christianity the doctrine of detachment, one can build up a system of morals that shows the individual the way out of individual selfishness but not the way out of *social* selfishness. It is all very true to say that "disinterestedness" in self is accomplished by greater concern for the social group, but what will free man from selfishness for the social group? It is all very well to free man from individual pettiness, but who will free him from social pettiness? This modern morality might be compared to a father who, being anxious to escape the inheritance-tax by an act of "disinterestedness," gives his property to his sons while he is living, only thereby to fall into the sin of group-selfishness.

Why, it may be asked, is such a moral system socially selfish? For the same reason that its individual morality is free from individual selfishness, namely, because it looks out to the good of something outside itself, namely, the good of the social group. Now how can the social group or society be freed from social selfishness? Only by looking out to a goal outside of society, or, in other words, by beginning to be disinterested in itself. When Our Divine Lord said: "Be not solicitous for your life, what you shall eat, nor for your body, what you shall put on," He was not stating only a moral doctrine. He was enunciating a principle of perfectly good hygiene. He was saying that the only way to develop self is to forget self; that the only way to grow physically mature is to think of other things besides halitosis, fallen arches, and pyorrhea, or better still to be "disinterested" in these things, and to look out to something outside self. Now thus far the new morality is perfectly sound: Interest in the group is the cure for individual selfishness.

Now, why should not the same principle hold for the group? To say that the group must be interested in itself is to say that the group must be selfish, for the common good is really common to all the members. If there is to be such a thing as "social disinterestedness," then the group, or society, must begin to think of other things besides itself, and one of those things is what Pilate thought about for many days until his death: "There is no power given to you except from above." To work truly for the good of society, one must be carried away by enthusiasm for something outside society. Humanism of itself is insufficient. Detachment from the individual can be accomplished by attachment to society, but detachment from society can be accomplished only by attachment to God. For this reason there never was enunciated a principle better destined to affect social disinterestedness than that of Him Who said: "Seek ye first the Kingdom of God and His justice and all these things will be added unto you."

Such a morality is good so far as it goes, but it does not go far enough. It explains bodily maturity but not spiritual maturity: it escapes individual selfishness but not social selfishness, and the reason is the same in both cases—it has refused to anchor outside of the ship in which it is sailing. It is not a bad moral system; it is a truncated system, not yet grown to its full stature, immature with the immaturity of dwarfishness, and disinterested in the perfect development of man's noblest qualities. It will probably do much for those who do not want morals in the strict sense of the term. It will be a temporary morality for a few select Humanists, but it will never be a morality for humanity: it will explain why we should love the best, but will never explain why we should love the moron.

A dead body can float downstream: it can go with the current: it can "be in the swim." To resist the current, even the current of popular opinion, is the property of a live body. There is one system of morals that has been resisting the current of the way men live for centuries, a system which believes that every man is a shining silver arrow shot out from the bow of this world to the mark of eternal happiness. There are other moral systems that float downstream, and the new pre-faces to morals are of this kind. The "new morality" of May will be the "antiquated morality" of June. Then a new carcass will be thrown into the stream, and as it floats the vultures of the air will feed upon it as their food for the month, and when night shall have passed away and the sun shall have risen over the eastern hills, Christ will be seen walking on the waters.

Henry Davis
1866-1952

The average Catholic is unaware of the complex systems of canon law and moral theology that underlie the simple declarations of right and wrong, according to which he lives his life. Traditional moral theology is a carefully worked out science. It moves logically and exhaustively, from the basic concepts of human acts, law, sin and virtue to the commandments of God, the precepts of the Church, the sacraments, indulgences, censures, the clerical state, the religious state and the duties of lay-people. Each of these topics is divided and subdivided, analyzed and carefully defined. The ensemble serves as the intellectual support system for the life activities of the members of the Church.

Because it is so technical and so logical, the science of moral theology runs the constant risk of becoming cold, of losing contact with actually existing human beings, and of descending upon the shoulders of men and women like a crushing weight. Clergy trained in moral theology, were they not extremely cautious in using it, could unknowingly drive good people away from a rich life of union with God and chain them to pillars of sin and guilt.

Many voices have risen up within Catholicism over the past few decades, either to warn against the risks involved in an overly scientific moral theology or to denounce it as antithetical to the original spirit of Christ. Actually, the whole field of moral theology is in a state of evolution at the present time. It may be another century before a sense of stability is recognizable.

The passage below is taken from the four volume work by Father Henry Davis, professor of theology at Heythrop College in England. It is entitled Moral and Pastoral Theology. *At the time of its appearance in 1934, the work was hailed as one of the finest works in moral theology in the English language. By 1949 it had gone through six editions. The work is an excellent example of how moral theology was understood in the pre-Vatican II era. The reader should take note of the precision that is used in clarifying a concept. In the particular chapter reproduced below, the topic is conscience. After establishing that conscience is an act of practical reason, the author discusses the various kinds of conscience, viz., the true and false, the certain and doubting, the perplexed, the scrupulous, and the lax. Recognizing the need for some moral system to guide one's behavior, the author explains Probabiliorism, Equiprobabilism, Probabilism, and Compensationism.*

There is no doubt but that clarity of insight is essential to responsible human action. As the Church forges ahead in its search for a new, more relevant statement of morality, it should be careful not to leave behind what is valid in the tradition of moral theology.

MORAL AND PASTORAL THEOLOGY

VOLUME I

CHAPTER IV

CONSCIENCE

SECTION 1. INTRODUCTORY

I n free human conduct, we find from experience that
we possess a consciousness of our acts, and we pass
judgment on them, considering whether we may or
may not or ought to do such and such an act, and whether we
ought to have done or omitted such and such another act. This
judgment is the moral conscience. The judgments which we
formulate are based upon certain moral principles of the most
general character, such as that good is to be done, evil avoided,
legitimate commands are to be obeyed, justice is to be maintained, promises are to be kept. The most general judgments are
immediately evident to all men and are the general moral
principles of human action. They have their origin in the natural
habit or aptitude, called *synderesis,* which is an endowment of
the nature that we have. This moral judgment, then, is a judgment on any specific act done or to be done, omitted or to be
omitted, in accordance with general moral principles.

This judgment is the proximate general rule or standard
of right action. It assumes the obligation of law to be known,
and it imposes on us the obligation of acting in accordance
with the law.

Conscience that is certain, that is, where its possessor is
clearly convinced that his conscience unhesitatingly imposes
a definite obligation here and now, in the concrete, must be
obeyed. Therefore, whether the speculative judgment which
precedes the dictate of conscience is true or false in point of
fact, the dictate following upon such judgment must be obeyed,
if it is certain. Thus, Abimelech (Gen. 20, 3-6) did what was
objectively wrong, but God excused him saying: "I knew thou

didst it with a sincere heart," and S. Paul (Rom. 14, 14): "To him that esteemeth anything to be unclean, to him it is unclean.

SECTION 2. DEFINITION OF CONSCIENCE

Conscience is an act of the practical reason. It tells us that an action which appears to us to be morally bad must be omitted, that an action which is here and now commanded must, if possible, be performed. The dictate of conscience is an act of the practical, not of the speculative, judgment. The intellect must, therefore, be considered as conscious of obligations. When, in considering the reasons for and against a given action, it expresses its approval or reprobation of that action, it goes through a process of reasoning, concluding with a practical judgment, namely, this may or ought to be done; that ought not to be done. But as it is an act of the practical reason, it addresses its premonitions to the will, putting before the will objects that are to be desired or shunned.

The intellect is and must be conscious that the source of the obligation to do or to omit an action is extrinsic to human nature, because it is inconceivable that man should be a law unto himself. Conscience has, therefore, a moral import. It is an undoubted fact, within ordinary experience, that in evildoing we are conscious of offending, not against nature and reason only, but against some law, deep-rooted in nature, which must have its justification outside us. Human beings recognize a Supreme Cause and Lawgiver; offences against reason are sins against God. It is with the utmost difficulty that a man argues himself into believing, for a time, that he can act against his conscience without violating some law.

SECTION 3. KINDS OF CONSCIENCE

Now if conscience were never interfered with by passion or ignorance there would be only one kind of conscience, namely, the true conscience, whose dictates would correspond with objective obligations. But passion and ignorance do interfere with advertence and free choice, so that we may rightly distinguish various kinds of conscience.

1. An erroneous or false conscience bases its judgment on what is *de facto* false; a true or correct conscience bases it on what is true, that is, on the actual objective law. The false conscience may be vincibly false, if a man could and ought to have made his intellectual inferences more carefully; it may be invincibly false, if he could not have done so.

2. Conscience is certain when the motive for practical judgment is certain, that is, when the conviction is apprehended to be a sound one. Conscience is a doubting conscience when the motive for action appears to be not certainly but only doubtfully valid.

3. Conscience is probable when one's judgment is based on reasons that are probably true but may, quite as well, be more probably false.

4. Persons of excessively strict conscience magnify obligations, or declare them to exist where they do not exist; those of lax conscience minimize obligations.

5. The scrupulous conscience is one that has not sound reasons for judging one way or the other, and yet gives its commands now in one way, now in another, basing its dictates on what it knows to be insufficient motives, yet in fear and apprehension leaning to the strict side. In brief, its motives are foolish and it knows them to be so when the mind is not obsessed by fear.

6. The judgment that goes before an act is called the antecedent conscience that settles the morality of our actions. Remorse, repining, terror, that sometimes follow upon an act, are called the consequent conscience; this consequent conscience has obviously no effect in respect of morality on the act that is already past and gone. The knowledge, therefore, that comes with years and experience cannot possibly affect the morality of our past actions; they were good or bad when they took place. Subjective culpability is derived from the will at the time of acting. When, therefore, we speak of conscience in respect of the morality of our actions, we mean conscience that is antecedent to an act.

From the definitions given above of the various kinds of conscience it will be at once evident that the conscience which is strict, lax, or scrupulous is a false conscience and should be corrected.

1. The True Conscience and the False Conscience

The false conscience, that is, the conscience that bases its judgment on what is *de facto* false, may be culpably or inculpably false, according as the ignorance, in consequence of which it exercises its command, is vincible or invincible. If this ignorance be wholly invincible before and during the act, it is clear that the false conscience is rather a misfortune than a fault. If, on the contrary, this ignorance be vincible, if it might have been dispelled and ought to have been dispelled by diligence commensurate with one's general opportunities and the importance of the issue, it is culpable. When, however, an act is performed whilst the mind is in the state of such culpable ignorance, the moral inordination of the act performed in consequence of this ignorance is to be measured by the degree of inordination of the ignorance, for at the time of acting, advertence is not directed, as we suppose, to the wrongfulness of the action. The guilt of an action, therefore, done in consequence of culpable ignorance is strictly measured by the guilt of the cause; the wrong was done when ignorance was not dispelled, and when the evil consequences were foreseen in some way or other. Now we must obey the dictates of conscience, whether it be true or false *de facto,* whether it be strict or lax, provided always it speaks to us with certainty. A man with a false conscience acts in good faith, it is supposed; he would act wrongly if he did not act according to the conscience which he has, since it is quite impossible for him to act according to a conscience which he ought to have but does not now possess. Therefore S. Paul says: "All that is not of faith is sin," that is to say, actions are sinful, if done without the conviction of doing what is right (in accordance with religious convictions).

Since, then, a person may sin formally, that is, may be guilty in conscience of violating law if he does not obey his conscience, and since wrongful actions done under the influence of a false conscience but in good faith, though not formally sinful are, nevertheless, objectively opposed to the moral order, it is of supreme importance that the conscience should be educated to discern right from wrong. This education must be acquired not only for more serious matters but for those which are less serious. Moreover, since there is a strict obligation on man to act rationally, to act as God would wish him to act, he must educate himself to appreciate that moral order which God has bound up with human nature, and the fulfilment of which is the good, the happy, and the rational life. Furthermore, it is a fact that if a man wants to become good he should try to become good. In the matter of conscience, religious education, being the only education that will create and foster a true conscience, should be most assiduously sought after. This must be obvious, because such education both teaches him what is right and provides the necessary sanction, namely, the will of the Author of Nature. Without this sanction, in time of stress and violent temptation, the conscience is apt, as we know, to lose its power; its voice is drowned in the clamorous insistency of passion, and fades away, a faint echo of its former self, or is even stifled altogether in the tumult of conflicting appeals. Right reason of itself will reveal to us its own first principles, and that very soon, for it is reasonable to think that we cannot remain long in ignorance of the great first principles of the Natural law. The child's reason soon tells it that it is wrong to steal, to tell lies, to disobey its parents. Apart, however, from the first principles of the Natural law and their immediate conclusions, the true conscience is a matter of education, mental, moral and religious. The true conscience, viz., that which tells one to do what is *de facto* in conformity with objective law, is the conscience that all men of good will strive to acquire by repeated reflection and moral education, thus preventing ignorance from misleading them and passion from anticipating reason. There is a certain conscientiousness in every art and science, whereby a man is circumspect in the use of materials, sources, inferences, and so on; in the good moral life, the true conscience is preceded by this intellectual circumspection in regard to obligations.

2. The Certain Conscience and the Doubting Conscience

Certainty of conscience depends on the certainty with which I draw my conclusions, consciously or implicitly, as to the morality of a given concrete act. Certainty based on evident principles is absolute certainty; if it is based not on evident principles but on what appear to be such good reasons, or on such sufficiently good authority that prudent doubt is excluded, the certainty is said to be perfect moral certainty. Neither absolute nor perfect moral certainty can always be obtained; we must, therefore, be satisfied sometimes with a degree of certainty that is imperfect, where a mistake is quite possible but not likely. A doubting conscience, on the other hand, is one in which I cannot make up my mind with anything like certainty as to a given line of conduct, either because I have discovered only moderately good reasons in favour of it, or because I have discovered excellent reasons on one side, whilst I am conscious of equally excellent reasons on the other.

If I doubt only in the abstract and speculatively, my doubt is speculative; if I am in doubt, here and now, as to the morality of a given concrete act which I am about to perform or to continue, my doubt is said to be a practical doubt. Obviously, I may not act in such circumstances, because I must act with a certain conscience, that is, with a conscience morally certain of the rectitude of a given act. If I did not wait for certainty but acted in doubt, I should be placing myself, quite deliberately, in the way of doing what my conscience cannot certainly approve. But the certainty here meant is not speculative certainty, for that is often impossible. What is here meant by certainty is practical certainty, that is, certainty that one may act correctly. What then is to be done in the case of doubt? Can we say that it is generally better to choose wrong than to spend the whole day in deciding? Surely not. Doubt must be dispelled to the best of one's ability, either by asking advice, or by reflection, or by acting on what appears to be a sufficiently good reason. Certainty, however, must be got. If, at the moment, there is no opportunity of asking advice or of discovering sufficiently cogent reasons, what is to be done? There are certain principles admitted by everybody in ordinary life and acted upon. The consideration of some of these principles may help one to arrive at that moral certainty which is sufficient. Some of these principles suggested for practical guidance are as follows:

1. Possession in good faith is a presumption of good title. For instance, I have come by some object or other, honestly, as I think, but I am not quite sure that the object really belongs to me. After taking the ordinary means of finding out the rightful owner and having failed, I may justify myself in retaining the object, on the presumption that actual possession gives me a good title to it, until the contrary is proved.

2. In positive doubt, a well-grounded presumption of title is a sufficiently good title.

3. Obligations may not be presumed to exist, they should be clearly established. Thus, if I doubt whether or not I have broken the fast before Holy Communion, should it appear to me after reasonable investigation that I did not, I may rightly say: The obligations to abstain from Holy Communion not certain; I may, therefore, receive Holy Communion with a good conscience, for the law of the Church is that Holy Communion may not be received after conscious violation of the Eucharistic fast.

4. That which ought to have been done in a given definite way to secure its valid performance may be presumed to have been correctly done. For example, a priest, in the habit of giving absolution with the correct form of words, remembers to have given absolution, and begins to doubt if he used the correct form. He may reasonably make up his mind that he did so; he cannot be obliged to repeat absolutions when mere passing doubts as these occur to his mind. He has acted in an ordinarily human way and may rest satisfied, unless his doubts are so strong as to amount to moral certainty.

It is obvious that one has to be circumspect in the use of such principles, for they are not meant so much for general guidance as for cases where persistence in doubt would lead to great mental anxiety; nor does such a principle as the above, which is sound in itself, excuse a man from using diligence proportionate to the importance of the issues at stake. This is especially so when a penitent is in need of absolution, a matter which will be dealt with later.

5. In doubt concerning an accessory circumstance of an act, I may presume that the whole act in substance is good and valid, and I need not repeat the act nor any portion of it.

6. In doubt, the safer course must certainly be followed, where a very definite object is to be attained at all costs. Thus, for example, when Baptism is to be administered, it would be wrong to run the slightest risk of invalid administration, except, of course, in a case of extreme necessity, when the best that can be done must be done at once, even if there be some misgiving as to the validity of the act. The Sacraments are for man's use, so that where it is a matter of the salvation of a soul, means, even the least likely to be of any use, may and must be used where no other means are available. But even in such cases, the safer course, that is, the course which best guarantees the result, is obviously to be followed, if possible under the circumstances, although there be only the slightest probability of the result being achieved. It is better to do so much than to do nothing at all.

With the help of these few principles, which are found to be nothing more than enunciations of common sense, one may succeed in arriving at moral certainty in regard to the lawfulness of a given act, whereas, without some such reflection, the doubt may remain, and may render a man inactive when action is imperatively called for.

3. The Perplexed Conscience

This is the state of conscience of one who has alternatives set before him, each of which seems to be sinful. The perplexed conscience is not a scrupulous conscience; the latter is in constant dread of past and present sin, basing its erroneous judgment on ridiculously insufficient reasons. The perplexed conscience is in a worse plight, because sin appears to be simply inevitable. What is the victim of a perplexed conscience to do? The following practical rules have been suggested by S. Alphonsus and others:

1. He should seek the counsel of a good director or some prudent friend and follow it.

2. If this cannot be done and the perplexity remain, he should choose that which seems the less of two evils. No sin will be then committed because he is not a free agent. Thus, for example, it may appear absolutely necessary to do one or other of two wrongful acts. It is clear that, under the circumstances,

the victim of a perplexed conscience thinks himself obliged to do wrong; that conviction is so obviously subversive of morality, that he may be assured that in avoiding what appears the greater evil and choosing the less he is doing right, and, therefore, doing a good action.

Of course, in point of fact, it is never necessary to do wrong; there never is, in fact, a choice to be made between two necessary moral evils. An example of the perplexity contemplated would be the case of one who thought, erroneously, that in a Court of Law he ought to perjure himself, in order not to bear witness against a friend. The fact is that one must tell the truth always for no loyalty to a friend can ever justify the smallest lie. Again, a mother might erroneously think it a sin to miss Sunday Mass in order to attend to her sick child; she has the two alternatives placed before her, and she must, so she thinks, stay at home and sin. But a true conscience would tell her that to miss Mass under the circumstances is not a sin, because there is no obligation of going to Sunday Mass under every conceivable circumstance. Her perplexed conscience is an erroneous one.

4. *The Scrupulous Conscience*

The scrupulous man is the victim of an imaginary spiritual impediment to his free action; he is tormented in every action, even the most harmless, with the thought that he may be committing sin, or that he is out of the grace of God. He then does his best to recover divine grace, and is momentarily satisfied; but the demon of unrest comes again to suggest that his choice was wrong. The fear of sin is a waking nightmare; the victim knows, in his saner moments, that his fears are groundless, yet he falls back again into his sad state, and there alternates between despair and hope. At almost every step of his spiritual journey, some personal agency, God, his Angel, or Satan, is at his side warning him, as he thinks, to clear his house of the seven devils that inhabit it. When he has chased them out, other seven have taken their place. He has no peace; he is seldom happy. Nobody understands his case; others have been scrupulous, but not quite exactly as he is. Though his anxiety is groundless, his malady is very real.

The scrupulous conscience is not to be confounded with the conscience that is tender. A person is often said to be scrupulous when his conscience is very delicate. We have sanctioned this confusion by speaking of a very honest man as scrupulously honest; his honesty is said to have the defects of this good quality. The tender conscience, if a true conscience, is, however, an eminently desirable conscience to possess, for its owner will rightly regard even slight sins as matter for regret and avoidance. The tender conscience differs from the scrupulous in that it is true and is founded on reasonable convictions; whereas the scrupulous conscience is always erroneous.

Scruples may have their origin in the natural temperament or in the physical state, each acting upon the scrupulous to render him timorous, nervous, dejected. In that state, scruples once getting possession, the victim goes from bad to worse, action and reaction succeeding one another with painful regularity.

Secondly, God may permit the presence of scruples in the soul, whatever their source may be. He cannot, however, be supposed to wish the scrupulous state to persist, if it lead to moral evil, such as despair, distaste for His service, neglect of prayer, or preoccupation with worldly pursuits.

Thirdly, Satan may, with God's permission, so effectually disturb the imagination, that the soul almost insensibly and as a natural consequence falls into the scrupulous state. If God permits scruples, He does so for a good purpose. This purpose will be evident at least to the spiritual director of the scrupulous. The divine purpose in permitting scruples to oppress a soul is that the sufferer may have greater humility, greater confidence, and achieve more rapid sanctification.

If Satan is the source of scruples, since he is man's enemy, they will never lead to peace or any spiritual benefit; more usually they will lead to disquiet, despair and moral disorder. If scruples are due to temperament or physical defect, they may be said to arise from one of several sources, such as a tendency to melancholy, fickleness, timidity, want of well-balanced judgment, pride and obstinacy, adherence to a species of rigorism, by which a man tries, under all circumstances, to choose the safer course, and forces himself to adopt ideals that are either not true at all, or not meant for him in particular. Since, therefore, scruples so often lead to great disorders both in the spiritual and in the physical life, it is of first importance to get rid of them, unless, indeed, God manifests in some way or other His Divine Will that we should endure them as we endure other spiritual afflictions permitted by Him. If, in spite of implicit obedience to our spiritual director, the state still persists, God knows how to draw good from scruples, and we must wait upon His good pleasure to deliver us from them. They will bestow this amount of good at least, namely, they will increase obedience, humility, self-distrust, confidence; they will teach us by our own sad experience how to sympathize with and direct others in a similar state.

The scrupulous conscience is usually exercised about three distinct classes of actions:

1. Firstly, about past confessions. These are judged to have been sacrilegious, either from want of true sorrow, or from having concealed a grave sin, or from lack of lucid explanation. This morbid state of mind is supposed, by the enemies of the confessional, to be a necessary consequence of Catholic practice; but like a good and wise physician, the Church has ready remedies for this state, and it is no more a consequence of the good practice of confessing sins, than hypochondria is a consequence of the study of medicine.

2. Secondly, the scrupulous conscience is exercised about possible or probable consent to evil thoughts in the past.

3. Thirdly, scruples are entertained concerning the pervading presence of sin; it is lurking in every action of the waking life; what appears quite harmless to ordinary people is moral poison to the scrupulous. He is so preoccupied with the thought of possible or unforgiven sin, that he has no peace; he becomes diffident, hesitating, introspective. From whatever point of view he examines the past, he cannot give a reasonable or even a coherent account of his motives. They may have been good, but they must have been wicked, so he thinks. A dissection of motives is hopeless; it is too complex a process and brings no lasting peace with it, even if it be attempted and appear to succeed for a time.

Ordinarily, it is of little use to suggest remedies to the scrupulous. The remedies proposed by spiritual directors may, however, be of some help to those who are not scrupulous, so that at the slightest indication of the advent of scruples in themselves or in those whom they can direct, such remedies may be ready at hand, and may be applied with kindly but firm insistence. The following rules of conduct for the scrupulous person have been suggested by experienced directors:

1. He should convince himself that he is really scrupulous, and that scruples do not necessarily lead to sanctity; that, therefore, he will make up his mind to attend to the health of both body and soul.

2. He should seek the guidance of one good confessor and not of many confessors. He should render obedience to his director, convinced that even if the director should err now and then, the penitent will not be held responsible for such occasional errors of judgment, which, most probably, will be very trivial.

3. He should be humble and resigned to God's Will, looking upon Him as kind, generous and merciful, and he should frequently make acts of confidence and love.

4. He should be brief in examining his conscience and in stating his difficulties.

5. He should never give way to scruples on the plea that for once in a way, it is better to have peace of mind than to continue resistance. The enemy grows stronger by every victory gained over the scrupulous.

6. He must boldly follow the advice given to him, convinced that by so doing he cannot be committing sin.

7. After gaining a victory now and then, he should learn to rely upon his own judgment without frequent recourse to his confessor.

8. He should be thoroughly convinced that doubtful sin is not certain sin, and that he need not confess doubts but only certainties.

9. He should act as other good people act. What is right for them is right for him. Therefore, he should not pry into his motives curiously and persistently, but do what he is doing with despatch and vigour.

10. When he is in doubt concerning his consent to evil thoughts, he may take it for granted that there was no consent. When in doubt about the quality of past confessions, he may assume that they were good. When in doubt about sufficient sorrow in confession, he may be assured that the very act of going to confession is, in his case, a sufficient act of sorrow. When in apprehension about final perseverance, he should say: "I will leave that to God. He will see to it. In Thee, O Lord, have I hoped. I shall not be confounded for ever. I can do all things in Him Who strengtheneth me."

The scrupulous person may well take any one of the proposed remedies without trying to use several. But if he should think that not even any one of them suits his case, he would be giving but one more manifestation of the protean character of his conscience. Rather, he should persuade himself that all these rules, derived from the experience of confessors during many centuries, exactly suit his case, and he should proceed to act upon some of them without delay.

5. The Lax Conscience

This kind of conscience is an erroneous one; it is a minimizer. It falsely judges actions to be harmless which are gravely sinful. Since this conscience is an erroneous one, it is obvious that if a man knows that he has such a conscience, he cannot lawfully follow its dictates without some endeavour to correct it, because otherwise he is deliberately exposing himself to violate God's moral order; that, in itself, is a contempt of law. It is quite true that in any given concrete case, such a man may be acting in good faith, for without advertence to his state and to the possibility of wrong-doing, he will not be guilty of formal sin. Nevertheless, God has established an objective moral order and cannot be supposed to be indifferent to its maintenance. By neglecting to correct what we may call his personal error, the owner of a lax conscience is allowing the error to become so great that he may become warped to such an extent as ultimately to confound right and wrong. These men shelter themselves under the comfortable doctrine of predestination in view of Christ's infinite merits, without any personal co-operation; a theory, or rather what does service for a theory, that makes the lax conscience still more lax, until conscience and caprice come to be indistinguishable. Such a conscience is the essential outcome of the principle of private judgment. The man who is a law unto himself in beliefs and morals has no sure foothold on which to take his stand when assailed by passion and temptation. If greater evils have not followed in the wake of this pernicious principle, we may be sure that they have been held back by God's preventing grace and His loving providence.

The remedies for a lax conscience are to meditate on the truths of Christian doctrine, to frequent the Sacraments, to examine the conscience, and to read good spiritual books.

6. The Probable Conscience

The probable conscience is the conscience of one who, antecedently to action, has good and solid reasons for thinking that a certain line of action is morally correct, though he is aware at the same time that there are better, sounder and more cogent reasons for thinking that it is not. His convictions, or perhaps it would be better to say, his inferences, are not certainly true but they are only probably true; they may be false, but they may be true and in accordance with fact. He does not know for certain in which category they are, otherwise he would be said to have a certain or sure conscience; as it is, his speculative judgment is only probably correct, so far, that is, as he knows. It is to be observed that in the analysis of moral action, the speculative judgment precedes the practical dictate of reason. In this context, when speaking of the probable conscience, we are considering only the speculative judgment, or that intellectual act which weighs and ponders reasons for and against an action, and not being able to arrive at certainty, arrives at probabilities only. With this proviso, we may adhere, without danger of confusing the issues, to the term commonly applied, and call that species of conscience a probable conscience which, before action, has arrived at speculative reasons that are probably true.

It is not claimed that the moral system to be presented in this section is the official teaching of the Church. There are several systems permitted to be taught in the Church, and each system is held and defended by able theologians. In this matter, as elsewhere in Moral Theology, very great latitude is allowed until the Church expresses its mind.

To prevent misunderstanding, it is necessary to say at once that no Catholic theologian of any school teaches that it is a good moral proceeding to take the benefit of the doubt, and to act on probable reasons, so as wilfully and consciously to expose oneself to commit formal sin. The concept of the moral system of Probabilism formulated by its opponents is something as follows: "This act is probably wrong; therefore, so long as I am not certain, I may do it." Such a procedure could not be dignified with the name of any moral system ever in vogue in the Church.

Dr. H. Rashdall thus caricatures Probabilism. He says: "Everything was done to attenuate the discrepancy between the ordinary pleasures and practices of the world and the requirements of Christianity, to offer the man of the world the maximum of indulgence which was compatible with sub-mission to the minimum requirements of the Church, and with the use of his influence and authority in its service" ... "Valu-able assistance was given by the intrinsically immoral doctrine of a fundamental distinction between two classes of sins—mortal and venial—a distinction depending upon the nature of the external act, and not upon the degree of moral guilt which it implies." Of all people to quote, Dr. Rashdall quotes Pascal (*Les Provinciales*), whose criticism is very witty but very irrel-evant. One more amazing misrepresentation: "Men were taught," he says, "how, if they wished to sin, they could nearly always—so long as they recognized the authority of the Church, and complied with certain ecclesiastical regulations—ensure that new sins should be only venial, even when the casuists' ingenuity failed to remove even this barrier to inclination." Possibly, like Pascal, he might find one or other lax casuist speaking thus, but it was not common teaching. And yet, Dr. Rashdall is him-self a Probabilist, as witness what he says (p. 442): "Consulted as to what a man ought to do under such and such circum-stances, the Moral Philosopher will not, *qua* Moral Philosopher, say: 'You should do this or that,' but rather he will explain the relevant ethical principles, apply them to the facts of the case, and then say: 'If you think, for instance, that these experiments have such and such a *chance* of saving pain; if you think that the pain they *may* save is equivalent to what they must cost; if you think that the good to humanity which they *may* effect is morally more than equivalent to any hardening of the heart which they *may possibly* bring with them, then perform these experiments; if not, don't.' "

7. The Need of Some Moral System

The making up of one's mind in respect of certain lines of action is not always an easy matter, if we regard speculative reasons alone; no more easy is it to come to conclusions on philosophical matters. In the latter, when faced by the apparent contradictions involved in one's concepts of Time, Space and Motion, we are well content to adopt that system which has already approved itself after some thought, keeping at the same time an open mind for further enlightenment.

Fortunately, our practical behaviour in the events of ordinary life, such as walking, eating, sleeping, does not depend in any way on the particular philosophical system which we may have adopted. The Idealist enjoys his exercise and meals equally with the Dualist, though he may or may not have quite the same intellectual satisfaction. But in matters of moral conduct it is very different. Here, we have to make up our minds that our line of conduct is certainly upright. To make up our minds, we possibly may have recourse to the advice of others; but that advice is sometimes conflicting. We may weigh the *pros* and *cons* and find ourselves no nearer a solution after hours of thought than we were before we began to reflect. Therefore, a correct moral system for cases of speculative doubt is necessary. In matters of ordinary conduct, men have not much difficulty in arriving at clear conclusions, because the force of habit, convention, the general consensus of mankind, common sense, all of these help to sanction or reprobate certain actions. But there must come occasions in life when we honestly doubt, and really cannot, on speculative grounds, choose between alternatives.

What are we then to do? If we act in doubt as to the rectitude of an action, we are acting with a bad conscience;

if we go on weighing reasons, we shall never act. Consequently, in order to be able to act conscientiously and without unreasonable delay, it is important to discover some guiding principles. The theologians of the Catholic Church have formulated several systems, some of them now obsolete, others still held by the various schools, but they have so laboured over the task for centuries, that the conclusions arrived at seem to these various schools to be completely justified by argument, and therefore several of these systems have nowadays their capable defenders and are used freely and unrestrictedly to guide personal conduct and to direct others.

It would be superfluous to describe at any length each of the systems hitherto devised; but it is necessary to present three of them, being those that have supplanted all the others, so that the arguments in favour of that system which is here presented as the most reasonable may be the better appreciated, without of course unfairly belittling the force and cogency of the other two. The three systems go by the names of Probabiliorism, Equiprobabilism and Probabilism.

It may be asked, why should there be any system other than one's own honest convictions? The answer to the question is that there need be no other, if we regard the matter subjectively. But we may be permitted to ask a question in turn, namely, if, as is said, you take each case as it comes before you, and act according to your honest convictions, how do you arrive at your conclusions in cases of doubt? That is the test of any system that claims to deal with doubt. A teacher who sets about the task of showing us how to behave so as to behave well both morally and meritoriously, must present us with some definite system of conduct where a system is most of all needed, namely, in cases of indecision, insoluble doubt and anxiety. He must prove his system to be reasonable in these crucial cases, otherwise he will have omitted to offer that guidance and help that are needed most of all.

Catholic theologians, therefore, boldly faced this task of formulating a moral system for cases of doubt. But they have certainly found the task no light one, since for centuries they have been sifting and reviewing the reasons alleged for and against each system, as it has been proposed by one school and another. It will be to our purpose to state and examine very briefly two of the three prevailing systems, and to devote more careful consideration to the system of Probabilism, which, as it seems to us, may be adopted to the exclusion of the other two.

8. Probabiliorism

The fundamental axiom of this system is that it is wrong to act on an opinion that favours liberty, unless the opinion is more probable than that which is in favour of the obligation.

The system of Probabiliorism, though in existence long before the sixteenth century, gained many capable defenders in consequence of the reaction against certain lax doctrines, propounded and defended by a school of writers who, in their efforts to extend the domain of reasonable liberty, fell into grievous error, and whose system, which has been called Laxism, was condemned by Pope Innocent XI in 1679. The revival of Probabiliorism, due mainly to the patronage of Popes Alexander VII and Innocent XI, was widespread and vigorous; it was the system adopted by the foremost writers amongst Dominicans, Franciscans, Augustinians, Carmelites and others. Some notable Jesuits also defended it. The system was, in fact, more generally taught than any other up to the nineteenth century.

The arguments used to establish the truth of this system of Probabiliorism were and still are as follows:

1. If the arguments in favour of liberty, as opposed to the obligation of a doubtful law, are distinctly less probable than the arguments in favour of the obligation, it would seem that in the conflict of these two sets of arguments, those that are the less probable should never avail to exert any influence whatever on a reasonable and prudent man. The more probable arguments become practically convincing. In everyday life, men certainly feel that they act with sufficient moral rectitude, when they act in accordance with an opinion that is more probably true than its contrary, and in fact, they judge that to act upon the less probable view would be unreasonable and hazardous, more especially where the issues at stake are important.

But this argument in favour of the system is not satisfactory, because, if a system is to be of any practical utility, it must be applicable to all cases. But we find, as a fact, that it is impossible to appreciate the various degrees of probability, and to say, even after long reflection, that such and such an opinion is really more probable than its contrary. In such cases we are still left in a state of doubt and are unable to apply this particular system to action.

It would, of course, be quite different if the probabilities on the one side were so obviously and overwhelmingly greater than those on the other, that the contrary opinion appeared highly improbable; but, as a fact, obvious ways out of difficulties do not present themselves when we need them most. Furthermore, in addition to the unpractical nature of this system, it is not true to say that, when an opinion is much more probable than its contrary, the lesser probability of this latter vanishes altogether and ceases to be probability at all. To maintain that, would be to do away with probability altogether, because it is of the very nature of probability that a more probably true opinion is not a certainly true opinion, corresponding with fact; therefore, a contrary opinion that is less probable may be really the true one in point of fact; it still retains its own degree of probability.

2. A second argument used by Probabiliorists is this: In the sphere of abstract reasoning, we ought to assent to that view which is the more likely to approach truth and to exclude error; that is to say, if we must assent at all, we should surely not assent to what is apparently the less likely to be true. Of course, we may withhold assent altogether; yet, as a fact, men do usually assent to what seems to them to be nearest the truth. So, too, in practical matters of conduct; if one line of action is more likely both to be conformed to moral order and to exclude moral disorder than the opposite line of action, then a man who wishes to act honestly and conscientiously ought to run no risks, and ought to adopt the more probably correct line of conduct.

The argument is unconvincing. For it is to be observed that if the system is consistently held and is applied all along the line—as it ought to be applied—then it follows that we should always choose the more probably correct line of conduct in everything we do. From this it would seem to follow that we should be obliged to try to follow the way of the Counsels rather than merely the way of the Commandments, since in the former way we should assuredly be travelling along a more secure road to salvation, for one who aims at perfection is the more likely to attain to salvation.

The conclusion is so obviously absurd that the fundamental axiom of Probabiliorism must be exceedingly wrong. In other words, the system logically leads to the obligation of choosing the safer course in all matters. But since we shall have done our duty if we choose the safe course, it is clear that we need not be Probabiliorists, and certainly should not impose such a system on others. Thus, then, on its practical side, the system of Probabiliorism would lead to very great inconvenience. But if we examine the second argument from another standpoint, it is surely not necessary to maintain that one is obliged, either in intellectual honesty or in practical life, to adopt an opinion which seems to be more probably true than its contrary. For if the less probable opinion be nevertheless really probable, it may afford us sufficient grounds for practical conduct, without troubling about our assent to it. We are not intellectually forced to assent to anything short of evidence; the more probable opinion will never oblige us to assent to anything except its greater probability. When two contrary probable opinions are in conflict for one's adherence, one can never assent absolutely to either. Though one must admit that the less probable opinion is the less likely to be true, nevertheless, if it is really probable at all, it may really be true, and may, therefore, be quite a reasonable opinion to act upon.

9. Equiprobabilism

Certain theologians of the eighteenth century, not willing to adopt the system just explained, and at the same time dreading the laxity in moral conduct and principles to which Probabilism was thought to lead, effected a sort of compromise. They were greatly encouraged by the prestige of S. Alphonsus, who seems to have abandoned Probabiliorism and to have adopted a less rigorous system, namely, that under discussion. But he certainly seems to have passed through several stages of thought in the matter, concluding, as it is supposed, by being a firm and convinced Equiprobabilist, and rejecting quite explicitly the milder doctrine of Probabilism. However that may be, for there is some doubt as to the exact meaning of his terms, this great theologian has had followers of insight and erudition, who have adopted Equiprobabilism, and have persistently rejected the milder system. These two systems, namely, Equiprobabilism and Probabilism are now the chief systems left in the field. Each is openly taught in the Catholic schools; anyone is free to adopt either system, though, in point of fact, the tendency of the great majority of modern theologians is towards the gentler and more liberal system: *"Quod si res dubia est, vincat humanitas et facilitas,"* S. Gregory of Nazianzen well says in another context; that is to say: "If the matter is doubtful, let humanity and gentleness prevail." Since, therefore, Equiprobabilism is still taught and defended by a large school of theologians, it will be of interest to present some of their arguments, and briefly to examine the cogency of them. The system is expressed in the three following propositions:

1. When conflicting opinions in regard to the existence of a law are equally or nearly equally probable, one may follow the opinion in favour of liberty; that is, the doubtful law need not be obeyed.

2. When in doubt whether a definite law has ceased to bind or not, in the conflict of equally or nearly equally probable opinions, one must follow the opinion in favour of the law, that is, the law must be obeyed, because the law is in possession.

3. When the opinion in favour of a law is certainly more probable than the contrary, it is unlawful to follow the less probable opinion in favour of liberty.

The first of these propositions is directed against Probabiliorists; the second and the third propositions are against Probabilists. The first proposition need not detain us, because all Probabilists accept it. The proof of it is that a law that is doubtful in the strict sense, that is to say, whose existence is doubtful, is one that does not and cannot bind here and now, for the reason that man's liberty should not be curtailed by a doubtfully existing obligation. It is obvious that a law should be known to be binding in order to bind in conscience; but the reasonable doubt as to its existence is equivalent to absence of promulgation. Furthermore, in strict doubt, liberty is in possession.

The second proposition, namely, in doubt as to the cessation of a law one must fulfil the law where the conflicting opinions for law and liberty are equally or nearly equally probable, is proved by Equiprobabilists by the following arguments:

(a) Just as when a law is not certain, human liberty is in possession and need not be curtailed, so it would seem that when a law has been certainly promulgated but its revocation is doubtful, law is in possession until its revocation is known to have taken place.

In reply to this reason it must be obvious that there is no valid distinction to be drawn between the existence of a law and the obligation of the same law. If it exists for me, it binds me; if it does not exist, it does not bind. Now when its revocation is doubtful, its persistence is also doubtful; consequently, its continued existence and obligation are both doubtful. If, then, the probabilities are evenly balanced or nearly so, between revocation and continued existence, what sensible man would impose on others the definite and certain obligation of fulfilling a law that may have been revoked? It is of little use to say with Equiprobabilists that the law is certain, because the phrase under the circumstances means nothing; no law is certain when it has probably been revoked. Human liberty is always in possession until certainly curtailed by law. Obligation is inconceivable without the connotation of something subject to obligation, which antecedently was free. The human will must be considered antecedently free before any obligation is laid upon it. Therefore, the burden of proof is upon the law; it must be proved certainly to exist before a certain obligation is imposed upon an antecedently free agent. It is not correct, therefore, to say that in the conflict of two nearly equal probabilities for and against the cessation of a law, the law must be obeyed.

(b) A second proof is based on the moral aspect of an action performed when the law probably still binds. It is said that if the law probably still exercises its binding power, the non-fulfilment of it cannot be morally right, since in such a case, the conscience cannot arrive at moral certainty as to the lawfulness of acting. But the conscience, it may be answered, can quite legitimately arrive at moral certainty in favour of liberty for this reason, that a law which does not certainly bind, does not exercise a clear and certain obligation. That is a fact, and the conscience can be morally certain of it. What would be the state of the anxious and scrupulous conscience, if its possessor were obliged to fulfil all obligations a second, a third and a fourth time, which he had probably already fulfilled? To say this is not to misrepresent the Equiprobabilist position; but it shows into what painful situations the system would inevitably bring anyone with a tender conscience; this is, in fact, a *reductio ad absurdum*.

The third proposition of Equiprobabilists is no more defensible. It is this: When the opinion in favour of a law is certainly more probable than the contrary, it is unlawful to follow the less probable opinion in favour of liberty. It must be stated at once, so as to avoid misconception, that there is no question here of moral certainty in favour of the law. If that were so, all schools would concur. But we are still in the region of probabilities, and it must be insisted that greater probability is not any more than probability; it is not certainty.

The arguments brought forward to prove this third proposition are as follows:

(a) Pope Innocent XI strongly urged the defence and teaching of the system expressed by this third proposition. That is admitted, but there is no suggestion that he urged it from any other point of view than as a personal opinion. It was at that time the personal opinion of many eminent teachers. But a strong recommendation of one opinion cannot be regarded as the condemnation of the contrary opinion, except perhaps on disciplinary grounds in the case of those to whom the recommendation was personally addressed. Others were left free to teach in their own way, and the two systems continued to be taught side by side, until, in course of time, the opinion of Pope Innocent XI was set aside by many theologians. Furthermore, the toleration in the Church during the last three centuries of the milder system, and the well-known tendency of later theologians to adopt Probabilism, are sufficient proof that Pope Innocent XI did not wish to impose the severer system on theological schools.

(*b*) A second argument in favour of the third proposition of Equiprobabilists is that a law is sufficiently promulgated and therefore binding, if it have in favour of its existence a greater probability, because this greater probability amounts practically to moral certainty. As stated above, the obligation of the law is obvious in the case of moral certainty as to its existence, since existence and obligation are correlative. But probability, however great, will never amount to moral certainty, provided always that there exists a solidly probable opinion to the contrary. It is quite true to say that a man who acts on greater probabilities is acting reasonably, and men usually act in this frame of mind; but it is another thing to say that there is an obligation to act in virtue of greater probabilities. On the contrary, one would be quite as reasonable if one said: I am not convinced; I choose to act on the contrary view, which, being really probable, may be quite true. The greater probability of a view, if short of moral certainty, will never oblige one intellectually to assent to that view.

(*c*) The third argument in favour of the third proposition is that a man is bound to act in conformity with the moral order. Now, just as a more probable opinion approaches the more nearly to objective truth and recedes the more certainly from error, so a more probably good action approaches the more nearly to the objective moral order, and recedes the more certainly from inordination.

In reply to this argument we may urge two considerations:

Granting that the proof were a valid one, it would follow that one should become a rigorist and always follow the most probable, nay even the most safe opinion, and thus be the more sure of acting in conformity with moral order, since this would be the most effectual method of getting at truth and at absolute goodness. But such a conclusion is admitted by no theologian, not even by the severer Probabiliorist, and has been condemned by the Church, because it is untrue, it is an impossible ideal to carry out in practice, and would lead to an utterly false concept of God's justice and goodness.

But the proof labours under the false assumption that greater probability more nearly approaches the truth. This is by no means the case. Opinions that have been held as more probably true, have often, in the event, proved to be false. Degrees of probability are not degrees of truth. Similarly, an action is either conformed to the moral order or it is not; it cannot, under identical circumstances be partly conformed to objective morality and partly at variance with it. Thus, a statement that is made on evidence that is even very probably true, may, nevertheless, be no statement of fact at all, and similarly, an action that is most probably a good moral action may, in point of fact, be objectively entirely out of order. Thus, I might have very strong reasons for thinking that I had paid a certain debt, but my creditor quite possibly might never have been paid at all.

10. Probabilism

The principle of Probabilism is that in cases of doubt as to the lawfulness of any concrete action, if there exists a really probable opinion in favour of liberty, i.e., of disregard of the law, although the opinion in favour of the law is more probable, I may use the former opinion and disregard the latter, and in doing so, I am acting with complete moral rectitude.

This moral system of Probabilism did not spring ready-made from the head of some Olympian. It was a slow process of growth, having traces of its presence far back in theological speculation, and in the writings of the Fathers, not unlike many of the conclusions, now so readily accepted in the Church, that once were vague, uncertain, debatable, and had to be elaborated by the diligent care of very many theologians. The theory was, it is said, first formulated with something like clear consistency by the learned Dominican, Bartholomew Medina, about the year 1577. Neither in its origin nor in its early elaboration can it be attributed to Jesuit theologians. In fact, far from having invented Probabilism, Jesuit theologians moderated its application. One of the Superiors General, Fr. Gonsalez, was anxious to impose on all the members of the Order the obligation of teaching the stricter system of Probabiliorism. He failed, and before his election to his high office, his book in defence of this system was refused publication by his censors. After his election, he published his book—somewhat modified—but his teaching was not adopted. He even engaged the sympathy of the Pope, Innocent XI, who highly praised the opinions of Fr. Gonsalez, and ordered that all Jesuits should be allowed freely to teach Probabiliorism, and to attack Probabilism. This order was issued by the Holy Office (an. 1680). The order was really unnecessary, for all members of the Society were and had been allowed freedom in the matter.

Until about 1638, the theologians of all Catholic schools with few exceptions followed the teaching of Medina. The most honoured names are found in the list of those who defended the theory. It was thus put on a firm basis, and subsequent opposition to it, extensive and vigorous, has not been able to shake its foundations so well laid by the theologians of the seventeenth century. As stated above, the theory did not make a sudden appearance in theological consciousness. Clear indications of it were traced by those who first formulated it, in the writings of SS. Augustine, Jerome, Ambrose, Gregory Nazianzen, Basil; still clearer indications were traced in the works of certain theologians who lived at least a century before Medina. It is true that it suffered partial eclipse during the Jansenistic controversies. It was thoroughly misunderstood and ridiculed by Pascal with much pleasantry and great unfairness. It was even misapplied by too ardent devotees, whose chief fault was that they unwarrantably extended the meaning of the term 'probable' in supposing that any opinion held by any author might be looked upon as probable, a phenomenon that is not very uncommon in young students today.

The system was, however, applied in unreasonable ways; some casuists arrived at absurd conclusions which shocked common sense. But these excrescences were soon cut away, and the system was gradually understood and was applied, as it is applied today, in a sane logical way.

The Basis of Probabilism

In its ultimate analysis, Probabilism is common sense; it is a system used in practical doubt by the majority of mankind.

People rightly say: I am not going to debate all day before acting in doubtful matters; there must be some very obvious way of making up my mind. At all events, If I cannot make up my mind for myself, I will act as some good people act, though many other good people might disapprove. That practical solution of doubt is common sense, and it is Probabilism. It is also morally correct, as will be shown.

Degrees in Opinion

Among men of all classes, some opinions are held to be morally certain, some are held as very probably true so that the contrary opinion is thought to be very improbable, others are held to be more probably true than their contrary, others, in fine, are merely probable, because they are motived by good reasons, although the contrary opinion has better and more numerous reasons in its favour. In every case, either of the two contrary opinions may be the true one.

When the truth of an opinion or the sufficiency of available evidence is debatable, one can never say that either the affirmation or the negation of it is certainly true. The greater probability of one opinion does not and cannot destroy the probability of its contrary. Therefore, it must be admitted that in the conflict of two opposite probable opinions, since either may be false, it is not paradoxical to say that the less probable opinion may be the true one. This is a fundamental presupposition of Probabilism and it is reasonable. Unless this is admitted, the system of Probabilism would be considered very lax. For want of appreciation of this basis of the theory, it is taken for granted by its opponents that Probabilism is a method of searing the conscience and of turning human liberty into licence. It is not maintained by any Probabilist, as we here understand the term, that the system ought to be the rule and standard of conduct in all circumstances; everyone is perfectly free to adopt any approved system of solving his doubts. He may, if he so choose, be severe with himself, but he may not exaggerate the obligations of other people.

301

The Value of Probabilism

The whole value of the system lies in this, that in the case of persons in a state of intense and painful doubt who seek advice, it is of first importance to console and help them by any legitimate means, and not the least reassuring amongst these means is to explain to them that obligations which are not clearly and certainly manifested in conscience are not certainly binding. A confessor may well advise the timorous and the scrupulous to act in accordance with the theory of Probabilism, and at the same time exhort those who are morally strong not to confine themselves within the limits of strict obligations, but to be generous and magnanimous. It is certainly to be feared that one who is everlastingly debating about his strict obligations will become deadened to higher ideals; but the good and earnest men who believe in Probabilism as a reasonable system of conduct in speculative doubt, would never advise others to be for ever prying into the precise extent of their obligations. Nevertheless, in quest of some system to be applied to the difficult and harassing moments of doubt, they would think it a veritable perversion of truth and common sense to impose doubtful obligations.

It is, furthermore, to be observed that probability is said to be intrinsic when the reasons for an opinion are cogent but not conclusive; it is called extrinsic, when the authority, learning, prudence, of other people are taken as a proof that the opinion in question is a probably true opinion.

Of course, the opinion of any chance theologian is not contemplated in this context as constituting a probable opinion, unless he is pre-eminent in his treatment of a given question; for when Probabilists speak of probable opinions, they define their own terms and these have to be accepted as they are defined. They define a probable opinion as that opinion to which a prudent man would give his assent, and they lay it down as fundamental to the system that a prudent man often does give his assent to one of two contrary probable opinions, although he fully admits that there is a good deal to be said on the other side.

Again, once given a probable opinion as the basis of good moral action, it might seem consistent to be able to use several probable opinions at one and the same time, and thereby to claim privileges and shake off obligations. Thus, for example, a man might accept a particular legacy because it is probably valid in conscience though void in law, and at the same time feel tempted to repudiate the obligations annexed to the legacy, on the ground that, being void in law, it is probably void in conscience also. The mere statement of this supposition shows this application of the system to be inconsistent and unreasonable; in fact, such cases do not and cannot fall within the scope of Probabilism. It is a misrepresentation of Probabilism to say that when two particular laws regarding one and the same act only probably bind, they may both be disregarded. Either may be disregarded, because neither is certainly in possession, but both cannot be disregarded in one and the same matter, because one or the other would certainly be violated. The example usually cited is that of a person whose watch on Friday night points to 11.45 p.m. and whose clock points to 12.15 a.m. Such a person could not lawfully eat meat on the ground that Friday was probably past, and also consider himself probably fasting from midnight in view of receiving Holy Communion on Saturday.

If we accept a favour, we accept it as it is with its circumstances; to evade obligations annexed to it is not reasonable or just. Whatever may be the sanction a man finds for keeping the legacy mentioned above, he will find contained within that sanction the implication that he must take on obligations as well. No Probabilist could defend any other line of action, because no Probabilist can condone an act that offends one or other of two laws.

No Exceptions to Probabilism

Since the system is one that has been formulated chiefly to help those who are in a state of doubt, it would be of little practical use if there were numerous exceptional circumstances in which the system could not be applied. The remedy for the scrupulous or timorous conscience, offered by Probabilism, would be almost as disquieting as the disease. We should never be quite sure whether or not this or that circumstance prevented the application of the system in our case.

It is the merit of Probabilism that there are no exceptions whatever to its application; once given a really probable reason for the lawfulness of action in a particular case, though contrary reasons may be stronger, there is no occasion on which I may not act in accordance with the good probable reason that I have found.

This point has not, it seems, been appreciated by some recent writers, who import into the question the danger there may be in invading other people's rights, who lay great and unwarrantable stress on the sanctity of even a doubtful law, the scandal that others may take from such action. All these considerations must have already been taken into account in forming one's probable opinion; they are very pertinent indeed to every system of forming one's conscience. Without due weight being given to accidental circumstances that may quite easily render an otherwise good action decidedly inopportune and disorderly, there is always a manifest danger of violating specific laws that are certain.

If it were a question of probable danger only, probabilities would have to be measured; where it is a question of manifest danger, law is already in possession and urges its claims here and now. There is no room for Probabilism in such cases, because the obligations are not doubtful. There is, therefore, no exception to the application of Probabilism. But there are apparent exceptions as they have been called; cases that stand altogether outside the scope, not only of Probabilism, but of every other system that has been invented, except the system of choosing the most secure means to the end, the system called Tutiorism.

But the reason is not that Tutiorism, which has been condemned, holds a place of honour for certain typical cases, but because everyone must be a Tutiorist, must choose the safest means, in certain clearly defined cases, because he is antecedently bound to do so. These cases, however, are not exceptions to Probabilism. It is necessary, therefore, to examine briefly these so-called apparent exceptions; it will readily be understood that they are not matters of dispute between the defenders of the various systems.

Henry Davis

Limitations of Probabilism

1. Probabilism cannot be applied to those cases where a definite object, such as salvation, real Baptism, valid Orders, has to be secured beyond possibility of doubt; for the actual and objective attainment of such an object can be secured only by the actual and objective fulfilment of certain specified conditions. Such conditions are absolutely essential, and it is obvious that no amount of probability on the side of any opinion will avail, unless that which is necessary is actually done. Thus, no probably valid administration of Baptism can avail to establish the certainty of valid administration; in such a case, since actual Baptism, and no probable Baptism, is necessary for salvation, it is no use invoking probabilities; the child to be baptized will benefit only by having received actual Baptism, and will not benefit because the minister's opinion was a highly probable opinion.

2. Probabilism cannot be applied to cases which have speculative probability in their favour but are in practice unlawful, whether on account of some positive enactment, or by reason of an express or virtual contract, whereby we may be bound to relinquish one line of action in order to adopt another that is more probably correct, or safer, or absolutely safe.

The following illustrations of these two classes of apparent exceptions will explain these limitations.

(*a*) In the matter of salvation we must follow that road which is quite safe, not that which is probably safe.

(*b*) In the matter of the Sacraments, we cannot invoke probabilities outside cases of extreme necessity. For example, certain liquids, as rose-water, are doubtfully though probably valid for Baptism. It would obviously be absurd, outside those cases of extreme necessity when no other liquid could be got, to confer Baptism with such probably valid matter, when valid matter could be got, since the child will not be baptized at all if the matter happen to be invalid. It is, therefore, altogether unlawful to use such doubtful matter when other matter, that is certainly sufficient, can be got. It is not a probable opinion that such matter might be employed. Probabilism as a moral system is not applicable to such cases; neither are they excep-

305

tions to Probabilism. Similarly, it is not permitted to use, in conferring the Sacrament of Extreme Unction, the oil of Catechumens instead of the oil of the Sick, however probable it may be that the Sacrament would thereby be validly administered. But in cases of real necessity, doubtful matter may be used when no better can be got, because charity demands that in such cases we should do the best possible under the circumstances, even though there be only the very slightest probability that what is done is of some avail. But in such cases, the Sacraments must be administered conditionally, so that we may safeguard the reverence that is due to them, as being the institutions of Christ.

(c) A third series of cases, specifically outside the scope of Probabilism, are those where our neighbour has acquired definite rights by virtue of express or virtual contract. For example, a physician may not employ probably safe remedies when he is at liberty to employ such as are more probably safe, or such as are absolutely safe, that is, of course, if the patient is willing to accept them. In desperate cases he may, obviously, employ probably safe remedies when he can use no others, because he is then doing all that it is humanly possible to do. The physician, surgeon, solicitor, judge, juryman, overseer, agent, have all of them entered into contracts with their neighbours, who, in consequence, have acquired rights that are quite certain. Probabilism can never be extended to those cases where our neighbour's rights are certainly in possession. But such cases are not exceptions to Probabilism.

(d) Lastly, others may have certain natural rights which it is wholly unlawful for us to invade; even a probable invasion of such rights will be entirely wrong, where there is no countervailing probable right on our side. Thus, for example, an innocent man has a right to his life. Consequently, I may not shoot at an object which is very probably not a man at all, though probably it is. My very probable conviction that it is a wild beast will not, as a fact, safeguard the man, if a man happens to be there, and every man has a right that I should not take the risk of injuring or killing him. In the cases just passed under review, it will be seen that there is not a question merely of the lawfulness of an action, but that manifest obligations, real and pressing, intervene to change the whole character of the act.

Since, then, these obligations already exist, there is no ground for applying principles of Probabilism. It will thus be acknowledged that such cases are no exceptions to the principles of Probabilism, for Probabilism is altogether engaged in solving doubts when an obligation is doubtful. In all of the cases mentioned above, obligations are not doubtful but certain.

Enunciation of Probabilism

Probabilism is a practical working moral system in which it is maintained, as a clear guiding principle of correct moral action, that where obligations are doubtful, it is permissible to follow the line of action indicated by a probable opinion in favour of liberty, although the opinion in favour of the obligation is the more probable. By the enunciation of such a principle it is not meant to convey the impression that we may do that which is probably right but more probably wrong. Every Probabilist, as indeed every man of sense, holds that we may never consciously do what is even probably wrong. The objections that are raised against the system are founded, for the most part, on a serious misconception of it. When we act, we must do that which is certainly right, so far, that is, as our judgment of the matter is concerned. It would be sinful to risk committing a sin, and to act in only a probably correct manner would be to act wrongfully. What the system carefully formulates is this principle, namely, that when I have a solidly probable opinion in favour of my liberty as against law, then the obligation of law does not bind me, I shall certainly act morally correctly if I disregard the doubtful obligation. To act with such a conviction is to act with moral certainty as to the rectitude of my action. Probabilism as a system must establish that if it is to establish anything. If it succeed in establishing that principle of action it will be a system of good moral action.

It is also to be observed that the Probabilism here defended is a moderate Probabilism, that is, a system that takes as its starting point a really probable opinion such as any prudent man could assent to in the ordinary business of life.

Opinions that are only just remotely probable, to which a prudent man would be slow to give his assent in the practical issues of life, are here ruled out of court. The same arguments will appeal to various minds in very different ways and with widely varying cogency. If some persons buttress their actions by flimsy opinions which, they aver, are probable to them, we can only say that they are mistaken in their estimate; it is the business of the true and prudent Probabilist to apply principles sincerely and cautiously, since natural inclination adds its own momentum to all judicial decisions where self is concerned. But, as stated above, the abuse of Probabilism is no reason for denying its reasonableness.

Proofs of Probabilism

1. A law does not bind unless, in respect of the object which the law envisages, such as almsgiving, it imposes on our will a strict moral necessity of action or of omission. Now a law cannot do this when it is really probable that either action or omission is permissible. Thus, for example, on seeing a beggar, I may reflect that I am bound to bestow an alms on him; I have, however, other obligations which probably cannot be fulfilled if I part with my money. The probability in the latter case is real and solid, but yet it is not so great as the probability that I am bound, here and now, to assist the beggar. Would anyone insist on the bestowal of alms under pain of sin? Not at all; the obligation of almsgiving does not clearly exist in the case, precisely because the contrary obligation may exist. Most people, however, would doubtless bestow the alms. They would do well and would be acting charitably, and yet when it is not a question of a graver obligation superseding a lighter one, but only a question of greater or less probabilities, either course may be rightly chosen. To insist on the bestowal of an alms in the case would be to adopt a system of conduct wherein more probable obligations would have to be always fulfilled.

2. Conscience is the ultimate arbiter of right action. Now conscience does not and cannot tell me to act in accordance with a law if its existence is uncertain. Thus if after reasonable investigation, I conclude that the law probably does not exist at all or does not bind me, how can conscience tell me that I

am, here and now, certainly bound to fulfil a law that probably does not exist? I have, for example, good reason for thinking that I have already performed an obligatory task, but I am not sure; indeed, there are more probable reasons for thinking that I have not done so. However, the fulfilment having probably taken place, can conscience tell me to do the task here and now under pain of sin? Once given a really good reason for thinking I have fulfilled an obligation, I am at present free. Of course, I may come to realize the obligation more clearly later on; but provided that here and now I am not conscious of a clear and certain obligation, my conscience cannot issue any command.

3. It is reasonable to adopt a line of action that is probably right where the contrary line of action, more probably right, is not manifestly the only right one. That is, when in speculative doubt concerning the lawfulness of a given action, is it not eminently reasonable, after sufficient care has been taken to weigh the arguments on both sides, to act on a reasonable opinion? One can say: Seeing that I cannot solve my doubts, I believe it reasonable to act on either of two contrary opinions, each of which is probably true. What I do in thus making up my mind is quite reasonable. Consequently, a man who acts on a really probable opinion in cases where obligations are doubtful, acts prudently and reasonably. It is important, however, not to confuse speculative and practical doubt.

4. A man must be considered as a free agent first, and as subject to law secondly, for he cannot be subject to law unless he is conceived to have some faculty which is antecedently capable of being subjected.

Consequently, in the conflict between the obligation of law and the freedom of man's will, the *onus* lies on the law of proving possession and priority. Now where a man is probably free from obligation, although the obligation more probably exists, his freedom is in possession, for the reason that it is so and always remains so, until law can point to prior claim on account of certain and clear possession. Law certainly cannot do that, if its existence, here and now, is only probable, however high the degree of probability for it may be. Therefore, in doubtful obligations, a probable opinion in favour of liberty may be followed in spite of a more probable opinion to the contrary in favour of law.

It cannot be urged that since man is born subject to God's law, the law is, therefore, antecedent to liberty. Man is, indeed, born thus subject to God's law in general, but he is not as a moral agent bound by any particular law, until he comes to the knowledge of such law and realizes that he must subject a free will to it. He certainly could never realize such a possibility unless he were conscious of the priority of liberty. "God made man from the beginning and left him in the hand (under the command) of his own counsel. He added His Commandments and Precepts" (Ecclus. 15, 14).

5. A law that is uncertain (i.e., not certainly existing or not certainly applicable) cannot beget an obligation that is certain. In practice, an uncertain obligation is no obligation at all, since a true and certain obligation implies the following absolute judgment: "I am bound to do this or omit that." Now when the law is uncertain, the conscience need never admit the necessity of such absolute practical judgment, because the command of the legislator is not absolute and certain, and cannot, therefore, be revealed as such in consciousness. Law must re-echo in conscience with no uncertain sound.

6. In Religious Orders a subject may lawfully bind himself to obey his Superior in all that is not manifestly sinful; consequently, he can bind himself to do what is only probably but not certainly and manifestly right, or in other words, to obey in matters that, so far as his private judgment is concerned, are less safe and less probably right. Indeed, in doing so, he may be sure that he is obeying God. It might be urged that when a Superior commands what is not manifestly sinful, the subject must look upon the order as manifestly right by reason of the jurisdiction of his Superior, who is in the place of Christ our Lord. But this plea is hardly pertinent, for we are considering the subject matter of the Superior's orders and not the sanction which they have. Now it is obvious that the subject matter of precepts varies greatly in the moral sphere, since the moral value of what Superiors command, apart from the added worth of obedience, differs objectively in different cases; the objective moral value of an act of charity that is commanded is not the

same as the objective moral value of an act of temperance. The subject judges for himself, and cannot help judging the amount of apparent worth and lawfulness in that which is commanded. The order of the Superior does not add or take away from the apparent probabilities, otherwise there would be no point in permitting subjects to exercise their own judgment on the matter of commands, as they do when they apprehend, as is supposed, the lawfulness of an object in itself. This being so, it is obvious that Superiors may order what is probably right.

Now the subject in a Religious Order may take a vow to obey in matters that are less probably right, so far as his private judgment is concerned, always of course short of manifest sin. If, then, a vow can be taken to perform such actions, they must be in themselves perfectly lawful to perform. It is, then, lawful under these circumstances to follow the less probable opinion, and therefore if this is permissible in the case of those who have taken a vow of obedience, it must be permissible in general.

7. In the case of real doubt concerning the obligation of a law, that is to say, when there are good reasons for thinking that the law does not exist, a solidly probable opinion in favour of personal liberty as against the law is equivalent to invincible ignorance of the law, because, in order to be bound by law, a man must clearly apprehend its manifest obligation here and now. It is surely not sufficient that he is conscious of a doubtful obligation. It might be urged that, under the circumstances, he ought to be conscious of the obligation of choosing the safer course, and of fulfilling the law, doubtful though it may be. Such a plea undermines every system of moral action except Tutiorism.

Objections to Probabilism

1. "Those who defend Probabilism on the ground that a doubtful law cannot bind, might ask themselves whether non-observance of such a law may result in material sin, however you may have convinced yourself that the non-observance is justified."

This objection may be urged against every system of moral conduct, for whenever, acting even upon a morally

311

certain opinion that a law does not bind, an agent considers himself free from obligation, the law may nevertheless exist. Subjective certitude and high degrees of probability do not settle objective facts; they settle only obligations here and now.

Therefore, even in the most rigorous system of conduct, the law can be actually invaded, and material violation, that is, material sin may result. Probabilists, therefore, quite freely admit that material sin may result from the employment of their principles, but by the same reasoning it may result in every moral system except absolute rigorism. It certainly will result in any human system whatever, because one who does not possess divine knowledge cannot always be certain that his resolution of doubt results in an absolute equation between his conduct and objective moral law. All that we are bound to do is to be morally certain in our consciences that we are acting in accordance with what we conceive to be objective morality. Being endowed with only human intellects that have their limitations, we cannot do more. Moral certainty of right conduct is quite sufficient. We cannot always get metaphysical certainty. Material sin, then, may result from the employment of any system of conduct, but Probabilists maintain that their system certainly guarantees what is necessary in order to avoid material sin; to expect more than this, would be to expect man to be omniscient.

2. The objection continues as follows: "In case they [Probabilists] finds it so [find that non-observance of a doubtful law may result in material sin], they might think out the question how a law that does not bind can beget even material sin."

The question is not difficult to answer. A law that does not bind, here and now, because a man is invincibly ignorant of it, assuredly can beget material, though not formal sin, because the actual transgression—viewed materially—of a law that really exists, but is not manifested in his conscience because he is ignorant of it, is an actual transgression of law and order. This law and order exist, whether he thinks of them or not.

But since such an order objectively exists, when a man inadvertently performs an act in violation of the order, he must certainly be conceived as committing a disorderly act, in other words, a material sin. A drunkard, for example, who, in a fit of intoxication, inadvertently commits homicide, has committed material sin, but being irresponsible at the time and not having foreseen the possibility of homicide, he is not formally guilty of the sin. The distinction between formal and material sin is too obvious to need further comment.

3. An opinion that is said to be solidly probable appears to lose all its probability when opposed by an opinion that is much more probable, just as in a pair of scales, the heavier weight exercises a necessarily overwhelming influence, so that the force of the lighter weight is counteracted.

In reply to this often repeated objection it may be stated that provided the less probable opinion is still really probable, as it may be, if founded on good reasons, it will retain its power of appealing to me on its merits as probable. This is known to be the case in actual life, where a question is raised that cannot be demonstrably settled; there is found room for contrary opinions, even though one opinion be much more probably true than another. The human mind is not like a pair of scales, because assent to probable reasons, if they are good, is freely but not necessarily given. Assent is necessarily given only to reasons that are evidently true, but probably true reasons never oblige the mind to assent, and consequently, when I act on the strength of a probable opinion, I am always conscious that though I am morally right in so acting, since I act prudently, nevertheless, the opinion of others who do not agree with me may be the true view of the case. But that consciousness does not rob my present assent of all its value for me. I have once for all assented, quite freely and reasonably, to sufficiently cogent reasons. Who will say that I am deluding myself, and that I can never act on an opinion while admitting the probability of its contrary? Who will say that the reasons which influence me to give my free assent are not only not true reasons at all—which we may admit—but are not even sufficient reasons to warrant reasonable action? So long as a set of reasons does not demonstrably prove an opinion based on them to be absolutely correct, I am perfectly free to think that these reasons do not oblige me to assent to the opinion.

I may, therefore, quite reasonably hold a contrary opinion based on fewer and less good reasons, provided always that they are sufficiently good.

4. It might be said that it is more prudent to assent to more probable reasons, and that it is imprudent and unreasonable to assent to less probable reasons.

Probabilists reply that it is entirely prudent to assent to good probable reasons, and that they admit that it is also entirely prudent to assent to more probable reasons, but that there can be no question of any degree of prudence in the matter, because even very probable reasons are not strictly evidence, and it is quite possible, though less likely, that the better reasons may be false.

If, then, it will be urged, the more probable reasons are more likely to be true, why should we not accept the more probable reasons and so become Probabiliorists? The answer is that good probable reasons may be true and may represent objective fact; this being so, should we not admit that a man is prudent and reasonable when he adopts an opinion that may be quite true, though other opinions may be true also. Is he not acting correctly if he do so?

The Probabiliorist may continue: "But since more probable reasons more nearly approach truth, the Probabilist consciously recedes from truth by following a less probable opinion." More probable reasons do not evidently approach truth more nearly than a less probable reason; they, indeed, probably do so, but they may also be false. We cannot be obliged to give assent to greater probabilities.

5. The Probabilist, it is urged, exposes himself to the danger of violating law, and consequently he sins, because he might, if he wished, act upon a more probable opinion, and thus be less likely to violate law. This objection may be urged against every system short of absolute Tutiorism. Even the most probable opinion leaves one still open to material violation of law. Furthermore, by acting according to a less probable opinion, a man does not expose himself to the danger of certainly violating law; he is consciously violating no law at all, because the obligation is doubtful, and therefore for him nonexistent.

6. Probabilism, it is said, is an easy road to self-indulgence, it leads to the blunting of the moral sense, and it minimizes obligations. The objection, as stated, is valid in greater or less degree against every system yet invented by man, because personal error is certain to intrude itself into the application of any system. The Probabilist does not admit that his system is essentially conducive to laxity; a good thing may always be abused. Every system, Probabilism, no less than others, must be used prudently.

It is an entire misconception of Probabilism to take any chance opinion as a solidly probable opinion, or to suppose that any group of five or six chance writers on Moral Theology is sufficient to constitute a probable opinion. They must be noted for their learning and prudence. If their reasons on a given subject have been completely met and rebutted, their opinions will have become improbable.

Furthermore, Probabilism does not minimize obligations, it reduces obligations to their true proportions. It possesses this merit above other systems, that it does not impose obligations on one, unless it has been clearly proved that they exist. But as it is not a system to be used in every event of life, but only in cases of doubtful obligations, it cannot be said to be a method of driving a bargain with God. It is a reasonable application of sound principles. The Probabilist is quite conscious of many and serious obligations already existing, but he objects to adding doubtful obligations to the human burden.

7. A man who rejects the more probable reasons on the side of law, and acts on the less probable in favour of liberty, seems to be acting irrationally, since his judgment should be inclined to the greater probability.

This is an argument against Probabilism that derives its force from the confusion between the necessary assent given to evidence, and a free assent given to probability. The Probabilist always admits the greater probability, where it exists, of the contrary opinion, but he maintains that this is not evidence but probability only. So long as we confine our attention to probabilities, we are not obliged to give assent to them, however probable they may be. Since, therefore, there can exist, as we suppose, a good solid presumption on one side against even greater presumptions on the other, one may say: "I am not bound either by any moral law that I know of, or by the exigencies of intellectual honesty, to subscribe to an opinion that is only probable. I am free to choose either opinion and to act upon it. If, therefore, I freely assent to and act upon the less probable opinion, I am acting as a rational being, I am guilty of no intellectual dishonesty. I am using free will in a perfectly reasonable manner." Though we might elect to follow the more probable reasons in favour of law, and willingly curtail our own liberty of action, could we honestly impose that obligation on others? If we could not, that which is morally right to advise, is morally right to do, under similar circumstances.

8. I ought to aim in all my actions at conformity with the objective moral order. How can I be said to do so, when I follow a line of action that is opposed to it more probably than not, having abandoned a standard of action that is more probably conformed to the objective standard of God's Eternal Law?

The objection is valid if it confine itself to the enunciation of the general principle that in all actions of life we ought to aim at regulating action with right order. But although we all admit this in the abstract, when we come to particular concrete cases, in which it is impossible to discern what is certainly the right moral order, then such clear perception being, as we suppose, impossible to attain, how can it be said that we are obliged to conform our actions to a standard that is not discernible? For it cannot be said to be discernible, if we do not and cannot, in a concrete case, perceive it. Furthermore, if it be said that we are obliged at least to tend in a direction towards more probable conformity with law, the Probabilist will reply that we must always tend towards absolute conformity with law. It is to be presumed that we do so in reality, whenever we fulfil manifest obligations, so soon as they become manifest. The Probabilist is in the habitual disposition of desiring to conform to law whensoever it imposes obligations upon him that are manifest; he does not feel bound to conform to law that is doubtful.

9. The Probabilist contention seems to be that you may do that which, more probably, is wrong.

Probabilists reply that if a less probable opinion in favour of liberty be acted upon, the action is altogether right. It is not true to say that it is only probably right and more probably wrong; it is certainly right. The greater antecedent speculative probability has nothing to do with the morality of the action in the concrete. The same argument might be employed against every system of conduct, short of Tutiorism, for however a man acts, he would, if judged by antecedent speculative reasons, probably be wrong, unless he chose absolutely the safest course.

But, in truth, the objection takes no cognizance of this important fact, namely, that action on a probable opinion against doubtful law is right, if the opinion is sufficiently probable to give good guarantee that the law is truly doubtful; and furthermore, such action being right, it cannot at the same time be more probably wrong, even although the law more probably exists.

10. In Ecclesiasticus (37, 20) we are told: "In all thy words let the true word go before thee, and steady counsel before every action"; our Divine Saviour is the Truth by which we must guide all our lives; the gate is narrow and the way is strait that leadeth to life. It is urged against Probabilists, that they attempt to make the gate very wide and the way very broad that leads to life, that they aim, not at truth, but at probabilities by which to guide life, and that before every action they expect and are satisfied not with the true but with probable reasons. He is, therefore, it is said, sophistical, and is under the condemnation uttered in Ecclesiasticus: "He that speaketh sophistically is hateful, he shall be destitute of everything."

The objection is specious; it arises from a radical misconception of the theory. Even Probabilists teach without any uncertainty whatever that the law must be obeyed to the letter; they teach that we may not expose ourselves to probable sin; that the truth is that standard of conduct by which we must endeavour to guide our lives, and that the gate still remains narrow and the way strait in every approved system of moral conduct. But what they are at pains to make clear is this, namely, that where we cannot get at manifest truth, where we are the prey to anxious doubt, where there are reasons for and against a particular line of action, it is not the part of a wise counsellor to impose on others obligations that do not clearly exist. Such a system of morality would impose intolerable burdens; it would lead to a species of rigorism, which, as a fact, good people do not feel obliged to adopt in their own case; it would be a remedy that is worse than the disease it is intended to cure, and finally, it has no sanction in Holy Scripture, nor in the universal teaching of the past.

It is true, indeed, that he who loves the danger shall perish in it (Ecclus. 3, 27), but the Holy Writer speaks there of the man of hard heart, who loves the perilous state of grievous sin, and in spite of grace, perseveres in such a state; it becomes a moral certainty that he will persist in his grievous state. The Probabilist, far from loving the danger of sin of any sort, makes it his special purpose before acting, to be quite sure that he is not infringing any known law of God. In such an attitude, he maintains and rightly so, that his conscience is correct and conformed with obligations. That is the sum and substance of his contention; that is what, as it seems to him, he succeeds in proving.

If it be said that S. Paul warns us against Probabilism in these words: "But prove all things; hold fast that which is good; from all appearance of evil refrain yourselves" (I Thess. 5, 21, 22), because in following the less probable of two opinions we do not seem to be avoiding the appearance of evil, it may be replied that if these words referred to a standard of moral conduct, they would be equally effective against the severer systems mentioned above, and would lead to a definite Tutiorism. S. Paul cannot be thought to convey such an impossible view. His words, on the contrary, primarily refer to prophecies that have to be tested and approved by competent authority. Secondarily, they may relate to conduct, but they should undoubtedly be read: "Keep yourselves from every form of evil." The exhortation of S. Paul is, of course, carried out in every Catholic system of moral conduct, not excepting that of Probabilism.

To sum up: The entire controversy between Probabilists and every other school of thought on the subject of right moral action really turns on this question: Is it incontrovertible that *a doubtful law does not bind*? If that proposition is certain, Probabilism is certain. It appears obvious to Probabilists that the statement is incontrovertible. They find it in S. Thomas and even in S. Alphonsus, two of the greatest masters of Moral Theology, not to speak of a vast array of other theologians. Indeed, the difficulties that issue in every system that rejects the proposition are so serious as to make right moral conduct extremely difficult, if not, indeed, humanly impossible.

11. Compensationism, or the Principle of the Sufficient Cause

Some authors, dissatisfied with the current moral systems, thought out what they have called a system of Compensationism. The most notable writers on this system were Manier, Laloux, and Potton. The latest adherent to the system, Prümmer, thus states the case for it (I, n. 351): All former systems labour under grave objections, and in practice impede rather than help the confessor. Every lover of truth adopts what is certainly the more likely to be true. In order to avoid a greater evil, a confessor may adopt a probable opinion in preference to one that is more probable, but it is never permitted to act thus without a grace and proportionate cause. In practice the system of Compensationism, or of Sufficient Cause, or of Christian Prudence, is to be preferred to all others.

In this system, when the case arises in which we wish to know if it is permissible to follow a really probable opinion in favour of liberty and to abandon the more probable opinion in favour of law, we must prudently examine all the circumstances. The holier and more important the law, and the more probable its obligation, the more cogent ought to be the reason we allege for favouring liberty; contrariwise, the greater the benefit that is hoped for in respect of the penitent, the more easily shall we permit the use of a probable opinion that favours liberty. Having stated the terms of the system, Prümmer proceeds to explain it. In practice, he maintains, this system is advised, for by employing it we avoid splitting on the rocks of Probabilism, Equiprobabilism, and Probabiliorism, and we act in accordance with Christian prudence, a virtue that directs all the other moral virtues, and is very necessary for the good life. Up to the time of Medina, he continues, none of the other modern systems was known to confessors, and yet very holy and prudent confessors administered the Sacraments of Penance, and did so with great fruit. Are modern confessors wiser than those? Are the sins committed to-day different from the sins of former times? The confessor who prudently examines the conditions of life of his penitent and the circumstances of his acts will pass a correct judgment if he attend first of all to the principle, 'In doubt, we are to be guided by presumptions'; and then carefully consult good authors, and not trust too much in his own judgment. Acting on such principles, he will be applying the best of all systems, one that is rightly called the system of Christian Prudence. Of that virtue, it is written: "Her ways are beautiful ways and all her paths are peaceable" (Prov. 3, 17).

Criticism of Compensationism

The adherents of the three modern systems, set forth in these pages, adopt all the principles as explained by Prümmer, and, indeed, they could not fail to do so, for they all regard presumptions, they consult good authors, and they distrust their own judgment to the extent of admitting the probability of the contrary system, but like Prümmer, they think their own system the best. If they are faithful to their own principles, they will act with the utmost Christian prudence, and in settling obligations they must always weigh the gravity of the law and the spiritual benefit of the penitent.

It seems, then, that Prümmer's quarrel with modern systems is not so serious as would appear, but it is useless to invoke another system and call it the system of Christian Prudence, if, as we maintain, that system already exists in Probabilism. If, on the other hand, Prümmer believed that a more serious law, if really doubtful, had any advantage, so to speak, over a less serious law which is also doubtful, he would have gone some way towards Tutiorism. The system of Compensationism, as explained by others than Prümmer, appears to approach Tutiorism, a system which ordinarily we are not bound to adopt. Yet other writers invoke, in proof of Compensationism, the strange principles: "A law imperfectly known imperfectly binds," and, "a law that is doubtful has greater

binding force than no law at all." These principles are meaningless.

Gerald Vann
1906-1963

Christian morality is a way of life. In order to be properly understood, it must be seen within the full context of the Christian mystery. It is only within this context that one begins to sense the richness of the moral life. Right and wrong, good and evil, virtue and vice all take on specific meanings in the light of Christian faith and Christian worship.

The selection below, taken from The Heart of Man *by Father Gerald Vann, a Dominican theologian, offers a necessary corrective to contemporary discussions of moral problems. In the heat of a debate over birth control, abortion, war, authority, divorce and similar important issues, it is all too easy to forget that the resolution of any human question must be anchored in a rich vision of life if it is to lead to the enrichment of the person or persons involved in the question.*

Morality should never be misidentified as a mere list of Do's and Don'ts. This simplistic approach to life, though it may appear clear and orderly, is actually an exercise in missing the point. It leads inevitably to a rigid, shallow type of existence.

Is there an alternative? Yes. Seen within the context of doctrine and worship, Christian morality becomes a process of rebirth of the self in God, a recognition that God, not the ego, is the center of self. Whereas the prohibition approach stresses only the minimum, Christian morality as a celebration of love invites the human to experience life to the maximum. Prohibitions and commands are ultimately wrong, for they make it impossible for us to love.

Obviously the level of morality discussed by Father Vann calls for tremendous maturity and a mastery of the human condition. But the Christian is the one who is committed to such a level and will settle for nothing less. He has mastered the material of life and acquired the art of living. He is the man of vision and the man of power, which meet at the summit of his moral life and become one. The mature Christian knows that true morality is God-centered, sacramental and liturgical. He knows that the end of morality is wholeness of life and creative energy. He knows that when you live in love, you cannot live alone, you cannot think or will or act alone. He knows that in the fullness of the vision of the Godhead there is nothing that we cannot love.

Need it all be only a wistful dream? The poetic vision of a few men and women who have anchored their daily lives in prayerful meditation? If the approach to morality proposed by Father Vann is the true one, what has happened in and to Christianity? Why, in the face of a vision of life that is so exhilarating and enriching, will most Christians choose to back off and settle for security in a list of Do's and Don'ts. Father Vann's work is worthwhile reading, for it presents what Christian morality is really all about. It is also bothersome reading, for circling around it is that haunting question: Why has the twentieth century chosen to say no?

THE HEART OF MAN

T he way back to God is the way of worship. If all that
we are and become and do in our many-leveled life
could be made one in worship, we should be saints.
Some people think that Christian morality is no more than a
series of Don'ts; others a little less ill-informed think it is no
more than a series of Do's. These things are included, for being
and doing are interdependent; but it is being that comes first in
importance; and Christian morality tells us first of all not what
we should do, still less what we should not do, but what we
should be.

That is why you cannot possibly separate, as some people
would have us do, the Church's moral teaching from its beliefs
about God's revelation of Himself to the world. You cannot
possibly separate them, because the moral teaching is entirely
determined by the doctrine; and if you try to isolate it, you
destroy it. You could isolate this or that element in it; you
could cling to the ideals of justice, kindness, generosity, fortitude; but these virtues would then cease to be the Christian
virtues, because they would be divorced from worship.

You find a marked similarity on the surface between
the *Ethics* of Aristotle and that part of the *Summa* of St.
Thomas which deals with morality; but the similarity is far less
striking than the difference. Aristotle will tell you how to act
wisely and well in accordance with reason, and what he says is
often so true and so salutary that St. Thomas is at pains to
repeat it; but all that is secondary, all that is relatively unim-
portant; you can obey all these precepts and acquire all these
good habits and still find at the end that the "good life" has
been led by the false self and not by the true. These things are
secondary; what is of first importance is the reality whose
presence kindles and whose absence kills them: the rebirth of

the self in God, the recognition that God and not the ego is the center of the self.

You remember the Pharisee and the publican in the Temple. The Pharisee was living the "good life"; but notice what he says: "I give thanks . . . I fast . . . I give tithes," and the good deeds turn to ashes because it is always "I"; it is the self which competently acts, the self which is served; there is no suggestion of need of the Other, the hunger of the heart is forgotten because pride has repressed it. The publican probably fails miserably to live the "good life," but he has the core of Christian as opposed to pagan morality, he has the one thing necessary, the pearl of great price, because he has learnt that he must say with his whole being not "I" but "Lord."

Christian morality is worship. There are prohibitions: they are the minimum though many of us find that even this minimum is more than we can achieve. Thou shalt not kill, thou shalt not steal, thou shalt not commit adultery, thou shalt not covet: it is not always easy to keep these and all the lesser prohibitions of anger and injustice and intemperateness which they include. But notice how Christianity changes them. Thou shalt love: this is the essence of Christian morality; and to love is to dethrone the false self and be able to say, "It is thou." You are forbidden, then, to kill and steal and covet; but you are forbidden *because* these are sins against love, because they hurt those with whom you should be living in love. The proud man may refrain from these things because it is to his own interest; the Christian must refrain from these things primarily because if he does not he cannot love, he cannot live life in its wholeness, he cannot worship.

But a second thing follows. If it is love that leads you to refrain from injustice, it will lead you to more than that. As love grows deeper and wider in you and you come nearer to the fulness of life, you will find that this minimum becomes hopelessly insufficient; you will find the negative carried further and further over to the affirmation of its opposite. The saint's love prompts him not to kill in the service of the false self, but to sacrifice his own life if need be in the service of God and men; not to steal for himself, but to share all that he has with others; not to destroy a family life by wrecking its unity, but to give

326

himself, even perhaps by forgoing his own family life, to restoring the family life of the world. Whatever he does is done thus as worship of the One and of the many in the One. How terrible when we find ourselves thinking of the moral law as a denial of freedom and happiness. These things are not wrong because they are forbidden: they are forbidden because they are wrong; and they are wrong because they are alien to the nature of man in general—because freedom and a full and dignified human life are impossible until they are outlawed; but principally because they make it impossible to escape from isolation, they make it impossible for us to love.

The lover does not find that love takes his freedom from him; on the contrary, he is tied and unhappy only if he is impeded from serving what he loves. If we obey the commandments because we fear that otherwise we shall be punished, we are not yet emancipated from the "bondage of the law" of which St. Paul speaks, we are not yet free. If we keep the commandments because we recognize that they are the necessary pattern of our own perfection, we are free but not yet happy, for we are still alone. But if, while accepting the commandments, as men, because they are the pattern of perfection, we yet obey them primarily because we are living in love, then we are fully free and fully happy, we are both man and child.

Christian morality tells us what we must be. We must be whole. If we are whole, or trying to be whole, we shall act in a certain way, the way of love and worship. If we love and worship, we shall refrain from acting in ways that hurt love and destroy worship. That is the Christian order. Our Lord did not say, "I am come that you may have a code of ethics," though He told us much about the way we should act; He said, "I am come that you may have life, and have it more abundantly."

The moral way is the way of rebirth. The new life is given chiefly through the sacraments; to receive it adequately and respond to it, we must be men of prayer and virtue; the power is from God, but God waits upon our will.

We must be men of prayer. Some people think that prayer just means asking for things, and if they fail to receive exactly what they asked for, they think the whole thing a fraud. Prayer does mean asking, though it means far more than that; but it must be not the proud self but the lover who asks. The lover may ask for gifts; but he will not want to ask against the will of the other, and he will not want to ask for gifts that would hurt love; he cannot, because his deepest wants are not his own. There is nothing very mysterious, still less is there anything superstitious, about the kind of prayer that is asking, if you accept the idea that there is spiritual energy and power as well as physical, and that the first can and does influence the second. Spiritual power unaided—the power of a personality—can produce physical changes in men and cause them to act uncharacteristically in this way or in that; and similarly the power of spirit in the universe may be taken to be capable of influencing physical events. One thing is immovable, being perfect, the will of God; but we do not suppose that prayer can alter God's providence, we believe that God's providence includes the power of prayer among the many converging influences which, under His will, produce events. What is superstitious is to suppose that prayer can, in fact, compel God's will, to suppose that prayer is magic, to suppose that if I pray for a coat, a coat will infallibly appear in my wardrobe. We pray within the design of God's providence, not against it.

But even if you take the superstition out of it, you are still far from real prayer unless you pray as a lover. "Give me this gift, but only if you want to." "Let this chalice pass from me, but not my will but thine be done." Love has such power that it can extort; but to extort is the last thing it wants to do. (That is why it is so terrible when the lover sinks back into the false selfhood which grasps and utilizes; for then he extorts, and perhaps only long after realizes he has hurt or destroyed love.) To pray is to ask as lover of God; it is also to ask as lover of the world. We are a family. Not only, "Give me this gift if you think it will be good for me," but also, "Give me this gift if you think it will be good for the family." We pray not for ourselves merely but for the world; and even when we pray for ourselves, we have to remember the good of the world.

But prayer is much more than asking. If we kept it to that, we might forget the Giver in our concern for His gifts. If we follow the example of the Church in the Mass, we shall begin with confession and penitence, the prayer of the publican; we shall go on to adoration and praise and the still, wordless prayer of wonder; and only then shall we ask, when our attention is fixed on the true Center of the self; and even so, though we pray for our own private needs and desires, we shall remember the "Collects"—the united prayers for the united needs of the world. And indeed, just as we see things at their most real when we see them and love them in God, so our prayer is most powerful and most of value when it is gathered up into the cosmic prayer of Christ and His Church. As we take the whole world to the Mass to be offered and blessed and restored, so we take our prayer to be offered and empowered. The first thing that prayer can do for us is to make us humble: to make us realize that the source of power—the power to pray, the power to live the life of virtue—is not primarily in ourselves, but in God. When prayer has thus taught us the Christian approach to morality, we shall begin to turn the whole moral life into prayer.

The Christian life, then, is always the life of the child. Yes, indeed; but it is also and equally the life of the man. There is the twofold progress: to live more and more in the life and the power of God, to grow more and more in strength and maturity of mind and will and personality. The more deeply and fully you become the Other, the more deeply and fully you become yourself. And as the ultimate purpose and motive of all activity is the giving of glory to God's love, which is also and at the same time my own perfection and happiness, so the means to the end is worshiping obedience to God's power and will within me, which is also and at the same time my own labor and effort. We believe that through baptism we are given the power to live the life of virtue; but that I should act here and now virtuously depends on my own long and laborious efforts to translate the power into practice, to acquire the habit of so acting. We have to train ourselves to freedom, to think for ourselves and judge for ourselves and act for ourselves, for only free acts can be the material out of which the good life is fashioned; and the training consists in constantly acting as we ought so as to form the habit of acting as we ought, for acts are in the realm of doing but habits are in the realm of being, and it is only when we *are* good that we have the good life. So we become good in so far as we become free *men;* but the freedom we acquire is the freedom to obey love, the freedom to live the life of the *child.*

We believe that the moral life is the search for wholeness. Some have taught that the end in view is to become the perfectly rational man, and that the way is to suppress the passions and emotions lest they sweep like a gale through the trim temple of reason and disturb the worshipers. It is Talleyrand's *surtout point de zèle,* and the correctness of eighteenth-century religion and the eighteenth-century God. We have seen already what happens when you repress half the personality. But what a religion! You would be saying to God, "Oh yes, I worship you; but only with that portion of your handiwork which I find it possible to consider respectable." You might attempt to praise God thus: but you would stifle yourself with the starchy formalities of your illuminated address. You could praise Him with logic and science, never with timbrel and harp, never with poetry and ecstasy and ardor, never with love. Christian morality is worship: not the worship of the divine mind by the human reason, but the worship by the whole man of the whole God. You worship with the whole man in so far as instincts, passions, emotions, mind, will are integrated and fulfilled in the unity of the personality by being "harnessed to the service of the Light." And again, how is this process brought about? By childlike obedience to the power and sharing in the life of God; by laboriously acquiring the maturity and mastery of manhood.

Virtue is defined as the enduring possession of the power to act with facility and readiness in a certain way. You can speak instead, if you will, of a "good habit"; but it is not a question of a mechanical habit in the sense of a mannerism which is often unconscious and unconsciously acquired. The musician acquires by long hard practice the enduring ability to play well; if you have acquired the habit of temperateness or generosity you will normally and spontaneously be gentle and generous. But it is more than a technique. The musician must have the technical skill; but technical skill alone does not make the musician. To bring the technique to life, you must have music in the soul. Vision without skill is dumb; but skill without vision is dead. So with the moral virtues: there is the acquired skill, but underneath the skill, the vision. You must know the presence of God in the soul.

First, then, maturity of mind, mastery, autonomy: not the proud, assumed autonomy of the false self which tries to master God, but the real autonomy of the man who has learnt to master himself. You must acquire knowledge, you must be critical and learn to judge, you must be able to make up your own mind, you must try to be wise: because the judgment, "This is the right action and not that," must rest, in the last resort, with that power in the mind to make practical moral decisions which we call conscience. Then you find the four great modes of right action, prudence, justice, fortitude, temperateness, as elements in every virtuous action; but these things are the possession of the mature personality; they mean the exercise of reason, courage, and control. And each particular virtue in its turn means a similar mastery of the particular material involved. The man of virtue is master and maker; for he has mastered the material of life and acquired the art of living.

But behind the skill, the vision. The temperate man is usually absolved from the labor of reasoning out how to act temperately here and now; he knows by a kind of instinct; and he knows because he not only *has* tenderness and the humility of the flesh, but *is* humble and tender. So you find in him a childlike freshness and spontaneity that are denied to the purely rational man.

Then again, all virtue is grounded in humility and is a mode of worship; and again you have the dependence and smallness of the child.

There is a third thing. The moral life as a whole is rooted in the life shared directly with God, the life of faith, hope, and love. And by faith we are led, not against reason but beyond reason, to the knowledge of God in Himself and therefore of ourselves. By hope we are kept young of heart; for it teaches us to trust in God, to work with all our energy but to leave the future to Him: it gives us poverty of spirit and so saves us from solicitude. And by love we are not told about God, we are brought to Him; we are brought down into the depths of the soul to become one with Him there, to learn through sorrow and repentance to be reborn and say, "It is thyself"; and then it drives us out again to rediscover the world and to make all men and things our brothers, to show us the unity of the family of creation: and so we have still more emphatically the affirmation that God is the center and that, if we live, we live in Him.

And then, finally, there is the direct influence and impulsion of the Spirit upon the soul; for though the power of God that is given us is expressed through the virtues, the vitality of the virtues themselves is limited by the fact that they are the possession of finite human mind and will. We try to hold the infinite in human hands. We see as in a glass, darkly; however fervent the faithful Christian, there is an imperfection in faith itself because in itself it is obscure; there is an imperfection in the moral life because the apprehension of the good is limited in itself by the narrow compass of the human mind. But as the wind that bloweth where it listeth, so is everyone that is born of the Spirit: it is the breath of the Spirit that gives us the freedom of the sons of God because it raises human action above the confines of the purely human. All the powers of the personality will be given this enlightening and energizing impulsion if we can learn to accept and respond to it: the mind's darkness illumined by a direct experience of God, an intuitive perception of divine truth, a sense of the Christian life both in theory and in action; the moral life deepened and strengthened by an immediately God-given sense of worship and reverence, and by a childlike confidence that is proof against all dangers, together with an "insatiable desire" to overcome them all in His service.

Here, when this direct loving obedience to the Spirit is perfect (for here, too, God waits upon our will), we have the fulness of the moral life, the immensity of power and personality of the Christian saint. Think for a moment of a type of man with whom we are too familiar. At his most characteristic he is somewhat stout and red of face from heavy food; he is capable in office or shop or factory; when he leaves it he likes a good meal, though he is hardly discriminating; he reads the paper or glances at a magazine or two; he likes a tot of whisky, though he is inclined to bolt it a little thoughtlessly; he may while away the time uncritically at a cinema; if he talks about anything at all outside his own immediate work or pleasures, he will probably repeat in slightly garbled form the political views of his morning paper; he calls his friends "old boy" and his wife "old girl," and if he is what is known as a clean-living man he will probably develop an irritability or some other mild form of mental or physical disorder which he will ascribe to business anxieties; he will never get to know his son and daughter and would find it impossible if he tried, and when he is dying he will possibly shed a secret tear or two over his dog, whom he has never understood either. Could we say that this was a moral life? We could not, for the simple reason that it was not a life at all. Morality is a sort of life, not a sort of death.

If ever we feel forced to conclude that the great majority of a nation is like this, we shall have to conclude also that the nation is doomed. It is possible to be dead in every sense that matters and still go on catching the train to the office in the morning. When a whole nation does that, it is better perhaps that it should do the thing thoroughly. Thank God, there are still an enormous number who have not had life and wisdom smothered and killed by what is called education. The other day in a village inn an old man spoke to me of the farmlands in the village and the quality of the soil and the way the fields were being ruthlessly torn and plundered and left in ruin by the men who wanted the iron ore and had no concern for the land; he spoke with knowledge and sense and wisdom; he did not know about the land merely, he knew the land, he had the feel of the land in his soul, he was alive. Thank God, there are still many like him. But he was old.

"I have said, Ye are gods." And yet we have known men who were dead though the fact had not occurred to them; and we have seen squalor and stupidity and the pettiness that poisons and kills. Where are these gods? Look at the saints. We think of gods as having a greater intensity of life, a greater power and a greater freedom than we. And here in the saints we have the "insatiable desire" for meeting difficulties and braving dangers; we have the "hunger and thirst after justice"; we have the charity that reaches to the ends of the world; we have the fullest possible intensity of life because we have the infinity of the life and power of God. The man who is dead in spirit was once alive when he was a child and was one with the universe; and here we have the complete obedience to the Spirit, the power to see with the eyes of God and judge with the mind of God and desire with the will of God which mean that the life of the child is preserved and fulfilled in the heart of the saint. We think of the gods as having a greater intensity of life than we. And here we have the fulness of a life that is whole; a life in which instincts and emotions and desires and thought and will are all gathered up and given a more than human vitality by being made to share in the life and express and fulfil the purposes of the Infinite. We think of the gods as having a greater power than we; and here we have the faith that moves mountains, the strength that laughs at perils, the love that sweeps like a gale wind through the world because it is one with the Love that is a burning and a consuming fire. We think of the gods as having a greater freedom than we. And here we have the freedom that always does what it wants; the freedom that has gone beyond the freedom from the slavery of sin and the pseudo self, beyond the bondage of the law which seems like an external restraint because it is obeyed only from fear, beyond the clash of finite with infinite will, because we have here the man who has found that the heart is only fully free when it is living in love, and that then it is free because there are no longer two wills but only one. "I am come that you may have *life*, and have it more abundantly."

At the summit of the moral life you come to the point where lover and master, child and man, the man of vision and the man of power, meet and are one. And in so doing, you come also to the answer of the greatest paradox that confronts the moralist. "If I seek for virtue I seek for my own perfection; but if I seek for my own perfection I am selfish, and selfishness is the essence of vice." It is an argument that seems to hold against the ethic of Aristotle; it will not hold against the morality that is worship. When you speak of love, you cannot really distinguish giving from getting, for each is indistinguishably both. You cannot take the desire for joy out of love without destroying it; but the desire for joy is itself a desire to give, and the joy is desired only provided that it is a gift. *Nihil unquam in te nisi te exquisivi;* when you seek virtue you desire God, who is your joy; but the more deeply you are living in love, the more fully you will live in Him, and therefore, even though you more and more desire your own happiness with Him, you will more and more think of your happiness in terms of serving Him.

The end of the moral life is wholeness. But it is wholeness of life; and life is creative energy. All living is seeing and loving; but all living is also making. The vision of the artist impels him to express what he has seen; the love of the lover impels him to give. The man who is dead in spirit is not dead merely because only a minute fragment of his personality exists; he is dead because he leaves the world unenlarged. The morality which is worship is both vision and love; and you cannot see it fully unless you see it as it affects the world. The whole human being is more than an individual body-spirit, a closed system: he is an individual in an environment, and on every level he is related by a thousand bonds to that environment, which he must affect for good or for ill. To be just or temperate is to deal justly or temperately with persons and things. If you are unjust and cruel, you may ruin another human life; if you are gentle and generous, you may make it enduringly happy. We are individuals in an environment; we are individuals in an environment which is largely in the power of evil, and for which we are largely responsible. Morality, then, is worship; but that sort of worship which fulfils in the world the purposes of God. This is the insatiable desire of the saints: to help to restore the world to God. It is not enough to be all things; we have to help and to restore all things. It is not enough to "realize the idea of the Good" in our own lives; we have to realize the idea of the Good in our environment. For indeed, the Good we have to express in our lives is God; and God is self-diffusive Love.

The morality which is ultimately self-centered is of necessity individualist also—even the service of others can be a form of selfishness; but the morality which is God-centered, though it necessarily involves the perfection of the self, looks directly to the purposes of God. So when we think of the moral life from God's side, in terms of the giving of His power and life through the sacramental system, we cannot forget that this power is given not for ourselves alone. The Church's office is to bring the truth and the life of God to the world, to restore it; sometimes this power is given to individuals entirely for the sake of others; you read in the New Testament of the gifts of "tongues" and prophecy and the rest, which served and empowered the Church as a whole; you read especially of the gift of healing, the healing of body and soul alike, by prayer and the laying on of hands; and still today the Church's office and privilege is to bless and to heal—to bless the earth and the fruits of the earth, to bless the animals, to bless mankind, and to heal the sick in body and mind, to heal by prayer and blessing, to heal through the liturgy which has such power to restore and integrate the unconscious, to heal through the touch of the waters at Lourdes where faith makes whole. But that is not all. The life and power that are given to the individual for the individual are given to the man in his environment, are given to the man as taking part in the cosmic struggle, and so are given in their turn for the blessing and healing of all things.

Think first of baptism. It gives us the new life, which is to say precisely that it frees us from the bondage of the spirit of evil and makes it possible for us to live and work for the purposes of God. Its first concern is with the individual personality; but we necessarily affect our environment not only by what we do but by what we are; and as baptism creates in us the responsibility of being members of the Church, the responsibility of being lovers of one another, so it gives us the power to fulfil our responsibilities.

Faith is life, for it means living in God; but the life of God is something that has to be slowly and painfully realized in us— we have to do and experience in our own way what Christ did and experienced for us; and this personal progress is part of a much vaster cosmic process, the long travail whereby the world must learn eventually to "put on Christ" and to be made whole. As we are dependent on and determined by the past, so we, in our own lives, fashion the future. Just as we ourselves in the present are weakened (because the Church is weakened) by every individual betrayal and strengthened (because the Church is strengthened) by every individual fidelity, so if we succeed in realizing the life of God within us we build up the future, if we fail we destroy.

336

Gerald Vann

What Christ did for us, we in our own way must do. If you are a Christian, you must be a mediator. Living in union with Christ, you must labor to bring the life and power of Christ into the world to which you are bound by the solidarity of sin; the Church, like the individual, is not a closed system, but a power and an energy that come from God and go out to the world in order to bring the two together; by baptism you are made a sharer in the power and the energy and, therefore, in the work that has to be done.

The sacraments correspond to the deep enduring needs and also to the great landmarks of human life. Baptism is the sacrament of rebirth, the sacrament of the child. Confirmation is the sacrament of the youth approaching manhood, about to face the world as an independent person. He will have to face a world that is largely hostile to his true self; he may have to face an environment that will oppose all his deepest desires and dreams; and he will have to be strong if he is to resist submersion and retain his independence. This sacrament of strengthening is given us to bring about the victory of independence; it is given us to make us spiritually adult also. Catholics speak of the Church as a mother: her motherhood is the correlative of the humility of the child; but just as the growth of human life implies a growth of independence, of the power to make one's own life, so too we become spiritually adult in so far as we arrive at maturity of judgment and conscience and the ability to play our own part in the cosmic struggle on the side of the good—serving the Church and not merely relying on her. Hence the symbolism of this sacrament: oil denoting strength and the warrior spirit, the anointing on the forehead for courage, the tap on the cheek for endurance of hardship and suffering, the pentecostal fire which symbolizes growth as the water of baptism symbolizes birth. We are come to the fulness of social responsibility; we are to be masters and makers and not merely children; we are to bring holiness to others by being holy ourselves, to set others on fire by contact with the fire within us.

So the sacrament of confirmation is associated with the old traditional idea of the common priesthood of the laity: the official sharing in the priestly power and office of Christ. If you are looking for the essential meaning of the Church, do not stop short at the organization, the legal and juridical aspects, do not isolate the teaching authority, for this, too, is only a part: you will find the essential meaning of the Church and its claims when you see it as a torrent of life and power—the life and power that teach and sanctify and rule—descending from God to man.

The Church is essentially Christ living and acting in the world. But we must think of Christ as the "total Christ": Christ acting in and through the authority and power of the Church, and thence in and through the whole family of Christians. So that if His power is not opposed but on the contrary more and more fully recognized and received by the Christian—received precisely through loving obedience to the Church—then the Christian is fully a Christian at last because at last he is bearing the Christ within him out into the world which as yet knows not Christ; he is living the Christian life in something of its fulness because he is receiving from Christ in the Church the life and power that can restore the world, and turning with love to the task of restoring it. Notice how at the first Pentecost it is not to individuals merely but to the Christian family that the Spirit comes, and comes as fire: it is the bringing of a common power for this common task—the task of restoring all things in Christ.

But unhappily, we can never think of the cosmic struggle as though it were a clearly defined battle between the forces of good and the forces of evil. It is waged by the Church; but it is waged also within the Church. We betray what we love. We try to fight for the restoration of the world, for the coming of the kingdom; but the coming is postponed, and the power of the Church to heal and make holy is curtailed, by the persisting presence and power of evil within us. My personal sins reinforce the power of evil; but I am responsible for more than this. We are one in the love and life of God, but we are one also in the solidarity of sin. Whenever I sin I first of all weaken the Church; and through that weakening there are other sins, and I am in part responsible for them. But the mercy of God will repair this damage too. We see the sacrament of penance in its fulness and greatness if we see it thus against the background of the total struggle. It has as its first purpose to restore the individual to life in God; but it is medicinal also to the life of the Church as a whole. We retard the Church's work by our sins; we help it on by our use of this sacrament—building up our own health and power, we help to build up the corporate health and power of the community of Christians also.

Penance is the sacrament of healing, the healing of the individual for the strengthening of the Church. It is not a negative thing—the wiping out of something that is past; the past is never abolished. Its whole purpose is positive and creative. Just as personal sin repeats over again the primal sin, so penance repeats the work of baptism: freeing us from the power of evil, restoring us to the Church, strengthening us to overcome the weakness that sin leaves in us, so that we may work again in the Church for the victory of the Good. But the cross must precede the resurrection. Penance is given us not to lull us into a feeling that all is well, but to shake us from complacency into self-knowledge, into a realization of our responsibility for the continuing power of evil in the world, into a deeper realization of God's love for humanity and the shallowness and unreality of our love for Him. We can fight for the world only when the sense of sin has turned our half-hearted repentance into the sorrow of love, shown us to what extent we are traitors to God's purposes, and so caused us to begin with humility to put our trust not in ourselves but in Him. Unless the grain of wheat die, itself remaineth alone.

But after the death, the resurrection; after sorrow and repentance, the life and power of the living Bread. There follows the greatest of all the sacraments, which brings us not divine power merely, but the Source of divine power. It is the Eucharist above all which empowers us to fight for the Good, and to fight as a family. There are the two dangers: of independence in isolation, the man without the child; and of uniformity without maturity, the child without the man. The Eucharist is the supreme way to wholeness. The Mass is first of all a sacrifice, an affirmation that God and not the false self is the center; it is the sacrifice of the whole man gathered up into the sacrifice of the whole Church, which itself is gathered up into the sacrifice of Christ; and then again it is the sacrament which effects the oneness first of all of the individual with Christ and then of the family of Christians with one another— the Communion is preceded by the kiss of peace, as it was preceded in the primitive Church by the agape, the love feast. When the Mass is over and the *Ite missa est* is said, it is not simply a number of individuals who are sent out to serve and restore the world: it is a family.

True, a family is a unity, not a uniformity: there is diversity of gifts, even though the same Spirit; the first thing the Eucharist effects is the wholeness of the individual Christian. But it is the sacrificed Christ who is received; and it is part of the purpose of the receiving that through it the Body of Christ should be built up in love and unity, and that, through the unity of the Body, the restoring power of Christ should be made visible and active in the world.

What a tragedy when the immensity of this coming of the Infinite into the soul is made a purely individual thing and we forget the family! How can we fail to note the insistence of the liturgy on the fact that it is our *common* sacrifice that we are offering, and the *common* sacrament that we are receiving, a sacrament of unity symbolized in the kiss of peace; and how can we fail to realize that, when we come down from the altar after the Communion, it is in a wholly new and richer sense that we are "all one in that One!" But what a tragedy also if we forget the larger family of creation!

When a Christian is sick and bedridden it is the office of the priest to bring the sacramental Christ to the house; and the preparations that are made, the solemnity of the reception of the priest who bears the Host, enact once again the humility and wonder of the centurion, "Lord, I am not worthy that thou shouldst enter under my roof." But we do not always notice that, when we come down from the altar and return into our houses, the same thing is done; we in our turn are God-bearers; and if it must be with a new sense of reverence and a new sense of oneness that we salute one another, we cannot but remember also the thing that is done in and to the world. How terrible if we allow ourselves to sink back into the pettinesses that kill love and oneness, how terrible if we fail to find courage to meet and conquer the spirit of hatred and evil, since we bear

within us the power of the presence of the Good Himself! How
terrible if we are content to leave mankind in its loneliness,
when we bear within us Him who came to take away the sin
and, therefore, the loneliness of the world!

We are all meant to be mediators. But we need not think
it necessarily our duty to be forever attempting to argue these
things; we need never think it our duty to preach at others;
nothing is more depressing and more illogical than aggressive
Christianity; we preach as we ought if we are what we ought to
be, and we preach best if we are what we most ought to be, a
family living in love and in God. To the sacrament of marriage,
with all that it has to tell us of the duties and power of love in
the world, we turn later; but the root of the matter is already
here. "See how these Christians love one another." If we who
are Christians could make the world say the words again as it
said them first, with awe and wonder, we should have fulfilled
the first part of our work as Christians; and the second would
follow automatically, for we could not to that extent love one
another without loving the world.

But we shall not so love one another if, in fact, we adopt
a selfish sectarian attitude to the world. When men see that the
building of the Church is a labor of love, the labor of a family,
and that it is the building not of a fortress but of a home whose
doors are always open, an invitation to enjoy the light and
warmth within; when they see that we are ready to live and die
for one another because we know that our duty together as a
family is to live and die for the world Christ came to restore,
then they will begin to say seriously that Christianity is love in
practice as well as in theory, and if they look for Christ they
will not dismiss the possibility of finding Him, despite our
sinfulness, in our midst.

The way back to God is the way of worship, the worship
given by the whole human being, man and child, to God. But
the whole human being precisely as such does not worship
alone. When you are living in love you cannot live alone, you
cannot think or will or act alone; when you live in Christ you
think and will and act in Christ, and it is the "total Christ," it
is Christ as gathering to Himself the totality of created things.
In the prayers of thanksgiving after Mass is included the canticle,

"Bless the Lord, *all* ye works of the Lord." We go back to God in company with those we love, helped and helping. To help all created things, that is the measure of our responsibility; to be helped by all, that is the measure of our hope. Do you think it childish and superstitious to look for help to the saints or the angels? We look to our friends for help; what is childish is to suppose that we cannot be helped except by things or persons we can see or touch. We live in the world of space and time, but we live in eternity too, in the eternal present; the world is a haunted house, but not all the spirits that inhabit it are mournful ghosts or spirits of evil; the mystery of iniquity is offset by the glory of the communion of saints. Do you think that the mother who dies is no longer in contact with her children, that lover is hopelessly separated from lover? And these great ones of God set no limit to their love of those who at any moment of our time-world are trying to play their part in the cosmic struggle. The modern West has reached a chilly cerebral stage in its evolution; think how it might be helped and perhaps saved from complete desiccation by the might of the seraphs, those spirits whom Christian tradition associates especially with fire, with the burning love which is the prayer of wonder.

We begin to live the moral life in the Christian sense when we begin to turn all that we do and are into worship; and if we do that, the false self will die within us, and we shall begin to be made whole; and we shall forget to be grasping, even about the things of the spirit, because we shall want to serve the world. But in fact we shall walk in all the power of God and His saints and angels, we shall walk in the company of all who love Him and of all the things He loves, and so we shall reach the breadth and height and depth of the infinite skies, and lose our fear of what can hurt us and our fear of what we can lose, and beneath all the pain of the world that is in us—for nothing now will suffer without our suffering too—there will be the unquenchable joy of the saints.

Then there will be only the final consummation to wait for, when, in the company of those who have loved and helped us and those we have loved and served, we shall enter into the ultimate fulness of integrity, we shall see Him as He is and all things in Him in their glory, and so we shall know at last the

complete oneness for which we have been so long unsucess-
fully striving because in the fulness of the vision of the Godhead
we shall find at last that there is nothing that we cannot love.

Gabriel Honore Marcel
1889-1973

The great war of 1914 destroyed the moral foundations on which western cultures were established. Along with the postwar efforts to rebuild cities, economies and populations, the nations involved in the war had to set about the awesome task of reconstructing moral concepts that could be of use to mankind as he moved into a new era. Rising up in Europe, particularly in France and Germany, were the intellectuals who have come to be known as the existentialists. They had experienced the horror of the war, realized that there was no way to turn back the hands of time, and sought to explore the directions that mankind might take in his efforts to declare himself a moral being.

Gabriel Marcel was one of the great existential thinkers, though he never really liked the term. He was born in Paris in 1889. His mother died when he was four years old. Throughout his life he made reference to her maternal presence which served as a stimulus to his attempts to probe the realm of the unseen within the human condition. He grew up in an environment of religious indifference, yet he had a natural sense of transcendence which supported his search for God. A series of debates on religious topics led eventually to his entry into Christianity and Catholicism. Marcel's adult life was filled with teaching, lecturing and writing. Besides being a philosopher, he was a dramatist and a musician. He died at the age of 83 in Paris.

In the face of contemporary moral issues, Marcel rejected the traditional approach of handling a question abstractly. He insisted that the better we know the concrete individual, the better we can resolve the human issue. But he understood the individual as a pathway to the mystery of existence. Far from developing a simplistic pragmatic approach to morality, Marcel strove to push through the individual (without losing sight of him) to the foundations of all human existence, a level at which he was convinced man could again discover God. Once man arrives at this point, true resolution of moral issues is a possibility.

Marcel's terminology and approach to morality may seem distant to the more common twentieth century technique of treating life as a problem. He was aware of this and argued that there simply is nowhere to go as long as we look at life as problem. For him, love, justice, sexuality, faith and the like are not and cannot be things that people possess, though that is how they are usually understood. Rather they are ways of experiencing the human condition, manifestations of the richness of existence.

From among a wealth of essays and reflections, we have selected a chapter of his book Homo Viator, *entitled* The Mystery of the Family. *In it, he probes the dynamics of human relationships as they unravel in time and dwells upon dimensions of human life that go unnoticed by the majority of mankind. It is his hope to evoke serious reflection on themes such as family, life, creative fidelity, communion and consecration, all of which are essential to human survival. To a world that appears to be caught in a web of hopelessness and frustration, Marcel offers a philosophy of hope and confidence.*

HOMO VIATOR

THE MYSTERY OF THE FAMILY

C learly I owe you a few words of explanation concerning the title under which this lecture has been announced. I must admit that it is rather a surprising title, which may seem oddly sensational. Why not have called our discussion "The Problem of the Family"? For numerous reasons: first, the family does not suggest just *one* problem, but an infinity of problems of every description which could not be considered as a whole; you have already heard several of them discussed with a competence which I lack. But it is above all because the family seems to me to belong to an order of realities, or I should rather say of presences, which can only create problems in so far as we are mistaken, not so much with regard to their special character, as to the way in which we human beings are involved in them. I apologise for being obliged to quote myself here; for I need to employ a distinction which I attempted about ten years ago to introduce into the domain of concrete philosophy and of which the importance still seems to me considerable.

I said that there can only be a problem for me where I have to deal with facts which are, or which I can at least cause to be, exterior to myself; facts presenting themselves to me in a certain disorder for which I struggle to substitute an orderliness capable of satisfying the requirements of my thought. When this substitution has been effected the problem is solved. As for me, who devote myself to this operation, I am outside (above or below, if you like) the facts with which it deals. But when it involves realities closely bound up with my existence, realities which unquestionably influence my existence as such, I cannot conscientiously proceed in this way. That is to say, I cannot make an abstraction of myself, or, if you like, bring about this division between myself on the one hand and some ever-present given principle of my life on the other; I am effectively and vitally involved in these realities. This holds good for instance in the case of the union of body and soul, or, in more precise terms, the bond which unites me to my body. I cannot make of this bond a pure idea to be placed in front of me and considered as an object, without misunderstanding its essential nature. Thus it follows that every term by which I try to qualify it as a relationship or to determine its function will invariably prove to be inadequate: I cannot exactly say that I am master of my body, or that I am the slave of my body, or that I own my body. All these relationships are true at once, which amounts to saying that each one of them taken by itself is false, that it does not so much *translate* as it *traduces* a certain fundamental unity. This unity is less a *given* principle than a *giving* one, because it is the root from which springs the fact of my presence to myself and the presence of all else to me. Thus it encroaches upon its own data and, invading them, passes beyond the range of a simple problem. It is in this very definite sense that the family is a mystery, and it is for this reason that we cannot properly and without confusion treat it simply as a question to be solved. Anticipating what is coming later, I want to point out right away that there is deep similarity between the union of soul and body and the mystery of the family. In both cases we are in the presence of the same fact, or rather of something which is far more than a fact since it is the very condition of all facts whatever they may be: I mean incarnation. I am not, of course, using this term in its theological sense. It is not a question of our Lord's coming into the world, but of the infinitely mysterious act by which an essence assumes a body, an act around which the meditation of a Plato crystallised, and to which modern philosophers only cease to give their attention in so far as they have lost the intelligence's essential gift, that is to say the faculty of wonder.

I assure you that I am not proposing to introduce anything in the nature of an exposition of doctrine here. I am dealing rather with a series of *enquiries* leading us towards a point which thought could not reach directly. Why? Because this point is situated at the same time too close up to us and too far away to be found in the strictly limited zone of objective knowledge. I have said too close and too far away, but, in reality, these contraries are found to coincide here, and I am inclined to think that this coincidence of that which is quite close and that which is infinitely far away is precisely what characterises every kind of mystery, even religious mysteries, which we are not dealing with here.

On the one hand, when I speak of my family, the primitive idea this word evokes is that of a certain pattern or constellation of which, as a child, I spontaneously take it for granted that I am the centre. Am I not the object of all those solicitous glances which sometimes touch me, sometimes overwhelm and sometimes irritate me, glances of which not a shadow escapes me for they all seem to be aimed at me personally in the same way as the voices whose inflections pass from gentleness to severity, from persuasion to threats. It is only little by little that I discern the relationships which bind these being to each other, thereby discovering that each one has his own life, his inviolable relationships with all the others, and also that for some of them I am a cause of preoccupation and a subject of discussion when I am not present, so that, I only receive a partial presentation, an adaptation for my personal use, of the thoughts and feelings which I arouse in these beings of whom only one side, and that always the same, is turned towards me. From this moment, everything becomes strangely complicated, new relationships are hiding themselves from me, how can I avoid the temptation of hiding myself from them in my turn? But at the same time strange contours appear in my personal life, it becomes furrowed with valleys and split up into compartments as well. The simple unspoilt countryside of my first years becomes complicated and clouded over. My family draws away from me, while remaining as near and as much a part of myself as ever: a tearing process? Let us rather say a traumatisation as difficult to heal as possible. That is not all, it is not even the beginning. Under the abstract words of paternity and sonship, I have gradually come to guess at occult and forbidden realities which make my soul dizzy. They attract me, but because they attract me, and because I think I should commit a sacrilege if I gave in to this attraction, I turn away from them. At the very least, I come to believe that, far from being endowed with an absolute existence of my own, I *am*, without having originally wished or suspected it, I *incarnate* the reply to the reciprocal appeal which two beings flung to each other in the unknown and which, without suspecting it, they flung beyond themselves to an incomprehensible power whose only expression is the bestowal of life. I *am* this reply, unformed at first, but who, as I become articulate, will know myself to be a reply and a judgment. Yes, I am irresistibly led to make the discovery that by being what I am, I myself am a judgment upon those who have called me into being; and thereby infinite new relationships will be established between them and me.

On the other hand, I have to recognise that behind the lighted but much restricted zone which I call my family there stretches, to infinitude, ramifications which in theory at any rate I can follow out tirelessly. Only in theory, however, for in fact an impenetrable darkness envelops this *upstream* region of myself and prevents me from exploring any further. I can discern enough, however, to enable me to follow this umbilical cord of my temporal antecedents, and to see it taking shape before me yet stretching back beyond my life in an indefinite network which, if traced to its limits, would probably be co-extensive with the human race itself. My family, or rather my lineage, is the succession of historical processes by which the human species has become individualised into the singular creature that I am. All that it is possible for me to recognise in this growing and impressive indetermination is that all these unknown beings, who stretch between me and my unimaginable origins whatever they may be, are not simply the causes of which I am the effect or the product: there is no doubt that the terms cause and effect have no meaning here. Between my ancestors and myself a far more obscure and intimate relationship exists. I share with them as they do with me—invisibly; they are consubstantial with me and I with them.

By this inextricable combination of things from the past and things to come, the mystery of the family is defined—a mystery in which I am involved from the mere fact that I exist: here, at the articulation of a structure of which I can only distinguish the first traces, of a feeling which modulates between the intimate and the metaphysical—and of an oath to be taken or refused binding me to make my own the vague desire around which the magical fomentation of my personal existence is centred. Such is the situation in which I find myself, I, a creature precipitated into the tumult; thus am I introduced into this impenetrable world.

To evoke the mystery of the family is then far less to attempt to resolve a problem than to try to recapture a reality and to awaken the soul to its presence. The consciousness of this reality has become tragically obliterated during several generations, and its clouding over has been one of the contributory causes for the precipitation of men into the hell where they are struggling to-day.

But this evocation, which appears to be simple enough, is in reality extraordinarily difficult to accomplish. For a mysterious reality can only be made actual for him who not only rediscovers it but who has the sudden consciousness of having rediscovered it, simultaneously realising that previously he had entirely lost sight of it. I have to strive then to make you aware of this negative evidence, thankless as such an undertaking may appear.

Nothing seems to me to give more direct evidence of the blindness from which a great number of our contemporaries are suffering in the matters we are considering to-day than the increasing number of controversies of a strictly spectacular order which arose in the period between the wars, whether in the Press or in public meetings, in connection with marriage, divorce, the choice of a lover, the practices of birth-control, etc. For whom, before what sort of spectators, did this ceaseless and all too often poisonous controversial stream flow? Before idlers, more and more incapable of living, I will not say their life, but *a* life of any sort, who led a ridiculous and sinister existence on the margin of reality, waifs without knowing it, shipwrecked mariners who did not even know that their ship was lost. These puppets made no effort to grasp a truth and derive nourishment from it, but they had an unhealthy craving to hear what they called a discussion of ideas. A discussion, that is to say a clash of ideas, not dealing with experience, for all experience worthy of the name has a certain weight and value—but professions of faith, challenges, prosecutions. Everything that happened in this realm seemed to show that a flow of words and argumentation were the actual sign of a total absence of experience and genuine thought. No doubt I shall be stopped here: "Are you not tending" it may be asked "to exaggerate arbitrarily the importance of discussions which have never held the attention of the sane and healthy elements in our country? The family is not an institution which has lost its meaning, it is still a living reality. We only need to look around us. How many families, even during this lamentable period, kept their vitality and preserved their unity!" I think that we must stop here and fearlessly face some very painful truths. Certainly there is no question of denying for one moment that a great number of people—mainly but not exclusively Christians—have preserved the meaning of family life in spite of the unwearied efforts of propaganda of every description which tried systematically to weaken it. Nevertheless we cannot fail to recognise the seriousness of the crisis which has begun in our time, a dangerous and perhaps in the long run a mortal crisis, as is proved by incontestable statistics: the huge increase of divorce, the general spreading of abortive practices, etc. These are facts which force us to penetrate deeper in order to expose the roots of these "social facts," roots which are to be found at the actual level of belief, or more exactly, *unbelief* where, for my part, I am inclined to see a cardinal principle of the spiritual biology of our era. These are the roots which the philosopher has to discover with the cool self-possession of a surgeon making an incision into a wound.

May I at this point be allowed a short digression, which actually is not a digression at all?

When I recall my experience as a member of the university and that of some of my friends, I see that it had become increasingly difficult to deal with problems concerning the family before a class of young students. I remember very well the embarrassment I felt on a particular occasion when it fell to me to speak of divorce, not simply as a recognised fact but as a practice which, taken all round, is disastrous and blameworthy. I knew quite well that I had in front of me the sons of divorced parents and that there was a risk of their bringing all the weight of my judgments against their parents, unless they revolted, as indeed they had a right to do, against strictures involving their most private feelings—feelings which indeed had to be respected. On these grounds, what a temptation there was to maintain a prudent reserve and to keep to vague and meaningless generalities!

But on the other hand how can we help seeing that if these great realities of marriage, generation, etc., are not approached directly and with fearless sincerity, they degenerate into nothing but material for rhetorical arguments. Conventionality is thus substituted for life, conventionality of which for my part I shall never weary of denouncing the poisonous influence, for it will never be anything but a waste product of thought, something which cannot be assimilated. This then is the dilemma confronting so many of those responsible for education at the present time. Should we, with no fear of appearing dogmatic, courageously tackle these questions while in so doing we risk upsetting and scandalising impressionable young beings; or should we confine ourselves to the hollowest of phrases or to historical or so-called historical facts and thus, in the latter case, help to encourage the loose relativity which has tended in our day to weaken all real moral judgment so prejudicially? If I insist thus on a difficulty which only seems to affect specialists, it is because I see in it a symptom revealing a state of things so grave that we can no longer shut our eyes to it. If we took the trouble to consult the text-books of morals and sociology which for twenty years or more were in favour with the high priests of official teaching, we should see to what an extent they encouraged the tendency to view problems in an almost exclusively historical setting and to emphasise the changing character of family institutions ever destined to grow more flexible. This tendency cannot be compensated for by what is at bottom no more than the wordy and superfluous reiteration of a few general principles earmarked by an out-worn rationalism. We might already notice at this point, so that we can probably return to it later, that, by a paradox worthy of our attention, these sociological moralists came in the end to preach the most disintegrating individualism, whilst all the time proclaiming and heralding the establishment of a socialism which was to subordinate personal initiative, in every field, to State control.

It will doubtless be objected that I am referring here to a period of our history which is happily passed and that for the last two years a vigorous and healthy reaction has taken place concerning this point and a great many others in favour of what we sometimes rather ingenuously term "right-mindedness." I most certainly do not wish to underestimate the importance and value of this reaction. It seems to me, all the same, that we must be careful to avoid an optimism which might have many disappointments in store for us. The multiplication of catchwords and well-known slogans in official speeches and in the Press should not mislead us. There is nothing there to lead us to believe in an effective conversion of hearts and minds: it is certainly not by mere methods of publicity that we shall succeed in reaching the most deep and hidden springs of individual wills. It is even permissible to fear that there may be a serious relapse and that the evils, from which we have already suffered so much, will reappear later with increased violence.

What is needed first of all is that by reflection, the only weapon at our disposal, we should project as clear a light as possible upon the tragic situation in which so many are living. These people are unable to explain to themselves a vital uneasiness, an anguish of which it is only in their power to grasp the most exterior causes or the most superficial symptoms. It seems to me that we should indeed be setting to work in the wrong way if we started merely from a moral crisis, from the increasingly deliberate repudiation of general principles which would have been accepted without question up to a certain time in history. I should prefer to say that these principles are in themselves nothing but the approximate and imperfect expression of a certain mental attitude towards life. It is in reality this attitude itself which has been transformed. In order to make the meaning of the words I am using more precise, I suggest that what has come about is much more a vital weakening than a transgression, or a denial. In a fine passage, recently quoted by Mr. Albert Béguin, the great Swiss author Ramuz, writing some years ago, spoke of a certain sense of holiness "which is the most precious thing the West has known, a certain attitude of reverence for existence—by which we must understand everything which exists, oneself and the world outside oneself, the mysteries which surround us, the mystery of death, and the mystery of birth, a certain veneration in the presence of life, a certain love, and (why not acknowledge it?) a certain state of poetry which the created world produces in us." It is precisely this sense of holiness, this fundamental reverence for life and for death, itself considered as the nocturnal phase of life, it is this state of poetry produced in us by the created world which, during the last decades, and more particularly of recent years, has given way to the pressure of pride, of pretentiousness, of boredom and despair; and for reasons, which will very easily appear on analysis, it is in the domain of family reality that the dire consequences of this giving way have first become apparent, actually threatening more and more directly the integrity of the individual considered in his structure and his own particular destiny.

He who refuses to face the danger goes on obstinately repeating that the family exists. But the word to exist is here the equivocal and therefore the most deceptive of terms. If the family is a reality it cannot be simply expressed or objectively established like a simple succession. Let us even insist that it is infinitely more than what appears from pure and simple entries in civil registers. It exists only on condition that it is apprehended not only as a value but as a living presence.

A value first of all. I think that here we must make an attempt to relive—but in such a way that we think it out and elucidate it—an experience which was shared by most of us when we were children, an experience which it is actually very difficult not to distort when we try to express it, because it includes a certain pride. This pride if we are not careful might seem to be confused with vanity, but this is a degradation of it. We are proud to belong to a certain community because we feel that something of its lustre falls upon us. Pride, as I recently had occasion to write, is a certain response made from the depths of my being to an investiture of which it behoves me to prove myself worthy. Such pride is experienced on my own account. It in no way aims at impressing some other person with the awe and fear which would flatter me. Thus it is a constructive sentiment, helping to give me inner foundations on which to establish my conduct. Vanity, on the other hand, by the very fact that it is turned outwards towards the rest of the world, is essentially sterile, or even, in the last analysis, disintegrating. But it is through this sentiment of pride that we can trace in what way the family is a value. It is a recognised hierarchy, and I do not merely have to integrate myself into it by recognising the authority vested in its leader; I have actually been caught up in it from the origin. I am involved in it, my very being is rooted in it. This hierarchy cannot fail, this authority cannot be abolished without the family bringing about its own destruction as a value. After that, in my eyes, it can no longer be anything but a net in which I feel I have been caught by mistake and out of which there is nothing left for me but to extricate myself as soon as possible.

In speaking of a presence, I introduce a somewhat different shade of meaning here, which it will be as well to explain more precisely. Again in this case each one of us must refer back to his childhood memories which, when we are dealing with realities of this sort, seem to me to play the part belonging to reminiscence in the philosophy of Plato. Each of us, with the exception of a few rare and unhappy individuals, has, at least on certain occasions, been able to *prove by experience* the existence of the family as a protective skin placed between himself and a world which is foreign, threatening, hostile to him. And there is no doubt that nothing is more painful in the destiny of an individual than the tearing away of this tissue, either by a sudden or a slow and continuous process, carried out by the pitiless hands of life or death, or rather of that nameless power of which life and death are but alternating aspects. The similes associated with and alas! abused by a feebly sentimental or didactic kind of poetry, the similes of cocoon, nest or cradle are those which most exactly illustrate what I should be ready to term the downy element in the reality of the family.

But here by an analytical effort we must free ourselves from metaphors themselves. We must make ourselves aware of the primitive *us,* this archetypal and privileged *us* which is only normally realised in family life. This *us* is in general inseparable from a *home of our own.* It is certainly not by chance if all the forces which have been working towards the destruction of the family house have at the same time been preparing for the overthrow of the family itself. This privileged *us* cannot, even on the humblest levels of this life of consciousness, be separated from a permanent habitation which is ours and which in the course of our existence has gradually become consubstantial with us. The spontaneous and immediate consciousness of an *always,* a perpetual life, is associated with the familiar objects among which we live, with the setting in which daily tasks are carried out, with the feelings which can scarcely be formulated of a tutelary presence incarnated in these things and this background and which, as it were, deepens and colours the daily outlook. All this seems to me in principle indissolubly bound up with the existence of the family considered both as a fact and a value. I want no other proof than the one (negative it is true) afforded by the mental upheaval, and often the heartbreak, so frequently brought upon a child by the common event of a house-move. It is brought upon a child and often enough even upon an adult if he has kept the childlike character, the tenderness of tissue which persists in some people throughout all the battering and bruising of personal experience. But inversely we must recognise that all which tends to destroy the sense of a habitation and of permanence in the surroundings of a being in process of formation will contribute directly to the weakening of his consciousness of the family itself. In passing, I may say that I am convinced that therein lies one of the chief causes of the disappearance of family consciousness among the working population of the great industrial centres, where nomadic life, not of tent and caravan, but of lodgings and furnished rooms, is the order of the day. The family tends to become simply an abstract idea instead of the very essence of the atmosphere a human being almost unconsciously inhales, an essence which imperceptibly impregnates and saturates his thinking, his appreciation and his love.

You may say that all these remarks only bear upon the outward and temporary conditions of life. But the more one strives to understand the meaning of existence, the more surely one is lead to the conclusion that the outward is also the inward, or rather to the realisation that this distinction has no meaning where the actual growth of a being is involved. It is moreover obvious that the disappearance of the settled habitation, or rather of the home, is inseparable from the fading away of traditions. Actually these traditions are to the inner man what the family setting is to the visible one. We cannot just say they are his environment; they help to form him. Without them there is a risk of his becoming the plaything of every chance influence; his development is exposed to all the dangers of incoherence. But the traditions of which I am here thinking bear upon the continuity of the family itself: they are first of all the records and examples which secure the bond between the generations. But there is yet another thing: every family which has real vitality produces a certain ritual without which it would be in danger of eventually losing its solid foundations. It is all this delicate architecture which is compromised and which, for nearly a century, has been cracking. Why? The reasons for this decrepitude appear to me to be very varied and to go very deep. Some are obvious. They have to do with ideology, with the diffusion of a mythology of which revolutionary spirits of every description have made themselves the channels. Some of them can scarcely be analysed. But we can say with certainty that the amazing transformation of the material conditions of life brought about by the industrial revolution tends to relegate to an almost legendary distance those who lived, thought and struggled before it. This upheaval was in reality too complete, too massive to be understood by those very people who witnessed it, and who became its victims instead of gaining anything from it. It was first of all a change of rhythm. Men were not able to recognise it; rather, they submitted to it by an inner adaptation, and this was not effected without causing the most serious psychological damage in many cases, and bringing about a real deterioration of the mental fibre. It was inevitable that this extraordinary acceleration of the rhythm of life should tend more and more to prevent the slow sedimentation of *habitus* which seems surely to have been from all time the essential condition at the origin of all realities connected with the family. Still more, such an acceleration could not take place without a reckless waste of the reserves slowly accumulated by living. Gustave Thibon in some illuminating passages has brought out most marvellously this tragic aspect of contemporary life. He denounces the fearful squandering of reserves which has taken place before our eyes; he points out most clearly that we are in danger of causing the worst possible confusion by preaching the duty of improvidence; for it is essential to make "the distinction between the improvidence of the saint who does not worry about the future because he has laid up his treasure, the source of eternity and life, within him, and the improvidence of the decadent man whose unstable soul has become the plaything of the moment and of every passing temptation, and who, equally incapable of waiting or of making a decision, constantly yields to the *immediate* suggestions of an egoism without sequence or unity. For the least economical person is also the most selfish. To economise in the sane and strict sense of the word means above all: to keep in order to give more effectively. No doubt there is a foresight which is miserly and self-contained, which is opposed to true human exchanges. But its legitimate child, absolute improvidence, is perhaps even more the enemy of giving and communion. In the material order, as in the spiritual, liberality and munificence are only possible for him whose strict vigilance has been able to create large reserves within and around himself. Such virtues have died out to-day."

Let us here notice that the great contemplative, in whom reflection and vision have become fused, is capable of unlocking doors which ard hidden from the vulgar gaze. Technical progress, considered not in itself, not of course from the point of view of the principles which made it possible, but as we see it incorporated into the daily life of individuals, has not been effected without the loss of human substance. This loss is indeed its none too easily detected counterpart. It is on the plane of craftsmanship that this loss of substance appears most clearly. But where it is a question of secret relationships between people, the ravages brought about by the technical revolution are harder to recognise and to understand. It is certain that they are due in great measure to the growing standardisation of individuals for which the first responsiblity is to be laid at the door of far too uniform an education, having much too little respect for local customs and peculiarities. Then there is the Press, whose degraded character can never be denounced resolutely enough. In addition there is a close connection between the acceleration of the rhythm of life and the appearance of a humanity which is inwardly more and more impoverished, more and more interchangeable. A metaphor, or rather an analogy will show what I mean. To take some region full of an inner soul, such as Brittany, for example; is it not noticeable that when we cross it rapidly it seems to be emptied of this spiritual quality, this mystery, which however we rediscover if we take the trouble to go through the country in a leisurely manner? The phenomenon which I have in mind here is of the same order, but it touches on human reality where being and appearing can never be truly separated. Moreover, even the mystery of places always conceals a human presence, maybe diffused; things are impregnated with the feelings they once awoke in souls. It is from the point of view of a philosophy of duration that we can succeed in understanding the unity, I would even go so far as to say the identity, of two phenomena which, for a superficial observer appear at first to be distinct. I mean to say on the one hand the depopulation of the country, and on the other the dissolution of the family. I think then that I shall not be wandering from my subject, if I try to expose the tragic inner reality of which these two phenomena are but two inseparable aspects.

Let us notice, first of all, that existence in towns makes a certain pretension, at any rate implicitly, of triumphing over the laws of alternation to which living beings are subject. The town-dweller strives, without the slightest success be it well understood, to inaugurate an order of life wherein there are no seasons. It is a lamentable and ridiculous application of the fateful sentence, *eritis sicut dei*: you shall be as gods, you shall be set free from the vicissitudes to which the animal world is subject. The large American cities are, as it were, the prototypes of a world where preservative processes, forcing and fakes are employed to provide specious satisfactions for the need we have developed to escape from the cosmic rhythm and to substitue for it I know not what inventions caricaturing the eternity for which we still yearn nostalgically. But hard experience seems to show that this exclusive human rhythm tends in fact to become that of a machine or an automation, for it is a rhythm which is not super-organic but sub-organic. Thus the danger arises of a most fatal disorder invading the very heart of existence, for the man who is apparently striving to become a machine is nevertheless alive, although he ignores more and more systemtically his condition as a living being. The inexpressible sadness which emanates from great cities, a dismal sadness which belongs to everything that is devitalised, everything that represents a self-betrayal of life, appears to me to be bound up in the most intimate fashion with the decay of the family. This sadness is sterility, it is a disavowal felt by the heart; a disavowal which, as we shall see more and more clearly, concerns the very conditions of life. It is really a question of what we might be tempted to call the very colour of existence; but yet we must understand that a colour can be looked at and as it were absorbed by the eye, whilst what we are dealing with is lived experience as such. In order to make my meaning clearer I will ask you to think of those changes, at first almost imperceptible, which tend to weaken the ties between us and our near ones. Each of us knows from experience how an intimacy can lose its transparency, how the current bearing two beings and uniting them dynamically can lose its fluidity, so that the individualities, which a moment ago still felt themselves to be fused and enveloped in the bosom of a tutelary and vivifying element, are now separated, colliding with each other in a succession of instantaneous clashes, each as brutally hurtful as a blow. I cannot help thinking that during the last centuries of our civilisation a dislocation of the same kind has taken place between man and life, and it is related to the obscure and organic misunderstandings in which so many married existences come to ruin. Thus the family has been attacked in the double spring whence it derives its special vitality: fidelity and hope.

The idea which I want to bring out here is difficult and from the rational point of view almost impossible to grasp, so, in order to avoid expressing it in academic terms which might distort it, I propose to say quite simply how it was recently borne in upon me in a concrete form.

We had just been through one of those almost completely depopulated villages which are to be found in hundreds in the departments of the south-west. A woman with whom we had exchanged a few words had complained to us of the quietness of the place, of the monotony and lack of amusements. Suddenly my thoughts were concentrated on everything which this word amusements stands for. "Assuredly." I said to myself, "it is above all the search for amusements which sends the villagers away to the towns. On the other hand, as these out-of-the-way places become more and more empty, life in them becomes more and more boring so that in a way the exodus creates its own justification. But in reality what do we mean by amusements? Amusement is diversion, a turning away, but what from? And how does the need for diversion show itself? This is the real problem. It is only too clear that the town with its 'amusements' has exercised a regular power of suction over the country districts; we might also say that the town dweller has brought about a gradual contamination of the peasant. But all the same, the soul of the peasant, which held out so long against this infection, had become open to it. It is said, not without reason, that the uncomfortable conditions which are so frequent in the country, the lack of air and light in the cottages, etc., have helped to depopulate the fields. But why have the inhabitants not devoted their energy to improving their rural dwellings as in certain mountainous districts such as the Grisons or the Tryol? It is not enough to speak here of a certain natural laziness, there had to be a preliminary disaffection before this disastrous diversion could take place. And once more the question confronts me with an irritating persistency; diversion? Why do they seek it, from what do they turn away? How can we help seeing that the question is identically the same as that which confronts us when we enquire into the causes of the breaking up of the family?" Immediately, however, I saw the answer with a clarity which since that time has never been eclipsed. The need for amusement, as each of us knows from his own experience, is bound up with a certain ebbing of life's tide. But this is still insufficient and even ambiguous. It may indeed happen that vitality decreases without the manifestation of this need, and on the contrary this decrease may even result in the disappearance of all curiosity: indifference settles down on the soul, the being reacts less and less, he gives himself over to debility, he covers himself with veils. The ebb of life of which we are thinking here is quite different in character. The being imagines he regains his life by seizing every occasion by experiencing violent sensations of no matter what order. But these so-called stimulants afford but precarious protection against boredom. What then is this boredom? One of the most intelligent men of our time who held an important post in the government until these last weeks, said to me shortly before the war: "France is suffering from a metaphysical malady: she is bored." It was a diagnosis which went deep and which I have never forgotten—a diagnosis which has been tragically confirmed by our misfortunes. At the origin of diversion, of the will to be diverted or amused at any price, there is an attempt to escape, but from what? It can only be from oneself. The *ego* is without any doubt faced with a dilemma: to fulfil itself or to escape. Where it does not attain fulfilment, it is only conscious of itself as of an unendurable gaping void from which it must seek protection at any price. Anyone who is absorbed does not know this void; he is as it were caught up in plenitude, life envelops him and protects him. Boredom, on the contrary, is not only bound up with inaction but with a dismantling process. Thus we can very well understand that in the country the woman is far more subject to it than the man. If it is true to say that she suffers more than he does from discomfort and inconvenience, it is because she has more time to think about such things, unless she is continually taken up by the incessant occupations of motherhood, which actually means that these tasks are not only a burden but a support for her. "One is borne along only by one's responsibilities," Gabriel Séailles said most excellently. If we start from this point we can understand the causes of the ebbing of life or rather of consciousness, wherein this consciousness comes gradually to repudiate its fundamental commitments. What then are its commitments? Here we are coming down to essentials.

It seems as though it were necessary to postulate the existence of a pact, I should almost say a nuptial bond, between man and life; it is in man's power to untie this bond, but in so far as he denies the pact he tends to lose the notion of his existence. What is exactly to be understood by this bond? I may be accused of being led away by a metaphor, of unduly exaggerating abstractions. But however we interpret this fact philosophically, we must recognise that man is a being—and the only one we know—capable of adopting an attitude towards his life, not only his own life, but life in itself. He is then not a mere living being, he is, or rather he has become, something more, and we might say that it is through this faculty for adopting an attitude that he is a spirit. M. Jean Lacroix in his fine book *Personne et Amour* very rightly reminds us that one of the essential charactertistics of man is his ability to expose himself voluntarily to death. This is, however, only a particular expression, the most striking of all, of a much more general truth—the truth of his transcendance over life and death. A human act, whatever it may be, presupposes it. It is this which makes it really possible and even legitimate to speak of man and of life as of two realities which are not confused or which have ceased to be confused. From this it follows that in speaking of a pact between man and life we have in mind on the one hand the confidence which man promises life and which makes it possible for him to give himself to life, and on the other hand the response of life to this confidence of man. But it is precisely the family, considered in relation to the act by which it is constituted, which shows us the working out of this pact, for it is in fact the pact's incarnation. And it is inversely in the acts by which families are disunited that the breaking of this same pact takes place before our eyes. It is not difficult to illustrate this very general idea by concrete examples.

The essential act which constitutes marriage is obviously not the pure and simple mating which is only a human act, common alike to men and animals; it is not just a momentary union, but one which is *to last*; it is something which is established. A family is founded, it is erected like a monument whose hewn stone is neither the satisfaction of an instinct, nor the yielding to an impulse, nor the indulgence of a caprice. From this point of view we should probably not hesitate to say that there are innumerable false marriages (of course, I am not using these words in the sense of "faux ménges"). I am thinking here of those unions which are perfectly legal, but where there is nothing in the inward depths of character, nothing in the very centre of the will which corresponds to the socially binding form or even, alas, to the strictly sacramental character of the union entered into. It is more than probable that in a society where divorce is not only accepted, but regarded in many circles as a more or less normal contingency, a time must inevitably come when the irresponsibility with which so many unbelievers lightly and heedlessly get married, is communicated from one to another until it infects even those who by tradition, human respect or some remnant of faith are still impelled to take a vow of fidelity in the presence of God, only to find out too late that by this contradiction they are themselves caught in a trap from which it is not possible to escape except at the price of a scandalous renunciation or dishonourable subterfuge.

Here we must also touch on the difficult question of knowing whether the bond of marriage can really be compared with a simple contract. I must own that on this point the opinion of jurists matters little to me, for it seems very probable that reflection should be free of the categories which they employ. Indeed, the more marriage is regarded as a simple contract, the more one must logically come to admit that it can be renounced by common accord, that it can even become no more than a temporary promise. The more one forms an exclusively rational idea of marriage, the more one is led, not perhaps theoretically but in fact, not only to admit divorce as, at the most, a possibility in exceptional cases, but to incorporate with one's notion of the marriage bond the idea that it can be revoked. Or alternatively one may proclaim that in the interests of society the individual should be sacrificed in this as in many other matters to the agonising pressure of convention. But this solution which may perhaps satisfy the legislator or the sociologist has the serious defect of setting up the most tyrannical heteronomy in the realm where the individual person seems most justified in claiming his inalienable right to be an exception.

The only condemnation of divorce which can be justified, at least in theory, in the eyes of those very people who suffer most under it, is the condemnation which they must recognise as being pronounced in the name of *their own* will—a will so deep that they could not disown it without denying their own natures. If one postulates that in principle the conjugal union finds its consummation, and even its sanction, in the appearance of a new being in which the husband and wife fulfil and pass beyond themselves, it becomes obviously absurd to consider it quite natural that this same married couple should become free again whenever the sentiments which prevailed at their union change for some reason or another. They are no longer simply united by a reciprocal act which by common accord they can annul, but by the existence of a being for whom they are responsible and who has rights over them which cannot be set aside—unless we are cynically to argue from the fact that in the animal species there comes a moment when male and female lose all interest in their offspring because it no longer needs them. One can scarcely deny, I fear, that the innumerable human beings who to-day invent for themselves the most loose conception of the married state, argue from the example of the animals to justify themselves. Moreover it is worth noticing how easy it is to slide from what professes to be a completely rational notion of marriage to the grossest form of naturalism which claims to remove all lines of demarcation between man and other living creatures, in order that he may enjoy all the licence which goes with the natural state. But we know only too well the aberrations people can fall into when they claim to draw positive conclusions concerning what can and should be considered natural and consequently justifiable, particularly in matters of sex, from their observations of animal habits.

We can in reality be certain that where the mind oscillates between an abstract formalism and an animalism with pretensions of a pseudo-scientific or poetically mystical nature, it condemns itself to lose sight of the unity apart from which it is impossible to think of the mystery of the family. "The heads of families, those great adventures of the modern world," said Péguy. What does this mean except that a family is not created or maintained as an entity without the exercise of a fundamental generosity whose rightly metaphysical principle must be examined. We must, of course, leave on one side the man who generates by chance, who produces his offspring like the animals without accepting the consequences of his act. He does not found a family; he produces a brood. In the true head of a family, the harmony which is attained between consciousness and the life force is established in a sphere which is not easily accessible to us by analysis. Perhaps there is even a danger that such a method might prevent us from understanding how this harmony is possible. As is so often the case, our thought has to work negatively and can only reach its objective by exclusion.

It is obvious on the one hand, as we have seen, that where the family is conceived as a reality any idea of marriage as a mere association of individual interests must be ruled out. It seems as though the marriage must in some way regulate itself in relation to the offspring, for whose coming preparation has to be made; but it is not less certain, and this observation is of the greatest importance here, that a marriage concluded simply with a view to procreation is not only in danger of degeneration because it does not rest on a firm spiritual basis, but, still more, it is an attack upon what is most worthy of reverence in the specifically human order. There is something which outrages the very dignity of the person when the joining of two beings is envisaged merely as a means of reproduction. The operation of the flesh is thus degraded and terrible revenge is in process of preparation for the time when the misunderstood and stifled powers in the depths of the human soul shake off the yoke which has been tragically imposed upon them. So it is certainly not true to say that procreation is the end of marriage. We must rather admit that both form complementary phases of a particular history which each one of us has to live out and through which he accomplishes his destiny as a creative being. The meaning of this word "creative" is very precise here: it denotes the active contribution each soul is at liberty to bring to the universal work which is accomplishing itself in our world and doubtless far beyond it. In this connection the condition of a human being of whatever kind is not essentially different from that of the artist who is the bearer of some message which he must communicate, of some flame which he must kindle and pass on, like the torchbearers of Lucretia. Everything seems to happen as though on the human level the operation of the flesh ought to be the hallowing of a certain inward fulfilment, an out-flowing not to be forced since it springs from an experience of plentitude. Perhaps I should make myself better understood by saying in a way which actually is not exclusively Christian that the operation of the flesh loses its dignity and degenerates from its true nature if it is not an act of thanksgiving, a creative testimony. But, from this point of view, what a deep difference we must establish between husbands and wives who prudently secure for themselves an heir to succeed them, an heir who is nothing but a representative or a substitute for them—and those who, in a sort of prodigality of their whole being, sow the seed of life without ulterior motive by radiating the life flame which has permeated them and set them aglow.

These observations, which actually should be infinitely shaded, make it possible to catch a glimpse of the meaning of the sacred bond which it is man's lot to form with life, or, on the other hand, to stretch to a breaking-point after which he remains alone in a darkened and defiled universe.

There is assuredly a sense in which it is absolutely true to say that in such a realm all generalisations are deceptive. It is not even enough to remember that there are only particular cases. The truth is rather that there are no cases at all, each soul, each individual destiny constitutes a microcosm, governed by laws which, at least to a certain degree, are only valid for that soul. Hence it follows that in questions concerning particular people, such as a certain childless couple, or a family centred upon an only child, we have no right to judge. We never know—it is not our business to know—what disappointments, what secret trials underlie that which we might at first be tempted to condemn as selfishness, cowardice or voluntary sterility. And indeed we can be glad of it, for in principle it is intolerable and undistinguishable from the most odious pharisaism that any of us should invade the privacy of others with our judgments. We regain our right to judge, however, in matters concerned with realities of a social order, such as the increase of divorce, the spread in the use of contraceptives or the practice of abortion. We can above all exercise our judgment with full knowledge and complete justice against an abominable propaganda which aims at making such methods appear rationally justifiable.

But from my own point of view, it will be understood that the question is not really one of proclaiming the immoral or anti-social character of any action or conduct. I have rather to discuss the symptoms in such action or conduct of a disaffection of beings from Being which, to tell the truth, does not imply the denial of an explicitly formulated promise, but the drawing back by which a spiritual organism dwindles, shrivels, cut itself off from the universal communion in which it found the nourishing principle of life and growth. But what we should notice here is that by a serious perversion of the mind this sclerosis is interpreted as an emancipation, this atrophy as a blossoming. This is the unforgivable sin of which a certain ideology has been guilty; they imagined that they were liberating the person when all the time they were suffocating it. To borrow the famous comparison of Kant, I should say that thinking to lighten the weight of the atmosphere which presses upon human souls, they have transported them into a rarefied medium, where it is not possible for them to breath normally. But what is tragic in the world of the soul is that there is no clear indication of mortal dangers as on the physical plane, where unmistakable symptoms or sufferings afford the most imperative of signals and force the organism to react. Here, alas! the coma of the dying can last for generations without the patient, misled by his physicians, realising his condition even in his death agony. Actually this expression is not strong enough, for the threat here is not merely that of death, which after all is essentially a purification, it is one of degradation and perversion under the innumerable forms possible to human nature, and these forms, by the very diversity of their character, are the counterpart or countersign of the dignity and vocation of man.

Perhaps we shall now be able to discuss why the mystery of the family can truly be said to be a mystery of fidelity and hope. Analysis shows that the crisis in our family institutions can be traced to a deeper and deeper misunderstanding of the virtues through which the unification of our destiny both terrestrial and super-terrestrial is consummated.

First of all a fundamental error or illusion must be disposed of concerning fidelity. We are too much inclined to consider it as a mere safeguard, an inward resolution which purposes simply to preserve the existing order. But in reality the truest fidelity is creative. To be sure of it, the best way is to strive to grasp the very complex bond which unites a child to its parents. There we have a relationship which is always exposed to a double risk of deterioration. Some, professing a strict and narrow traditionalism, tend to consider the child as entirely in the debt of those who gave it life; others, on the contrary, minimising this debt, if they do not actually deny it altogether, will tend to treat the child as the creditor, for they view life not as a blessing but a crushing burden which the parents in the heedless selfishness have already had occasion to remark that the phenomena of the breaking up of families which is increasing so rapidly at the crushing burden which the parents in their heedless selfishness have already had occasion to remark that the phenomena of the breaking up of families which is increasing so rapidly at the present day is probably connected with this systematic depreciation of life. The advocates of birth control claim more or less sincerely that it is out of pity for their possible descendants that they refuse to give them the chance of existence; but we cannot help noticing, all the same, that this pity which is bestowed at small cost, not upon living beings but upon an absence of being or nothingness, is found in conjunction with a suspiciously good opportunity for indulging the most cynical egoism, and can scarcely be separated from an impoverished philosophy which measures the value of life by the pleasures and conveniences it provides. It is no less certain that pure traditionalism presents an unacceptable position here as elsewhere. Life, as it is transmitted in the act of procreation, is really neither a blessing nor a curse in itself. It is a possibility, an opportunity, a chance for good or evil. But this possibility is only achieved in so far as the being to whom it is granted appears from the moment of his birth as a subject, that is to say as able to enjoy and above all to suffer, and capable of one day attaining to the consciousness of what he has at first only felt. This being has to be armed in such a way that the two-sided possibility which has been given him appears to him as a precious opportunity when, on reaching the stage at which he adopts his own attitude to life, he can appreciate it. It is, then, the sacred duty of parents to behave in such a way towards their child, that one day it will have good reason to acknowledge that it is in their debt. But if ever they are to be justified in considering that they have a *credit* here it will be exclusively in so far as they have succeeded in discharging a debt themselves, which to tell the truth cannot be likened to a payment of account but rather to the production of a work of art where their only share is the laying of the foundations. This amounts to saying that the debt and credit are strictly correlated and connected together on the child's side quite as much as on that of the parents. But is not this to recognise implicitly that such categories are too narrow, that they are no longer applicable except where the mystery of the family has been somehow desecrated from within by beings who have ceased to share its life and have transported themselves onto a plane where each one demands his due? In the same order of ideas it is very interesting to notice that though these notions of credit and debt tend sometimes, alas, to be accepted in limited families where a special

function seems to be vested in the child by his parents through a
pseudo-agreement in which he will always be justified in saying
he has had no part, they will be found quite inapplicable to
large families where the husband and wife, with no niggardly
calculations and no pretensions to dispose of life as of their
savings, have generously given themselves up to the creative
spirit which penetrated them. It is still necessary, of course, that
the children should share in the spirit of the family. Unfortunately, it does not always follow that they do. If they allow
themselves to become infected with the prevalent individualism
they will be tempted in many cases to pose as the victims of the
blameworthy thoughtlessness of those who brought them into
the world. So then in the end everything comes back to the spirit
which at the same time is to be incarnated or established, and
maintained, the spirit spreading beyond the self; and it is precisely this spirit which is expressed by the words "creative fidelity."
The more our hearts as well as our intellects keep before them
the idea of our lineage, of the forbears to whom we are answerable—because in the last analysis it is from them that we receive
the deposit which must be transmitted—the more this spirit will
succeed in freeing itself from the shroud of selfishness and
cowardice in which a humanity, more and more cut off from its
ontological roots, is in danger of becoming gradually enveloped.
Inversely, the more the sense of a lineage tends to be lost in the
fading consciousness of a vague and nameless subsoil, the less
human soul will be able to discern its ultimate responsibilities
and the more the family will tend to be reduced to an association
with common interests, a sort of limited company of which it is
lawful and even normal that the constitution should become
increasingly flexible.

I think that it is indispensable here to stress the fact that
creative fidelity such as I am trying to define depends in no way
upon the acceptance of any special religious belief, although
Christian dogma gives it a transcendant justification and adds
infinitely to its splendour. We must, I think, recognise on the
one hand that there exists a form of Christianity, heretical no
doubt but all the same unimpeachable, which, by the predomi-
nance given to the eschatological side can dangerously weaken
or even undermine the soul's love of life. This love of life I should

readily call the ethico-lyrical impulse which controls the human swarm. Many souls under Jansenistic influence have no doubt succumbed to the temptation of abjuring what is human and deserting the earth, without perhaps getting much nearer to heaven by so doing. But, on the other hand, I should be quite disposed to think that *a religio* exists of which the pagans themselves have left us admirable signs, a reverence for the dead and for the gods presiding over the home which apart from any essentially Christian spirituality gives evidence of the pact between man and the life-force to which I have so often had occasion to refer: and it is only too easy to understand that where this *religio* has given way to the pitiless pressure, not of technics but of a mentality fascinated and unsettled by the progress of technics, we see as at the present time an increasing number of violations of that natural morality and order still recognised as such by our forefathers. I am tempted to think that it is this *religio* which we must first restore and that unfortunately a Christian super-structure, which only too often is nothing but a camouflage can very well disguise how fatally it is lacking. Unquestionably this point seems to me the most important in the whole tangle of considerations which I have tried to set before you to-day. The men of my generation have seen carried out before their eyes with extraordinary tenacity a work of systematic subversion which is no longer directed against revealed doctrines or principles hallowed by tradition, but against nature itself. Man, whatever brainless biologists may think about him, will never be on the same level as the animals. Wherever he is truly himself, wherever he is faithful to his vocation, he is infinitely above them. Wherever he deliberately renounces his true calling, he falls infinitely below them. As for the humanism for little Voltaireans on the retired list, offered by those who advocate a return to the just mean, to average virtues, to prudent calculations and methodical precautions, we now know with tragic certainty that it is the tremulous forerunner of the worst individual and national disasters.

This is not all: if so many souls to-day seem to be deaf to the call of creative fidelity, it is because these souls have lost all sense of hope. I must here briefly recall the fundamental ideas which I developed a few weeks ago on this theological virtue, the mysterious source of human activity. I said that hope cannot be separated either from a sense of communion or from a more or less conscious and explicit dependence on a power which guarantees this communion itself. "I hope in Thee, for us," such is the authentic formula of hope. But the more this "for us" tends to confine itself to what concerns the self instead of opening onto the infinite, the more hope shrivels and deteriorates, and, in the domain of the family, the more it tends to degenerate into a short-sighted ambition and to fix its attention on ways of safeguarding and increasing a certain Having which actually need not take a grossly material form. But I added that it is only by breaking through Having that hope can effect an entrance into our soul. By the term Having I did not mean exclusively the visible possessions of which each of us can make an inventory, but rather the armour of good or bad habits, opinions and prejudices which makes us impervious to the breath of the spirit, everything in us which paralyses what the Apostle calls the liberty of the children of God. Perhaps in this connection it would be well to follow the example of one of the greatest thinkers of our day and to concentrate our attention on a central fact in the psychology of contemporary man; I mean anxiety, and particularly the anxiety which is less the result of bitter experience than a mortifying anticipation, the anxiety which is like the premature decay of those who have never lived. There is indeed scarcely one of the collective influences of this age which has not tended to mark the foreheads of our adolescents with the sign of this decay; school, the Press, forms of entertainment even, have helped to impair the youthful freshness, the candid voice, the limpid gaze, the purity of heart, without which youth ceases to be a quality and a grace and becomes no more than a title, a dimension entered on an identity card. It would be unpardonable to undervalue the reaction which has been taking place for the last few years in movements which are, or hope to be, the prelude to a renaissance in our unhappy country. But there is no disguising the fact that the task is crushing and is far beyond the power of the movements in question. The atmosphere is still saturated with germs of decay which can only be swept away by an entirely new spirit. I think it is clear that on the one hand such a renewal can only spring from a religious principle but that on the other it cannot surely be the work of Christians alone, if by that we mean those who are regular members of a definite church. Finally, I am persuaded that though we certainly do not want public authorities to be patrons, since this only too often compromises a movement, we can at least ask them not to paralyse the initiative of people of all complexions, as they unite in a common effort to stimulate and revivify society. It is very much to be feared, indeed, that the State, the modern State, all of whose organs have been successively overdeveloped, will tend finally to kill everything which it claims to sanction or foster in the human being, for it is beyond its power either to give life or to reveal and recognise it.

Life: I confess that I have doubtless misused this word, the ambiguity of which I am the first to acknowledge and deplore. But whatever may be the confusion to which this ambiguity exposes loose or untrained processes of thought, it none the less has the special positive merit of revealing to us, like a drop of water in the desert, the existence of the mystery of incarnation to which I drew your attention at the beginning. The family, inasmuch as it is the matrix of individuality, is really the meeting place of the vital element and the spiritual. Still more it is an evidence of our inability to separate them, unless it be when we claim to abide by the wager of a purely speculative reason which follow from its introduction into the world of beings, to throw off the shackles proper to the state of a creature. In the last analysis it is on this elementary yet generally misunderstood notion of the state of a creature, the condition of a creature, that we must here place the decisive accent. By a paradox which well deserves our attention, the more man, misled not by science but by a certain elementary philosophy of science, comes to regard himself as a mere link in an endless chain, or as the result of purely natural causes, the more he arrogates to himself the right of absolute sovereignty in all that concerns the ordering of his personal conduct. The more he is theoretically humiliated by a materialistic philosophy which claims to deny any special identity to himself or his actions, the more does he actually develop a practical pride which impels him to deny the existence of any human order to which he might owe obedience. It is natural that under such conditions the family should be choked between the claims of two systems apparently opposed, but actually converging and reinforcing each other. In fact, it only assumes its true value and dignity through the functioning of a central relationship which cannot be affected by any objective causality and which is the strictly religious relationship whose mysterious and unique expression is found in the words *divine fatherhood.* Certainly this analogy may seem very far from a natural fatherhood, which is established by methods belonging to positive consciousness. The analogy, however, is not simply a spiritual way of looking at things. It is of a constructive character; it provides a key. We are here approaching a paradoxical truth upon which all the metaphysical understanding of the family depends. Far as we may be from claiming that theology arbitrarily transposes natural relationship into the sphere of divine realities, we must undoubtedly recognise that, inversely, all the so-called natural relationships which, as we have seen, can never be reduced to simple experimental data, not only symbolise transcendental relationships towards which they direct our devotion, but they also tend to weaken and dissolve precisely in so far as these relationships are misunderstood and denied. In other words, contrary to the persistent humanistic illusion, we have good reason to assert that family relationships, like human matters in general, afford no consistency, no guarantee of solidity. It is only when they are referred back to a superhuman order, which here below we cannot grasp apart from its signs and indications, that their truly sacred character becomes apparent. Accordingly, as events have gone on showing for the last quarter of a century, wherever man betrays faith in man, wherever treason becomes a habit and then a rule, there can no longer be room for anything but insanity and ruin. It can scarcely be different wherever the claim is made to establish a way of private life which disregards the vow of fidelity. The truth is that humanity is only truly human when it is upheld by the incorruptible foundations of consecration—without such foundations it decomposes and dies. Do not let us say, however, that it returns to nothingness. If this word has any meaning, which is not certain, it is on a level of reality far below the human structure. When man, by denying the existence of God, denies his own, the spiritual powers which are dissociated by his denial keep their primitive reality, but disunited and detached they can no longer do anything but drive the beings of flesh and soul back against each other in a despairing conflict—those beings which, had their union been safeguarded and preserved, would have gone forward towards eternal life. What all this amounts to is that if, as is certain, we have to recover to-day the sense of a certain fundamental reverence towards life, it cannot be by starting from below, that is to say from a biology of racialism or eugenics infected with ill-will. On the contrary, only an affirmation which reaches far beyond all empirical and objectively discernible ways of living can gain for us a sense of life's fullness and, besides this, set the seal of eternity upon the perpetually renewed act of creation, that act by which the whole family preserves its being and grants to the soul, which it forms and guides, the fearful power of completing or, alas, of repudiating it.

Maurice Gustave Nédoncelle

1905-

Love, as a theme, haunts the twentieth century. The number of films, songs and books on love is overwhelming and reveals the degree to which love has become a major concern in our time. Tragically, though the human condition is incomprehensible if not established on a rich concept of love, very few men and women seem to have arrived at an accurate understanding of love. For the person who does want to approach the theme of love responsibly and maturely, the book Love and the Person, *by Maurice Nédoncelle, is an excellent starting point.*

The author, born in France in 1905, studied at Saint Sulpice and the Sorbonne. He earned a doctoral degree in philosophy and letters at the Sorbonne, as well as a Doctorate in Theology from the University of Strasbourg. He has dedicated his life to writing and teaching. His excellent knowledge of the contemporary movements of existentialism and personalism has provided him with the background necessary to grasp the intellectual structures that support modern man and to gauge the pressures that have built up around man in this century.

Realizing that twentieth century man is easily described through terms such as lost, insecure, lonely and frightened, Nédoncelle has chosen to focus attention on two of the most significant and dynamic terms in the human vocabulary, love and person. Though he treats them separately for the purpose of clarification, he is quite aware of the link between them. In fact he is convinced that love proceeds only from persons and is directed only toward persons. Should it take on any other form, love would be incomplete.

Love, for Nédoncelle, is a will to promotion. The I that loves wills above all the existence of the thou. Love demands that the I go out to the thou, not as a thing to be possessed or controlled, but as an interior existence having perfect subjectivity. With this insight, Nédoncelle begins his exploration of love, one of the most important spheres of human encounter. He is convinced that the will to promote the other's well being lies behind and permeates every relationship described by the word love. After isolating the purest and truest meaning of the word, he discusses love as an expression of human relationship and love as a value in itself. What does Love seek? Is it the supreme value? the supreme reality? These are fundamental questions which must be examined if love is to be more than a mere word in today's world.

Love takes on its fullest meaning only when lived by actually existing persons; but this can be accomplished only to the degree that persons consciously and deliberately establish their relationships on the most authentic concept of love. Maurice Nédoncelle's work makes this concept available. His style and terminology are demanding, for he is quite serious about his task and challenges his reader to apply his intellectual abilities to the question at hand with vigor. The reward is an expanded and highly enriched appreciation of a word that deserves the total commitment of all human beings.

LOVE AND THE PERSON

A Will To Promotion

Among all the concepts attached to a given word we should choose the most authentic one, the one that can help us understand even the anomalies, twists and distortions to which the word is liable. Now, the concept that satisfies these requirements and that should enter into the definition we are looking for is the following: love is a will to promotion. The *I* that loves is willing above all the existence of the *thou;* it subsequently wills the autonomous development of the *thou;* and finally wills that this autonomous development be, if possible, in harmony with the value the *I* anticipates for the *thou.* Any other desire would be either a timid hesitation on the threshold of the temple or egoistic delight in a mirrored reflection. There is no love properly so-called unless there are two, and unless the *I* undertakes to go out to the *thou* in order to regard him in the truest possible sense, not as an object of curiosity, but as an interior existence having perfect subjectivity.

Max Scheler defined love in a way that coincides partly with our proposal but ultimately differs from it. According to him, love is an intentional movement causing a superior value to appear in a concrete being. It is never motivated by the knowledge of a value that that being may have already acquired in its empiric existence. Thus one can love a criminal as well as a saint: in both cases the lover rises toward an excellence inherent in the one of whom he is enamored; and this excellence subsists in the realm of value no matter what may have been the conduct of the loved one up to this time. But what is the object of love? It may be three-fold: I can become attached to the vital being of the other, and the highest value I see in him—the exaltation of sexuality for example—becomes the nobility of his being. I can place myself on a higher level and love the psychic reality of the other; this new orientation will lead me to values of culture and truth. Finally, at the highest level, it is his spiritual nature that enthralls me, and the value I then perceive is the very person of the other. Only personal love is moral; here the good is not extrinsic to the *thou,* it is the *thou* itself.

There is much to be retained from this analysis. But Scheler adds certain refinements to his thesis that make it very debatable. In love, as he sees it, there is never anything to be accomplished. "What," he asks, "can a mother really will as she lovingly contemplates her sleeping child?" Certainly, the active, educative attitude may be a consequence of love, but it would not be essential to love itself. It is, in effect, impossible for Scheler to insert the will into love, for according to him, the will is purely executive in character; it is devoid of any intentionality or direction of its own.

I fear that his decision to limit love to an emotional contemplation is a grave error. If we separate sentiment and self-sacrifice at the base of love, love itself is destroyed. The primordial drive of the self is not only an impulse toward the other and toward the inner value of the other, as Scheler so admirably showed; it is also an efficient energy that wants to contribute to the existence and development of the other. Thus it is not a question of directing him toward some extrinsic end nor of using him as a means for the triumph of a value foreign to his unique vocation. It is a question of giving him the solidity and perfection of his singular personality and striving for the boundless liberty of his unfettered being. Love is not a lazy repose in the beauty of an image, but a vital involvement, a vigorous commitment, a straining toward the fulfillment of the *thou.* Even in contemplation there should be an active desire.

Does this mean that the will to advancement is a will to creation? Perhaps. In principle, the lover longs to engender wholly the being of the beloved. However, a human person cannot, in fact, pretend to such a thing. We try to consolidate the existence of the *thou* or contribute to his growth. But we always fall short at some point. Often our control goes no farther than our imagination, as in the case of the novelist who brings his characters to life on paper; sometimes he manages to stammer out a new essence but his phantoms evolve in a misty existence, powerless to come fully alive. We give a child bread to help his physical growth; we may come to the assistance of a friend, influence a mind and modify its qualities. But man does not create man.

Someone will object, saying that he procreates him. Is this truly an objection? On this point I find myself again in agreement with Scheler: procreation is not a relation of spiritual causality. There is no direct continuity between the parents and the soul of their child. The *ingenium* of the son descends from heaven to earth. To the degree that the son is himself he is not hereditary; he is not proportionate to the paternal *ingenium*. His arrival is basically independent of the designs of the parents. The sex act is subjectively the expression of conjugal affection and implies in itself nothing more in this respect. The fact that conception may take place without any thought being directed to the possibility of offspring should suffice to show up the weakness of the alleged creative powers of the procreators. Conjugal love may indeed include the desire for the child and penetrate the sex act with an intention it did not originally have. The moralist will be generous with good advice on this subject. But the fact remains that the arrival of the child is always a gift and a surprise. What is hereditary is not owing to the will of the parents; it is only the resemblances of repetitious qualities that are transmitted from one generation to the next.

Now, a child is something other than a mass of qualities, he is a new germ of personality who will have to make his own choice from among the totality of traits to which he is liable and integrate them little by little according to an unforeseeable design. Strictly from the viewpoint of causality, which supposes a conscious will to advancement, influence cannot begin unless the child is already there. We never create another personality, we discover it. Between it and us there is an initial gulf that cannot be crossed. In the geometry of souls the lines are at first parallel; only later do destinies touch and intersect.

Wise old Plato was right on this point. He maintained that in our human experience love originates in the loveableness of the beloved. We receive the beloved, we discover in him reasons for cherishing him even if he be vile or vilified. The stream of love then flows from the beloved to the lover and back again, enriched in its content and intensified in its movement. But Plato, I will admit, does not take into sufficient account the gratuitous initiative of the lover—an initiative proportionate to the nobility of his love. Even though love may be rooted in necessity it flowers in freedom; it is perception, but it is also creative imagination; the autonomy love would give, it first acquires itself; and if, to some extent, it always receives what it gives, it is simply to learn to give more and more while receiving less and less. The very act of receiving tends to be the result of a conscious work; the act is experienced in order to be confirmed; and from then on it is willed.

If the lover is not entirely the creator, must we conclude that he means to withdraw for the greater good of the *thou* and that this good is realized only by his retreat? This extreme does not necessarily follow. When it is a question of material goods, sincere love should, it is true, be disposed to share them even at considerable cost to self and one may soon suffer want of support. But however painful the results of his catering to the needs of the beloved, the lover suffers no mutilation or suppression of his fundamental will to advance the beloved. He cannot deny the act that is constitutive of his own being, i.e., willing himself for the sake of the other; and how could the effacement of the self automatically produce positive progress in the other? Recourse to voluntary self-limitation solves nothing.

All this brings us back to our original statement and calls for this additional remark: the self is convinced that in love it can influence another center of consciousness and produce, to a degree, the growth of an interior character that exists for itself in his presence. Every lover has this ambition, and to take it away from him is to take away his love itself. Illusory or not, his intention rests on this fundamental belief in a transitive action of one consciousness on another.

Maurice Gustave Nédoncelle

A Will To Mutual Promotion

To love implies the desire to be loved, and in a certain sense, the fact of being loved. I am well aware that this double affirmation will cause some astonishment. Those who disagree with me will cry shame, as though I were introducing egoism into the heart of generosity. They will also accuse me of mistaking chimeras for realities; it is only too evident that affection is not always requited. However, I do not see how I can relinquish my paradoxes.

In my defense I will first expound and evaluate the contrary opinion. It has recently been brilliantly presented by Anders Nygren in *Agape and Eros*. This Lutheran philosopher conceives of two kinds of love. One is *Eros,* the desire for the best: the aristocratic aspiration of the human self that would wish to raise itself to the level of the divine; it cannot be satisfied except by taking God Himself for its object. It is motivated by the perception of the beauty residing in this supreme object.

The other type of love is *Agape:* it is the gift and sacrifice of self for the loved one; it creates the value of its object; it is spontaneous and kind; it is not in the least motivated by the excellence of the beloved. Eros is centripetal; agape is centrifugal. They are two spiritual movements that have nothing in common.

This psychological opposition, continues the author, is rooted in history. The Greek philosophers knew eros; it was Christianity that revealed agape. Within the Greek perspective, love expresses man's nature and responds to his tendency toward perfection. We must not confuse the popular Venus with the celestial Venus: eros is, of course, noble. But it is a superior egoism, none the less. It postulates a human soul with a divine value buried in its depths; its goal is the divinization of the self. Through love, the soul is awakened to the desire to arrive at the absolute perfection from which it is exiled here below and for which it has an indestructible nostalgia. The lover is enamored of himself and therefore seeks to possess God in order to become divine. As for the love of other human beings, it can be, under these conditions, only an instrument for going toward self and toward God. The neighbor is a step on the ladder to the divine and we can appreciate our fellow men only insofar as they serve as means to our ascension: we love them *propter Deum.*

On the other hand, agape is the supernatural love emanating from God himself and subsisting in Him alone; it is bestowed on us gratuitously as a consequence of a sacrifice of the Most High. We who are the object of this love and receive it, are nothing but miserable creatures; our self has nothing lovable in itself, no rights, no intrinsic value. If we love our neighbor it is because the divine agape in us, by passing through us as an efficient and not as a final cause, impels us to act thus. In the true Christian tradition the other need not fear he will be treated as a simple means *propter Deum.* . . . Man is loved by man because the gift which comes from God demands it, and this gift is entirely disinterested: it is free of any egoistic infiltration. Agape alone respects and establishes true "philanthropy." This is strikingly evident in the evangelical precept to love one's enemies. Such an attitude is inconceivable to pagan philosophers, totally concerned as they are with allowing the delectable riches of the Good-in-itself to flow into them.

Nygren thinks that any synthesis of these two historic forms of love is impossible. St. Augustine forged a hybrid notion, *Caritas,* which mixes the Greek eros with the New Testament agape. Theologians of the Middle Ages often prolonged this error or erected it into a system; but the cement has never held. Their compromise raised insoluble difficulties and engendered repeated crises in the speculative order. However, these attempts have been useful, for their failure has helped place the exact notion of agape in bolder relief. Through successive "reforms" the Christian conscience has stood out with greater clarity, it has understood its own originality and supernatural character. The salvation of love is not from man, whose nature is all desire; salvation comes from heaven; it overcomes and transcends desire, for it is gift.

Such is Nygren's thesis: neat, elegant, and basically dualist. Here and there it lends itself to admirable developments. But I must admit that on the whole I cannot subscribe to it. My first objection is that it reduces man's role to nothing and makes impossible any dialogue between the creature and the Creator, or even between the beloved and the lover. It suppresses the very notion of a return of love. All it leaves is the divine solitude. Indeed, to what could our response to the Lord be reduced? An acceptance of grace? Submission? But is that love? If so it would be either eros or agape: if eros, the attitude of the beloved is egoistic and to be condemned. If agape, it ought to be in a form that can flow from the creature. Now, it seems to me that this is not a love that descends from God and has not yet met our being, but a love that is implanted in us to be reborn and rise again in newness toward God. Thus we are brought back either to the notion of a good eros excluded by Nygren or else to that kind of created grace that duplicates agape and makes us imitators of God by elevating our nature to a supernatural state without destroying its personal spontaneity. In its communion with God the self is saved from its supposed fundamental perversion; personality responds freely to Him who calls it; it is not a stranger to transcendence but blossoms forth in it. But at this point we do not understand in the same way as Nygren the vicissitudes of a divine love loving itself in us. So we abandon his thesis to save the possibility of a loving exchange.

There is a final hypothesis possible: that obedience to grace would be neither eros nor agape. But by definition it would no longer be love, since love, it is maintained, can take only these two forms. We must conclude, then, that for Nygren the creature loved by God is itself incapable of love. If God expects something from us it can be only the docility of the slave. Under these circumstances should the divine liberality be called a work of love? It is the omnipotence of an artist who brings passivities to light; it is not the gift of a goodness that causes personalities to unfold.

No doubt one could answer that the attitude of the soul submissive to God has a name, and that that name is faith. However, the difficulty still remains. Either faith has, indeed, been aroused in us by divine charity without ever being called to consummation in an act of love (but this affirmation, hardening as it does the theological distinction between faith and charity, would have the paradoxical result of making Nygren more Catholic than the Catholics themselves: under pretext of respecting the originality of faith, the whole religious life of man would be imperviou s to love). Or else, on the contrary, in keeping with the tradition of the Reformation, faith is formed by charity, and that formula would have to be interpreted in this instance as the affirmation of a loving response by man to God (but then we find again in our supernatural state and, under cover of faith, the difficulties regarding eros and agape I have already pointed out). Thus we shall either have to reject the thesis or deny any particle of generosity in man.

Actually, dialogue is essential to the reciprocity of love, and if there is to be dialogue between the Creator and the creature, the creature must be something other than a necessary reflection or an automatic echo. He must be capable of disinterestedness, and that by free choice. This living response supposes that the loved one desires to share in the perfection of the supreme lover in order to offer him an autonomous image of it. In a word, the love of God urges us and compels us, not in order to constrain us as things, but to oblige us to be free.

Let us suppose that we have this liberty and that Nygren accepts it. His doctrine would not be any more satisfactory; it would lead straight to a new impasse and strip human beings of the dignity proper to them: the power to delight and to grieve their Creator. It makes any disappointment of the divine Lover impossible. If the gift alone counts, if true love is centrifugal, the attitude and response of the beloved matters little; the lover can only cease being interested in the use the beloved will make of his freedom.

By an odd coincidence we come upon that unforgettable passage in which Goethe exclaims: "If I love you, what is that to you?" No doubt this proud cry represents a lofty state of soul; between unilateral love and spiritual beggary Goethe chooses unilateral love, and rightly so. Reciprocity is elusive; he fails to achieve it and resigns himself to choose the lesser of two evils. This designates a makeshift and not the perfection of love. The inevitable consequence of his protestation is the challenge: "If you don't love me, what is that to me?"

All these haughty questions are dangerous. There are two ways of being disappointed: one is to feel oneself thwarted, the other is to discover the moral mediocrity of the one loved. Now these two ways merge into one for the perfectly loving soul; for, unresigned to evil, it says: "My satisfaction is your value; my sorrow is your refusal to fulfill the value that was in you and that my love wants to help you to realize to the fullest."

Finally, just as the gift of the Creator includes the desire to elevate the beloved toward the harmony He offers, so also the mounting desire that moves the beloved, leads him to seek supreme perfection and admit that it consists in generously giving oneself. There is an eros of the agape, a need to possess the spirit of dis-possession, a desire to find one's soul in losing it. Why should eros be only a will to monopolize and use? It is the desire of the best, and as such is destined not to use everything but to learn that it ought to serve the spirit of generosity. The contrast proposed by Nygren is a psychological error. He condemns eros, whereas it is only the limits imposed on eros that are condemnable, limits which a sincere eros itself condemns, since it discovers that its vocation is to be converted to generosity.

Setting aside these theological discussions, let us turn to the direct and more modest analysis of the reciprocity of centers of consciousness—it will lead to analogous conclusions. Above all, it leads us to believe that every lover wants to be loved and all love finds at least a minimum of reward.

1) There is a *minimum of reciprocity* in the fact that love originates in the perception of the lovableness of the beloved. If it is truly another that I love and not an impersonal quality pinned on him, it is he who, in a sense, has begun to love me. He has advanced me and enriched me simply by his very presence open to my perception. My love for him ought to begin in a kind of thanks, and I can tell him with the poet: *"C'est moi qui te dois tout, puisque c'est moi qui t'aime."* ("It is I who owe you everything since it is I who love you.")

It will be objected that this person does not even know that virtue has gone out of him, and he may be unaware of my existence. How can you say he is my benefactor? I answer: he has not willed me by name, he has not turned toward me as a result of a special decision, but he has given himself to the world, he has willed this in willing to display his activity and allow his personality to be glimpsed there. Thus it is that he has caused his being to shine in my own.

Nietzsche speaks of an enriching virtue—*schenkende Tugend*—emanating from certain personalities. This radiance is not the prerogative of a Socrates or a St. Francis of Assisi; it is inseparable from all personal existence. To be in the world is to be a minimum of goodness publicly exposed. Human centers of consciousness are hidden in many respects by the cosmic masquerade; but there is one aspect under which they cannot do otherwise than show themselves and communicate their share of excellence to those who contemplate them. There are so many tragic and absurd angles to the human condition that we can only rejoice to discover this happy feature of our destiny. To be in the world is *to be able* to dissimulate and to wreak havoc, that is true; but first of all, before ugliness sets in, it is to open one's soul to other souls and bring them an initial presence which is itself a gift. A countenance that appears is a reality surrendered, a secret cautiously unveiled, a value poured out and not taken back. Everyone knows there is a play of light behind the lattice wall, and in the weakest or most retiring mind there is a fundamental will that continues to sing the joy of this necessary and innocent gift. The person is an expression and a role: he soon learns to calculate his effects or to poison the atmosphere. But in the beginning he is unaware of his grimaces and is all freshness and trust. Love is always watching for this initial moment, and that is why it is born in mutuality even though it must often sink into solitude.

2) But love does not have a hermit's vocation; it always seeks a *maximum of reciprocity*.

The response that a person to whom I am attached can give me may exhibit four successive degrees:

At the lowest, the other responds to my will to promotion by the *simple fact of his existence and growth*. The little child or the unconscious patient may never be aware of the care I lavish on them. My reward is that they live; their very existence is a recompense.

Then there is the reciprocity that is already psychological if *the other is aware of my project,* even though he rejects it or, while being aware of it, does not know its author. I provide him with a new theme. I plant in his being a virtual personality. Whatever variations he may weave on the theme or whatever may be his ignorance of the fact that he received it from me, he has truly received it and the theme is truly in him. My loving intention remains in his presence, at least under the form of an anonymous ideal of his self. It is a path that may be barred or that he may choose not to take; but something of my will is, as it were, really knit into his substance. Newman wrote in this fashion on the subject of the kind of presence that faithful Christians can have even in their persecutors: "They have a friend of their own in each man's bosom, witnessing for them; even in those who treat them ill." This statement is rich in meaning and expresses in a particular instance the larger truth I am trying to define.

3) At the third level of reciprocity the *thou ratifies the loving design of the I for the thou.* He has accepted the theme offered him, and the variations he composes are in harmony with it. It is thus that the disciple repays the master and the child honors the education he has received. It is not a question of copying an effect or slavishly aping a model but of adopting a spiritual orientation and freely responding to a source of inspiration.

4) Lastly, reciprocity is complete when *the beloved in turn wills the advancement of the lover* and turns back to him with the same intentness that had turned the lover toward him, choosing the lover's personal development as the goal of his activity. At this moment the circuit of love is complete.

If we now analyze the gift of self that characterized the impulse of the loving person, we see that that person implicitly wants the four degrees of reciprocity whose progression we have just noted. By the very fact that he wants to help another be himself, the lover seeks to obtain, insofar as circumstances and the attitude of the loved one permit, the perfect constitution of the full circuit of love. This is equivalent to saying that by loving he aims somehow to be loved: the two movements inevitably converge.

What does it mean to *give oneself to another?* It is to commit oneself to be concerned about him, to make him exist more fully. But the lover would deny the worth of his love did he not desire the beloved to share it and be loving in his turn. To will that the other be loving is to will that he love in me what makes me able and willing to love him; it is to will that he love me. "I belong to you" means: depend on me for yourself, I dedicate myself to you. But the expression is equivocal and it is logical that it be so. It also means: I depend on something in you to help me so that I can be worthy of you and useful to you. Help me to help you. I want you to be such that I, in my turn, can place myself in your hands and receive a greater value from you. By the fact that I attach myself to you, I make it possible for you to transform me for yourself. In one and the same act I believe in you and in myself; I hope in you and in myself; my love is an invocation that I address simultaneously to you and to me.

Doubtless, when I love you I first will that you be loveworthy and, perhaps, even that your generosity turn away from me, in order to turn toward the world and give it a greater value. It is thus in conjugal love and friendship: I want the other to be able to forget me temporarily, should that be necessary for him to better fulfill his duty; I wish, in certain circumstances, that he go to those who need him before he concerns himself with me who can do without his help; I wish, in a word, to be able to esteem him. This is particularly so in parental love: a popular saying has it that parents do not rear their children for themselves, and that love descends from the older to the younger generation instead of rising from the younger to the older. These aphorisms not only express a fact of nature, they indicate an order of duty. But by consenting to my request that he leave me, the beloved richly rewards me at the very moment he seems to ignore me. And at the end of his charitable action, will he not meet me again? As the object of his act will I ever be absent from his horizon? It is only from his work, and in appearance, that he had to exclude me. I am not excluded from the deeper impulse that inspired his work. It was from me he drew the noblest reason for his withdrawal, since it was I who said: "If you love me, leave me."

Neither sacrifices nor delays can shut me out from the circuit that would draw my beloved toward me—it would be contradictory if they could. The journey of the beloved will be complete only if it comes to an end in me after having encompassed, in a way, a universe of other selves. Even in the cases in which a physical distance is morally indispensable to the work of love, the lover wishes implicitly that the beloved, while setting forth from him, should come back to him in the end. The four degrees of reciprocity indicated above are in the will of the lover from the beginning; but he cannot fully live them except by stages, and he would destroy the purity of his intention if he omitted the intermediate steps through pride or impatience.

Thus, in the gift of self the *I* enhances the *thou* and this constitutes an agape; and the *I* is enhanced by the *thou,* which constitutes an eros. This circle is inevitable. What is willed is a manner of being of the *thou* and the *I* which derives directly from the loving will and has its origin in it. A sincere eros leads to agape; a sincere agape brings us back to eros; each leads to the other while remaining present in the other, once it has led there. The lover who has understood the implications of eros does not desire the other as an instrument to be subordinated to his use, but as an end that is equal or perhaps superior to himself. An analogous statement is true for the lover inspired by agape. If we raise these statements to the level of the principle that sustains them, we discover their transcendent unity: Plotinus taught that God is eros itself; his definition, properly understood, is meant to be illuminated and completed by the Johannine word: "God is agape."

The love of self, therefore, is not necessarily a form of egoism. It should culminate in self-sacrifice and is indeed implied by it. The two ways, while apparently opposed to each other, are really complementary. In principle they are inseparable. But whence comes *the inveterate distrust of moralists with regard to one of these two?* These men are severe toward eros and well disposed toward agape. The reasons for their attitude are mysterious and more difficult to explain than one would think. The facts are clear and no educator can doubt them. To suggest to a child that he take as his ideal the fullest development of his personality is to risk making a hard-hearted person of him, unsympathetic and unfeeling. He may become an "angelic epicurean" but he will still be an egoist. On the other hand, to exhort him to self-sacrifice and renunciation is to point out a short cut to perfection and propose a healthier and safer method of education.

The facts are clear . . . it is the reason for them that is obscure, and we cannot be satisfied with an argument *in terrorem*, or a pious sermon by way of explanation. Why, then, is the cult of self so equivocal and so apt to turn us away from the fullness of love instead of leading us to it?

A first reply would be as follows: the love of self is a spontaneous, constant and incoercible tendency. The gift of self, on the other hand, is fragile; it demands effort, which alone is meritorious. —That reply is, basically, quite insufficient. Let us rid ourselves of our prejudices and look at things impartially. What do we observe? On the one hand, in order to reach its goal, the desire for the best demands a host of sacrifices and heroic decisions. The lower self must be constantly immolated to the higher. In Plato's temple of wisdom there is an altar for holocausts; and even Nietzsche, who downgrades the will-to-good in favor of the will-to-power, is not a gentle master in this respect: in order to fulfill himself he tears himself like a corybant. —On the other hand, is it true that self-sacrifice for the sake of others is a disposition that is parsimoniously distributed among mankind and always hard to cultivate? I would be tempted to believe the contrary. Altruistic tendencies are as spontaneous as the others. There is a prodigal sacrifice of self all around us. But how many of these sacrifices are blind or stupid! . . . Many people will deprive themselves of necessities and spend themselves recklessly for a dog or a parrot. There are some who, in times of disaster, would rather lose their lives than be separated from a favorite house plant. Agape, too, has its excesses, its mistakes in perspective, and its perversions, sometimes touching, sometimes scandalous. The solution must be sought elsewhere.

A second reply is more satisfactory. It would have us note the ease with which love, whether it be selfish desire or self-sacrifice, ceases to be directed toward a *thou* properly so-called, and turns to impersonal objects. Thus it is that we become attached to things or institutions without making of that attachment a means for advancing personal subjects but rather a frontier that limits and satisfies us. But if it is an impersonal being we love it is impossible to give it true autonomy. A plant, a dog, or even a social form, such as the fatherland or humanity, are not subjects endowed with a free inner life. They are not universal perspectives like you and me. It follows that the loved one is, in this case, unequal to the lover; and even if the lover were to immolate himself for an object of this kind, he would be using it much more than he would be serving it. The will to possess necessarily gets the better of the will to give. If I realize that my dog is a dog, I shall never be able to love him for himself as much as, or in the same way that, I love him for myself. A kind of generosity and even reciprocity may unite us, but they are not of the same species as when the *thou* is a person. There will be a difference of level between an eros that is personal and an agape that cannot be so. True, I can forget that my dog is a dog and naively treat him as a friend and equal. But this naivete is suspect: I pretend to be unaware that the dog is not a personal self because in that way I can imagine that I am dominating a free being. The love of animals, and of children, too, affords us, at little cost, what we obtain only with great difficulty in the love of adults: security.

Besides, this illusion will not restore the balance between the two aspects of love, self-centeredness and self-sacrifice, for the failure of a frank and total reciprocity between the loved one and myself maintains a difference of nature between my desire turned toward my subjectivity and my devotion turned toward the weak form of consciousness that is my dog's. Willy-nilly the reach of my devotion will be shortened and the level of my objective will be lowered; the love I have for myself will direct and utilize my devotion in a tyrannical fashion. And this is normal.

But the psychological habit we contract in our relations with natural creatures or social institutions is apt to contaminate our relations with personal beings. We are tempted to transpose into inter-human love a behavior that is unjustifiable, since it makes us regard the other as a thing or an idea, and leaves us on the periphery of his subjectivity. At last we understand why moralists distrust the ways of eros and warn against its dangers. We understand it all the better when we see how facts confirm their fears. The attitude proper to the pseudo-love that persons bear toward things often invades the mind and spoils the love one bears toward other persons.

This explanation is interesting; but it calls for additional comment. The great mystery is the malady that impels eros and agape to stop short in their elementary stages and lazily rest there. We lack ambition for ourselves and others. But to this weakness it shares with agape, eros adds another of its own. Love of self is more quickly and thoroughly corrupted than devotedness. Whenever there is gift there is inevitably self-desire, too: we love ourselves as being able to help the *thou* we have chosen. On the other hand, where there is love of self there is not necessarily gift also; I can love myself in such a manner as to rid myself of all devotedness to others. In this sense, any gift, mediocre though it be, involves a certain attention to the interests of the self, it considers them and respects them; while the love of self, if it is mediocre, can wrap itself up in a strictly private pleasure and preclude any turning toward others. It is greedly and in too great a hurry. Thus the spell of evil paralyzes eros more completely than it does agape.

Nevertheless, evil does profit from the growing pains that hamper agape. If I renounce the noble love of self, it is because of deep-seated inertia. If, on the contrary, I get discouraged in my generosity toward others, it is not only from a lack of energy that has its source in me (and for which I am to blame), it is also occasioned by the ingratitude I experience on the part of others or their refusal of the value I wish to offer them. The inclination to give oneself meets with obstacles from within and without; the love of self finds them only within; its value and success depend, ultimately, on the self alone. In both cases, the soul suffers defeat; but morality, which is concerned only with what depends on us, will insist on the duty to fight against egoism and profess as an *a priori* mistrust of the search for self. Renunciation and devotedness will be, in its eyes, the sole way of access to virtue.

Abandoning these subtle, irritating discussions, we shall next consider the most frequent symptoms of the disease that strikes love. The first is bitter jealousy. The self strictly limits the scope of its generosity, it goes out to the *thou* to the exclusion of others or against them. The second symptom is a slowing down in the soul's ascent toward value, or a descent into the cheap marketable values of sensuality; it is a sealing off of approaches from above, a kind of monstrous insensibility to spiritual perfection. In jealousy and sloth are summed up the majority of love's tragedies. On the one hand there is belligerent tension and bitterness; on the other, the "vertiginous sweetness" of the rests or *decrescendos* that used to disturb Baudelaire.

To be cured, one has to go to the moralists. And the reform they propose will be first to stop loving one being at the expense of another. The avid and exclusive soul is already half converted when he can get along without rivals. Many couples feel the need of eliminating a third party and making him suffer in order to taste the happiness of their union. Their intimacy is heightened by these battles. This smiling sadism that persecutes everyone else in order to realize a sweeter life for two alone, has been little studied. It is, however, as mysterious as, and more frequent than, the frowning kind! Charles Lamb alludes to it humorously in his "A Bachelor's Complaint About the Behavior of Married People": "What I am complaining about," he says, "is that you can't be in their company a moment without being made to feel, by some indirect hint or open avowal, that *you* are not the object of their preference."

Conversion is complete when it is realized that to truly love a person one must wish to make him infinitely lovable, for in this radical wish the need for all the values stands out. My partner will not be infinitely lovable unless he infinitely loves the universe of persons and makes himself worthy to be loved by them. I wish to raise him to a point where my jealousy is wiped out once and for all and where all the doors of the world are wide open to him. The will to advance the beloved is demanding: it tolerates neither pettiness nor laziness; it leads us much farther and higher than we had suspected at first; it implies, in effect, an unlimited development of the *I* and *thou;*

and in the personal identity it pledges to confer on the lovers, it is the identity and development of all conscious beings that it is logically committed to promote, step by step, to the point where there is a mutual interpenetration of all by God and God by all.

Love Links Persons Into A Spiritual Community

The reciprocity we have just analyzed is a journey of the *I* toward the *thou* and the *thou* toward the *I*. From the outset there is a vague perception of the bond that unites two centers of consciousness and all others in them. In a word, the relationship now takes the form of a *we*. But there are many forms of the *we*. F. Perroux distinguished the *we* of similitude (*I* as *thou*), the *we* of association (*I* with *thee*), the *we* of dilution (*I* in *thou*), and the *we* of love (*I* for *thee*). Though the list is incomplete and tentative, it suffices to introduce the problem of the nature of the *we* of love and how it is distinguished from the others.

1) To understand its special character, let us take as an example an old man who loves the charm of a child. Shall we say that he seeks to acquire the child's charm and share it with him? Evidently not. It is not a question of fusing or confusing their respective domains. The old man wants the child to have its own charm and to keep it in the measure that it is a gift having its own nuances proper to the development of the little one. The child, who is attached to the old man, in his turn ratifies and advances, after a fashion, the wisdom or goodness of the old man. Each is happy to improve a wealth he does not possess in himself. Each has an asset in the other: it is a centrifugal possession. What is more, it is an existence of each self in the other, for it is their very being that grows and lives on in another being. Their inner will establishes itself in an outer world, and what is most intimate to it lodges in a stream of life different from their own. Thus it is in every personal love. It is hard for us to translate this situation into metaphorical language because it cannot be conceived as a community of bodily qualities or as a natural possession. We imagine presence in another as a good separate from the gift: thus we see the old man as possessing the loveliness of the child in the same way a

wealthy man has his fortune at the bank. Matters of love are more subtle. The qualities which express each self do so only by being born in the other self and in developing for his sake. It is through him that they come back to the lover in an atmosphere which is an offering in return.

The *we* of love is the very meeting of these two subjects whose having is in the other, and it is the awareness of this double, generous transposition that is its very being. More vital or more actual according to the degree of reciprocity attained, this is what characterizes all love. The communion of the subjects is but the coexistence of these two out-of-center series in which individual qualities can finally circulate in the continuity of persons. No other experience enables us to understand so clearly the reconciliation of the one and the many in the life of the spirit. *Aut duo, aut nemo.*

2) It follows that the *we* of love is a *heterogeneous* identity of the *I* and *thou*. It is the community of two subjects as subjects. Too often in the past philosophers have maintained that every identity is homogeneous. They regard as identical any two elements that we are unable to distinguish upon the most methodical examination. But while reason wishes to identify everything, reality opposes this reduction. The notion of an absolute identity may even be contradictory. This is what Plato was forced to conclude in his metaphysical dialogues on the same and the other. Closer to our own time, Bradley rejects identity as well as diversity in the world of appearances. And Meyerson admits that identity breaks down unless there is irrational diversity subsisting in contrast with it.

We should be spared many a philosophical dilemma if we admitted that identity is heterogeneous and does not concern objects but subjects. Just as Bergson abandoned the false continuity of homogeneity and introduced the idea of a profound continuity with irreducible aspects, it seems we must realize that true identity is heterogeneous and supposes the diversity of subjects and their irreplaceable character. Far from causing confusion, this identity, which is the identity of love, abolishes errors. It disengages and dissolves the inferior, woolly form of identity; it forces us to sacrifice what obstructs the originality of personal subjects and prevents them from being

397

themselves. It does not rest on the similarity between its participants but on their harmonious originality. Certainly it leads us to state, without fear of presumption, that the *I is the thou,* but only in the perspective in which it *causes the thou to be,* and is itself willed by the *thou.* By this will, the subjects identify with each other, and do so only in the measure in which they become different.

3) On the other hand, the *we* of love is inactive in the sense that it does not create the *I* and *thou* but simply expresses their mutuality. Friendship is not something added to two friends like a third individual, or even like a third force separable from their two wills. It does not establish them in their love by a kind of feedback; it simply accompanies them; it is the spiritual nature of their persons. We are tempted to believe the contrary because we thoughtlessly assimilate the community of minds with the community that results from a juridical contract sanctioning social engagements. It is quite true that the contract is separate from the contracting parties and subsequently binds them before the law no matter what changes may have occurred in their inner disposition. But though the loving exchange does constitute a new situation, it does not create it in the same way a contract would. It is in the very tissue of the subjects who make the agreement, and if they separate, it is torn apart. It leaves them as the sparkling of the sea flees with the setting sun.

If the exchange is active, it is through the weight of the past that has been inscribed in a common biography and which, in this regard, is indestructible and active even in the separate biographies. The *we* is dynamic from another point of view: it is a broadened, stimulating awareness that urges its participants to further progress, with due regard for their free decision. It is not a prop that forces us to grow just so, nor a technique for retraining ourselves. It is an energy and an attraction inviting us to make a common effort toward the highest values. Its own impulse—if it can be said to have one of its own—is to perceive vaguely a superior power of identity, more cohesive than the one previously experienced. The *we* is more or less closely knit: each degree of union it expresses awakens the dread of disunion and impels us to seek an ever closer reciprocal belonging.

Finally, even though the subjective *we* may be indifferent, in principle, to the number of its associates and capable of an indefinite extension without its form undergoing any radical change, in the human condition the *we* seems to be limited to a dyad: subjective awareness does not achieve real reciprocity except between two personal beings. Such is our situation. The biblical notion of Adam and Eve is to be taken seriously. Even the dyad itself is weak, intermittent, and maintained in fragmentary fashion. *Nec sine te, nec tecum.* How often trajectories cross only to move apart from each other! Even the fairest climates have their fogs and tempests.

Naturally, there are many possible dyads (Eve and Abel, Abel and Cain, etc.). But the existence of a triad or a quadrad is rather problematical: I mean a community in which three or four individuals are simultaneously translucent to each other in such a way that each turns lovingly to the others as if they were but one and receives from them simultaneous and equal attention. The triad has the formula: a—b, a—c, b—c. The family group would seem to furnish its elementary type; but who will maintain that father, mother, and child are each able to think of the other two at the same time without some faltering on the part of one of the three? Two beings can unite personally in the devotion they have for a third person: the dyad accompanied by a "for him" is frequent. But does the third party then turn to the other two with the same refinement of perception and without any loss of contact?

This distribution, if it occurs at all, and if it truly concerns the will to mutual advancement, is certainly very unstable. Either there is a swift passage from one dyad to another, or the triad descends below the personal level we are presently considering and sinks into a confused impression of community, as in a team or a group. In that case it is the idea of a common task and not their individual selves that unites the members of the group. In place of the subjective *we* there is substituted, in a sense, the image of the other or others, i.e., an objective *us*. It is by the mediation of an objective *us* and the shift from one dyad to another that love maintains its power to unite morally all men, in spite of their discontinuity, and according to the demands already implicit in the sincere relationship between two lovers. But these vast horizons are always enclosed in a more humble form; they are reflected obliquely in the narrow mirror of the dyad.

CHAPTER 3

THE VALUE OF LOVE

We have already noted that love pursues a value or reposes in it when it has found it. Precisely what value does it seek? This is the first question we must take up. In the second place, what value does this pursuit or satisfaction possess? That is to say, what value does love itself have? This second question reveals a final one: what reality does the value of love actually have?

What Does Love Seek?

The inner logic of love impels it to develop until it has achieved the total fulfillment of its potentialities. It is not inevitable that it reach its utmost limits, for every human being is free up to a certain point to oppose it or respect it or, more exactly, to sink or rise in the current of love that bears him along. But each time we correspond to the essential demands of that impulse we are aware of implicitly willing the infinite perfection of the beloved and, indirectly, of ourself as loving. We commit ourself to make the other and ourself utterly lovable and loving. But for a consciousness to be so it must embrace the whole universe and strive for the promotion of all other centers of consciousness according to the same value system. The human love of one person leads to the love of all persons. First of all, it wishes their existence and makes it an initial value. Next, it desires that their perfection or eternal essence be revealed, for it is through this eternal essence that the successive images of the ideal it has of itself are manifested to the discriminating conscience. Finally, love desires the autonomous development of individuals in time to be in as harmonious accord as possible with that ideal, which is their call to perfection. Briefly, the sincere lover wills the total order of persons and strives to encourage, insofar as he can, the growing identity of each self in its vocation to value. *Aut omnes, aut nemo.*

In order to clarify these ideas it may be useful to define more accurately the word that the problem of love obliges us to repeat over and over: "person." For the sake of simplicity we will abstract from the nuances that could be established between person and personality and simply say: *personality is the condition of the self that obliges it to seek its progressive fulfillment by itself, according to a perspective at once unique and universal.* This definition implies the notion of irreversible duration: each person is an historical development; at least we have no experience of a form of personality other than this. It supposes, besides, a self-creating continuity, that is, the presence of free causality in the self. And finally, it establishes the self in a vocation to totality; it recognizes in the self, by that very fact, the highest form of finality and value. The person must reach out to everything without consenting to dissipate itself in triviality or enclose itself in egoism; it is called to possess itself in order to give itself and, by this double movement, fulfills itself in an equilibrium at once mobile and continuous. In appearance a human being is only a tiny drop of psychic awareness; in reality it is a crucible wherein the spiritual universe seeks to give and receive all its energy in an irreplaceable individuality.

The real difficulty with the notion of person is that it has to be defined as a universal perspective, i.e., by the juxtaposition of two seemingly incompatible terms. How can a perspective, or individual consciousness, be total without losing its very individuality? This cannot be seen at first glance. Thus the ordinary tendency of philosophers is to classify person with bio-social individuality and regard the life of the mind as impersonal. This was, as is well known, the policy adopted by M. Brunschvicg. He used to tell me: "The farther I go, the more impersonalist I become." He would add that in formulating the *cogito* Descartes certainly had no intention of proclaiming *ego sum Cartesius.*

But such a position, no matter how noble the motives, is unsatisfactory. In the first place, it conflicts with the fact that the representation of the impersonal is an eminently personal act; this representation does not make the self disappear, it purifies it by contact with objectivity and the intellectual exercise of anonymity, which is not the same thing as mere impersonality. Is it not remarkable that the strongest personalities, those whose unique character is revealed in genius, should be precisely the ones who are the least embarrassed by the conscious awareness of their best and deepest self, or by their immersion in the absolute of the spiritual life? We may find it difficult to imagine the survival of a weak individuality in the ocean of infinite truth, beauty, and goodness where it would be rudely thrown and obliged to grow; but it was in a divine milieu that Aristotle, Beethoven, and Shakespeare accentuated the traits of their original consciousness, instead of allowing them to fade away there. The imprint of their personality is deeper in proportion as their elevation is greater. The higher they are the more readily they can be discerned. If there is any conclusion to be drawn, it is that the growth of inwardness and personality, far from conflicting with each other, run a parallel course.

Finally, and above all, the reconciliation of the self and the spirit is evident as soon as one analyzes the fact of love: in it, and in it alone, we understand that the self can keep and increase its singular self-awareness by becoming universal; for the self, by loving, wills to promote other selves and reach the entire universe of the spirit through them, step by step. The very act by which the individual consciousness is determined, leads it to all things and bids it develop them, i.e., understand them and help them to understand themselves and to be. In this way the route by which we were seeking to unite the subject and the absolute, the one and the many, the individual perspective and the universe, is opened wide to us. Thus, just as the person is basically committed to love, the purpose of love is to constitute persons; it cannot will a self without having to will at the same time the other selves to keep pace with the perfection of its movement. They and it do not draw away from the spirit, and the spirit cannot withdraw from them. The unique is thus bound to totality, and totality does not destroy the multitude of unique subjects but gives them consistency.

But experience teaches us that the valorization of the self is accomplished by means of a hierarchy of physical, social, or moral processes without which the self could never awaken to its proper destiny and grow in it. From the viewpoint of love this means that it cannot carry out its program all at once in itself or others: each being and each form of being is for it so many stages on an endless road. This is why the values it pursues are fragmented and arranged in degrees. We cannot, for instance, love the Chinese except through our own countrymen, or work for the prosperity of future generations except by dedicating ourselves to our contemporaries. We have noted that the fundamental form of this dedication may be narrow and that the dyad is at every moment the receptacle in which universal cooperation must be both contained and deepened. There follows not only a segmentation of the values of love but a relative opposition between them: the farthest become the rival of the nearest. It is quite evident that the exclusive service of one of these terms would make us neglect the other; however, can a person succeed in the one without at the same time including something of the other? The end of love is always beyond the immediate task; the value it seeks is ultimately measured by the balance of its tentative and partial efforts. Nothing, therefore, prevents our maintaining our original position: love wills the total order of persons, even though it may approach it only by degrees, for no other values can satisfy here.

It remains for us to determine how love uses the means to promote each consciousness. The means are of two kinds: at one time it will be *persons* themselves who serve to love other persons, at another it is *things*, i.e., material beings or anonymous ideas. In the first instance the means should also be ends in themselves: when I use the other for the good of a third person, my act is immoral and my love contradictory if I do not respect in that living instrument a destiny as precious as that of the third party. The consciousness I call an instrument ought to be in some respect a collaborator and an equal. Things, on the contrary, are pure means; their end is projected beyond themselves into the consciousness that accepts them: they are worthy of respect only by that title, as vehicle or enrichments of personal beings.

Whether they be living or inanimate, the instrumental values love seeks will have as their role either to directly advance persons or bring them back to the level from which they may have fallen. They lend themselves to a technique of ascending progress or salvific redemption. We understand why the spirit of redemption, love's most generous invention, submits first to the exigencies of a justice that is often powerless to achieve by itself its work of retrieving the past. The love that wills the growth of the other is turned toward the future from the very outset; but redemptive love reaches it only by a return to the past which it attempts to convert and endow with new value.

Is Love The Supreme Value?

Were we to follow the movement of liberation and reformation at the heart of human love, we would see that it tends to sublimate itself, to unfold itself, and to reveal within itself a love that is no longer human but absolute, since it is the principle of the universal synthesis in which human love is situated. When my consciousness seeks to promote another without reserve, it discovers an infinite plan of action that it did not initiate and whose justification depends on the infinite itself. All we do is apply in a particular case of our own the cosmic desire for harmony that is proposed to our activity and gives us our vocation. Our imperfect love is rooted in a perfect order that is our autonomous model and whose value is placed above all the others, since it confers on them a definitive meaning and is presented as the value of values. From the very first it wills the infinite, not only in the manner that the true and the beautiful may will it, but still more by uniting in itself the exigencies of the true and the beautiful, for it envelopes the whole symphony of values in its own.

Love dares to aspire to the conquest and explanation of all realities: the task it assumes is to take the universe as it is and transform it according to its own law. It is the ideal that, under penalty of destroying itself, recoils before nothing. The moment it despaired of overcoming evil it would be completely annihilated. Any timidity is its ruin. It is ready to create and to destroy, to assimilate and regulate the diversity of beings. It commits itself to acquire the fullness of the real if it does not yet possess it. It is a voracious and agile value that wants to leave nothing without relation to itself and cannot rest unless it is allowed to control all destinies. It alone aspires to bear the weight of the world; indeed, it must do so by reason of its original *élan;* if it refuses, it is cut off at the root and disintegrates in contradiction.

Thus, love cannot accommodate itself to the "coordinate" role assigned to it by some thinkers: it must be all or nothing. This is where love differs so much from other values which meet an absolute limit of their power or validity, or else evaporate at a given moment of their development. I do not mean simply the utilitarian or instrumental values that bear within themselves the testimony of their subordination; even the true and the good, although they are universals and cannot be made the means of other values, are incapable of *saturating* the universe. When I have looked at all things *sub specie bonitatis* I can subsequently view them *sub specie veritatis.* . . . Love, on the contrary, contains, or summons before it, these points of view; it does not use them, it is their soul and their plenitude. They are only aspects; it is complete vision. By its essence love is the value to which no higher value can be added and to which no value can be foreign. In attributing this privileged place to it we do no injustice to the federation of values or their multiplicity of dimensions. Analysis shows that no other value can claim such primacy without diminishing the others or using them as instruments. Love alone can animate them all while respecting them all. Its determination is to be the soul of all determinations.

But the mode of relation that binds love to all ultimate values is not the same one that binds it to instrumental values nor to the various forms of concrete existence. The variety of its relationships with each being is unlimited. That is why it would be ridiculous to imagine that a metaphysics of charity could *deduce* the content of experience and the unfolding of history. Love is committed to a polymodal justification; in truth, each individuality, each idea, each fleeting trait of the universe is bound to it according to a special and unpredictable relationship. Just as mathematics is the domain of order and yet each new theorem is an original expression in that order, so, too, the bonds binding each being with love are the inexhaustible invention of an ever new relationship. The dialectic of love is constantly bursting the rigid molds in which people try to enclose it. At one time it is the principle of deduction, at another it is the rule of equilibrium, at still another it responds to the anguish of the world with a cry that overwhelms anguish and transforms it, even when it seemed beyond the possibility of transformation. Now it may show itself by a swift descent to the depths of an idea, and then it may slowly turn another one over and over. The way it deals with life is still more ingenious than its manner of combining ideas. Love fulfills some beings by gentle growth; others it breaks in order to perfect them. Its immanences are the indefinitely renewed activity of its transcendent freedom. Love is the only value that can claim *a priori* the distinction of being regarded both as the final cause of the universe and a cause strong enough to draw all the other types of causality in its wake.

Is this theoretic *pretension* a theoretic *success?* I do not deny that he who tries to justify the universe philosophically by love does so at a great risk. A perfect human interpretation of the world is impossible in a world that is itself imperfect. But it is possible to show with certitude that the promise offered by the value of love is always kept in the particular cases that the philosopher can analyze. However, for another reason it must be admitted that here the ambition exceeds the execution. This is because the philosophy of love is still at foundation level; it has scarcely advanced since Plato. Has anything in this area been systematically studied in modern times, with the possible exception of the relationships between love and knowledge or justice? Max Scheler tried to single out sympathy for special study; but do we have even a single important monograph on its relation to hatred, indifference, or severity? Kierkegaard offered some suggestions along these lines, but nothing more. The Anglo-Saxons, MacTaggart in particular, have begun to speak of its relations with the absolute. Theologians are the ones who have more closely examined the conflicts between charity and evil and their possible reconciliation. But even these regions hold unexplored secrets! Most of the attempts to discover them have been superficial; they do no more than pipe conventional tunes.

Philosophers should come to grips with this great theme instead of abandoning it to the novelists and poets. Love would go bankrupt if it could not be clarified by the reflection it provokes, and if it did not shed some light on such fraudulent imitations as are fabricated by thinkers who conspire to overthrow its eternal order with all the more temporal force as they are the more popular and united.

Should an example be needed of this masterful virtuosity that is love's privilege, let us examine how it is associated on the one hand with knowledge or will, and on the other with hate. As to the former, it is an analytic relationship; as to the latter, it is a victory over the irrational. Real knowledge is an extract of love: it wills, in its own way, the other as other. As the scholastics saw well, it has something of an altruistic character. One could comment, in this sense, on the statement of Cardinal Vital du Four: *quanto clarius intelligo, tanto ardentius diligo.* Doubtless, if the human intellect, according to St. Thomas, becomes in a certain manner all things, it is because things measure it and gratuitously communicate their form to it. But this initial subordination of our intellect only proves that the creature receives the altruistic impulse in the understanding before making it its own by the formation of concepts; the altruism of knowledge is, in a word, simultaneously a gift and an act. In this philosophy it is more completely altruistic than in subjective idealism; it is so even in the understanding of earthly things, which is inferior, discursive, and liable to end in the concept without attaining to beings. Inversely, real love contains knowledge and develops it in its depths as a germ indispensable to its own essence. In this respect, Father Rousselot transposes into philosophy a theological statement of St. Thomas: *qui plus habebit de caritate, perfectius Deum videbit.* This could be denied only by substituting impoverished forms of love for the rich ones: the *amor sensitivus* for the *amor intellectivus,* that is, by confining it to an emotional impulse, or else by reducing it to the state of an inert fruition and suppressing at the same time the possibilities it might offer for psychological and metaphysical investigation.

A similar demonstration shows the relationships between love and the will. From the very first our fundamental will thrusts us beyond ourselves toward an infinite Good, and invites us to constitute ourselves for others; no will is perfect except in being perfect love. Opinions may differ on the hierarchical order of intelligence, will, and sentiment in love, but we cannot help seeing their connection; and, truly, when one deduction opposes another too violently in this matter, it may be that the aspects of the soul are being regarded as quite separable, thus killing the living organism that penetrates them.

The analysis of impartiality may illustrate the innermost character of this union. Only the impoverished forms of love are partial in the pejorative sense of this word; they cure through failure, so that one may say that disappointment becomes the principle of true knowledge. When the passions turn into indifference, truth appears. But this correctness is the point of departure, or rather the first manifestation, of a new love containing the knowledge and willing the determinations of the being known in its essential reality. Impartiality is thus the fruit of true love; it is at least its first degree. If love develops subsequently beyond this minimum, which opens to disinterested knowledge and action, it will no doubt seem to return to the attitude of partiality. That is because love will not be satisfied to place all real determinations on the same level; it espouses their best and most secret movement to dispose them according to the ideal order of the loving will in its most fervent intention. This new partiality does not have the drawbacks of the other; it is not deceitful: it simply rises to the being of the ought-to-be. The intellect and will are no longer the dupes of the heart but its associates in the service of value. And the real is not deformed but surrenders totally in the penetrating and active sympathy that now envelopes it. Reality is no longer limited to achievements, past or present. It now embraces the intellect and will subsisting in and being perfected in love. We must conclude in favor of the basic inherence of the intellect and will in love, and even of their ultimate perfection in it.

Contrariwise, there is no intrinsic connection between love and hate on the spiritual plane. No matter how often they are associated at the level of dramas of passion and instinct, such an alliance is unthinkable when one rises above mutilated experience and examines the essences of these two states. Between hatred and the will to promote the other there is a chasm that pure dialectics cannot bridge. We ask: whence the need to cause suffering to one who loves us and whom we do not love, or whom we love but who does not love us? Why the frenzy to humiliate the other and inflict struggle and defeat on him under this bitter, refined, and implacable form? No one would seriously think of cultivating hate in pursuit of a perfect love, as if hatred were a novitiate of personality or a means to its normal development. Neither can anyone maintain that in detesting the other we chastise him to make him love us, for that is true only of banal hatreds and does not constitute the most deep-seated purpose of detestation. Hatred does exist, and facts oblige us to a manner of being in it that is at once unforeseen, contingent, and scandalous. The simultaneous presence of love and knowledge or will is necessary; the co-existence of love and hatred is mysterious: it supposes a kind of mental derangement and decline having a motive and a mechanism no human mind can completely fathom. Philosophers can certainly try to discern how an absolutely good charity could cause a state of things in which hatred is possible; but they are always baffled at a certain point in their investigation and cannot see things entirely from the point of view of a supreme Providence whose action is beyond their ken. At this point philosophy must perfect itself in faith and hope. Dialectics is thus forced to supplement its deductive method of reasoning with a surrender to the infinite love it is still exploring. The connection it makes so easily elsewhere now escapes its grasp and will be found only in the sacred resources of transcendence. This science has to consent to a kind of sacrifice of its own vision if it is to continue on its course.

Where a knowledge of origins is lacking, dialectics can at least perceive a recurrence and help to correct hatred with love. It is no longer a question of deduction and analysis but ascension and homage in which evil recoils before a principle stronger than itself. The supremacy of love is certainly verified again, but it is a proof toward which we must grope our way, blindfolded. The certitude that results is strong, but it is indirect and transposed in a strange style, just as hatred and evil, too, were strange.

The principle of this last demonstration could be summarized as follows: let us suppose that hatred wanted to realize itself completely—the only way it could do so would be to constantly transform its methods and object so that finally it would attack and condemn itself, tearing at and even destroying itself. When it is akin to anger it is only too plain that it cannot last long; for it aims at suppressing the one it hates, that is, suppressing its reason for being, and by so doing aim at its own annihilation. It must therefore bind the one hating to the hated one; it must wish the eternity and perfection of the being it hates in order to become itself eternal and save its mystery. What is more, it must also will that the hated one be as generous as possible in order to be itself fully gratuitous and perverse; it must ennoble its enemy and make him its benefactor and god. It is thus immediately vitiated by a contradiction that disfigures and bruises it; it must work lovingly for this god and be his servant so as to succeed in hating him more, like the wicked angel of the Old Testament who had to get his orders from the Lord before he could tempt the just ones of the earth. But hate is thus limited to a formal attitude and deliberately deprives itself of all effectiveness in order to save the insignificant domain of its intention.

Nothing prevents hatred in a free being from resting in this strange defeat as in a victory. But by resisting its enemy in the very act in which it asks him to please raise it morally, its challenge is a weakness and its effort a sham. Hatred diminishes in proportion as it attempts to realize itself. What alternative is left for it but to regain a little substance? None, no doubt, except to shift the position of its revolt and blame its god for the ontological depression in which it is struggling. In this perverse and gratuitous hatred it can escape a mortal anemia only by accusing the Other of having tried to destroy its spiritual value. The accusation then takes on a tragic grandeur and everyone knows that we do not really pardon a person whom we suspect of having degraded us; it is no longer a being full of goodness that we oppose but an evil and pernicious one. Thus the one whom we regarded a moment ago as clothed with love, we now decide to identify with the principle of evil. Hatred denies itself. However, if it regards love as detestable, it is guilty of a grave error and it knows it; so it decides to blind itself—and then where is the enlightened will that animates every serious hatred? Besides, this lie, dangerous for itself and ineffectual as regards the hatred being, draws the hating one to demand his right in the name of the justice and love of which he pretends to have been defrauded. But this is a new and decisive failure, for the malicious person reintroduces in his act the cult of the moral values he had undertaken to deny. The diabolic scheme, in short, falls to pieces under its own blows, and can subsist only by never completely willing itself, that is, by trying to fix itself on shifting sands. The person who hates decides to enclose himself within limits he must will and not will at the same time. He has no alternative but to take pleasure in his own failure; and when he does, hate is dislodged and begins again its interminable, infernal dance, for the pleasure in question can no longer be that of pure hatred; it is already an intrusion of the power of loving in the very orneriness of the rebellious spirit; it is a homage his vice must render to virtue.

The loving will respects this stubbornness, however, by penetrating it with its peaceful victory; for while love makes us face ourselves involuntarily, it does no violence to us in the development it impels us to foster in ourselves voluntarily, once we are brought face to face with ourselves. But if the hate-filled spirit of revolt, wearied of itself, finally allows its iciness to melt before the fires of grace, if the rebellious will is vanquished by suffering and humility, we have a feeling that its conversion will be for it the beginning of a new series of metamorphoses. Reversing its aim one last time, hatred subsequently directs itself against hatred and its odyssey ends in repentance. Love, as the evil genius and death of death, encounters it and gently draws the self out of the morass in which it had fallen, no longer allowing it to cast itself against anyone, no matter how wicked, even should he be wickedness in person; for hatred can no longer direct its blows against anything but the self's culpable idea and evil mask. Hate bids the self destroy the reality of the evil, allowing it to perpetuate only the memory of it so as to shrink from it in an esthetic revulsion or find in it a stimulus for good. From the former fault there then proceeds an innocent and unprecedented youth. The fall from which the sinner rises is productive of good; he finds himself rewarded, as if love wanted to compensate for the former ugliness by the introduction of a new kind of beauty.

A chain of events of this kind shows us how unlimited are the means to self-fulfillment at the disposal of love's universal synthesis. Although at times we may lack direct light to help us follow its course, we do not doubt that it can always continue on its way and arrive at its goal, even while respecting vagrant freedoms. Viewed from any angle, the value of love convinces us of its supreme power in fact of the world and invites us to reassess this world at all levels of existence and according to all the procedures available to the mind.

This immense program meets with a final difficulty. Is it its own value that love wills? Is it not rather the value of the person? Does it not subordinate itself to the promotion of freedoms? And hence should one not say that the supreme value is not love but personal freedom? The true end would then seem to be the fulfillment of the consciousness, freed of its tutors and open to an independent destiny.

But a twofold reply can be made to the objection. First, love does not will free personality for the sake of its freedom; it wills freedom because it is the condition of a truly loving personality. It penetrates the person with love. And then love penetrates our abstract notion of love with personality: not only does it express itself in the spiritual society of centers of consciousness but, what is more, it can be the supreme value only if it is itself a super-personality. This last thesis is equivalent to maintaining that love is the essence of God and that in it all the divine attributes are reconciled. Such an assertion is difficult to prove entirely by the sole effort of a philosophy that refuses to have recourse to the teachings of supernatural revelation. Nevertheless, reason has an intuition that love would stop midway and be irrational if it were not itself a living consciousness in which our own personality finds its source, its support, and its end. There is nothing that forbids this assertion, and all the data of our experience urge us to accept it.

Is Love The Supreme Reality?

Love appears to us as the highest of values and its purpose is to assume in itself all reality, to the point that it justifies reality's existence by the vocation it confers on it. But what degree of reality does this purpose have? Is it positively accomplished? Is the exigency of absolute synthesis eternally satisfied? In short, does the reality of this value ever completely catch up with the reality of existence?

If we limit ourself to what the temporal order offers us visibly in the human spectacle, it would seem we should have to answer in the negative. The final cause remains beyond the world, in the realm of the possible. Pure love is a spirit which soars above facts, and the light it sheds on them is refracted in disparate colors. Absolute love is subdivided into a host of relative forms as soon as it touches our earth, and its forms sometimes clash. N. Hartmann, for example, places the love of those nearest to us at the bottom of the scale, then the love of those more distant, then the generosity emanating from the radiant person; he does not always pronounce clearly on the hierarchy of these values, but he thinks it is possible to affirm that personal love, properly so-called, should be placed above them. Now, does one not serve one of these loves at the expense of the others? We alluded above to one of these conflicts, the rivalry between devotion to the nearest and devotion to the more remote; we showed that it is not unsolvable, but in practice it certainly is the cause of delicate cases of conscience. It is not easy to know when it is permitted to die oneself or take the life of another for future humanity. . . .

What is still more serious is that the ideal, even fragmented and obscure, penetrates very slowly into the reality in which our lifetime struggle is carried on. In its works *ad extra,* in the film of mundane history, love seems so weak! Its essential demands keep it far removed from the program of life as announced. Are proofs necessary? Let us examine the humblest dyad at the very beginning of the act that incarnates the ideal in observable facts. Love desires the influence of one consciousness on another. This ambition is never totally illusory, but its realization is often infinitesimal. Is it not often hopelessly

413

optimistic to believe that the *I* can change the *thou* or even change itself for the sake of the *thou?* "Every choice has already been made," says Alain; what we imagine to be a free metamorphosis of beings is ordinarily only the implacable turning of their mechanism. Besides, human reciprocities are weak, and when autonomy asserts itself, even if it is nurtured in the goodness of the other, it turns away from the mother-soul and fulfills itself in revolt.

However, so much emphasis is placed today on that somber aspect of the question that in the end the facts are often exaggerated and distorted. Perception of others and reciprocal influences are real; and sometimes they even really attain their maximum. Lovers are not deceived in this: they know very well that they are bound by a mutual gift. If in the *Satin Slipper,* Rodrigue and Prouhèze were mistaken in this regard, the whole atmosphere of the drama would be changed. Similarly, were I not loath to demean the discussion by a coarse reflection, I would say with Marcel Proust: "The husbands who are deceived and know nothing know everything just the same." This is also true outside the pages of literature: life testifies in this sense when it renounces its passionate prejudices and consents to recollect itself and listen to the sincere voice speaking within. We have to insist that reciprocal knowledge, despite its blunders, is very often true, and everyone is, deep down, convinced of this. The skeptics, when they stop writing books and seriously face the *other,* are just as convinced as the rest.

In a certain psychology that passes for realistic, it is good form to pretend that the successes of human love are owing to the imagination and that we never either know or change another being. "Love is nothing but a hypothesis changed into a fixed idea," P. Janet teaches; "the person we love will be credited with having the power to console us when we are sad, restore our courage when we are weak, point out the path of life, and generally help us. He really does not have this power at all; he does not dream of having it; he is incapable of having it; but that makes no difference. We pretend he is this kind of person. This is what constitutes love."

The cynicism of the last sentence does not do away with the enigma presented by the facts, and it masks the rarest and most precious part of it. That the mind should be able to feed only on vapor is, on reflection, the strangest of mysteries. Even if reciprocity is only a double illusion, there is absolutely no proof that the agreement of two illusions is itself an illusion. That agreement is perceptible and sometimes maintained by a double consent is what keeps a spark of truth alive in the most pitiful attachments. But we must go farther. Is it so disastrous that imagination should be an integral part of love? People vilify the loving imagination without noticing that, granting a certain discipline, it can become a positive factor in the success of love. What they call illusion is perhaps quite simply an anticipation. This it is that binds the past state of the lovers to their future; it is by this that they can model each other according to an ideal. Without the image they would be unable to pass from contemplation to action. It is thanks to it that the popular antinomy of love can further be resolved: it is blind, they say, and yet it reveals. Blind to what limits and deforms, it reveals what develops and reforms. Such, at least, is love's role in a consciousness capable of escaping the equivocal enchantments of any kind of intermediary and bending itself to a spiritual purpose. Far from leading us necessarily into error and solitude, the imagination can lead us to a fine perception and mutual fulfillment that is far from mythical.

But no matter what the successes of human love may be, they are episodic and partial. They are springtimes between two winters; summer is not for this world. And so these successes alone do not allow us to conclude to the reality of a divine Providence whose plan would always be favorable to us and include the whole world. We arrive at that kind of conviction by other roads, and in particular by philosophical reflection on the origin and consistency of persons, independently even of their earthly supports. These inquiries are not our subject. Thus it would be intellectually foolhardy to claim at this point to have proved that an absolute and eternal Goodness really does direct the total cosmic reality. Certainly nothing prevents an infinite and supreme Will from being entirely perceptible in a limited experience. However, it is a fact that this transcription has not yet been achieved in our world. Love is the highest and most demanding value—that is certain. Is it also the supreme reality and the master obeyed by every other reality? What we have said does not give an absolutely precise knowledge of it, but it does permit us to believe it, and in affirming it, to choose wisely. To reflect on the implications of human love is to dispose oneself, if not to see God, at least to believe in Him; it is to discover something of His essence, if not of His existence. The phenomenon of human reciprocities, feeble though it be, draws us far above ourselves and allows us to catch a glimpse of the fact that every being is already subject to an ever vigilant and victorious Charity.